After Victory

PRINCETON STUDIES IN

INTERNATIONAL HISTORY AND POLITICS

Series Editors
Jack L. Snyder
Marc Trachtenberg
Fareed Zakaria

Recent Titles:

After Victory

INSTITUTIONS, STRATEGIC RESTRAINT,

AND THE REBUILDING OF ORDER

AFTER MAJOR WARS

G. John Ikenberry

PRINCETON UNIVERSITY PRESS

PRINCETON AND OXFORD

Copyright © 2001 by Princeton University Press
Published by Princeton University Press, 41 William Street,
Princeton, New Jersey 08540
In the United Kingdom: Princeton University Press,
3 Market Place, Woodstock, Oxfordshire OX20 1SY

Library of Congress Cataloging-in-Publication Data

Ikenberry, G. John
After victory : institutions, strategic restraint, and the rebuilding of
order after major wars / G. John Ikenberry
p.cm. — (Princeton studies in international history and politics)
Includes bibliographical references and index.
ISBN 0-691-05090-2 (alk. paper — ISBN 0-691-05091-0 (pbk. : alk. paper)
1. World politics. 2. Military history, Modern—19th century. 3. Military history,
Modern—20th century. 4. Peace. 5. Security, International.
I. Title. II. Series
D363 .I46 2000
327.1—dc21   00-034681

This book has been composed in Janson

The paper used in this publication meets the minimum requirements
of ANSI/NISO Z39.48-1992 (R1997) (*Permanence of Paper*)

www.pup.princeton.edu

Printed in the United States of America

7   9   10   8   6

ISBN-13: 978-0-691-05091-1 (pbk.)
ISBN-10: 0-691-05091-0 (pbk.)

To Lidia, Jackson,

and the memory of Tessa

In crossing a heath, suppose I pitched my foot against a *stone*, and were asked how the stone came to be there. I might possibly answer, that, for anything I knew to the contrary, it had lain there forever; nor would it perhaps be very easy to show the absurdity of this answer. But suppose I had found a *watch* upon the ground. . . .
—Reverend William Paley, *Natural Theology*, 1802

CONTENTS

PREFACE

THE CENTRAL question of this book is: What do states that have just won major wars do with their newly acquired power? My answer is that states in this situation have sought to hold onto that power and make it last, and that this has led these states, paradoxically, to find ways to set limits on their power and make it acceptable to other states. Across the great postwar settlements, leading states have increasingly used institutions after wars to "lock in" a favorable postwar position and to establish sufficient "strategic restraint" on their own power as to gain the acquiescence of weaker and secondary states. Leading postwar states might ideally want to tie other states down to fixed and predictable policy orientations and leave themselves institutionally unencumbered. But in seeking the institutional commitment of less powerful states—locking them into the postwar order—the leading state has to offer them something in return: some measure of credible and institutionalized restraint on its own exercise of power. The type of order that emerges after great wars hinges on the ability of states to restrain power institutionally and bind themselves to long-term commitments.

Viscount Castlereagh in 1815, Woodrow Wilson in 1919, Harry Truman in 1945—each sought to use newly preponderant state power to mold a postwar settlement that bound other states to each other and to them. American officials again found themselves in this position after 1989. But to lock other states into a desired order, these leading states did not simply exercise power—they sought the acquiescence of other states by agreeing to set limits on the use of that power. The order-building power of these leading states was partly rooted in their ability to limit that power institutionally. The changing capacity of states to do so has had a profound impact on the type of international order that has emerged after great wars.

My interest in postwar junctures and peace settlements began in the late 1980s, when the debate about the character and significance of American hegemony was in full swing. My interest was not in the decline of hegemony but in how hegemonic order is created in the first place, and in how political order more generally is created.

The end of the Cold War made my question even more compelling. It also raised the stakes of my initial question about order formation in two ways: first, with the end of the Cold War, scholars and pundits began to argue that the United States was again at a major postwar juncture, a historical watershed not unlike 1919 and 1945. The question immediately became: What can we learn from early postwar settlements about how to create a stable and desirable postwar order? The other way the stakes were raised was that the end of the Cold War sharpened certain theoretical debates. It was now possible to determine whether external threats were the essential element in cohesion and cooperation among the industrial democracies. During the Cold War, the explanation for stable and cooperative relations among these countries was overdetermined. Both neorealists and liberals had plausible explanations, but it was impossible to determine precisely which variables mattered most. When the Cold War ended, these two theoretical traditions generally expected divergent outcomes and the possibility existed for more careful adjudication of their respective theoretical claims.

In the fall of 1991, I traveled to Washington, D.C., to spend a year working on the Policy Planning staff of the State Department. It turned out to be a very interesting time to be in Washington. Soviet Premier Mikhail Gorbachev went on holiday in August to the south of Russia, and while he was out of Moscow a coup was launched. The drama unfolded before the world on live television. A rising Russian reform politician, Boris Yeltsin, stood on a tank in front of the parliament and shook a defiant fist in the air. The military was rallied, and democratic forces took back the government, but in the meantime the old Soviet empire quickly unraveled. The Cold War was over.

Viewing this drama from the State Department was revealing. American diplomats frantically worried about the viability of the civilian government led by Yeltsin. The winter of 1991–1992 was severe in Russia, and there was worry that food riots and human distress would strangle the struggling democracy at its birth. The largest assemblage of foreign ministers ever brought together at the State Department met in January 1992 to coordinate food, medical, energy, and housing assistance to Russia.

But beyond the immediate crisis, American officials wondered privately about the future. The Cold War was over, so what would come next? Containment and strategic rivalry between the Soviet Union and the West had dominated international relations for a long time. The celebration of "winning" the Cold War was mixed with anxiety about the organizing strategies and purposes of American foreign policy after it was over. One of the great worries at the time was about the future cohesion of the industrial democracies, the so-called "free world" countries that had just won the Cold War. The external threat that had fostered cooperation was suddenly gone. What would keep the advanced industrial powers together now? One of my colleagues at Policy Planning kept asking the question: What is the "glue" that is going to hold the system together? This was the big question at the time, and it remains a critical question in theoretical debates about international order after the Cold War.

Another way to ask this question is: What are the sources of order among industrial democracies? In this book, I argue that the best place to look for an answer is the situation after wars, when states are grappling with fundamental questions of order. This is when order takes shape. My answer draws upon both realist and liberal theoretical traditions. Realism asks many of the right questions about power: Who has it, how is it exercised, how do other states react to huge concentrations of it? Or, as I pose the question in this book: How is power turned into order? But realists, or at least modern neorealists, do not have all or even the most important answers to their own questions. Certain types of states—mature liberal democracies—have capacities to deploy institutions that, together with the openness and accessibility of democracy itself, allow postwar states to overcome the problems of resistance to and suspicion of power that pervade these historical turning points. States have faced similar problems of building postwar order over the centuries, but the "solutions" have changed. Today, at least among the Western democracies, the solutions look a lot like the solutions to the problem of order *within* their states.

It remains a puzzle to neorealists why powerful states might agree to contain or bind themselves within international institutions. Why would a newly unified Germany, emerging as the most powerful economy in Europe in the 1990s, agree to insert itself within a binding European monetary order? Or, to ask the historical question explored in this book: Why would the United States, emerging from World War II as the most powerful country the world had yet seen, agree to spin a dense web of international institutions and place itself squarely within them? Neorealists have generally not granted much significance to institutions and therefore do not have a good answer to these questions. The answer this book gives is that these states are playing a more sophisticated power game than neorealism appreciates; but it also argues that in order to understand the role of institutions in these situations, it is necessary to move beyond the rationalist and contractarian theory of institutions that liberalism offers. Doing so allows us to appreciate how, even within highly asymmetrical power relations, democratic industrial states can create stable and legitimate order.

There is more "glue" among the advanced industrial countries than many scholars expected. This is a book about how and why this is so.

ACKNOWLEDGMENTS

WHATEVER the failings of this book, they would have been far greater without the kind help of friends and colleagues. That this book bears little resemblance to the first paper I wrote on the subject over a decade ago is a tribute to the richness of the intellectual encounters I have had along the way. Joe Barnes, Robert Gilpin, Peter Katzenstein, Andrew Moravcsik, Nicholas Onuf, and Jack Synder read the penultimate draft of the manuscript and provided invaluable comments. I am particularly indebted to David Lake and Michael Mastanduno for their lucid commentary on multiple drafts of the manuscript. I also acknowledge Tom Callaghy, Judith Goldstein, Joseph Grieco, Charles Kupchan, John Hall, Joseph Lepgold, Daniel Lindsay, Charles Lipson, Michael O'Hanlon, John Rohr, Duncan Snidal, and Rob Sprinkle for helpful suggestions on earlier chapters and papers. I am also indebted to Daniel Deudney for stimulating my thinking through collaborative writing and a jointly taught research seminar at the University of Pennsylvania on "The Logic of the West." I have also been helped by talented research assistants, including Thomas Sisk and Peter Funke.

The book has also benefited, fittingly, from institutional support. The Woodrow Wilson International Center for Scholars in Washington, D.C, where I was a fellow during 1998-1999, provided research support and a congenial setting needed to revise the manuscript. I am also pleased to acknowledge the financial assistance of the University Research Institute and the Christopher H. Browne Center of International Politics at the University of Pennsylvania. I am also grateful to the Council on Foreign Relations and the Hitachi Foundation for an International Affairs Fellowship during 1997–1998. I thank the Brookings Institution and its Director of Foreign Policy Studies, Richard Haass, for inviting me to be a Visiting Scholar during Spring 1997. I am also indebted to Malcolm Litchfield and Chuck Myers at Princeton University Press for taking an interest in my project and shepherding the manuscript to completion, and to Margaret Case for excellent copyediting.

My greatest debts are personal. This book is dedicated to my wife, Lidia, and our two children. Work on the book manuscript began in earnest about the time of the birth of Tessa in 1995 and, in an extraordinary confluence of events, it was completed within a week of the birth of Jackson and the sad passing of Tessa in 1999. The joy and anguish of these life passages have put into perspective the struggles and pleasures of writing this book. So I am most grateful to Lidia, whose unflagging support and wise counsel made this book possible.

After Victory

Chapter One

THE PROBLEM OF ORDER

At RARE historical junctures, states grapple with the fundamental problem of international relations: how to create and maintain order in a world of sovereign states. These junctures come at dramatic moments of upheaval and change within the international system, when the old order has been destroyed by war and newly powerful states try to reestablish basic organizing rules and arrangements. The end of the Cold War after 1989 is seen by many contemporary observers as the most recent of these great historical moments. With the dramatic collapse of the bipolar world order, the question not asked since the 1940s has recently been posed anew: how do states build international order and make it last?

The great moments of international order building have tended to come after major wars, as winning states have undertaken to reconstruct the postwar world. Certain years stand out as critical turning points: 1648, 1713, 1815, 1919, and 1945. At these junctures, newly powerful states have been given extraordinary opportunities to shape world politics. In the chaotic aftermath of war, leaders of these states have found themselves in unusually advantageous positions to put forward new rules and principles of international relations and by so doing remake international order.[1]

This book raises three fundamental questions about order building at these great junctures. First, what is the essential logic of state choice at these postwar moments when the basic organization of international order is up for grabs? That is, what is the strategic circumstance common to these ordering moments, and what are the choices that the leading states face in rebuilding postwar order? Second, why has the specific "solution" to the problem of order changed or evolved across the great postwar settlements? In particular, what is the explanation for the growing resort to institutional strategies of order building, beginning with the 1815 settlement and most systematically pursued after 1945? Third, why has the 1945 postwar order among the advanced industrial countries been so durable, surviving the dramatic shifts in power that accompanied the end of the Cold War?

The great postwar junctures share a set of characteristics that make them unusually important in providing opportunities for leading states to shape international order. The most important characteristic of interstate relations after a major war is that a new distribution of power suddenly

---

[1] For a list of European and global postwar settlements, see Appendix One.

emerges, creating new asymmetries between powerful and weak states. These new power disparities are manifest precisely as the old order has been destroyed, and there are opportunities and incentives for states to confront each other over the establishment of new principles and rules of order. Major postwar junctures are rare strategic moments when leading or hegemonic states face choices about how to use their newly acquired power—choices that ultimately shape the character of postwar international order.

A state that wins a war has acquired what can usefully be thought of as a sort of "windfall" of power assets. The winning postwar state is newly powerful—indeed, in some cases it is newly hegemonic, acquiring a preponderance of material power capabilities. The question is: what does this state do with its new abundance of power? It has three broad choices. It can *dominate*—use its commanding material capabilities to prevail in the endless conflicts over the distribution of gains. It can *abandon*—wash its hands of postwar disputes and return home. Or it can try to *transform* its favorable postwar power position into a durable order that commands the allegiance of the other states within the order. To achieve this outcome, it must overcome the fears of the weaker and defeated states that it will pursue the other options: domination or abandonment.

Historically, the leading states at the great postwar junctures have had incentives to take the third course, but the means and ability of doing so has changed over time.

There are three central arguments of this book. First, the character of order after major wars has changed as the capacities and mechanisms of states to restrain power has changed. The ability of these states to engage in what can be called "strategic restraint" has evolved over the centuries, and this has changed the way in which leading states have been able to create and maintain international order. The earliest postwar power restraint strategies of states primarily entailed the separation and dispersion of state power and later the counterbalancing of power. More recently, postwar states have dealt with the uncertainties and disparities in state power with institutional strategies that—to varying degrees—bind states together and circumscribe how and when state power can be exercised.

An historical pattern can be identified. Beginning with the 1815 settlement and increasingly after 1919 and 1945, the leading state has resorted to institutional strategies as mechanisms to establish restraints on indiscriminate and arbitrary state power and "lock in" a favorable and durable postwar order. The postwar order-building agendas pursued by Britain after the Napoleonic wars and the United States after the two world wars entailed increasingly expansive proposals to establish intergovernmental institutions that would bind the great powers together and institutionalize their relations after the war. These postwar institutions did not simply solve functional problems or facilitate cooperation; they have also served as mechanisms of political control that allowed the leading state (at least to some extent) to lock other states into a favorable set of postwar relations and establish some measure of restraint on its own exercise of power, thereby mitigating the fears of domination and abandonment.

Second, the incentives and capacities of leading states to employ institutions as mechanisms of political control are shaped by two variables: the extent of power disparities after the war and the types of states that are party to the settlement. The more extreme the power disparities after the war, the greater the capacity of the leading state to employ institutions to lock in a favorable order; it is in a more advantaged position to exchange restraints on its power for institutional agreements and to trade off short-term gains for longer-term gains. Also, the greater the power disparities, the greater the incentives for weaker and secondary states to establish institutional agreements that reduce the risks of domination or abandonment. Likewise, democratic states have greater capacities to enter into binding institutions and thereby reassure the other states in the postwar settlement than nondemocracies. That is, the "stickiness" of interlocking institutions is greater between democracies than between nondemocracies, and this makes them a more readily employable mechanism to dampen the implications of power asymmetries.

Third, this institutional logic is useful in explaining the remarkable stability of the post-1945 order among the industrial democracies—an order that has persisted despite the end of the Cold War and the huge asymmetries of power. More than in 1815 and 1919, the circumstances in 1945 provided opportunities for the leading state to move toward an institutionalized settlement. Once in place, the democratic character of the states has facilitated the further growth of intergovernmental institutions and commitments, created deeper linkages between these states, and made it increasingly difficult for alternative orders to replace the existing one.

Indeed, the institutional logic of post-1945 order is useful in explaining both the way the Cold War ended and the persistence of this order after the Cold War. It tells us why the Soviet Union gave up with so little resistance and acquiesced in a united and more powerful Germany tied to NATO. Soviet leaders appreciated that the institutional aspects of political order in the West made it less likely that these states would take advantage of the Soviets as they pursued reform and integration. The institutional structure of the Western countries mitigated the security consequences of an adverse shift in power disparities and the rise of a united Germany, and this gave the Soviets incentives to go forward with their fateful decisions sooner and on terms more favorable to the West than they would have otherwise been. And institutional logic helps account for why the major Western institutions continued to persist despite the collapse of bipolarity, even if (in the case of NATO) there was no immediately apparent function for it to perform. These institutions continue to persist because they are part of the system of mutual commitments and reassurances whose logic predated and was at least partially independent of the Cold War.

Behind this argument about the changing character of postwar orders is an argument about how democracies—employing interlocking institutions—can create an order that mutes the importance of power asymmetries within international relations. To the extent that institutions play this role, the political order that results increasingly takes on "constitutional" characteristics. Fundamentally, constitutional political orders reduce the implications of "winning" in politics. Institutional limits are set on what a party or a state can do if it gains an advantage at a particular moment—for example, by winning an election or gaining disproportionately from economic exchange. In other words, constitutional orders "limit the returns to power." Limits are set on what actors can do with momentary advantages. Losers realize that their losses are limited and temporary, and that to accept those loses is not to risk everything or to give the winners a permanent advantage.

Seen in this way, it is possible to argue that the constitutional character of political orders—whether domestic or international—can vary. The degree to which the institutions within that order limit the returns to power vary, and therefore the overall constitutional character of the order can vary. Historically, international orders have exhibited very few institutional limits on the returns to power. Orders built simply on the balance of power or the coercive domination of a hegemonic state exhibit no constitutional characteristics whatever. But if institutions—wielded by democracies—play a restraining role that is hypothesized in this book, it is possible to argue that international orders under particular circumstances can indeed exhibit constitutional characteristics.

This is a claim of considerable theoretical significance. It is widely understood that domestic and international politics are rooted in very different types of order. Domestic politics is governed by the rule of law and agreed-upon institutions, whereas international politics is governed by the exercise of state power. In domestic politics, power is "tamed" by a framework of institutions and rules, whereas, it is argued, international politics remains an untamed world of power politics. In the most influential formulation, the two realms have fundamentally different structures: one based on the principle of hierarchy and the other on anarchy.[2] But it may be more accurate to say that domestic and international order can take many different forms. In some countries, politics can be extremely ruthless and coercive, whereas some areas of international politics are remarkably

---

[2] Kenneth Waltz, *Theory of International Politics* (Reading, Mass.: Addison-Wesley, 1979).

consensual and institutionalized. The domestic-international divide is not absolute.[3]

When war or political upheaval results in the rise of a newly powerful state or group of states—that is, where there exist highly asymmetrical power relations in an international environment where the basic character of order is in transition—leading states will be presented with the choice to dominate, abandon, or institutionalize the postwar order. When the incentives and opportunities exist for the leading states to move in the direction of an institutionalized settlement that binds states together so as to limit and constrain state power, including the power of the leading or hegemonic state, the postwar order begins to take on constitutional characteristics.

The rest of this chapter looks more closely at the puzzles of postwar order that have eluded explanation, the hypotheses and institutional argument developed in this book, and the larger theoretical implications that are at stake in the debate over how states create and maintain order.

THE PUZZLES OF ORDER

Order formation in international relations has tended to come at dramatic and episodic moments, typically after great wars. These shifts in the system are what Robert Gilpin calls "systemic change," moments when the governing rules and institutions are remade to suit the interests of the newly powerful states or hegemon.[4] The irregular and episodic pattern of international order formation is itself an important observation about the nature of change. The importance of war, breakdown, and reconstruction in relations among states speaks to a central aspect of international change: that history is, as Peter Katzenstein argues, a "sequence of irregular big bangs."[5]

[3] For other arguments along these lines, see Helen Milner, "The Assumption of Anarchy in International Theory: A Critique," *Review of International Studies*, Vol. 17 (January 1991), pp. 67–85; David A. Lake, "Anarchy, Hierarchy and the Variety of International Relations," *International Organization*, Vol. 50 (1997), pp. 1–33; Barry Buzan and Richard Little, "Reconceptualizing Anarchy," *European Journal of International Relations*, Vol. 2, No. 4 (1996), pp. 403–39; and Helen V. Millner, "Rationalizing Politics: The Emerging Synthesis of International, American, and Comparative Politics," in Peter J. Katzenstein, Robert O. Keohane, and Stephen D. Krasner, eds., *Explorations and Contestation in the Study of World Politics* (Cambridge: MIT Press, 1999), pp. 119–46. For a discussion see G. John Ikenberry, "Constitutional Politics in International Relations, " *European Journal of International Relations*, Vol. 4, No.2 (June 1998), pp. 147–77.

[4] Robert Gilpin, *War and Change in World Politics* (New York: Cambridge University Press, 1981), pp. 41–44. This type of change is contrasted with "systems change," which refers to change in the basic character of the actors within the global system; and it is contrasted with "interaction change," which refers to change in the political, economic, and other processes among actors.

[5] Peter J. Katzenstein, "International Relations Theory and the Analysis of Change," in Ernst-Otto Czempiel and James N. Rosenau, eds., *Global Changes and Theoretical Chal-*

World politics is marked by infrequent discontinuities that rearrange the relations between states.

Although the most consequential reordering moments in international relations have occurred after major wars, the specific character of the orders these settlements produced have changed over the centuries. The settlements grew increasingly global in scope. The Westphalia settlement in 1648 was primarily a continental European settlement, whereas the Utrecht settlement in 1712 saw the beginning of Britain's involvement in shaping the European state system. The Vienna settlement in 1815 brought the wider colonial and non-European world into the negotiations. In the twentieth century, the settlements were truly global. The peace agreements also expanded in scope and reach. They dealt with a widening range of security, territorial, economic, and functional issues and they became increasingly intrusive, entailing greater involvement in the internal structures and administration of the defeated states; they culminated in 1945 with the occupation and reconstruction of Germany and Japan.[6]

Most important, in the settlements of 1815, 1919, and 1945, the leading states made increasingly elaborate efforts to institutionalize the postwar security relations between the major powers. Rather than rely simply on balance-of-power strategies or preponderant power, they sought to restrain power, reassure weaker potential rivals, and establish commitments by creating various types of binding institutions. The strategy was to tie potentially rival and mutually threatening states together in alliance and other institutions. Robert Jervis notes this logic in the Vienna settlement: "The conception of self-interest expanded, and statesmen came to believe that menacing states could best be contained by keeping close ties on them."[7]

The postwar settlements of 1919 and 1945 saw postwar order-building strategies that were even more far-reaching in their use of institutions to bind and reassure potential adversaries. The explanation of how and why this practice of using institutions to tie states together emerged in 1815 as

lenges (Lexington, Mass.: Lexington Books, 1989), p. 296. For a recent survey of alternative conceptions of change within international relations theory, see Michael Doyle and G. John Ikenberry, eds., *New Thinking in International Relations Theory* (Boulder, Colo.: Westview Press, 1997).

[6] See Redvers Opie et al. *The Search for Peace Settlements* (Washington, D.C.: Brookings Institution, 1951), pp. 2–5. For surveys of the major postwar settlements, see Robert Randle, *The Origins of Peace: A Study of Peacemaking and the Structure of Peace Settlements* (New York: Free Press, 1973); Charles F. Doran, *The Politics of Assimilation* (Baltimore: Johns Hopkins University Press, 1971); Kalevi J. Holsti, *Peace and War: Armed Conflicts and International Order, 1648–1989* (New York: Cambridge University Press, 1991); and Charles W. Kegley, Jr., and Gregory A. Raymond, *How Nations Make Peace* (New York: St. Martin's Press, 1999).

[7] Robert Jervis, "A Political Science Perspective on the Balance of Power and the Concert," *American Historical Review*, Vol. 97, No. 3 (June 1992), p. 723.

an alternative to a simple balance-of-power order, and reappeared in even more extensive form after the two world wars, is an important historical and theoretical puzzle.[8]

After 1945, the United States pursued a strategy of postwar order building that involved the unprecedented creation of new intergovernmental institutions. In the aftermath of World War II, the prewar order was in ruins, the European great powers were beaten down, and the United States was poised to dominate world politics. From this commanding position, between 1944 and 1951, the United States led the way in establishing the Bretton Woods institutions, the United Nations, the North Atlantic Treaty Organization (NATO), the U.S.-Japan security treaty, and other alliances in Asia. Postwar institutions came in many guises—regional, global, economic, security, multilateral, and bilateral.

There have been many great wars and many moments when newly powerful states were in a position to organize the postwar order. But never has a single state emerged so dominant after so consequential a war; and never has there been a great power that has sought to institutionalize the postwar order so thoroughly. The specific contrast can be made between American and British hegemonic periods, for the United States has made much more extensive use of institutions than Britain did in the nineteenth century.[9]

Why would the United States, at the height of its hegemonic power after World War II, agree to "institutionalize" its power? The United States did attempt to lock other states into these institutions while simultaneously leaving itself as unencumbered as possible. But the postwar institutions inevitably also set some limits on how America could exercise its hegemonic power. Why would it agree to these institutional limits? It is also a puzzle why weaker and secondary states would agree to become more rather than less entangled with such a powerful hegemonic state. To do so is to risk domination, and if these weaker states believe that the hegemon's power will ultimately decline, they might argue that it is better not to lock themselves in, and wait until they can get a better deal later.

It is also a puzzle that the 1945 order has been so durable. One of the great surprises of the post-Cold War period is the remarkable stability of relations between the United States and the other advanced industrial

[8] Robert Jervis argues in his study of the 1815 concert system that scholars "don't know enough about why this practice emerged." Ibid., p. 724.

[9] For comparisons of American and British hegemony, see Robert Gilpin, *U.S. Power and the Multinational Corporation: The Political Economy of Foreign Direct Investment* (New York: Basic Books, 1975); David Lake, "British and American Hegemony Compared: Lessons for the Current Era of Decline," in Michael Fry, ed., *History, the White House, and the Kremlin: Statesmen as Historians* (New York: Columbia University Press, 1991), pp. 106–22; and Joseph S. Nye, Jr., *Bound to Lead: The Changing Nature of American Power* (New York: Basic Books, 1992).

countries. Despite the collapse of the Soviet Union and the end of bipolarity, relations among the United States, Europe, and Japan continue to be relatively open, reciprocal, legitimate, and institutionalized. Many observers expected the end of the Cold War to trigger major changes in relations among these countries, such as the breakdown of multilateral institutions, the rise of regional blocs, and the return to strategic balancing by Japan and Germany.

The end of the Cold War has not only eliminated a source of cohesion among the industrial democracies; it has also led to a unipolar distribution of power. In both economic and military spheres, the United States leads its nearest rival by a larger margin than has any other leading state in the last three centuries. Yet despite this concentration of American power, there is very little evidence that other states are actively seeking to balance against it or organize a counterhegemonic coalition. Again, the puzzle today concerns what has not happened: In a decade of sharp shifts in the distribution of power, why has there been so much stability and persistence of order among the industrial democracies?

THE DEBATE ABOUT ORDER

The debate about the sources of international order is typically waged between those who stress the importance of power and those who stress the importance of institutions and ideas.[10] This is a false dichotomy. State power and its disparities determine the basic dilemmas that states face in the creation and maintenance of order, but variations in the "solutions" that states have found to these dilemmas require additional theorizing. The character and stability of postwar order hinge on the capacities of states to develop institutional mechanisms to restrain power and establish binding commitments—capacities that stem from the political character of states and prevailing strategic thinking about the sources of international order. But prevailing theories of institutions also miss the way institutions play an ordering role as mechanisms of political control.

The realist tradition advances the most clearly defined answers to the basic question of how order is created among states.[11] The fundamental

---

[10] For a useful discussion of "optimistic" (Kantian) and "despairing" (Rousseauian) intellectual traditions on the question of international order, see Ian Clark, *The Hierarchy of States: Reform and Resistance in the International Order* (Cambridge: Cambridge University Press, 1989). For a survey of theories of international order, see John A. Hall, *International Order* (Cambridge: Polity Press, 1996), chapter one.

[11] According to Talcott Parsons, the original articulator of the "problem of order" was Hobbes, who argued that individuals operating in the state of nature would not be able to create order among themselves—that is, establish stable, recurrent, and cooperative social relations. The solution would ultimately require the imposition of order by a hierarchical

realist claim is that order is created and maintained by state power, and shifts in order are ultimately driven by shifts in the distribution of state power. Built on this view, realism—and its neorealist revisions—offer two relatively distinct images of order formation in world politics: balance of power and hegemony.

Balance-of-power theory explains order—and the rules and institutions that emerge—as the product of an ongoing process of balancing and adjustment of opposing power concentrations or threats among states under conditions of anarchy.[12] Balancing can be pursued both internally and externally: through domestic mobilization and through the formation of temporary alliances among states to resist and counterbalance a threatening concentration of power. Under conditions of anarchy, alliances will come and go as temporary expedients, states will guard their autonomy, and entangling institutions will be resisted. Balance-of-power realists differ greatly over how explicit and self-conscious the rules of balance tend to be. The order that emerges is thus either the unintended outcome of balancing pressures or a reflection of learned and formalized rules of equilibrium and balance.

A second neorealist theory holds that order is created and maintained by a hegemonic state, which uses power capabilities to organize relations among states.[13] The preponderance of power by a state allows it to offer incentives, both positive and negative, to the other states to agree to ongoing participation within the hegemonic order. According to Robert Gilpin, an international order is, at any particular moment in history, the reflection of the underlying distribution of power of states within the system. Over time, this distribution of power shifts, leading to conflicts and ruptures in the system, hegemonic war, and the eventual reorganization of order so as to reflect the new distribution of power capabilities. It is the rising hegemonic state or group of states, whose power position has been ratified by war, that defines the terms of the postwar settlement and the character of the new order.

These neorealist theories are helpful in identifying the strategic dilemmas that emerge at postwar junctures: the problem of creating order in highly asymmetrical power relations. But neither version of neorealism can make

---

sovereign. See Parsons, *The Structure of Social Action* (New York: McGraw-Hill, 1937), pp. 89–94. Albert Hirschman shows that the modern intellectual response to Hobbes, leading to Adam Smith's *Wealth of Nations*, was to cast doubt on Hobbes's problem of order by suggesting that certain human motivations kept others under control and, most importantly, that the pursuit of political and economic self-interest was not typically an uncontrollable "passion" but a civilized, gentle activity. See Hirschman, *The Passions and the Interests* (Princeton: Princeton University Press, 1977).

[12] See Waltz, *Theory of International Politics*. For extensions and debates, see Robert O. Keohane, ed., *Neorealism and Its Critics* (New York: Columbia University Press, 1986).

[13] See Gilpin, *War and Change in World Politics*.

complete sense of the rising role of institutional strategies of order building by leading states or the sequence of postwar orders that emerged. Neither version allows international institutions to play a primary role in the
organization of relations among states.[14] In a simple neorealist view, hegemonic order is established and maintained by the continuing use of inducements and threats that are available to the preponderant postwar state,
which relies on such material capabilities as military power; control over raw
materials, markets, and capital; and competitive economic and technological
advantages.[15] As I will argue later, there is evidence that hegemonic states—
Britain in the nineteenth century and the United States after the world
wars—acted according to a more sophisticated understanding of power and
order. They sought to establish mutually agreed-upon rules and principles
of order, and they appeared to realize that to do so required not just wielding
material capabilities but also restraining the use of that power.[16]

Likewise, the continuing stability of the Western postwar order challenges most neorealist theories of balance and hegemony. With the end of
the Soviet threat, balance-of-power theory expects the West, and particularly the security organizations such as NATO, to weaken and eventually
return to a pattern of strategic rivalry.[17] Neorealist theories of hegemony

---

[14] Waltz's classic statement of neorealism assigns little significance to the role of international institutions. For recent discussions of international institutions within the realist tradition, see Randall L. Schweller and David Priess, "A Tale of Two Realisms: Expanding the
Institutions Debate," *Mershon International Studies Review*, Vol. 41, Supplement (May 1997),
pp. 1–32; and Robert Jervis, "Realism, Neoliberalism, and Cooperation: Understanding the
Debate," *International Security*, Vol. 24, No. 1 (Summer 1999), pp. 42–63.

[15] Few scholars are satisfied with an understanding of hegemonic order built simply around
the exercise of material capabilities. Robert Keohane, for example, notes that "theories of
hegemony should seek not only to analyze dominant powers' decisions to engage in rule-
making and rule-enforcement, but also to explore why secondary states defer to the leadership
of the hegemony," and stresses that these theories "need to account for the legitimacy of
hegemonic regimes and for the coexistence of cooperation." Keohane, *After Hegemony: Cooperation and Discord in the World Political Economy* (Princeton: Princeton University Press, 1984),
p. 39. Likewise, Robert Gilpin argues that the "governance" of the international system is in
part maintained by the prestige and moral leadership of the hegemonic power. Although the
authority of the hegemonic power is ultimately established by military and economic supremacy, "the position of the dominant power may be supported by ideological, religious, or other
values common to a set of states." Gilpin, *War and Change in World Politics*, p. 34.

[16] Why principled agreement is sought by leading postwar states and how it might be
secured among unequal states are important questions that neorealist hegemonic theories
cannot answer. See G. John Ikenberry and Charles A. Kupchan, "Socialization and Hegemonic Power," *International Organization*, Vol. 44, No. 3 (Summer 1990), pp. 283–315.

[17] John J. Mearsheimer, "Back to the Future: Instability of Europe after the Cold War,"
International Security, Vol. 15 (Summer 1990), pp. 5–57; Mearsheimer, "Why We Will Soon
Miss the Cold War," *Atlantic*, No. 266 (August 1990), pp. 35–50; Conor Cruise O'Brien,
"The Future of the West," *National Interest*, No. 30 (Winter 1992/93), pp. 3–10; and Stephen
M. Walt, "The Ties That Fray: Why Europe and America Are Drifting Apart," *National
Interest*, No. 54 (Winter 1998/99), pp. 3–11.

have argued that the extreme preponderance of American power will trigger counterbalancing reactions by Asian and European allies, or at least a loosening of the political and security ties that marked the Cold War era.[18] Some neorealist accounts have been advanced to explain the absence of European or Asian balancing responses in the face of renewed American hegemony. One such explanation looks at American post-Cold War grand strategy and its seeming ability to use material resources to coopt and reassure allies, thereby forestalling balancing and resistance.[19] Another realist answer is that contemporary American power is so much greater than that of other states that counterbalancing would not work.[20]

Nonetheless, the basic thrust of these neorealist theories is that the advanced industrial states will again have to deal with the problems of anarchy after the Cold War: economic rivalry, security dilemmas, institutional decay, and balancing alliances. The external threat of the Cold War is gone, and even if the United States remains predominant, it has lost a critical source of cohesion among the allies. The fact that post-Cold War relations among the Western industrial countries have remained stable and open, and institutionalized cooperation in some areas has actually expanded, is a puzzle that can only be explained by going beyond neorealism.[21]

Liberal theories are also relevant but incomplete in understanding the politics of order building after major wars.[22] These theories provide particularly promising leads in explaining aspects of the 1945 postwar order, but they do not provide a full explanation of its features or the sources of its

---

[18] See, for example, Christopher Layne, "The Unipolar Illusion: Why New Great Powers Will Arise," *International Security*, Vol. 17, No. 4 (Spring 1993), pp. 5–51; Layne, "From Preponderance to Offshore Balancing: America's Future Grand Strategy," *International Security*, Vol. 22, No. 1 (Summer 1997), pp. 86–124; and Josef Joffe, " 'Bismarck' or 'Britain'? Toward an American Grand Strategy after Bipolarity," *International Security*, Vol. 19, No. 4 (Spring 1995), pp. 94–117.

[19] See Michael Mastanduno, "Preserving the Unipolar Moment: Realist Theories and U.S. Grand Strategy after the Cold War," *International Security*, Vol. 21, No. 4 (Spring 1997), pp. 49–88; and Robert F. Lieber, response to Walt, "The Ties That Fray," in *National Interest*, No. 55 (Spring 1999), p. 114.

[20] William C. Wohlforth, "The Stability of a Unipolar World," *International Security*, Vol. 24, No. 1 (Summer 1999), pp. 5–41.

[21] See Daniel Deudney and G. John Ikenberry, "The Nature and Sources of Liberal International Order," *Review of International Studies*, Vol. 25, No. 2 (Spring 1999), pp. 179–96.

[22] Theories of the democratic peace, pluralistic security communities, complex interdependence, and international regimes all identify important features of international relations, and they are particularly useful in explaining aspects of relations among the Western industrial countries in the postwar period. For overviews of liberal theories, see Mark W. Zacher and Richard A. Mathew, "Liberal International Relations Theory: Common Threads, Divergent Strands," in Charles W. Kegley, ed., *Controversies in International Relations Theory: Realism and the Neoliberal Challenge* (New York: St. Martin's, 1995). For an important synthetic statement of liberal theory, see Andrew Moravcsik, "Taking Preferences Seriously: A Liberal Theory of International Politics," *International Organization*, Vol. 51, No. 4 (Autumn 1997), pp. 513–53.

stability.[23] Liberal theories are less concerned with the asymmetries of power between states and the constraints on cooperation that are engendered as a result. They miss the prevalence of institutional binding practices as an alternative to traditional balancing and the way in which the open and democratic American polity has combined with international institutions to mitigate the implications of postwar power asymmetries.

Liberal theories see institutions as having a variety of international functions and impacts that serve in various ways to facilitate cooperation, modify state power, and alter the ways in which states identify and pursue their interests.[24] Liberal theories have also identified and stressed the importance of institutions among states that serve as foundational agreements or constitutional contracts—what Oran Young describes as "sets of rights and rules that are expected to govern their subsequent interactions."[25] But there has been less attention to the ways that institutions can be used as strategies to bind states together so as to mitigate the security dilemma and overcome

[23] No single theorist represents this composite liberal orientation, but a variety of theorists provide aspects. On the democratic peace, see Michael Doyle, "Kant, Liberal Legacies, and Foreign Affairs," *Philosophy and Public Affairs*, Vol. 12 (1983), pp. 205–35, 323–53. On security communities, see Emanuel Adler and Michael Barnett, eds., *Security Communities* (New York: Cambridge University Press, 1998); and Karl Deutsch, *Political Community and the North Atlantic Area* (Princeton: Princeton University Press, 1957). On the interrelationship of domestic and international politics, see James Rosenau, ed., *Linkage Politics: Essays on the Convergence of National and International Systems* (New York: Free Press, 1969). On functional integration theory, see Ernst Haas, *Beyond the Nation-State: Functionalism and International Organization* (Stanford: Stanford University Press, 1964). On the fragmented and complex nature of power and interdependence, see Robert Keohane and Joseph Nye, *Power and Interdependence* (Boston: Little, Brown, 1977). On the modernization theory underpinnings of the liberal tradition, see Edward Morse, *Modernization and the Transformation of International Relations* (New York: Free Press, 1976); and James Rosenau, *Turbulence in World Politics: A Theory of Change and Continuity*) Princeton: Princeton University Press, 1991).

[24] The liberal literature on international institutions and regimes is large. For overviews, see Stephen Krasner, ed., *International Regimes* (Ithaca: Cornell University Press, 1981); Steph Haggard and Beth Simmons, "Theories of International Regimes," *International Organization*, Vol. 41 No. 3 (Summer 1987), pp. 491–517; Volker Rittberger, ed., *Regime Theory and International Relations* (Oxford: Oxford University Press, 1995); and Andreas Hasenclever, Peter Mayer, and Volker Rittberger, *Theories of International Regimes* (Cambridge: Cambridge University Press, 1997). For an excellent survey of institutional and regime theory, see Lisa L. Martin and Beth Simmons, "Theories and Empirical Studies of International Institutions," in Peter J. Katzenstein, Robert O. Keohane, and Stephen D. Krasner, eds. *Exploration and Contestation in the Study of World Politics*, pp. 89–117. The seminal statement of neoliberal institutional theory is Keohane, *After Hegemony.*

[25] Oran Young, "Political Leadership and Regime Formation: On the Development of Institutions in International Society," *International Organization* Vol. 45, No. 3 (Summer 1991), p. 282. See also Young, *International Cooperation: Building Regimes for Natural Resources and the Environment* (Ithaca: Cornell University Press, 1989). The concept of constitutional contract is discussed in James M. Buchanan, *The Limits of Liberty* (Chicago: University of Chicago Press, 1975), esp. chapter 5.

incentives to balance. Liberal theories grasp the ways in which institutions can channel and constrain state actions, but they have not explored a more far-reaching view, in which leading states use intergovernmental institutions to restrain themselves and thereby dampen the fears of domination and abandonment by secondary states.

The approach to institutions that I am proposing can be contrasted with two alternative theories: the neoliberal (or "unsticky") theory and the constructivist (or "disembodied") theory. Neoliberal theory sees institutions as agreements or contracts between actors that function to reduce uncertainty, lower transaction costs, and solve collective action problems. They provide information, enforcement mechanisms, and other devices that allow states to realize joint gains.[26] Institutions are employed as strategies to mitigate a range of opportunistic incentives that states will otherwise respond to under conditions of anarchy.[27] Institutions are thus explained in terms of the problems they solve; they are constructs that can be traced to the actions of self-interested individuals or groups.[28]

Constructivist theory sees institutions as diffuse and socially constructed worldviews that bound and shape the strategic behavior of individuals and states. Institutions are seen as overarching patterns of relations that define and reproduce the interests and actions of individuals and groups. They provide normative and cognitive maps for interpretation and action, and they ultimately affect the identities and social purposes of the actors.[29]

[26] See Keohane, *After Hegemony*. The general theoretical position is sketched in Keohane, "International Institutions: Two Approaches," *International Studies Quarterly*, Vol. 32 (December 1988), pp. 379–96, and Keohane and Lisa Martin, "The Promise of Institutionalist Theory," *International Security*, Vol. 20, No. 1 (Summer 1995), pp. 39–51. See also Lisa Martin, *Coercive Cooperation: Explaining Multilateral Economic Sanctions* (Princeton: Princeton University Press, 1992).

[27] See Lisa Martin, "An Institutionalist View: International Institutions and State Strategies," in T. V. Paul and John A. Hall, eds., *International Order and the Future of World Politics* (New York: Cambridge University Press, 1999).

[28] The neoliberal approach argues that institutions are essentially functional or utilitarian "solutions" to problems encountered by rational actors seeking to organize their environment in a way that advances their interests. Kenneth A. Shepsle describes institutions as "agreements about a structure of cooperation" that reduces transaction costs, opportunism, and other forms of "slippage." Shepsle, "Institutional Equilibrium and Equilibrium Institutions," in Herbert F. Weisberg, ed., *Political Science: The Science of Politics* (New York: Agathon, 1986), p. 74.

[29] As Alex Wendt argues, "Constructivists are interested in the construction of identity and interests and, as such, take a more sociological than economic approach" to theory. Wendt, "Collective Identity Formation and the International State," *American Political Science Review*, Vol. 88, No. 2 (June 1994), pp. 384–385. Adopting a similar view, Peter J. Katzenstein argues that "institutionalized power can be seen to mold the identity of the states themselves and thus the interests they hold." Katzenstein, "United Germany in an Integrating Europe," in Katzenstein, ed., *Tamed Power: Germany in Europe* (Ithaca: Cornell University Press, 1997), p. 5.

Behind state interests and power are state identities—prevailing norms and ideas about the purposes and orientation of the state as an entity and as an actor in the wider international system. In this view, the organization of postwar order, in each historical instance, reflects the prevailing thinking among those party to the settlements about what the proper principles and purposes of international order should be. This prevailing thinking, in turn, is rooted in the principles and purposes that shape the fundamental identities of the states themselves.[30]

A third position holds that institutions are both constructs and constraints. Institutions are the formal and informal organizations, rules, routines, and practices that are embedded in the wider political order and define the "landscape" in which actors operate.[31] As such, institutional structures influence the way power is distributed across individuals and groups within a political system, providing advantages and resources to some and constraining the options of others. This approach gives attention to the ways in which institutions alter or fix the distribution of power within a political order. It offers a more sticky theory of institutions than the ratio-

---

[30] John Ruggie makes an argument of this sort about the relationship between the territorial state, sovereignty, and international institutions. Ruggie argues that multilateralism became the basic organizing principle that allowed the emerging interstate system to cope with the consequences of state sovereignty. Multilateralism—with principles of indivisibility, generalized rules of conduct, and diffuse reciprocity—provided an institutional form that defined and stabilized the international property rights of states and facilitated the resolution of coordination and collaboration problems. See John G. Ruggie, "The Anatomy of an Institution," in Ruggie, ed., *Multilateralism Matters: The Theory and Praxis of an Institution* (New York: Columbia University Press, 1993), pp. 3–47. See also Christian Reus-Smit, "The Constitutional Structure of International Society and the Nature of Fundamental Institutions," *International Organization*, Vol. 51, No. 4 (Autumn 1997), pp. 555–89.

[31] This theoretical view—often called "historical institutionalism"—makes several claims. First, state policy and orientations are mediated in decisive ways by political structures—such as institutional configurations of government. The structures of a polity shape and constrain the goals, opportunities, and actions of the groups and individuals operating within it. Second, to understand how these institutional constraints and opportunities are manifest, they must be placed within an historical process—timing, sequencing, unintended consequences, and policy feedback matter. Third, institutions have path-dependent characteristics—institutions are established and tend to persist until a later shock or upheaval introduces a new moment of opportunity for institutional change. Finally, institutional structures have an impact because they facilitate or limit the actions of groups and individuals—which means that institutions are never offered as a complete explanation of outcomes. The impacts of institutions, therefore, tend to be assessed as they interact with other factors, such as societal interests, culture, ideology, and new policy ideas. For surveys of the theoretical claims of this perspective, see Peter A. Hall and Rosemary C. R. Taylor, "Political Science and the Three New Institutionalisms," *Political Studies*, Vol. 44, No. 5 (Decemeber 1996); pp. 936–37; Kathleen Thelen, "Historical Institutionalism in Comparative Politics," *Annual Review of Political Science* (Palo Alto: Annual Reviews, Inc., 1999), pp. 369–404; and Sven Steinmo, et al. *Structuring Politics: Historical Institutionalism in Comparative Analsysis* (New York: Cambridge University Press, 1992).

nalist account, but unlike constructivism, it locates institutional stickiness in the practical interaction between actors and formal and informal organizations, rules, and routines. Because of the complex causal interaction between actors and institutions, attention to historical timing and sequencing is necessary to appreciate the way in which agency and structure matter.

The key focus of neoliberal institutional theory is the way in which institutions provide information to states and reduce the incentives for cheating.[32] But this misses the fundamental feature of the prevailing order among the advanced industrial countries: the structures of relations are now so deep and pervasive that the kind of cheating that these theories worry about either cannot happen, or if it does it will not really matter because cooperation and the institutions are not fragile but profoundly robust. Moreover, it is a question not only of *how* institutions matter but of *when* they matter. Neoliberal institutionalism argues that institutions matter most after hegemony; when hegemony declines, institutions sustain order and cooperation. But institutions are also critical at the beginning of hegemony—or "after victory"—in establishing order and securing cooperation between unequal states.[33] The theory of institutions advanced in this book incorporates assumptions about path dependency and increasing returns to institutions to explain their potential significance in overcoming or mitigating anarchy, balance, and strategic rivalry.

THE ARGUMENT

This book argues that the basic problem of order formation is a problem of coping with the newly emerged asymmetries of power. This is the classic problem of political order: How can a stable and mutually acceptable system of relations be established between strong and weak states? Max Weber took this problem as the central dilemma of politics—turning raw power into legitimate authority. Wars create winners and losers, they magnify the differences between strong and weak, and they destroy the old rules and institutions of order. In this situation, as has been said, leading or hege-

---

[32] The more general claim of the neoliberal approach, embodied in Keohane's pathbreaking work, is that states—in the rational pursuit of their self-interest—often find incentives and opportunities to establish institutions that reduce transaction costs and overcome other obstacles to cooperation. The argument advanced here builds on this seminal insight and attempts to extend it in two directions—where institutions matter and how institutional constraints are manifest.

[33] See Keohane, *After Hegemony*. For a discussion of how neoliberal institutional theory is useful in explaining distributive struggles and competitive security relations between unequal states, see Keohane, "Institutionalist Theory and the Realist Challenge After the Cold War," in David A. Baldwin, ed., *Neorealism and Neoliberalism: The Contemporary Debate* (New York: Columbia University Press, 1993), pp. 269–300, and Keohane and Martin, "The Promise of Institutional Theory," in *International Security*.

monic states can aggrandize their position, states can seek security in balances of power, or states can create more institutionalized political orders. Faced with similar postwar strategic situations in 1648, 1713, 1815, 1919, and 1945, the leading states pursued different strategies. The initial settlements dealt with the problem by separating and balancing power of the major states.[34] The settlements after 1815, 1919, and 1945 increasingly resorted to institutional strategies to establish strategic restraint and overcome fears of domination and abandonment. The central focus of this book is to understand the logic and variation in these postwar strategies and the implications for the stability of the 1945 postwar order.[35]

The argument advanced here is that the character of postwar order has changed as the capacities of states to restrain power and establish commitments has changed. The rise of democratic states and new institutional strategies allowed states capacities to develop new responses to the old and recurring problem of order.

Chapter Two specifies the book's dependent variables: the order-building strategies of the leading postwar states and variations in the character of postwar order. The primary empirical focus is on the choices and policies of newly powerful postwar states and, in particular, variations in the extent to which these states employed institutions as mechanisms to establish commitments and restraints.[36] The secondary empirical focus is the actual character of postwar order and, in this regard, a broad distinction

---

[34] This is not to argue that the pre-1815 postwar settlements did not also involve the creation of norms, rules, and institutions. Indeed, they did. Hedley Bull, for example, depicts the rise of sovereignty and the balance of power among European states and later the larger international order as a process of institution building within a society of states. See Bull, *The Anarchical Society: A Study of Order in World Politics* (London: Macmillan Press, 1977). But institutional strategies in the more restricted sense used here—binding intergovernmental institutions, such as security alliances, devised as mechanisms to establish commitment and restraint among the great powers—were not in evidence.

[35] I am seeking to explain variations in the extent to which leading states pursued institutional strategies of order building and the extent to which the resulting postwar order had institutional—or constitutional—characteristics. I am not seeking to explain the more general variations in the types of order—balance, hegemonic, and constitutional—across all major postwar settlements. If the objective were to explain the simple presence or absence of institutional strategies or constitutional characteristics, the focus would necessarily be on the contrast between pre- and post-1815 settlements. But the focus here is on variations among settlements that involve the use of institutional strategies and exhibit traces of constitutional order. The operative dependent variable is the order-building strategy of the leading state— as seen in its policies and actions during and after the war and the characteristics of the order that resulted. Hence the historical focus is on variations in the 1815, 1919, and 1945 settlements and not on the fuller set of postwar settlements.

[36] These strategies are distinguished in terms of their power restraint mechanisms. Strategies of institutional binding and supranationalism are specific ways in which states can introduce constitutional characteristics into postwar order.

is made between three types of order: balance of power, hegemonic, and constitutional. These varieties of order differ in the way that the distribution of state power is organized and restrained. This book does not seek to explain systematically variations in these three types of order. Rather, it looks for variations in the character of order as evidence of the extent to which institutional strategies of order building are advanced and successfully pursued by the leading postwar state.

These arguments about the institutional logic of order building and variations in its manifestation are developed in Chapter Three. Assumptions are made at the outset about the basic "problems" that leading states face in rebuilding order after major wars: the breakdown of the old order, the rise of new power asymmetries, and the basic choices that they face. These simplifications are made so as to clarify the basic strategic circumstances and choices. Explaining variations in the choice of order-building strategies—and the growing embrace of institutional strategies—is the puzzle that emerges from this construction of the problem.

Over time, postwar settlements have moved in the direction of an institutionalized order, and have begun to take on constitutional characteristics. Power in exercised—at least to some extent—through agreed-upon institutional rules and practices, thereby limiting the capacities of states to exercise power in arbitrary and indiscriminate ways or use their power advantages to gain a permanent advantage over weaker states. This model of postwar institution building is an ideal type. None of the major postwar settlements fully conforms to its ideal logic. The model allows, however, for the identification of a logic of order building that is more or less present in the settlements of 1815, 1919, and 1945, and that is most fully evident in the 1945 settlement among the industrial democracies. Chapters Four, Five, and Six examine these major modern postwar cases. The 1815 juncture provided Britain with a leading power position, but the establishment of binding institutions was limited by the nondemocratic character of the states involved. The proposed general security guarantee failed primarily because of the inability to the states involved to make binding commitments. Russian Tsar Alexander's highly personal and eccentric foreign policy was the most visible expression of this constraint. The 1815 case shows the leading state attempting to use institutions as a mechanism of power restraint, and there are some traces of constitutional order, but the episode also reveals the limits to which nondemocratic states can create binding institutions. In 1919, the prevalence of democracies among the Western postwar powers provided opportunities for institutional agreement, and Woodrow Wilson articulated ambitious institutional proposals. European leaders did worry about American domination and abandonment, and they did seek to draw the United States into a security commitment. An institutional bargain was within reach, and the reasons for failure are more idio-

syncratic than deeply rooted in the postwar circumstances identified by
the model. Wilson's stubborn convictions about the sources of law and
institutions, the poor exercise of American power, and missed opportunities were enough to doom the settlement, particularly in the face of conflicting interests among the allies.

The 1945 juncture provided the most pronounced incentives and capacities for the leading and secondary states to move toward an institutionalized settlement. The United States commanded a far more favorable power
position than it did after 1919 or than Britain did after 1815. It had more
capacities to make institutional bargains with other states, and the sharp
asymmetries in power made European governments particularly eager for
agreements that would establish commitments and restraints. The democratic character of the states involved made the institutional agreements
that resulted—however reluctantly they were initially entered into—more
credible and effective in mitigating the severest implications of power
asymmetry. The character of the American domestic system—which provided transparency and "voice opportunities"—and the extensive use of
binding institutions served to limit the returns to power and provide assurances to states within the order that they would not be dominated or abandoned. The order that has emerged is distinctive—multilateral, reciprocal,
legitimate, and highly institutionalized. The post-1945 American-centered
order has found a novel and effective way to overcome the problem of
order posed by the great asymmetries of power after the war.

Because the Cold War reinforced cooperation among the industrial democracies, it is difficult to evaluate fully the significance of the institutional
sources of order during this period. As a result, the pattern of relations
among these countries after the Cold War takes on added theoretical importance. As Chapter Seven demonstrates, the durability of relations
among the advanced industrial countries—despite the loss of the Soviet
threat as a source of cooperation—are consistent with the logic of institutional order and pose problems for alternative theories of contemporary
international order.

The book's implications for contemporary American foreign policy makers are explored in the conclusion. The United States has entered the new
century as the world's lone superpower. Whether that extraordinary power
can be put to good use in creating a lasting and legitimate international
order will in no small measure be determined by how American officials
use and operate within international institutions. It might appear that there
are few constraints or penalties for the United States to exercise its power
unilaterally and at its own discretion. But the theory and historical experiences explored in these chapters suggest otherwise. The most enduringly
powerful states are those that work with and through institutions.

Chapter Two

VARIETIES OF ORDER: BALANCE OF POWER, HEGEMONIC, AND CONSTITUTIONAL

It is widely agreed that domestic and international politics are rooted in very different types of order. Domestic politics is the realm of shared identity, stable institutions, and legitimate authority, whereas international politics is, as one realist scholar recently put it, a "brutal arena where states look for opportunities to take advantage of each other, and therefore have little reason to trust each other."[1] In the most influential formulation, the two realms have fundamentally different structures: one based on the principle of hierarchy and the other on anarchy.[2]

But are the two realms really so dissimilar? Both domestic and international order can take many different forms. In some countries, politics can be extremely ruthless and coercive, whereas some areas of international politics are remarkably consensual and institutionalized. Seemingly stable and legitimate polities, such as the United States in the mid-nineteenth century, can rupture into bloody civil war, and countries within Western Europe and the North Atlantic region have created a highly stable and integrated political order over the last high century, in which armed violence is largely unthinkable. The most useful insight might be that both realms of politics—domestic and international—face similar problems in the creation and maintenance of order, and the solutions that emerge are often different but sometimes similar.

Across the great historical junctures, leading states have adopted different strategies for coping with the uncertainties and disparities of postwar power and, as a result, have built different types of postwar orders. Variations in the extent to which leading states attempted to built order around binding institutions are manifest in the divergent order-building efforts of Britain in 1815 and the United States in 1919 and 1945. Thus the central empirical concern in the historical case studies in this book is with the policies and actions of these states relating to the reorganization of postwar relations among the major states. In what way and to what extent did these leading states advance institutional strategies for establishing restraints and

[1] John Mearsheimer, "The False Promise of International Institutions," *International Security*, Vol. 19, No. 3 (Winter 1994/95), p. 9.

[2] Kenneth Waltz, *Theory of International Politics* (Reading, Mass.: Addison-Wesley, 1979).

commitments? What determined the opportunities and constraints on the pursuit of these institutional strategies?

It is possible to draw inferences about the strategies of leading states by the type of order that ultimately emerges after the war. If leading and secondary states are willing and able to build order around binding institutions, the order will take on constitutional characteristics. Thus a second dependent variable is the character of the postwar order. This raises additional questions. How does constitutional order differ from more traditional balance-of-power and hegemonic orders? Along what dimensions do constitutional orders vary?

This chapter seeks to specify more precisely these variations in strategies and characteristics of postwar order. First, the chapter looks at the major types of political order—balance of power, hegemonic, and constitutional. Second, it sketches the variety of strategies that states have employed to build order and organize the way in which power is exercised and restrained. Finally, it discusses the sources of and variations in political stability of postwar order.

VARIETIES OF POLITICAL ORDER

The central problem of international relations is the problem of order—how it is devised, how it breaks down, and how it is recreated.[3] Yet it is not obvious what is meant by "order" in international relations, and therefore the "breakdown of order" or the "creation of order" are also ambiguous.[4] What is political order, how does it vary, and how can it be compared?

In his classic discussion of order, Hedley Bull distinguishes between world order and international order, the former composed of all peoples and the totality of relations among them, and the latter a system of rules and settled expectations among states. International order is defined as "a pattern of activity that sustains the elementary or primary goals of the society of states, or international society."[5] This distinction is useful in locating the different realms of order and illuminating both the deep structures of

---

[3] See Raymond Aron, *Peace and War* (Garden City, N.Y.: Doubleday, 1966), and Stanley Hoffmann, *World Disorders: Troubled Peace in the Post-Cold War Era* (New York: Rowman and Littlefield, 1998), chapter eight.

[4] Order is obviously only one feature of world politics. Critics of this focus argue that to give order analytical primacy is to give the study of international politics a static, statist, and Western bias. See Steve Smith, "Is the Truth out There? Eight Questions about International Order," in T. V. Paul and John A. Hall, eds., *International Order and the Future of World Politics* (New York: Cambridge University Press, 1999). For a discussion of the contested meaning of order, see Robert W. Cox with Timothy J. Sinclair, *Approaches to World Order* (Cambridge: Cambridge University Press, 1996).

[5] Hedley Bull, *The Anarchical Society: A Study of Order in World Politics* (London: Macmillan, 1977), p. 7.

international society and the evolving institutions and practices that compose relations among states. It is less useful in providing conceptual tools with which to probe historical transitions and contested junctures that transform rules and institutions of order.

In this book, political order refers to the "governing" arrangements among a group of states, including its fundamental rules, principles, and institutions. Political order is established when the basic organizing arrangements of the system are set up. When they are overturned, contested, or in disarray, order has broken down; when they are reestablished, order has been recreated. The focus is on the explicit principles, rules, and institutions that define the core relationships between the states that are party to the order. This limits the concept of order to settled arrangements between states that define their relationship to each other and mutual expectations about their ongoing interaction.

This conception of order is similar to what Robert Gilpin calls "systemic" order and change, which refers to "change in the governance of an international system." Governance change is "change in the international distribution of power, the hierarchy of prestige, and the rules and rights embodied in the system."[6] Systemic order does not refer to all aspects of international cooperation or agreements. It refers to the basic rules and principles of order among the states within the system. It refers to the rules of the game, even if these rules stipulate simply that governance is to be achieved through the balance of power or rule by the most powerful state.

Defined in this way, international order can take a variety of forms. A stable political order does not necessarily require normative agreement among its members. The order could be based simply on exchange relations, coercion, or the operation of the balance of power. Nor must stable order be based on explicit agreements among states. Order could be essentially spontaneous, the side effect of states acting separately. Indeed, neorealists argue that one of the virtues of a balance-of-power order is precisely that it requires so little agreement, normative consensus, or shared characteristics among the units. An order could also be based simply on a convergence of specific interests among states, or it could be an order based entirely on hegemonic coercion.

BALANCE-OF-POWER AND HEGEMONIC ORDERS

The three most important varieties of political order among states are those organized around the balance of power, hegemony, and constitutionalism. Each represents a different way in which power is distributed and

---

[6] Robert Gilpin, *War and Change in World Politics* (New York: Cambridge University Press, 1981), p. 42.

Table 2–1
Types of International Order

	Balance of Power	*Hegemonic*	*Constitutional*
organizing principle	anarchy	hierarchy	rule of law
restraints on concentrated power	counterbalancing coalitions	none	binding institutions
source of stability	equilibrium of power	preponderance of power	limits on the return to power

exercised among states—differences, that is, in the basic organizing relations of power and authority. They also differ in terms of the restraints that are manifest on the exercise of state power and in the sources of cohesion and cooperation among states. They differ, as well, in terms of the underlying conditions that render international order more or less stable.

Order based on balance, hegemony, and constitutionalism are ideal types. Actual historical orders have typically exhibited characteristics of several types. Balance and hegemonic orders—captured in neorealist theories of international relations—are well known and richly theorized. Constitutional order—at least as it is manifest in relations among states—requires more elaboration. The basic characteristics of these orders are summarized in Table 2–1.

A balance-of-power order is organized around the principle of anarchy, in which there is no overarching political authority. According to Kenneth Waltz, this is the essence of the international system. The "parts" of the system are made up of states that are alike ("like units") in their fundamental character, undifferentiated by function.[7] In a condition of anarchy, states do not stand in any fixed, formal, or hierarchical relation with one another. The last word in political authority is state sovereignty, which constitutes the formal rejection of hierarchy.

In a world of anarchy, incentives exist for states to balance.[8] Security—indeed survival—is the fundamental goal of states, and because states can-

[7] Waltz, *Theory of International Politics*, p. 95.

[8] Three assumptions lie behind the neorealist claim that balance of power is the only real solution to the problem of order. First, all states seek security, but because other states can always become threats, that security is never absolute. Second, the intentions of other states are inherently uncertain. A state can never be absolutely sure that its current allies will remain allies in the future or turn into adversaries. This is because all states have the capacity to threaten, and their intentions are unknowable. Finally, relative capabilities are more important than absolute capabilities to ensure the security of states, because security is derived from the relative strength of a state in relation to competing states.

not ultimately rely on the commitments or guarantees of other states to ensure their security, states will be very sensitive to their relative power position. When powerful states emerge, secondary states will seek protection in countervailing coalitions of weaker states. The alternative is to risk domination. As Waltz argues: "Secondary states, if they are free to choose, flock to the weaker side; for it is the stronger side that threatens them. On the weaker side they are both more appreciated and safer, provided, of course, that the coalition they join achieves enough defensive or deterrent strength to dissuade adversaries from attacking."[9] Alliances emerge as temporary coalitions of states formed to counter the concentration of power. As the distribution of power shifts, coalitions will shift as well. Order is based on the balancing actions of states—the necessary and inevitable outcome of states seeking to ensure their security in an anarchic system.[10]

Waltz contrasts balancing with "bandwagoning," which he argues is a typical strategy of competitors within a domestic political system.[11] When would-be leaders compete for leadership of a political party, for example, they often form coalitions to block the success of other contenders, much as states do within anarchy. But once a leader is finally selected, the losers tend to bandwagon—to throw their support to the winning leader. "As soon as someone looks like the winner, nearly all jump on the bandwagon rather than continuing to build coalitions intended to prevent anyone from winning the prize of power."[12] Losing candidates have an incentive to throw their support to the winner. "In a competition for the position of leader, bandwagoning is sensible behavior where gains are possible even for the losers and where losing does not place their security in jeopardy."[13] The contrast is critical to Waltz, and it goes to the heart of the neorealist claim that domestic and international orders are fundamentally different types: the stakes of winning and losing are lower in domestic politics, and the possibilities exist to experience gains even while cooperating with the powerful new leader.

[9] Waltz, *Theory of International Politics*, p. 127.

[10] For discussions of balance-of-power politics, see Martin Wight, "The Balance of Power," in Butterfield and Wight, eds., *Diplomatic Investigations* (Cambridge: Harvard University Press, 1966), pp. 149–76; Edward V. Gulick, *Europe's Classical Balance of Power* (New York: W. W. Norton, 1967); Inis L. Claude, Jr., *Power and International Relations* (New York: Random House, 1962), pp. 3–93; Claude, "The Balance of Power Revisited," *Review of International Studies*, Vol. 15 (April 1989), pp. 77–86; Ernst Haas, "The Balance of Power: Prescription, Concept or Propaganda," *World Politics*, Vol. 15, No. 3 (1953), pp. 370–98; Stephen M. Walt, *The Origins of Alliances* (Ithaca: Cornell University Press, 1987); Glenn H. Snyder, *Alliance Politics* (Ithaca: Cornell University Press, 1997); and Michael W. Doyle, *Ways of War and Peace* (New York: W. W. Norton, 1997), chapter five.

[11] On the tendency of balancing over bandwagoning in international relations, see Walt, *The Origins of Alliances*, pp. 17–33, 263–66.

[12] Waltz, *Theory of International Politics*, p. 126.

[13] Ibid., p. 126.

To bandwagon in international politics is to allow the emergence of a "world hegemony," which would leave weaker states at the mercy of the strong. In anarchy, the only effective check on the rising power of another state is to combine with other weaker states to resist domination. It is this timeless logic of balance within anarchy that gives shape to international order.[14] Alternative logics do not make sense because the stakes are too high and they are not sustainable.

Hegemonic order is also based on the distribution of power among states, but it operates according to a very different logic: the relations of power and authority are defined by the organizing principle of hierarchy. In a hierarchical international order, states are integrated vertically with highly defined superordinate and subordinate positions. Political authority is centralized, although there may be a great deal of interdependence and functional differentiation among the units. According to Waltz, this authority principle is seen primarily in the structure of domestic political orders, where politics is "centralized and hierarchic." In this situation, "the parts of domestic political systems stand in relations of super and subordination. Some are entitled to command; others are required to obey."[15]

But hierarchies can be established and maintained in different ways. Where hierarchical power relations and political authority are established by the rule of law and the operation of agreed-upon formal institutional processes—for example, where rulers are elected through representative government—this is actually better seen as a constitutional political order. It is hierarchical only in the sense that political and legal institutions operate to invest authority in specific high offices through which officials exercise rule. In contrast, where the hierarchy is established and maintained by the coercive wielding of power, this more clearly captures the character of

---

[14] The need to maintain a balance of power to prevent the triumph of a dominant power is the core idea in realist theory from Thucydides to the present day. An evocative statement of this thinking is found in a report of the British Foreign Office written before World War I: "History shows that the danger threatening the independence of this or that nation has generally arisen, at least in part, out of the monetary predominance of a neighbouring State at once militarily powerful, economically efficient, and ambitious to extend its frontiers or spread its influence. . . . The only check on the abuse of political predominance derived from such a position has always consisted in the opposition of an equally formidable rival, or of a combination of several countries forming leagues of defence. The equilibrium established by such a grouping of forces is technically known as the balance of power, and it has become almost an historical truism to identify England's secular policy with the maintenance of this balance by throwing her weight now in this scale and now in that, but ever on the side opposed to the political dictatorship of the strongest single State or group at a given time." Quoted in "Memorandum by Sir Eyre Crowe on the Present State of British Relations with France and Germany, January 1, 1907," in G. P. Gooch and H. Temperly, eds., *British Documents on the Origin of the War, 1898–1914* (London: H. M. Stationary Office, 1928), Vol. 3, Appendix A, p. 405.

[15] Waltz, *Theory of International Politics*, p. 15.

hierarchy within hegemonic orders. It is the underlying disparities of power capabilities that create the conditions for hierarchical rule.

The most extreme form of hierarchical order in international relations would be empire, in which weaker units are not fully sovereign and control is ultimately based on coercive domination. In actual practice, imperial orders have varied widely in their degree of hierarchical domination and control.[16] Hegemonic orders are also hierarchical, although within the order weaker and secondary states are formally sovereign and the extent and mechanisms of domination can be looser and less formal. But ultimately, hegemonic order is established and maintained by the preponderance of power of the leading state, and when that power declines or passes to another state, the order will break apart or decay.[17]

The logic of hegemonic order is captured in Robert Gilpin's model of war and change, in which international politics is a succession of orders imposed on the world by leading states. As Gilpin argues, "the evolution of any system has been characterized by successive rises of powerful states that have governed the system and have determined the patterns of international interactions and established the rules of the system."[18] Steady and inevitable shifts in the distribution of power among states give rise to new challenger states who eventually engage the leading state in hegemonic war, which in turn gives rise to a new hegemonic state that uses its dominant position to establish an order favorable to its interests. Rules and rights are established and enforced by the power capacities of the hegemonic state. Compliance and participation within the order is ultimately ensured by the range of power capacities available to the hegemon—military power, financial capital, market access, technology, and so forth. Direct coercion is always an option in the enforcement of order, but less direct "carrots and sticks" are also mechanisms to maintain hegemonic control.

[16] See Michael Doyle, *Empires* (Ithaca: Cornell University Press, 1986).

[17] For discussions of hegemonic power and hegemonic stability theory, see Charles Kindleberger, *The World in Depression, 1929–1939* (Berkeley and Los Angeles: University of California Press, 1973); Stephen Krasner, "State Power and the Structure of International Trade," *World Politics*, Vol. 28, No. 3 (April 1976), pp. 317–47; Robert Gilpin, *US Power and the Multinational Corporation: The Political Economy of Direct Foreign Investment* (New York: Basic Books, 1973); Robert Keohane, "The Theory of Hegemonic Stability and Change in International Economic Regimes, 1967–1977," in O. R. Holsti, R. M. Siverson, and Alexander George, eds., *Change in the International System* (Boulder, Colo.: Westview Press, 1980), pp. 131–62; Susan Strange, "The Persistent Myth of Lost Hegemony," *International Organization*, Vol. 41, No. 4 (Autumn 1987), pp. 551–74; and David P. Rapkin, ed., *World Leadership and Hegemony* (Boulder, Colo.: Lynne Rienner, 1990). For a review of the literature, see David A. Lake, "Leadership, Hegemony, and the International Economy: Naked Emperor or Tattered Monarch with Potential?" *International Studies Quarterly*, Vol. 37, No. 4 (December 1993), pp. 459–89.

[18] Robert Gilpin, *War and Change in World Politics*, pp. 42–43.

Gilpin also argues that a wider set of resources—ideological and status appeals—are integral to the perpetuation of hegemonic order.[19] But the authority of the hegemonic state and the cohesion of hegemonic order are ultimately based on the predominance of power of the leading state, and when that power declines, the hegemonic order is bound to break apart.[20]

The strong version of hegemonic order is built around direct and coercive domination of weaker and secondary states by the hegemon. But hegemonic orders can also be more benevolent and less coercive—organized around more reciprocal, consensual, and institutionalized relations. The order is still organized around asymmetrical power relations, but the most overtly malign character of domination is muted.[21] Where hegemony takes a more benevolent form, with real restraints on the exercise of power, the resulting order begins to lean in the direction of constitutionalism. Likewise, these differences in the character of hegemony lead to differences in why weaker and secondary states do not attempt to balance against the lead state in a hegemonic order. In a highly coercive hegemonic order, weaker and secondary states are simply unable to counterbalance. Domination itself prevents the escape to a balance-of-power system. In more benign and consensual hegemonic orders, where restraints on hegemonic power are sufficiently developed, on the other hand, the expected value of balancing is lowered, and the incentives to pursue it are reduced. In these circumstances of benign hegemony, the order takes on characteristics of what might be called "weak" constitutionalism.

Balance-of-power and hegemonic orders are both creatures of the international distribution of power. Balancing orders reflect predictable and patterned responses to the prevailing distribution of power; they are driven

---

[19] Gilpin, *War and Change in World Politics.*

[20] In another version of the theory, George Modelski argues that the global political system goes through distinct historical cycles of domination by power states. According to Modelski, four states have played dominant or hegemonic roles since A.D. 1500: Portugal until the end of the sixteenth century, the Netherlands in the seventeenth century, Great Britain in the early eighteenth century until the Napoleonic wars and again in 1815 to 1945, and the United States since 1945. Modelski argues, as does Gilpin, that each cycle of hegemonic domination ends with war, ushering in a new hegemonic era. George Modelski, "The Long Cycle of Global Politics and the Nation-State," *Comparative Studies in Society and History,* Vol. 20, No. 2 (April 1978), pp. 214–35; and George Modelski and William R. Thompson, *Leading Sectors and World Powers: The Coevolution of Global Economic and Politics* (Columbia: University of South Carolina Press, 1996). For a survey of the power cycle literature, see Torbjorn L. Knutsen, *The Rise and Fall of World Orders* (Manchester: Manchester University Press, 1999).

[21] The distinction between benevolent and coercive hegemony is made by Duncan Snidal, "The Limits of Hegemonic Stability Theory," *International Organization,* Vol. 35, No. 4 (Autumn 1985), (1985), pp. 579–614; Bruce Russett, "The Mysterious Case of Vanishing Hegemony: Or Is Mark Twain Really Dead?" *International Organization,* Vol. 39, No. 2 (Spring 1985), pp. 207–31; and Joseph Lepgold, *The Declining Hegemon: The United States and European Defense, 1960–1990* (New York: Praeger, 1990).

by the fundamental interest that states have to maintain their position and not to be dominated by an unchecked hegemonic state. As the distribution of power shifts, so too do the balancing coalitions. Hegemonic orders are established and maintained by the concentration of power, although the degree of direct coercion and manipulation of weaker and secondary states can vary. The ideological appeal and prestige of the hegemonic state are also relevant to its ability to form a stable order. But whereas a balance-of-power order is based on the checking or counterbalancing of concentrated power, a hegemonic order is essentially based on unchecked power. Both these types of order can be contrasted with constitutional order, where the checks on power are much more fixed and developed, rooted in relatively intractable institutional frameworks.

Constitutional Order

Constitutional orders are political orders organized around agreed-upon legal and political institutions that operate to allocate rights and limit the exercise of power. In a constitutional order, power is "tamed" by making it less consequential. The stakes in political struggles are reduced by the creation of institutionalized processes of participation and decision making that specify rules, rights, and limits on power holders. A constitutional order is neither identified nor ensured by the existence of a constitutional document or charter—although constitutional orders may in fact have a written constitution—but by the way in which agreed-upon and institutionalized rules, rights, protections, and commitments combine to shape and circumscribe the wielding of power within the order.[22]

Constitutional orders are most clearly seen within domestic polities, particularly within the Western democratic countries. The idea that relations among states can be organized in a constitutional order is much more uncertain and problematic. Limits on power are never clear-cut, absolute, or fully guaranteed in relations between states. "In the international system," as Stephen Krasner argues, "institutions are less constraining and more fluid, more subject to challenge and change than in more settled circumstances. The mechanisms for locking in particular institutional forms, such as socialization, positive reinforcement between structures and agents, or path-dependent processes, are weaker at the international level than in

---

[22] Most of the countries of the world have constitutions, but this in itself does not make them constitutional political orders. As a recent study of Eastern European constitutional experience notes, although these countries under communism did have constitutional charters or texts, "they were not meant to constrain and to obligate the power elites. They had little, if anything, to do with the idea of constitutionalism." Jon Elster, Claus Offe, and Ulrich K. Preuss, *Institutional Design in Post-Communist Societies: Rebuilding the Ship at Sea* (New York: Cambridge University Press, 1998), p. 63.

well-established domestic polities."[23] The underlying structural condition, even in highly complex and integrated international orders, is still anarchic. But where institutions can be established that provide some measure of binding restraint on states, and where domestic polities allow for the locking in of international commitments, the conditions exist for an international political order to operate with some measure of constitutionalism.[24]

As Giovanni Sartori argues, "constitutions are, first and above all, instruments of government which limit, restrain and allow for the control of the exercise of political power."[25] But even in domestic constitutional systems, limits and restraints are not absolute, and governments can vary widely in the depth and breadth of their constitutional controls. The incremental and piecemeal character of constitutionalism can be glimpsed in its early modern rise in Britain, when constitutional limits and restraints were contained in a variety of documents that were variously called covenants, instruments, agreements, and fundamental laws. The first written constitutions emerged in America and were enacted in 1776—the constitutions of Virginia, Maryland, and Pennsylvania.[26] In general, constitutional-type restraints on power are even less evident in relations among states, but if interstate political orders do manifest institutional restraints that shape and limit—at least to some degree—the way state power is exercised, we are in a position to ask the next question: Why are some international orders more constitutional in character than others?[27]

Three Elements of Constitutionalism

A constitutional political order has three essential characteristics. First, shared agreement exists over the principles and rules of order. Participation and consent are based on this shared agreement on basic principles and rules. There is a meeting of minds about what the "rules of the game" are within the political order, and these "rules of the game" will contribute to the operation of a stable and noncoercive order. Agreement at this basic level means that the rules and institutions of the political order are in some

[23] Stephen D. Krasner, "Compromising Westphalia," *International Security*, Vol. 20, No. 3 (Winter 1995/96), p. 117.

[24] These enabling conditions are developed in the next chapter.

[25] Sartori, *Comparative Constitutional Engineering: An Inquiry into Structures, Incentives and Outcomes* (London: Macmillan, 1994), p. 198. Constitutions entail both denials and grants of power. See Samuel H. Beer, *To Make a Nation* (Cambridge: Harvard University Press, 1993), p. 97.

[26] See Carl J. Friedrich, *Constitutional Government and Democracy: Theory and Practice in Europe and America* (Boston: Ginn, 1950).

[27] For a typology of regimes and constitutional agreements, see Alec Stone, "What Is a Supranational Constitution? An Essay in International Relations Theory," *Review of Politics*, Vol. 56, No. 3 (Summer 1994), pp. 441–74.

fundamental sense legitimate. Participants willingly embrace the rules of the game as appropriate and right. But, of course, the legitimacy of a political order does not by itself mean that it is a constitutional order. A balance-of-power order may be legitimate, but it is not a constitutional order.

Second, rules and institutions are established that set binding and authoritative limits on the exercise of power. Constitutions are a form of legal constraint on politics, manifest as a declaration of principles that specify rights, protections, and basic rules.[28] Constraints on power are also ensured through institutional devices and procedures such as the separation of powers and checks and balances. The end result is that holders of power must exercise that power within an institutionalized political process.

Constitutional political orders are those in which the fundamental political institutions within the polity have gained sufficient autonomy to shape and limit the play of deeper social forces. In such orders, as Samuel Huntington argues, "the power of each group is exercised through political institutions which temper, moderate, and redirect that power so as to render the dominance of one social force compatible with the community of many."[29] Historically, constitutional political orders emerged in the Mediterranean world when clan-based societies broke down, and more diverse and unequal social groupings threatened to destroy political community. Political institutions emerged as solutions to this rising diversity and inequality: they provided new formal ways to connect groups together, mechanisms to settle disputes, and a structure of government that restricted the ways wealth could be translated into political power.[30] Constitutional political orders are ones with political institutions that have achieved a high degree of autonomy—institutions that are not simply the reflection of specific social forces or class interests, and that dampen and mute the political implications of inequality within the society.

Finally, in a constitutional order, these rules and institutions are entrenched in the wider political system and not easily altered. Constitutional struggles happen only rarely, and once they are settled, politics is expected to take place within these legal and institutional parameters. In other words, there is a notion of political "path dependency" in arguments about constitutions and constitutional change. This logic of constitutional politics is advanced by Bruce Ackerman, who embraces a "dualist" theory of consti-

[28] For a discussion of constitutional constraints that emphasizes both the negative features of constitutional binding and its positive and dynamic purposes as a mode of institutional design, see Stephen Holmes, "Precommitment and the Paradox of Democracy," in Holmes, *Passions and Constraint: On the Theory of Liberal Democracy* (Chicago: University of Chicago Press, 1995), pp. 152–77.

[29] Samuel Huntington, *Political Order in Changing Societies* (New Haven: Yale University Press, 1968), p. 9.

[30] Ibid., p. 11.

tutional development and makes a basic distinction between "higher" and "normal" lawmaking in American political development. Most of what passes for politics and government decision making is "normal lawmaking," which takes place within defined constitutional limits. When elected leaders wish to change some aspect of the basic framework, they must engage in "constitutional politics"; "they must take to the specially onerous obstacle course provided by a dualist Constitution for purposes of higher lawmaking." To change the country's higher laws requires the mobilization of "the people"—a process that is required by constitutional rules and by the need to generate sufficient "democratic legitimacy" to make fundamental constitutional change. As a result, constitutional politics takes place at rare moments when popular struggle and political mobilization break out over basic questions of American politics, and sometimes culminates in constitutional revision.[31]

Reducing the Implications of Winning

In effect, constitutional agreements reduce the implications of "winning" in international relations or, to put it more directly, they serve to reduce the returns to power. This is also what constitutions do within domestic orders. They set limits on what an actor that gains disproportionately within the order can do with those gains, thereby reducing the stakes of uneven gains. According to Adam Przeworski, "Unless the increasing returns to power are institutionally mitigated, losers must fight the first time they lose, for waiting makes it less likely that they will ever succeed."[32] In this way, constitutions set limits on what power holders can do with momentary advantages. Losers realize their losses are limited and temporary—to accept those losses is not to risk everything, nor will it give the winner a permanent advantage.

The role of constitutional limits on power can be seen most clearly in mature Western constitutional democracies. When a party or leader wins an election and takes control of the government, there are fundamental and strictly defined limits on the scope of the power that can be exercised. A newly elected leader cannot use the military to oppress or punish his rivals, or use the taxing and law-enforcement powers of government to harm or destroy the opposition party. As a result, both parties can agree to stay within the system and play by the rules.[33]

---

[31] Bruce Ackerman, *We the People: Foundations* (Cambridge: Belkap Press of Harvard University Press, 1991), p. 6.

[32] Adam Przeworski, *Democracy and the Market* (New York: Cambridge University Press, 1991), p. 36. See also Jon Elster and Rune Slagstad, eds., *Constitutionalism and Democracy* (New York: Cambridge University Press, 1988).

[33] A growing formal theoretical literature is exploring the ways in which constitutions function to establish credible limits on the exercise of state power. Competitive markets and stable

The role of constitutional rules and institutions can be seen more clearly in countries with sharply divided social or ethnic groupings and without the natural social homogeneity and cross-cutting cleavages that typify most Western countries. Arend Lijpart's study of political order in the Netherlands is illustrative; it is a country with deep religious and class cleavages that create separate, distinct, and isolated population groups, but they nonetheless operate within political institutions that allow for "stable, effective, and legitimate parliamentary democracy."[34] How do these divided and self-contained blocs defend and promote their interests without resort to civil war or the threat of secession? Lijphart argues that some modest degree of shared national identity helps. But importantly, a politics of accommodation has emerged and become institutionalized in Holland, a politics that "resembles politics at the international level." A sort of confederal political structure has taken shape: a permanent institutional framework that ensures that each bloc will not become a permanent loser in the political system. In particular, the rule of proportionality in decision making and in the allocation of resources is critical to the politics of accommodation. Every group is assured of winning at least a bit. This rule of proportionality is followed in the government's cabinet structure. "Not all major parties are permanently on the cabinet, of course," Lijphart notes. "But being in opposition does not entail being excluded from the policy-making process. There is no sharp line between government and opposition parties."[35] The constitutional structure of government binds the blocs together and creates formal institutional mechanisms that ensure that each bloc has a stake in the process. No single bloc can win everything or all the time, but neither will any bloc lose everything or all the time.

It is precisely the absence of these constitutional structures that helps to explain the violence of other ethnically or religiously divided states. In these states, winning is potentially absolute and so, too, is losing. If one

democracy hinge on the ability of a polity to overcome the problem of "credible commitment," that is, its ability to establish and maintain guarantees of economic and political rights by providing binding assurances that state rulers or a majority coalition will not exploit their power position to confiscate wealth or oppress minorities. In this formulation, the constitution operates as a "self-enforcing agreement," solving coordination problems that allow citizens to police the state. See Barry R. Weingast, "Constitutions as Governance Structures: The Political Foundations of Secure Markets," *Journal of Institutional and Theoretical Economics*, Vol. 149, No. 1 (1993), pp. 287–311; and Douglass C. North and Weingast, "Constitutions and Commitment: The Evolution of the Institutions Governing Public Choice in Seventeenth-Century England," *Journal of Economic History*, Vol. 49, No. 4 (December 1989), pp. 803–32.

[34] Arend Lijphart, *The Politics of Accommodation: Pluralism and Democracy in the Netherlands* (Berkeley and Los Angeles: University of California Press, 1968), p. 2. See also Lijphart, *Democracy in Plural Societies: A Comparative Exploration* (New Haven: Yale University Press, 1975).

[35] Lijphart, *The Politics of Accommodation*, p. 136.

religious or ethnic faction wins control of the apparatus of the state, the other faction has no protections against domination or violent destruction. The stakes in these political battles are total: to lose is to risk losing one's life. As a result, the factions have an incentive to battle to the death. Only when each group has guarantees that laying down weapons and allowing the other group to wield power has more limited and temporary consequences can agreement be reached.

James Fearon identifies this problem in societies torn apart by ethnic and religious violence as a "commitment problem."[36] In societies—such as the former Yugoslavia—previously held together by imperial power, an ethnically and religiously divided majority and minority face each other. The minority must choose whether to participate in the new state and accept a share of the "gains" within the society, or launch a war of secession. It would prefer opting for some agreed-upon division of the gains to fighting a civil war, but only if it could be guaranteed that the majority would in fact implement the agreed-upon division in the new state. But the majority cannot credibly commit itself to the fulfillment of these moderate demands because once the new state is formed, it will have consolidated its power through control of the police and army. There is no effective check on its power once the state is formed. Fighting a war of secession is preferable to living in a postimperial state "with no credible guarantees on their political status, or economic and even physical security."[37] In this model, ethnic war is a sort of "preventive war" undertaken by the minority because of the majority's inability to commit to certain political bargains.

Constitutional institutions serve to mitigate this problem. If they are effective, they reduce or limit the returns to power of groups—or states—that momentarily possess greater power advantages. In reducing the returns to power, constitutional orders both reduce what a power holder is able to do with its power at any given moment and to ensure that its power advantages are not permanent.

How Constitutional Restraints are Manifest

There is considerable disagreement among theorists over the sources of constitutional authority, particularly among instrumental views and deeper views that center on goals and values. Constitutional orders create political frameworks that are difficult to change, but what exactly makes them so?

---

[36] James D. Fearon, "Commitment Problems and the Spread of Ethnic Conflict," in David A. Lake and Donald Rothchild, eds., *The International Spread of Ethnic Conflict: Fear, Diffusion, and Escalation* (Princeton: Princeton University Press, 1998). See also Fearon and David D. Laitin, "Explaining Inter-Ethnic Cooperation," *American Political Science Review*, Vol. 90, No. 4 (December 1996), pp. 715–35.

[37] Fearon, "Commitment Problems and the Spread of Ethnic Conflict," p. 118.

Some theorists stress the specific legal and judicial mechanisms that protect rights and create limitations on power. In this view, constitutions are a form of legal constraint on politics, manifest as a declaration of principles that specify rights, protections, and basic rules. In this way, the constitution provides a sort of "last word" on the essential principles and rules of political order, which can nevertheless be applied, interpreted, and extended. The argument made by some that the European Union is becoming a constitutional order stresses the spread of European judicial principles and practices, which serve to create a Europe governed by a "specified interstate governmental structure defined by a constitutional charter and constitutional principles."[38] Others stress the institutional architecture of constitutional orders, which create limits on power through the many institutional devices and procedures that they specify. Theories of institutional balance, separation, oversight, and judicial review have an intellectual lineage that may be traced from Aristotle to Locke and Montesquieu. In this view, constitutions create limits through institutional design. Finally, others argue that constitutional authority is really a reflection of (and therefore dependent on) the wider, shared consensus on political order within the polity. The stable functioning of a constitution requires a consensus on basic principles and rules. It is the diffuse authority of common values and political goals that creates the constraint on power.[39]

In this book, I stress the way in which power is restrained through binding institutions that tie states down and together, and thereby reduce worries about domination and abandonment. In this sense, constitutionalism depends heavily on the role of international institutions as shaping, constraining, and connecting mechanisms between states. It is precisely because institutions can in various ways bind (particularly democratic) states together, constrain state actions, and create complicated and demanding political processes that participating states can overcome worries about the arbitrary and untoward exercise of power.

Strong and Weak Constitutional Orders

Constitutional orders are political orders that limit or restrain the exercise of power through a framework of agreed-upon rules, institutions, and for-

---

[38] Joseph Weiler, "The Transformation of Europe," *Yale Law Journal*, Vol. 100, No. 8 (June 1991), p. 2407.

[39] Taking this view, Robert Dahl argues in regard to constitutional rules in the United States: "to assume that this country remained democratic because of the Constitution seems to me an obvious reversal of the relation; it is much more plausible to suppose that the Constitution has remained because our society is essentially democratic." Dahl, *A Preface to Democratic Theory* (New Haven: Yale University Press, 1956), p. 143. See also Dahl, *On Democracy* (New Haven: Yale University Press, 1998), chapter ten.

mal-legal authority. But institutional limits on the exercise of power, in both domestic and international orders, are never absolute. Political orders can vary widely in how and the extent to which constitutional arrangements limit the returns to power. Or, to put it differently, political orders may be more or less constitutional in character.

A strong constitutional order is a political order in which the rules, rights, and protections are widely agreed upon, highly institutionalized, and generally observed. Authoritative institutions and procedures spell out the principles and rules by which power is exercised. It is ultimately the sturdiness of basic political institutions—their resistance to manipulation by particular powerful group interests—that determines its strength as a constitutional order. If strong political or class interests can easily overturn or circumvent basic laws and political procedures, the constitutional order would be considered much weaker. Samuel Huntington argues that a highly developed political system has "procedures to minimize, if not to eliminate, the role of violence in the system and to restrict to explicitly defined channels the influence of wealth in the system."[40] This is precisely what defines the strength of a constitutional order—the autonomy and resilience of basic political institutions to their manipulation by social forces and power wielders.

An international order with strong constitutional characteristics is one in which the power capabilities of the relevant states are highly constrained by interlocking institutions and binding agreements.[41] In practice, constitutional characteristics within an international order are manifest in the degree to which international institutions bind powerful and weaker states together, creating a difficult-to-change institutional framework within which their relations are carried out, and thereby establishing some limits on the arbitrary and indiscriminate exercise of state power. Moreover, the strength of the order's constitutional characteristics will depend on the degree to which the wider set of relations among states are institutionalized in binding agreements and mechanisms.

Seen in this way, constitutional order can be contrasted with balance-of-power and hegemonic orders.[42] A balance-of-power order is one in which restraints on state power are maintained exclusively by countervailing coalitions of states. The concentration of power is checked by alliances that aggregate opposition power. Hegemonic power is effectively unrestrained power. Weaker and secondary states cooperate with the hegemon because

[40] Huntington, *Political Order in Changing Societies*, p. 21.

[41] In practice, an international order with strong constitutional characteristics may, in relative terms, look more like a domestic political order with weak constitutional characteristics. But the point is that constitutionalism—whether in domestic or international political order—varies, and therefore variations can be identified and explained.

[42] Actual orders may in fact exhibit characteristics of each of these basic types.

of threats and inducements. But once institutional constraints on the exercise of power are introduced, it is possible to imagine a wider range of mixed and varied political orders. The strong version of balance of power, as Kenneth Waltz argues, is based on the view that "bandwagoning" is a risky alternative for weak and secondary states. But if there are credible commitments and binding institutions that potentially mitigate the most extreme forms of exploitation of the weak by the strong, bandwagoning or a mix of balance and cooperation is potentially less unattractive. Likewise, in a hegemonic order where institutions can be put in place that inhibit or constrain the exercise of arbitrary and indiscriminate power by the leading state, the power asymmetries—and the returns to power—begin to lose their full significance.

POWER RESTRAINT STRATEGIES

In addition to looking directly at the overall character of political order that emerges after major war, it is also possible to look at the strategies of leading and weaker states as they attempt to construct the postwar order. The argument of this book is that the character of postwar orders have changed as the order-building strategies that states have had available to them have changed. These strategies can be delineated.

The postwar settlements of 1648, 1713, 1815, 1919, and 1945 all grappled with the problem of how to restrain and limit power. But the orders that emerged from the settlements differed—and evolved—in how they sought to do so. To appreciate these differences, it is useful to see these institutional restraint mechanisms as part of wider continuum of techniques and arrangements that states can employ to constrain and disperse power within the international system. These strategies include the promotion of state autonomy, the division of territory to disperse power, the creation of counterbalancing alliances, and the creation of binding institutions. This spectrum of power control strategies is summarized in Table 2–2.

The most basic strategy is to reinforce state sovereignty. Power is controlled through the fragmentation of political units into sovereign states. If states are given legal independence and political primacy within the order, this undercuts the aggrandizement of power by imperial and religious groupings. This decentralization of power is reinforced through the codification of state sovereignty in international public law. This was the most important objective of the Westphalia settlement: to confer ultimate sovereign autonomy to territorial states, which were subordinate to no other type of authority such as universal monarchy. The rights and sovereign autonomy of states were divorced from particular religions, and it extended international law by putting republican and monarchical states

TABLE 2–2
Power Restraint Strategies

Technique	Logic
reinforce state autonomy	fragmentation of political units undercut religious and imperial groupings
territorial/power distribution	disperse power capability into multiple units
	restrain power aggrandizement
counterbalancing alliances	check power aggrandizement through blocking coalitions of states
institutional binding	tie potentially threatening states together in alliances and mutually constraining institutions
supranational integration	share sovereignty with overarching political institutions/authorities

on a footing of equality.[43] Behind these mutual expectations about the role of religion and territorial sovereignty were understandings about Europe as a political order: that it had a unity and integrity as an organized political area within which rulers shared certain common orientations. The treaties of Osnabruck and Munster fixed by written instrument the political status of individual states, affirming the principle of territorial sovereignty in both religious and political matters. A shared legal notion lay behind the articulated norm: that the autonomy of states was a matter of law or legal doctrine, and as such it had a standing that military force alone could not challenge.[44]

This view of the Westphalia settlement emphasizes the efforts of the victorious states—particularly France and Sweden—to undermine or erode the religious universalism and hierarchical control of the Holy Roman Empire. As Kalevi Holsti argues, Westphalia "represented a new diplomatic arrangement—an order created by states, for states—and replaced most of the legal vestiges of hierarchy, at the pinnacle of which were the Pope and the Holy Roman Empire."[45] Territorial rulers were given the right to choose between Protestantism and Catholicism, territorial units were given legal status equal to the emperor, and Roman notions of exclusive territo-

[43] See Leo Gross, "The Peace of Westphalia, 1648–1948," *American Journal of International Law*, Vol. 42, No. 1 (January 1948), pp. 20–41.

[44] See Kalevi J. Holsti, *Peace and War: Armed Conflicts and International Order, 1648–1989* (New York: Cambridge University Press, 1991), chapter two.

[45] Ibid., p. 25.

rial property rights were rediscovered.[46] In these ways, the settlement strengthened the political and legal autonomy of emerging territorial states. As Stephen Krasner argues, the peace treaties themselves were not a sharp break with the past; they built on earlier practices and doctrines, and they reflected the specific territorial and political interests of the winning states. Post-Westphalia Europe remained a heterogeneous mixture of political and institutional types.[47] But the settlement did reflect an effort to counter Europe-wide religious-imperial domination by strengthening the legal and political autonomy of territorial rulers.

A second technique to control power involves the break-up or separation of territorial units so as to disperse power capabilities. The aim is to make sure that no state possesses sufficient territorial assets to dominate the other states in the order. At postwar peace conferences, the map of political order is literally on the table. Defeated states have few options to resist this redrafting exercise, and the collapse of failed hegemonic states, such as France after 1713 and 1815 and Germany after the world wars, opens up vast territorial domains to negotiation. In some cases, such as after the wars of the Spanish succession, the postwar territorial negotiations are explicitly concerned with the fragmentation and distribution of territory so as to disperse power potential; in other cases the breakup of huge territorial powers have been pursued in the name of self-determination, such as after World War I. The expansion of sovereign nation-states after 1945 also reflected efforts by major states to limit power by reinforcing state autonomy. By breaking the empires apart, the power potential of the developed countries was significantly limited.[48] Across these postwar eras, the strategy was the same: to constrain power aggrandizement by fragmenting and distributing territorial units.

The third strategy of power control is the most familiar: the balance of power. Here states develop arrangements that allow them to aggregate their power in temporary alliances to offset and counterbalance threatening powers in the international system, and this balancing behavior is conducive to international stability.[49] The specific mechanisms and processes of power balance can vary widely, and theories of balance of power reflect

[46] See John Gerard Ruggie, "Territoriality and Beyond: Problematizing Modernity in International Relations," *International Organization*, Vol. 46, No. 1 (Autumn 1993), pp. 139–74.

[47] Stephen D. Krasner, "Westphalia and All That," in Judith Goldstein and Robert O. Keohane, eds., *Ideas and Foreign Policy: Beliefs, Institutions, and Political Change* (Ithaca: Cornell University Press, 1993), pp. 235–64.

[48] See Robert H. Jackson, *Quasi-States: Sovereignty, International Relations, and the Third World* (New York: Cambridge University Press, 1990).

[49] For a recent survey, see Michael Sheehan, *The Balance of Power: History and Theory* (London: Routledge, 1996).

this diversity.[50] The working of balance may be more or less explicit as a principle of order, and alliance groupings may be more or less formal and institutionalized. But the essential logic is the same: the aggrandizement of power is checked by countervailing power.

The Utrecht settlement of 1713 was most notable in its enshrinement of the notion of balance as the source of power restraint, but it also drew on the strategies of enhancing state autonomy and power distribution.[51] The settlement articulated a shared understanding that the states were in fundamental ways equal and autonomous. That is, the states within Europe were self-determining entities that could not be dominated or dictated by other states. As Andreas Osiander argues: "The triumph of equality is evident from the fact that, at Utrecht, the idea of a hierarchy of actors was discarded."[52] But the core principle of the settlement was the notion of the balance of power. France acknowledged that a union of the French and Spanish monarchies was unstable—an effective violation of the terms of European order. At Utrecht, the notions of balance and equilibrium were central to the settlement of territorial and dynastic disputes.

The Vienna settlement also invoked notions of balance and equilibrium. Castlereagh, Talleyrand, and Alexander all resorted to these notions in advancing settlement goals. The British foreign minister believed strongly in the principle of balance and equilibrium; all other principles and arrangements were secondary.[53] As we will see, the actual postwar settlement involved more refined ideas about balance; it entailed balance defined less in terms of material power capabilities than as a mutually acceptable understanding about the maintenance of political equilibrium within Europe. In addition, the great powers—who gave themselves special standing at Vienna—agreed that they should work together to maintain a mutually acceptable order, a joint management that required the development of rules and institutional arrangements to make territorial adjustments and resolve disputes.

The fourth strategy is institutional binding. Here states respond to potential threats and strategic rivalries by linking states together in mutually constraining institutions. Institutions can have this impact because of their

---

[50] Organski, for example, identifies six methods by which states might attempt to maintain the balance of power: to arm, seize territory, establish buffer zones, form alliances, intervene in the internal affairs of other nations, or divide and conquer. A.F.K. Organski, *World Politics*, 2nd ed. (New York: Alfred A. Knopf, 1968), p. 267.

[51] See Mathew S. Anderson, "Eighteenth-Century Theories of Balance of Power," in Ragnhild Hatton and Mathew S. Anderson, eds., *Studies in Diplomatic History: Essays in Memory of David Bayne Horn* (London: Archon Books, 1970), pp. 183–98.

[52] Andreas Osiander, *The States System of Europe, 1640–1990: Peacemaking and the Conditions of International Stability* (London: Oxford University Press, 1994), p. 121.

[53] Ibid., p. 175.

potential to bind and lock in effects. States might ordinarily seek to preserve their options, to cooperate with other states but to leave open the option of disengaging. Through institutional binding, states do exactly the opposite: they build long-term security, political, and economic commitments that are difficult to retract. They lock in their commitments and relationships, to the extent that this can be done by sovereign states. Examples of binding mechanisms include treaties, interlocking organizations, joint management responsibilities, agreed-upon standards and principles of relations, and so forth. These mechanisms raise the "costs of exit" and create "voice opportunities," thereby providing mechanisms to mitigate or resolve the conflict.[54]

Institutional binding can itself vary in terms of its extensiveness. Security alliances are the most important and potentially far-reaching form of binding. Paul Schroeder argues that the alliance that formed the Concert of Europe was an early manifestation of this binding logic. In this and other subsequent cases, alliances were created as *pacta de controhendo*—pacts of restraint.[55] They have served as mechanisms for states to manage and restrain their partners within the alliance. "Frequently the desire to exercise such control over an ally's policy," Schroeder argues, "was the main reason that one power, or both, entered into the alliance."[56] Alliances create binding treaties that allow states to keep a hand in the security policy of their partners.

But alliances can also vary in the degree to which they entail binding relations. The post-1815 congress system loosely bound the European great powers to periodic consultations and a continuation of the anti-Napoleonic alliance. The 1949 security pact between the United States and Western Europe was a much more binding institution, particularly after it developed intergovernmental planning mechanisms, a multinational force, and an integrated military command. The range of obligations are more extensive, and the institutional mechanisms that ensure ongoing commitments are greater within the NATO alliance than in other security pacts.

Institutional binding can also be manifest in other types of institutions that lock states together in joint decision making, enmeshing states in deeply rooted forms of institutionalized cooperation. The practice of institutional binding only makes sense if international institutions or regimes

---

[54] These terms are from Albert Hirschman, *Exit, Voice, and Loyalty* (Cambridge: Harvard University Press, 1970).

[55] See Paul W. Schroeder, "Alliances, 1815–1945: Weapons of Power and Tools of Management," in Klaus Knorr, ed., *Historical Dimensions of National Security Problems* (Lawrence: University Press of Kansas, 1975), pp. 227–62; and Snyder, *Alliance Politics*, chapter nine.

[56] Schroeder, "Alliances, 1815–1945," p. 230.

can have an independent ordering impact on the actions of states.[57] The assumption is that institutions are sticky—that they can take on a life and logic of their own, shaping and constraining even the states that create them. When states employ institutional binding as a strategy, they are essentially agreeing to mutually constrain themselves. In effect, institutions specify what it is that states are expected to do and make it difficult and costly for states to do otherwise.

A final strategy is formal supranational integration, where the formal legal and institutional obligations between states within the union are essentially indistinguishable from internal legal and political institutions. The strategy is similar to institutional binding, but it goes beyond intergovernmentalism to include more formal merging or sharing of formal sovereign authority. The European Coal and Steel Community (ECSC) is one of the earliest examples of this strategy: the French government and other Western Europeans sought to tie postwar German industrial capacity to a wider European institutional structure. These industrial sectors—the core of war-making capacity—were reconstructed in a joint Franco-German enterprise. Rather than balancing against Germany or destroying its industrial base, France and Western Europe moved to bind Germany to the wider regional order.[58]

More generally, many observers argue that the European Union is increasingly taking shape as a supranational political order, and European lawyers and judges have begun talking about the EU as a "constitutional" polity.[59] In a supranational order, the "pooling" of sovereignty and political authority has been widely diffused across national and international levels, so as to make the unilateral assertion of national or state authority difficult to invoke fully or decisively.

Institutional binding and supranationalism share characteristics as power restraint mechanisms. Binding institutions, such as NATO and the World

[57] The assumption that institutions can have an independent ordering impact on states is discussed in chapter three below.

[58] French support for the ECSC was also driven by more practical and immediate commercial goals, such as gaining access to cheap German coal as an input to its steel production. The actual political and economic achievements of the ECSC are also widely questioned. See John Gillingham, *Coal, Steel, and the Rebirth of Europe, 1945–1955: The Germans and French from the Ruhr Conflict to Economic Community* (Cambridge: Cambridge University Press, 1991); Alan S. Milward, *The Reconstruction of Western Europe, 1945–1951* (Berkeley and Los Angeles: University of California Press, 1984); Milward, *The European Rescue of the Nation-State* (London: Routledge, 1993); and Andrew Moravcsik, *The Choice for Europe: Social Purpose and State Power from Messina to Maastricht* (Ithaca: Cornell University Press, 1998), chapter two.

[59] Frederico G. Manicini, "The Making of a Constitution for Europe," in Robert Keohane and Stanley Hoffmann, eds., *The New European Community* (Boulder, Colo.: Westview Press, 1991), pp. 177–94; Eric Stein, "Lawyers, Judges, and the Making of a Transnational Constitution," *American Journal of International Law*, Vol. 75, No. 1 (January 1981), pp. 1–27; and Joseph Weiler, *The Constitution of Europe* (London: Cambridge University Press, 1999).

Trade Organization, are established by multilateral treaties that specify commitments and obligations—treaties that, in effect, "devise systems of checks and balances whose main function is to keep under control the powers of the organization they set up."[60] The Treaty of Rome, which established the European Community, was also secured through a traditional multilateral treaty. As such, the resulting institutions are not—strictly speaking—constitutional agreements. Treaties that establish international organizations do not typically enjoy the same "higher-law status" as domestic law. Binding legal and institutional commitments agreed to in intergovernmental treaties do not recognize the legal supremacy of a higher judicial authority. The Treaty of Rome was also unlike a constitution in that is did not safeguard the fundamental rights of individuals as European citizens; member states retained the right to confer citizenship. In more recent decades, however, incremental steps have been taken to "constitutionalize" the treaty by the expansion of the authority and reach of the European Court of Justice and the incipient establishment of European citizenship rights.[61] As the EU moves further in this direction, supranationalism takes on a more formal-legal and federal character, and the resulting political order moves well beyond traditional treaty-based institutional binding.

Stepping back, the broader continuum of power restraints is defined by the degree of institutionalized cooperation and formal-legal authority that shapes and limits the exercise of power. In one sense, the strategies are all techniques that seek to balance power. As Carl Friedrich has argued, "the substitution of . . . an international organization for an international balancer is, in a sense, merely a specific instance of the general feature of all constitutions; a constitution seeks to balance various governmental powers and organizes a balance of interests . . . in the community."[62] Even in the case of the European Union, the move toward greater integration and shared institutions is at least partly driven by the balancing logic, most recently as European countries have grappled with the rise of unified and economically dominant Germany.[63] Nonetheless, when order is built around institutional binding practices and supranationalism, it is substituting interlocking institutional constraints for balance-of-power controls as the basic check on concentrated power. The logic of balance is to check power with power; the logic of institutional binding and supranationalism is to restrain power through the establishment of an institutionalized political process supervised by formal-legal authority.

[60] Mancini, "The Making of a Constitution for Europe," p. 178.

[61] Mancini, "The Making of a Constitution for Europe."

[62] Carl J. Friedrich, *Constitutional Government and Democracy*, p. 86.

[63] See Joseph M. Grieco, "State Interests and Institutional Rule Trajectories: A Neorealist Interpretation of the Maastricht Treaty and European Economic and Monetary Union," *Security Studies*, Vol. 5, No. 3 (Spring 1996), pp. 261–306.

As noted, it is possible to see both an evolution in the types of power constraint mechanisms employed by the postwar states and a general increase in the degree to which formal intergovernmental institutions were central organizing elements of the postwar political orders. The Westphalia settlement primarily sought to establish the religious and political independence of the European states, and its codification of the doctrine of state sovereignty served to parse and fragment power. Utrecht also upheld state sovereignty, but with the rise of more capable territorial states, the settlement also sought to restrain hegemonic power on the continent through self-conscious territorial distribution and the operation of the balance of power. The Vienna settlement and the world war settlements of 1919 and 1945 are notable for the new use of binding institutions to limit and restrain the exercise of power. The Vienna settlement relied primarily on mechanisms of consultation and great-power norms of restraint. The twentieth-century settlements involved the establishment of global and regional multilateral institutions and alliances, although the balance of power and other restraint mechanisms were manifest in these orders as well. Overall, the settlements reveal changes in the way in which power was regulated and restrained: the mechanisms have become increasingly more varied, sophisticated, and institutionally binding.

STABILITY OF POSTWAR ORDER

In addition to explaining the changing character of postwar order, this book poses the question of how we explain the stability or durability of the 1945 order among the Western industrial countries. In explaining the changing character of postwar order, is it also possible to identify features of the contemporary order that render it unusually durable?

The idea of stability is much more problematic than might appear at first glance.[64] Some scholars equate stability of an international order with the absence of war; thus stability and peace are interchangeable. John Herz argues that along these lines, "A system is (relatively) stable where changes are relatively slow, gradual, and peaceful; unstable where they tend to be sudden, far-reaching in impact, and frequently violent."[65] But some versions of balance-of-power theory suggest that war is sometimes necessary as a mechanism to maintain stability. Likewise, as Robert Jervis argues,

---

[64] See Robert Jervis, *Systems Effects: Complexity in Political and Social Life* (Princeton: Princeton University Press, 1997), pp. 94–98.

[65] John Herz, "The Impact of the Technological-Scientific Process on the International System," in Abdul Said, ed., *Theory of International Relations* (Englewood Cliffs, N.J.: Prentice-Hall, 1968), p. 115.

"Change can be peaceful without being slow and gradual, as the events in East Europe in 1989 remind us, and peaceful changes can be 'far-reaching in impact.' "[66] Slow and peaceful change can eventually result in a radical transformation of the order, which is not a mark of stability.

In this book, political order refers to the governing arrangements among a group of states, including its basic rules, principles, and institutions. Political order is created when these basic governing arrangements are put in place, and the political order is threatened or broken apart when these arrangements are overturned, contested, or in disarray. An essential element of political order in this view is that the participants within the order must have some acknowledgment or awareness of the order—its participants, rules, and mode of operation; it is not enough to identify patterned behavior or interconnections between actors. It is possible, as a result, that some historical periods and regions of world politics are without political order, at least as it is defined here.

Accordingly, a useful measure of stability is the ability of the political order to contain and overcome disturbances to order. Orders will differ in their ability to handle internal and external forces that threaten instability. Different governing rules, principles, and institutions will be better able to cope with disturbances—such as shifts in power distributions, the rise of new states, and changes in the goals and purposes of states—than other orders. But the simple durability or longevity of such an order is not in itself a complete measure of its stability. An order may last a long time, but not be put to the test in terms of its ability to contain disturbances, whereas an order that does have such characteristics may be overturned because of extraordinary circumstances.[67]

Assessing the stability of a political order, therefore, entails making judgments about how resilient it is in the face of disturbances. In the first instance, it is necessary to look at the durability of the order in the face of threatening forces from both within and outside. But it is also necessary to look within the order to see what sort of mechanisms are at work that allow it to adjust and stabilize itself in the face of such disturbances. Does the order's stability hinge on continuous and difficult-to-accomplish maneuvering by state leaders, or is the order's stability rooted in a wider set of more durable and resilient political structures?

Each of the three models of political order makes different claims about the sources of stability. An order based on balance is rendered stable when the competing states faithfully engage in the counterbalancing and produce an equilibrium of power. In the Waltzian formulation, stability is achieved

[66] Jervis, *System Effects*, p. 95.
[67] Ibid., p. 97.

through the ongoing competitive adjustments of states operating within anarchy. There is an automatic aspect to this stabilizing process. The system tends toward equilibrium, and so even war and great upheaval in the system can be understood as punishing states that do not respond more directly to the imperatives of balance, eventually paving the way to a return to balance and system equilibrium.[68]

At a closer proximity to specific international settings, however, stability—defined as the orderly and peaceful operation of the balance-of-power system—requires the ability of states to recognize and respond to shifting power distributions. Kissinger takes this view of the post-1815 order and emphasizes the importance of the cooperative and self-conscious management of a stable balance: "Their goal was stability, not perfection, and the balance of power is the classic expression of the lesson of history that no order is safe without physical safeguards against aggression." As a result, a "new international order came to be created with a sufficient awareness of the connection between power and morality; between security and legitimacy."[69] The failure of state elites to appreciate power shifts and respond with counterbalancing action is a source of instability. In this view, war is the result of the failure of successful balancing activity. Moreover, specific types of underlying power distributions may be more likely to result in stable power balances than others. A dispute continues as to whether bipolar or multipolar balances are more stable.[70]

---

[68] Waltz, *Theory of International Politics*, chapter ten.

[69] Henry Kissinger, *A World Restored: The Politics of Conservatism in a Revolutionary Age* (New York: Grosset and Dunlop, 1964), pp. 317–18. Hans Morgenthau makes the same argument in more general terms: "Before the balance of power could impose its restraint upon the power aspirations of nations through the mechanical interplay of accepting the system of the balance of power as the common framework of their endeavors. . . . Where such a consensus no longer exists or has become weak and is no longer sure of itself, as in the period starting with the partitions of Poland and ending with the Napoleonic Wars, the balance of power is incapable of fulfilling its functions of international stability and national independence." Morgenthau, *Politics among Nations: The Struggle for Power and Peace* (New York: Alfred A. Knopf, 1948), pp. 163–65.

[70] In the classic formulation of the argument, Kenneth Waltz argues that bipolar systems are more stable than multipolar systems, whereas Karl W. Deutsch and J. David Singer argue that multipolar systems are more stable. Both agree that a multipolar order entails a much more complex set of variables and power relations, creating more uncertainty about how particular balancing policies will impact on the wider system. The disagreement is really over whether this uncertainty creates more opportunities for false steps and destabilizing foreign policy or whether it encourages prudence and caution. See Waltz, "The Stability of a Bipolar World," *Daedalus*, Vol. 43, No. 3 (1964), pp. 881–901; Deutsch and Singer, "Multipolar Power Systems and International Stability," *World Politics*, Vol. 16, No. 3 (April 1964), pp. 390–406; and Richard Rosecrance, "Bipolarity, Multipolority and the Future," *Journal of Conflict Resolution*, Vol. 10, No. 3 (1966), pp. 314–27. For a review of the debate, see Jack Levy, "The Polarity of the System and International Stability: An Empirical Analysis," in Alan Ned

Hegemonic order remains stable as long as the leading state retains its preponderance of power. The problem, of course, is that hegemonic states inevitably experience relative decline, and the order that is created during the zenith of their power cannot be sustained as that power wanes. Rising states—embracing their own and often competing interests in creating a congenial international order—will eventually challenge the declining hegemonic state. The result has typically been strategic rivalry among the great powers, and hegemonic war. As a result, as Gilpin argues, "a stable system is one in which changes can take place if they do not threaten the vital interests of the dominant states and thereby cause war between them."[71] Or as Gilpin argues elsewhere, "An international system is stable (i.e., in a state of equilibrium) if no state believes it is profitable to attempt to change the system."[72] The hegemonic stability theory assumes that the long-term rise and decline of major states is the ultimate source of the instability of hegemonic order. But it leaves open the possibility that rising states might be accommodated within the existing hegemonic order, at least until the benefits of challenging the existing lead state outweigh the costs. This raises the possibility for variations in the ability of specific hegemonic orders to accommodate rising great powers, and the result will be variations across historical cases in the stability of hegemonic order.[73]

In constitutional orders, the sources of stability are the durability of political institutions, particularly the constitutional institutions that define the basic rules of the polity. If specific social forces or class interests are able to subvert legal and governmental rules, the polity loses its constitutional character, and the system reverts to the simple rule or domination by the powerful. Where the polity is held together by constitutional institutions that ensure power sharing and guarantee some mutually satisfactory distribution of gains, the failure of those institutions will usher in heightened conflict and political instability. As argued earlier, successful or effective constitutional orders specify the principles and rules by which power is exercised, and by so doing, they limit the returns to power. The implication is that the stability of the order depends on the ability of these constitutional arrangements to limit what the power wielders can do with their

---

Sabrosky, ed., *Polarity and War: The Changing Structure of International Conflict* (Boulder, Colo.: Westview, 1985).

[71] Gilpin, "The Theory of Hegemonic War," in Robert Rotberg and Theodore Rabb, eds., *The Origins and Prevention of Major Wars* (New York: Cambridge University Press, 1988), p. 16.

[72] Gilpin, *War and Change in World Politics*, p. 50

[73] There is a large literature that explores this process of power transition. See Gilpin, *War and Change*; Organski, *World Politics*; Organski and Jack Kugler, *The War Ledger* (Chicago: University of Chicago Press, 1980); and Richard Ned Lebow and Barry S. Strauss, eds., *Hegemonic Rivalry from Thucydides to the Nuclear Age* (Boulder, Colo.: Westview, 1991).

power. Stability requires that institutions function relatively autonomously and operate to ensure that there are no permanent losers.[74]

At the international level, stability of a constitutional order also depends on the ability of institutions effectively to limit the returns to power. Of course, formal constitutional orders do not exist between states.[75] But international orders nonetheless vary in the degree to which institutions have been established that shape and limit the exercise of state power. The logic and explanation for these variations is developed in Chapter Three. The stability of these orders hinge on the strength of intergovernmental institutions in the face of asymmetrical and shifting power relations. If binding institutions and credible commitments give way, the order loses its capacity to reassure otherwise threatened or insecure states. The constitutional logic is lost—it loses its stability—and it will move back toward a more traditional balance-of-power or hegemonic order.

Conclusion

This study seeks to explain variations in the extent to which leading states pursued institutional strategies of order building after 1815, 1919, and 1945. This chapter has specified the dependent variable in two ways. The most direct and empirically observable variable is the order-building strategy itself—the policies and actions of the leading state. A leading state may or may not pursue an institutional strategy, and if it does it may do so to a greater or lesser extent, with or without other strategies that employ different power restraint mechanisms. The leading state may also be more or less successful in establishing an order around binding institutions. The British in 1815 advanced less extensive institutional binding proposals than the United States did after 1919 and 1945, institutional arrangements that they understood would work alongside (but also modify) the traditional balance of power. The United States after 1919 had ambitious proposals for postwar order that involved the extensive use of institutions, but these proposals were only partially enacted and ultimately without American participation. The 1945 order entailed more extensive use of binding institutions than either 1815 and 1919, manifest most fully in the security commitments and restraints established between the United States and its postwar allies. But 1945 is also notable for the range of institutions that were established: global, regional, economic, security, and political.

Variations in the role and extensiveness can also be inferred less directly in the character of the eventual postwar order itself. As we have seen, three basic models of order—balance of power, hegemonic, and constitutional—

---

[74] See Huntington, *Political Order in Changing Societies*, chapter one.
[75] The European Union is a possible exception.

capture the most general variations. These models are ideal types, and each model is formulated as a "strong" version. Actual orders can vary. The balance-of-power order may be automatic and operate strictly in terms of material power-balancing requirements, or it can be a more managed order informed by self-conscious rules and norms. A hegemonic order may involve the direct and coercive domination of weaker and secondary states by the leading state, or it may be organized around more reciprocal, consensual, and institutionalized relations. The order is still built upon asymmetric power, but the extreme consequences of those power asymmetries are muted. The constitutional order can also vary in terms of the strength of the rules and institutions that bind the states together and limit the returns to power. Constitutional orders are identified in terms of the presence and functioning of an institutionalized political process. But these constitutional characteristics can vary: institutions may more or less bind states together and more or less ensure a mutually agreeable distribution of gains. Constitutional orders—like balance and hegemonic orders—can run along a continuum of strong to weak.

The "weak" versions of balance-of-power and hegemonic order involve the presence of rules and institutional processes that diminish the pure operation of balancing or hegemonic coercion. In both cases, institutions are intervening mechanisms that alter the underlying dynamics built around power distributions. As a result, these weaker—that is to say, institutionalized—versions of balance and hegemony can take on characteristics that make them look somewhat like a constitutional order. The constitutional structure described by Lijphart in the Netherlands has institutional arrangements that ensure that the weak-minority will not be a permanent loser in the national political system. Power sharing and confederal structures ensure a minimum degree of distribution of benefits. This constitutional "solution" to the problem of order in divided societies with unequal religious/ethnic groups is different more in degree than in kind from a highly institutionalized balance-of-power order or a highly institutionalized hegemonic order.

Chapter Three

AN INSTITUTIONAL THEORY OF ORDER FORMATION

THE AFTERMATH of major war presents the winning state with choices. The destruction caused by war and the breakdown of the old order provide opportunities to establish new basic rules and organizing arrangements that are likely to persist well into the future; the stakes are high.

At such postwar junctures, the leading state has three broad choices. One is to use its power to dominate the weaker and defeated states. It won the war and it has acquired the power to do so. Domination can be pursued in the settlement itself, by imposing severe penalties and extracting oversized reparations from the defeated states.[1] Domination can also be pursued well into the future, using superior power capabilities to bully other states over the entire range of economic and political relations. To the extent that this type of strategy gives shape to postwar order, it is a hegemonic or imperial order.

A second choice for the winning state is to abandon the other states and simply go home. In this case, the leading state would neither attempt to exploit its favorable power position for postwar gains nor try to use that power to achieve agreement with other states over new postwar rules and arrangements. The other states are left to their own devices. This choice by the leading state may not lead to a specific type of postwar order. But left to themselves, weaker and secondary states—faced with an uncertain, unpredictable, and disengaged powerful state—are likely to pursue some sort of balancing response.

A third choice is for the leading state to use its commanding power position to gain acquiescence and participation in a mutually acceptable postwar order. The goal would be to establish a set of rules and arrangements that are durable and legitimate, but rules and arrangements that also serve the long-term interests of the leading state. To seek agreement on postwar

---

[1] Domination can take many forms. An extreme version of this strategy was the imposition of Soviet rule in Eastern Europe after World War II. As part of this strategy, the Soviets stripped its parts of occupied Germany of factories, vehicles, and industrial goods and sent them back to Russia. As Stalin told Tito and Djilas: "This war is not as in the past; whoever occupies a territory also imposes on it his own social system. Everyone imposes his own system as far as his army can reach. It cannot be otherwise." Milovan Djilas, *Conversations with Stalin* (New York: Harcourt, Brace, & World, 1962), p. 81.

order leaves open what precisely these states would agree to. It might in fact be agreement to establish a balance-of-power order. The choice to seek a legitimate and mutually acceptable postwar order is separate, at least at the outset, from the choice to employ binding institutions to achieve this mutually agreeable order.[2]

Even if the leading state seeks to construct a mutually acceptable order, however, agreement is not certain. Weaker states have reason to fear that the leading state will pursue one of the other options: domination or abandonment. And so the leading state must reassure the other states that it will not exploit its favorable position and will abide by its commitments. Without these assurances, weaker states have incentives to resist the leading state, organize an alternative order if possible and, at the extreme, balance against it. In turn, the leading state must be confident that when secondary states agree to participate in the postwar order and abide by its rules, that they will do so well into the future. Otherwise, if the other states are free to exploit the situation, why should the leading state tie itself down and limit its options?

In general, a leading state will want to bind weaker and secondary states to a set of rules and institutions of postwar order—locking in these states to predictable patterns of behavior—but remain unbound itself, free of institutional constraints and obligations. But to get the willing participation and compliance of other states, the leading state must offer to limit its own autonomy and ability to exercise power arbitrarily. The willingness and ability of states to offer and enter into these self-binding bargains hinge on the types of states involved and the character of postwar power disparities. Democracies are better able to do so, but are also often unwilling. The greater the postwar disparities in power, the more opportunities the leading state has to lock in a favorable order, and the more weaker and secondary states will be attracted to institutional agreements that lower the risks of domination or abandonment.

This is the context in which the politics of postwar order formation is played out. The set of choices and calculations that leading and secondary

---

[2] The argument is not that these three options are regularly chosen by great powers. In general, all newly powerful postwar states should have an incentive to use their power to build an order that is seen as legitimate by weaker and secondary states who participate within it. Even the Soviet Union's post-1945 relations with Eastern Europe, which initially took the form of coercive domination and the extraction of short-term distributional gains, eventually entailed more elaborate efforts to elicit the allegiance of its weaker partners, manifest in COMECON and the Warsaw Pact. Likewise, the American failure to ratify the Versailles treaty in 1919—resulting, effectively, in an abandonment of efforts to create a postwar order—was more an unintended consequence of the peacemaking process than a strategic decision of the United States. The argument is that some states in some situations are better able to create an agreed-upon order than others, and the specific incentives and capacities of

states make at this juncture determine the character of the postwar order. We turn now to the logic of choice at this juncture, and after this we turn to the characteristics of states and institutional strategies that influence the attractiveness and availability of institutional strategies of order building.

THE CONSTITUTIONAL LOGIC

A state that wins a war has incentives to construct a postwar order that is legitimate and durable.[3] The war has left the state in a commanding position, but that dominance is not fully realized or stable if the postwar order in which the state operates is not legitimate. A legitimate political order is one where its members willingly participate and agree with the overall orientation of the system.[4] They abide by its rules and principles because they accept them as desirable; they embrace them as their own. In Rousseau's famous formulation: "The strongest is never strong enough to be always master, unless he transforms strength into right and obedience into duty."

The leading postwar state could choose not to seek a legitimate order, but there are incentives for the leading state to turn its momentarily commanding power position into a longer-term and durable advantage. In effect, in seeking a legitimate postwar order, the leading state is engaging in power management. To achieve a mutually acceptable order means to se-

---

leading states to use institutions to overcome obstacles to mutual agreement also vary across leading states and historical eras.

[3] The model presented in this chapter is a simplified and abstract representation of the circumstances and choices of states in the aftermath of major war, a stylization that is intended to clarify the underlying dynamics that I argue are most important in explaining how order emerges after wars. The actual historical circumstances of postwar order building are infinitely more complicated, and even the specific historical cases that are most fully captured by the model will diverge from it in important respects. But the specification of the model allows the cases to be compared with regard to how closely they conform to the model, and explanations for variations can be offered and evaluated.

[4] The distinction between legitimate and coercive orders is one of the most elemental ways of characterizing political systems. A leading state can secure its interests and the compliance of other states in two fundamental ways. One way is through coercion, where the leading state directly uses its material capabilities to induce other states to operate in a desired manner within the order. The other is through a process of rule making and institution building, where secondary states agree on their own to abide by the rules and expectations of the order. This distinction is made in G. John Ikenberry and Charles A. Kupchan, "Socialization and Hegemonic Power," *International Organization*, Vol. 44, No. 3 (Summer 1990), pp. 283–315. A similar distinction between types of acquiescence (or "acceptance") is made by Michael Mann: "*pragmatic* acceptance, where the individual complies because he perceives no realistic alternative, and *normative* acceptance, where the individual internalizes the moral expectations of the ruling class and views his own inferior position as legitimate." See Mann, "The Social Cohesion of Liberal Democracy," *American Sociological Review*, Vol. 35 (June 1970), pp. 423–39.

cure agreement among the relevant states on the basic rules and principles of political order. That is to say, the incentive to create a legitimate order after the war can make a constitutional settlement appealing.[5] The more institutionalized the order, the more that participants within the order act according to defined and predictable rules and modi operandi. To get this willing and institutionalized cooperation, however, the leading state must overcome weaker and secondary state fears of domination and abandonment. That is, it needs to make its commanding power position more predictable and restrained.

Strategic Restraint and Power Conservation

Why would a newly powerful state want to restrict itself by agreeing to limits on the use of its power? Because it has an interest in conserving its power. The leading state gives up some freedom on the use its power in exchange for agreed-upon principles and institutional processes that ensure a durable and predictable postwar order.[6]

A constitutional settlement conserves the power of the leading state in two ways. The first is by lowering the enforcement costs for maintaining order within the system. The constant use of power—and the coercion and inducements it implies—to secure specific interests and continuously resolve conflicts is costly.[7] It is less costly over the long term to create an order in which secondary states embrace its rules and principles on their own. It is far more effective over the long term to shape the interests and orientations of other states rather than directly shape their actions through coercion and inducements.[8]

---

[5] I am using the terms constitutional order (or settlement) and binding institutional order (or settlement) interchangeably.

[6] This model's assumption about the power goals of the leading state is broadly realist. The state seeks to use its power as efficiently as possible. It wants to preserve and extend its power position into the future, and it is willing to give up some "returns" on its power in the short run in favor of a greater longer-term return on its power if such a possibility exists. For discussions of alternative realist assumptions about the power goals of states, see Jack L. Snyder, *Myths of Empire: Domestic Politics and International Ambition* (Ithaca: Cornell University Press, 1991); Fareed Zakaria, *From Wealth to Power: The Unusual Origins of America's World Role* (Princeton: Princeton University Press, 1998); Randall L. Schweller, "Neorealism's Status Quo Bias: What Security Dilemma?" *Security Studies*, Vol. 17, No. 5 (Spring 1996), pp. 90–121; Charles L. Glaser, "Realists as Optimists: Cooperation as Self-Help," *International Security*, Vol. 19, No. 3 (Winter 1994/95), pp. 50–90; and Joseph M. Grieco, "Realist International Theory and the Study of World Politics," in Michael Doyle and G. John Ikenberry, eds., *New Thinking in International Relations Theory* (Boulder, Colo.: Westview Press, 1997), pp. 163–201.

[7] See Ikenberry and Kupchan, "Socialization and Hegemonic Power."

[8] This is true even if the leading state has to use more power resources at the outset to obtain agreement on basic rules and institutions, and even if it has to compromise (to some extent) for the sake of agreement on the character of those rules and institutions.

The leading state lowers its enforcement costs in a constitutional order by giving weaker states a stake in the system and gaining their overall support. As Lisa Martin argues, "a hegemon can expect fewer challenges to an institution in which smaller states have a say in joint decisions than to a unilaterally imposed arrangement."[9] In effect, a constitutional settlement is one in which the leading state agrees to extend decision-making access and rights to secondary states in exchange for their acquiescence in the order's rules and institutions. The resulting legitimacy of the order reduces the chance that secondary states will seek to overturn or continually challenge the overall order. Margaret Levi argues that a similar incentive exists for power holders in domestic systems: institutionalized bargaining is less risky for the dominant actor than the constant expenditure of resources to quell resistance. "Coercion is expensive, and its use often precipitates resentments that can fuel the flames of opposition. Thus, rulers will seek to create compliance that is quasi-voluntary."[10] A constitutional settlement reduces the necessity of the costly expenditure of resources by the leading state on bargaining, monitoring, and enforcement.

Second, if the leading state calculates that its heightened postwar power advantages are only momentary, an institutionalized order might lock in favorable arrangements that continue beyond the zenith of its power. In effect, the creation of basic ordering institutions is a form of hegemonic investment in the future. If the right type of rules and institutions become entrenched, they can continue to work in favor of the leading state even as its relative material capabilities decline—gains that the leading state would not realize in a noninstitutionalized order.[11] If this is so, the state's power

[9] Lisa Martin, "The Rational State Choice of Multilateralism," in John Gerard Ruggie, ed., *Multilateralism Matters: The Theory and Praxis of an Institutional Form* (New York: Columbia University Press, 1993), p. 110. This line of analysis builds on institutionalist theory pioneered by Robert Keohane in *After Hegemony: Cooperation and Discord in the World Political Economy* (Princeton: Princeton University Press, 1984).

[10] Margaret Levi, *Of Rule and Revenue* (Berkeley and Los Angeles: University of California Press, 1988), p. 32.

[11] Terry Moe argues that this same logic is frequently at work when a winning party takes over the reigns of government. "They can fashion structures to insulate their favorable agencies and programs from the future exercise of public authority. In doing so, of course, they will not only be reducing their enemies' opportunities for future control; they will be reducing their own opportunities as well. But this is often a reasonable price to pay, given the alternative. And because they get to go first, they are really not giving up control—they are choosing to exercise a greater measure of it ex ante, through insulated structures that, once locked in, predispose the agency to do the right things. What they are moving away from—because it is dangerous—is the kind of ongoing hierarchical control that is exercised through the discretionary decisions of public authority over time." Moe, "Political Institutions: The Neglected Side of the Story," *Journal of Law, Economics, and Organization*, Vol. 6 (Special Issue 1990), pp. 227–28.

position is conserved. The state's momentary power advantage locks in favorable future returns.[12]

This investment motive for a binding institutional order is based on several assumptions. First, the victorious state realizes that its favorable relative power position will not last indefinitely. It need not be pessimistic about its future power position; it need only acknowledge that the war has temporarily reduced the power capacities of the other major states, and that they will eventually rebuild and increase their relative power position. With this dynamic view of its own power position, the leading state has reason to calculate what impact various uses of that power will have on its future power position.

Second, the leading postwar state can make a choice between using its power capabilities to gain momentary advantages in particular distributional struggles and using those capabilities to invest in institutions that will persist into the future.[13] The implication is that there is a trade-off between these choices, and each will produce a different rate of return over the short and long term. In effect, the leading state enters the postwar period sitting on a declining power base. A binding institutional settlement allows that state to conserve its base by creating rules and institutions that will extend the stream of benefits and advantages into the future, beyond what would otherwise be the case.

Finally, institution building is a form of investment because rules and institutions are sticky, at least to some extent. Unless there is a substantial shift in state power and interests, postwar institutions are likely to persist and continue to shape and constrain state action even after the power that created them has declined.[14] If institutions simply track the distribution of

[12] These assumptions about the institutional conservation of state power are actually variables, and their presence or absence will have an impact on the possibility and appeal of a constitutional settlement. If a state does not conclude that its power will decline or be threatened, it will be less concerned with anchoring its position in a constitutional order. Conversely, when the leading state foresees declining power and rising conflict, the incentive for offering a constitutional settlement increases. On the changing calculations of a declining hegemon, see Duncan Snidal, "The Limits of Hegemonic Stability Theory," *International Organization*, Vol. 39, No. 4 (Autumn 1985), pp. 579–614.

[13] The classic statement of these state choices is Arnold Wolfers's distinction between "possession" and "milieu" foreign policy goals. See Wolfers, "The Goals of Foreign Policy," *Discord and Collaboration: Essays on International Politics* (Baltimore: Johns Hopkins University Press, 1962), pp. 73–74.

[14] The claim is that institutions can have an independent ordering impact on their environment even after the disappearance or decline of the actors that created them. See James G. March and Johan P. Olsen, *Discovering Institutions: The Organizational Basis of Politics* (New York: Free Press, 1989). Regarding international regimes, see Stephen Krasner, *International Regimes* (Ithaca: Cornell University Press, 1982); and Oran Young, *International Cooperation: Building Regimes for Natural Resources and the Environment* (Ithaca: Cornell University Press, 1989), chapter three.

power, and therefore change as state power and interests change, the investment motive loses its appeal. The more that institutions have lock-in effects, the greater their attractions to leading states at these critical junctures.[15] The assumption is that institutions can become embedded in the wider political order, where through the process of feedback and increasing returns to institutions states find that the costs of changing those institutions can grow over time, thereby increasing the shaping and constraining role of institutions.[16] Overall, the leading state extends the time horizon by which it calculates its interests. Weaker and secondary states are offered a good deal today in exchange for compliant participation in the future.[17]

The Constitutional Bargain

If institutions can have an independent ordering impact on states, and if leading postwar states have an incentive to take advantage of this path-dependent opportunity to lock in a favorable order that will persist beyond its power capabilities, why would weaker states accept the deal? Why not just resist any institutional settlement after the war and wait until they are stronger and can negotiate a more favorable settlement? Several factors might make this a less attractive option. First, without an institutional settlement, bargaining will be based simply on power capacities, and the hegemonic state will have the clear advantage. The weaker states will lose more

---

[15] The more confident that the leading state is that institutions can be constructed that will perpetuate its interests into the future, the more it will be willing to give up some gains in the short term in favor of a longer-term strategy. In effect, the greater the stickiness of institutions, the lower the leading state's discount rate for calculating its interests over the long term.

[16] The processes of feedback and increasing returns to institutions are themes developed later in the chapter.

[17] Albert Hirschman makes a similar argument about German trade policy in Eastern Europe in the 1930s. Hirschman argues that Germany, the leading state in the region, offered very generous trade arrangements with the smaller countries to the East so as to redirect trade patterns and promote their dependence on Germany. These new dependent economic relations would in turn gradually foster more favorable and compliant attitudes toward Germany. See Hirschman, *National Power and the Structure of Foreign Trade* (Berkeley and Los Angeles: University of California Press, 1980 [1945]), p. 29. Jonathan Kirshner notes: "Small states in this setting typically gain in an economic sense, often handsomely, as large states attempting to enhance their influence make overly generous concessions. Thus asymmetric economic relations offer an exception to, and in fact a reversal of, the concern for relative gains. This expands the core of mutually acceptable bargains and makes cooperation between them even more likely." Kirshner, "Great Power Economic Relations in the Pacific: Some Realist Expectations," in G. John Ikenberry and Michael Mastanduno, eds., *The Emerging International Relations of the Asia-Pacific Region* (forthcoming).

than they would under a settlement whereby the hegemonic state agrees to forego some immediate gains in exchange for the willing participation of secondary states. The option of losing more now to gain more later is not attractive for a weak state that is struggling to rebuild after war. The hegemon or leading state, on the other hand, will be more willing to trade off gains today for gains tomorrow. The difference in the two time horizons is crucial in understanding why a constitutional settlement is possible.

A second reason why weaker states might opt for the institutional agreement is that if the leading state is able credibly to demonstrate strategic restraint the others buy protection against the threat of domination or abandonment. As realist theory argues, a central concern of weak or secondary states is whether they will be dominated by the more powerful state. In an international order that has credible restraints on power, the possibility of indiscriminate and ruthless domination is mitigated. Just as important, the possibility of abandonment is also lessened. If the hegemonic state is rendered more predictable, the secondary states do not need to spend as many resources on "risk premiums," which would otherwise be needed to prepare for either domination or abandonment. In such a situation, the asymmetries in power are rendered more tolerable for weaker states.

In sum, the constitutional settlement involves a bargain: the leading state gets a predictable and legitimate order based on agreed-upon rules and institutions. It obtains the acquiescence in this order by weaker states, which in turn allows it to conserve its power. In return, the leading state agrees to limits on its own actions and to open itself up to a political process in which the weaker states can actively press their interests upon the more powerful state. The hegemonic or leading state agrees to forego some gains in the early postwar period in exchange for rules and institutions that allow it to have stable returns later, while weaker states are given favorable returns up front and limits on the exercise of power. Institutions play a two-sided role: they must bind the leading state when it is initially stronger and the subordinate states later when they are stronger.

Institutional and Substantive Agreements

To understand the logic of constitutional order, it is useful to make a distinction between substantive and institutional agreements. Bargaining may be over distributive outcomes; in this case, states struggle over the distribution of benefits in specific relationships.[18] On the other hand, it may reflect

---

[18] See Stephen D. Krasner, "Global Communications and National Power: Life on the Pareto Frontier," *World Politics*, Vol. 43 (April 1991), pp. 336–66.

what Oran Young calls "efforts on the part of autonomous actors to reach agreement among themselves on the terms of constitutional contracts or interlocking sets of rights and rules that are expected to govern their subsequent interactions."[19] The first type of agreement is a substantive agreement with outcomes that determine the distribution of material benefits between the states. The second type is an institutional agreement that specifies the principles, rules, and parameters within which particular negotiations over outcomes are conducted.[20]

For the leading postwar state to offer a constitutional settlement to other states does not mean it is seeking agreement or making concessions on specific issues. Constitutional agreements specify the rules of the game— that is, the parameters within which states will compete and settle disputes over specific issues. States may have divergent expectations about the settlement of various distributional conflicts. A constitutional agreement specifies the principles and mechanisms through which those conflicts will be settled.

If the leading postwar state seeks a constitutional settlement, it is making a calculation that although it is compromising on the formal or institutional settlement, within those newly created institutions, it will still be able to press its advantage. In return, the institutional agreements also lock in secondary and weaker states to a particular range of policies. The institutions make it more difficult for both the leading and lesser states to make radical shifts in their policy orientations, and they provides rules and expectations about how power is exercised and disputes are settled.

Thus, when a leading postwar state makes a choice between ways of allocating its power assets—between substantive and institutional bargaining—it is faced with alternative attractions and limitations. The use of power for short-term substantive gains is attractive in that the gains are relatively certain and they can be put to work immediately. On the other hand, if institutional agreements can be secured, they are a remarkable power-saving arrangement. They can potentially lock in agreements well into the future and provide an ongoing stream of benefits even after the state's power position has declined. As noted earlier, they can also reduce the ongoing need to use power resources to secure compliance and favorable outcomes.

[19] See Young, "Political Leadership and Regime Formation: On the Development of Institutions in International Society," *International Organization*, Vol. 45, No. 3 (Summer 1991), p. 282.

[20] For a useful discussion of the distinction between substantive and institutional agreements, see Adam Przeworski, "Democracy as a Contingent Outcome of Conflicts," in Jon Elster and Rune Stagstad, eds., *Constitutionalism and Democracy* (New York: Cambridge University Press, 1988), pp. 64–70.

The possibility of an institutional settlement stems from the ability to achieve agreement on institutional arrangements even if the underlying substantive interests remain widely divergent and antagonistic. For the powerful state, institutions are attractive because they can effectively rule out some outcomes that would harm its fundamental interests, and constrain other states well into the future.[21] Under the right conditions, these attractions can outweigh the loss of some autonomy and limits on the arbitrary use of power. For weaker states, the institutional compromise also rules out or at least lowers the risks of some outcomes that it fears, such as domination or abandonment by stronger states. Institutions are not neutral with respect to the interests of states; they do not make all outcomes equally possible. Agreement to abide by the new institutional rules comes from an understanding that within this framework, the arrangements will allow them to defend and protect their interests, at least enough to make it a more attractive option than the risky alternative.

Institutional agreements do shape and constrain the policy options of states and put some general parameters on the distribution of gains; indeed, this is why ordering institutions are attractive to both leading and weaker states. But this raises the question: why are the struggles over policy (and the distribution of gains) not simply reproduced in negotiations over institutions? In "multiple issue spaces" (such as after major wars) institutions "induce" particular outcomes or solutions to particular bargains.[22] If institutions matter in this way, then fights over specific issues will merely be displaced onto the institutions: the distinction between institutional and policy issues, as William H. Riker argues, "is at most one of degree of longevity."[23] In setting constitutional rules, states are also—indirectly at least—shaping and constraining future substantive policy outcomes. If this is so, why would agreement on ordering institutions be any more tractable than substantive agreements over the distribution of gains?

This problem is overcome partly because of a measure of uncertainty over specific outcomes of future distributive battles within the postwar institutional settlement. Institutional agreements specify a range of acceptable state actions, but they do not in themselves determine in advance the specific distribution of gains. The presence of some uncertainty or ambigu-

[21] Adam Przeworski makes this point: "Agreements about institutions are possible, even if the political forces involved have conflicting interests and visions because institutions shape the opportunities of realizing specific interests and the groups involved understand that institutions have this effect." Ibid., p. 70.

[22] Kenneth A. Shepsle and Barry R. Weingast, "Structure-Induced Equilibrium and Legislative Choice," *Public Choice*, Vol. 37, No. 3 (1981), pp. 503–19.

[23] Riker, "Implications from the Disequilbrium of Majority Rule for the Study of Institutions," *American Political Science Review*, Vol. 74, No. 2 (June 1980), pp. 444–45

ity about the specific distributional implications of institutional agreements allows competitive states to reach agreement.

But although some ambiguity about the specific outcome of future distributive struggles facilitates institutional agreement, too much uncertainty diminishes the attractiveness of these institutional agreements. Postwar ordering institutions need to be sufficiently determinative of future state behavior to make them attractive to both the leading and weaker states. The leading state needs to be certain that there will be continuity in the broad policy orientation of the other states—at least to the point that it is willing to impose self-restraints on its own autonomy in policy making and discretionary exercise of power. Weaker and secondary states need to be confident that the leading state is in fact credibly restrained—at least to the point that they are willing to lock themselves into a constitutional settlement. The constitutional agreement requires some degree of certainty that institutions will limit or mute the ability of states to turn power disparities into one-sided and permanent advantage.

After the institutional bargain is struck, the stickiness of institutions reinforces the stability of the postwar agreements. If institutions were not sticky, and if institutions were simply the crystallization of specific substantive outcomes, the problem that Riker identifies would be continuous and perhaps insurmountable. But, once established, institutions make it difficult for states to change policy direction fundamentally. The ability of states to agree on a constitutional bargain thus depends on a measure of separation—but not a complete divorce—between institutional and substantive agreements. If all distributive struggles hinged on the constitutional rules—and the complete substantive implications of the rules were knowable to all parties in advance—agreement might be impossible or at least much more difficult. But the implications of the institutions must be sufficiently clear, as well; specifically, it must be understood that power capacities will not completely determine substantive outcomes and that states can be locked into relatively stable policy orientations.

Such considerations underscore the importance of how the historical juncture that triggers order-building presents itself—particularly, the character and extent of the war and of system breakdown. The more complete the system breakdown, the more fundamental will be the discussion of institutional arrangements. Negotiations over basic principles and norms of order are more necessary, since the default option of not reaching some agreement is less available. There will be more basic discussion of institutions and less incremental assessment of how institutions are in practice serving to distribute benefits. Also more issues will be involved. This will increase the uncertainty; it will be more difficult for states to calculate the specific distribution of benefits that are shaped by the rules and institutions.

The willingness of the leading state to move toward an institutionalized order will also be influenced by its judgment about how effectively it can operate within such an order. To operate within an institutionalized order, it will need to bring organizational skills and capacities to bear in a political process that involves coalition building, bargaining, and compromise. Some leading states will be better able to do this than others.[24] As a result, they will respond to the basic constitutional incentive in slightly different ways. This is a crucial variable, which has shaped the willingness of military dictatorships to move toward a constitutional democracy: those that have political parties that can represent their interests within the electoral system will be more inclined to move toward democratic constitutionalism than those that do not have such operational capacities.[25] Likewise, some leading states will be better able to operate within a institutionalized political process, and this will alter the attractiveness of the constitutional logic.[26]

INSTITUTIONAL STRATEGIES OF RESTRAINT

The leading postwar state has a disproportionate role in creating confidence in postwar commitments. Because it has the most power, the leading state has the most capacity to break out of a commitment and take advantage of its position to dominate or abandon the weaker and secondary states. As Peter Cowhey argues, other states "will not become fully committed to working within the multilateral order unless they believe the dominant powers intend to stay within it."[27] Secondary states may have fewer options than the leading state, but their willingness to participate within the order—that is, to engage in voluntary compliance—will hinge on the ability of the leading state to demonstrate its reliability, commitment, and willingness to forego the arbitrary exercise of power. As a result,

[24] The observation has been made, for example, that the United States is better organized than Japan to operate within far-flung multilateral institutions, whereas Japan finds itself better able to operate within formal bilateral relations. Chalmers Johnson, lecture at University of Pennsylvania, 2 April 1996. The implication is that, as a result, their incentives to create and operate within multilateral institutions will differ because of these different internal organizational characteristics and orientations.

[25] See Przeworski, "Democracy as a Contingent Outcome of Conflict."

[26] The argument is made later that democracies are better suited to operate within institutionalized orders than nondemocracies, and that the postwar order favored by the United States after 1945 was one that was particularly congenial to Western democratic polities. Not only are democracies better able to establish institutions that serve to reduce the returns to power but also individuals within democratic polities are likely to be experienced and capable of operating effectively within them.

[27] Peter F. Cowhey, "Elect Locally—Order Globally: Domestic Politics and Multilateral Cooperation," in John Gerard Ruggie, ed., *Multilateralism Matters: The Theory and Praxis of an Institutional Form* (New York: Columbia University Press, 1993), p. 158.

the leading state will have strong incentives to find ways to certify its power: to demonstrate that it is a responsible and predictable wielder of power and that the exercise of power is, at least to some acceptable degree, circumscribed. To achieve this goal, the leading state can pursue several strategies of restraint—opening itself up, tying itself down, and making itself more predictable and accessible to weaker and secondary states.

Opening itself up means that the leading state makes its policy moves more transparent to other states, thereby reassuring them and providing access for other states to attempt to influence policy. One facet of this strategy is what Jon Elster calls "bonding." Elster argues that bonding is analogous to the efforts of a firm that is attempting to attract outside shareholders: "it must incur 'costs of bonding,' such as conservative principles of accountancy, in order to attract capital."[28] Potential shareholders are more likely to lend their capital to a firm that operates according to established and reasonable methods of record keeping and accountability. Likewise, a powerful elite or class can take steps to ensure its predictability and accountability as an inducement to other citizens to buy into their political predominance. When a state is open and transparent to outside states, it reduces the surprises and allows other states to monitor the domestic decision making that attends the exercise of power. When openness also entails accessibility by other states to decision making, this provides additional reassurance that power can be rendered responsible and predictable.

The implication of this argument is that democratic states have an advantage in the process of bonding. They already have the decentralized and permeable institutions that provide secondary states with information, access, and ultimately reassurance. But regardless of the domestic character of the leading state, it can take a variety of steps to reassure secondary states of its commitment to operate within the limits of the agreed-upon rules and institutions. This may entail specifying formal methods and procedures for the adjudication of specific conflicts. It may entail attempts to formalize the processes of making decisions within the leading state when they relate to secondary states, so as to convey a sense of predictability and transparency in the exercise of foreign policy. Most important, bonding might entail providing specific and formal mechanisms for secondary states to have a "voice" in the decision making of the leading state as well as of institutions and operations of the postwar order.[29] Again, democratic states have a built-in advantage in this regard, but even in the case of nondemocracies, mechanisms and procedures of consultation and participation can be created in the process of bonding.

---

[28] Elster, "Introduction," in Jon Elster and Rune Slagstad, eds., *Constitutionalism and Democracy* (New York: Cambridge University Press, 1988), p. 15.

[29] In terms of the business firm analogy, this would be equivalent to inviting shareholders to sit on the board of directors of the firm.

The leading state can go beyond simply opening itself up to weaker and secondary states by engaging in institutional binding; it can establish institutional links with other states, thereby limiting its own autonomy and allowing other states to have institutionalized "voice opportunities" in the decision making of the leading state. In effect, binding institutions create constraints on the way power can be used in the system, thereby rendering asymmetric power relations less exploitative and commitment more certain. The returns to power are reduced.[30]

These binding strategies have been explored by Joseph Grieco and Daniel Deudney. Grieco argues that weaker states within the European Union have an incentive to create institutional links with stronger states so as to have a voice in how the strong states exercise their power, and thereby prevent domination of the weaker by the stronger. Building on Albert Hirschman's classic work on exit, voice, and loyalty, Grieco argues that weak states might find institutionalized collaboration with stronger states attractive if the institution provides mechanisms to influence the policy of the stronger states. "States . . . are likely to assign great significance to the enjoyment of such effective voice opportunities in a cooperative arrangement, for it may determine whether states can obtain redress if they are concerned about such matters as the compliance of stronger partners with their commitments in the arrangement, or imbalances in the division of otherwise mutually positive gains that may be produced by their joint effort."[31] Put differently, the institutionalization of relations between weak and strong states, when it creates voice opportunities for the weaker states, can be a solution for these weaker states that want to work with but not be dominated by stronger states.

Deudney also describes the dynamic of binding, but emphasizes its other feature: it is a practice of establishing institutional links between the units that reduce their autonomy vis-à-vis one another.[32] In agreeing to be insti-

---

[30] For a discussion of how formal institutions provide ways for powerful states to convey credible restraint to weaker states, see Kenneth W. Abbott and Duncan Snidal, "Why States Act through Formal International Organizations," *Journal of Conflict Resolution*, Vol. 42, No. 1 (February 1998), pp. 3–32.

[31] Joseph M. Grieco, "State Interests and Institutional Rule Trajectories: A Neorealist Interpretation of the Maastricht Treaty and European Economic and Monetary Union," *Security Studies*, Vol. 5, No. 3 (Spring 1996), p. 288. See also Grieco, "Understanding the Problem of International Cooperation: The Limits of Neoliberalism and the Future of Realist Theory," in David A. Baldwin, ed., *Neorealism and Neoliberalism: The Contemporary Debate* (New York: Columbia University Press, 1993), pp. 331–34; and Grieco, "The Maastricht Treaty, Economic and Monetary Union and the Neo-Realist Research Programme," *Review of International Studies*, Vol. 21 (1995), pp. 21–40. The classic formulation of this logic is Albert Hirschman, *Exit, Voice and Loyalty—Responses to Decline in Firms, Organizations, and States* (Cambridge: Harvard University Press, 1970).

[32] Daniel Deudney, "The Philadelphian System: Sovereignty, Arms Control, and Balance of Power in the American States-Union," *International Organization*, Vol. 49 (Spring 1995),

tutionally connected, states mutually constrain one another and thereby mitigate the problems of anarchy that lead to security dilemmas and power balancing. According to Deudney, binding practices are particularly available to and desired by democratic polities that want to resist the state-strengthening and centralizing consequences of balance-of-power orders. Binding restricts the range of freedom of states—weak or strong—and when states bind to each other, they jointly reduce the role and consequences of power in their relationship.

The logic of binding is best seen in security alliances, which have often been created at least in part to allow alliance partners to restrain each other and manage joint relations. Alliances have traditionally been seen as temporary expedients that bring states together in pledges of mutual assistance in the face of a common threat, a commitment specified in the *casus foederis* article of the treaty. But as Paul Schroeder and others have noted, alliances have also been created as *pacta de controhendo*, that is, pacts of restraint.[33] They have served as mechanisms for states to manage and restrain their partners within the alliance. "Frequently, the desire to exercise such control over an ally's policy," Schroeder argues, "was the main reason that one power, or both, entered into the alliance."[34] Alliances create binding treaties that allow states to keep a hand in the security policy of their partners. When alliance treaties are *pacta de controhendo*, potential rivals tie themselves to each other—alleviating suspicions, reducing uncertainties, and creating institutional mechanisms for each to influence the policies of the other.[35]

---

pp. 191–228; and "Binding Sovereigns: Authorities, Structures, and Geopolitics in Philadelphian Systems," in Thomas Biersteker and Cynthia Weber, eds., *State Sovereignty as Social Construct* (Cambridge: Cambridge University Press, 1996), esp. pp. 213–16.

[33] See Paul W. Schroeder, "Alliances, 1815–1945: Weapons of Power and Tools of Management," in Klaus Knorr, ed., *Historical Dimensions of National Security Problems* (Lawrence: University Press of Kansas, 1975), pp. 227–62. As Schroeder notes, the internal constraint function of alliances was earlier observed by George Liska, *Nations in Alliance: The Limits of Interdependence* (Baltimore: Johns Hopkins University Press, 1967), pp. 9–11 and 20–21; and Liska, *Alliances and the Third World* (Baltimore: Johns Hopkins University Press, 1968), pp. 24–35. For an overview of alliance theory, see Stephen M. Walt, "Why Alliances Endure or Collapse," *Survival*, Vol. 39, No. 1 (Spring 1997), pp. 156–79.

[34] Schroeder, "Alliances, 1815–1945," p. 230.

[35] For a discussion of this dynamic, see Patricia A. Weitsman, "Intimate Enemies: The Politics of Peacetime Alliances," *Security Studies*, Vol. 7, No. 1 (Autumn 1997), pp. 156–92. For a formal analysis of intra-alliance dynamics under conditions of inequality, see James Morrow, "Alliances and Asymmetry: An Alternative to the Capability Aggregation Model of Alliances," *American Journal of Political Science*, Vol. 35, No. 4 (November 1991), pp. 904–33. Japanese-American security binding is explored in Peter J. Katzenstein and Yutaka Tsujinka, " 'Bullying,' 'Buying,' and 'Binding': US-Japanese Transnational Relations and Domestic Structures," in Thomas Risse-Kappen, ed., *Bringing Transnational Relations Back In: Non-State Actors, Domestic Structures and International Institutions* (New York: Cambridge University Press, 1995), pp. 79–111.

Elements of Institutional Binding

What makes institutions sticky? It is possible to identify a series of specific mechanisms that bind states together and lock in their policy orientations and commitments?[36] Individually and together, these institutional linkages and feedback effects can potentially serve to constrain and enmesh states in ways that serve the strategic interests of both leading and subordinate states. Treaty commitments, intergovernmental routines, and internationalized political processes—these and other interstate institutional connections raise the costs of sharp reversals in policy and create vested political interests and organizational inertia that reinforce stable and continuous relations.

Three large-scale processes can be identified. First, institutional agreements can embody formal legal or organizational procedures and understandings that strengthen expectations about the orientation of future state behavior. Institutional agreements set out a road map about how problems will be resolved, creating channels of communication and routines for decision making and consultation. Standards are set and expectations are formalized in agreements. Although states are certainly able to break an institutional agreement, the formal agreement itself creates political costs that would be incurred if it were broken.

When these institutional rules and procedures are implemented, they can take on some measure of autonomy and authority. They provide guidelines and other understandings that specify how relations are to be conducted. If an agreement, for example, mandates annual summit meetings or regular ministerial meetings, a framework is put in place for "doing business." Where rules and principles that spell out the terms on which disputes are to be settled are also agreed upon, this also strengthens expectations about future state behavior. In other words, institutional agreements can create "process rationality"; an institutional framework is created that specifies the appropriate and expected way in which states will conduct their relations.[37]

Moreover, when institutional agreements are ratified as formal treaties, this strengthens the agreement as a legal contract, with all the authority and force that such legal agreements have within each polity. Treaty-based

---

[36] The argument is not that these binding and locking constraints on states are ever absolute, only that if they operate at least to some extent, the model of the constitutional bargain presented earlier has some viability.

[37] On the "logic of appropriateness" and the "logic of consequences," see March and Olsen, *Discovering Institutions*; and March and Olsen, "The Institutional Dynamics of International Political Orders," in Peter J. Katzenstein, Robert O. Keohane, and Stephen D. Krasner, eds., *Exploration and Contestation in the Study of World Politics* (Cambridge: MIT Press, 1999), pp. 303–29.

agreements do not necessarily have the same standing as domestic law but they do have legal standing that again raises the costs of breaking the treaty. Treaties embed agreement in a wider legal and political framework that reinforces the likelihood that it will have some continuing force as state policy. Gerhard von Glahn argues that "inasmuch as the rules recognized by the states of the world as binding obligations are enforced in the courts of those states or have been approved officially and formally by the governments of those states, the rules must be considered rules of true law."[38] At the very least, the rules of conduct laid down in general treaties and conventions tend to be understood by those states that sign them to be legally binding obligations. "They are embodied in formally enacted compacts," as one scholar notes, "and it is the firmly established habit of foreign offices to consider that such compacts have legal force."[39] Regardless of the specific standing of these agreements as law, treaties and other types of institutional agreements create binding obligations that become part of the context of policy making; they provide presumptions in favor of policy that accords with treaty commitments and they create political costs for acting otherwise.[40]

Second, institutional agreements also often lead to transgovernmental connections, routines, and coalitions, which in turn give a certain momentum and continuity to specific state policies and commitments. Institutions are not just agreements, they are also interstate processes that require state officials to engage in ongoing interaction with other states. This requires that state bureaucracies be organized in particular ways—with mandates, missions, and routines. It may be easy for a state leader to make quick decisions, but government bureaucracies do not move as fast. Where institutional agreements become anchored in elaborate bureaucratic organizations, the constraints on state policy rise. When these bureaucratic networks and routines are extended into intergovernmental and international organizations as well, state leaders will have additional difficulties overcoming established patterns.[41]

[38] Gerhard von Glahn, *Law among Nations*, 4th edition (New York: Macmillan, 1981), p. 3.

[39] Fredrick Sherwood Dunn, "International Legisalation," *Political Science Quarterly*, Vol. 17, No. 4 (December 1927), p. 585. For a general discussion of the sources of international legal authority, see Anthony Clark Arend, "Do Legal Rules Matter? International Law and International Politics," *Virginia Journal of International Law*, Vol. 38, No. 2 (Winter 1998), pp. 107–53.

[40] Treaties and international agreements often require supplemental implementing legislation that further extends and integrates the institutional agreement into the domestic political system.

[41] This is the dynamic that Keohane and Nye seek to capture in their "international organization" model. "International organization in the broad sense of networks, norms, and institutions includes the norms associated with specific international regimes, but it is a broader category than regime, because it also includes patterns of elite networks and (if relevant)

The creation of intergovernmental planning and decision-making processes can also create interlocking and mutual organizational dependencies. This can have several implications. It extends the policy-making process to include participants from other states, making it more difficult for a state that is party to the institution to contemplate and plan abrupt shifts in policy in isolation—and this reduces surprises and reinforces continuity of commitment. Also, to the extent that joint decision making evolves toward some division of labor in the expertise and planning capacity, the costs of breaking those connecting links rise. The political process created by institutional agreement also provides opportunities for states to gain access to the thinking of officials in other states and to influence their policy by active engagement. International institutions thus provide channels for states to be part of the policy-making process in other states: in creating an ongoing interstate political process, institutions provide "voice opportunities" for states, mechanisms to influence what other states think and do.[42] The result is greater reassurance that opportunistic or threatening reversals in policy will not occur.

Where these intergovernmental groupings operate with special knowledge and expertise, this too strengthens their position and reinforces continuity in policy. These can take the form of "epistemic communities," transnational groups of experts that have acquired access to governmental policy making.[43] More generally, institutional agreements can facilitate the growth of transgovernmental groupings of bureaucratic and technical experts who support and reinforce particular policy commitments. The more these intergovernmental groupings can claim jurisdictional competence and specialized knowledge, the more authority and autonomy they will have within the wider domestic and international settings.[44]

Third, an institutional agreement can become an organizing vehicle for a wider set of reinforcing political activities and institutions. This is a sort of institutional "spillover" process. This happens, for example, in areas where institutional agreements oblige states to specific policy standards

---

formal institutions." They go on to argue that "[t]he international organization model assumes that a set of networks, norms, and institutions, once established, will be difficult either to eradicate or drastically to rearrange. Even governments with superior capabilities—overall or within the issue area—will find it hard to work their will when it conflicts with established patterns of behavior within existing networks and institutions." See Robert Keohane and Joseph Nye, *Power and Interdependence* (Boston: Little Brown, 1977), p. 55.

[42] See Grieco, "State Interests and Institutional Rule Trajectories."

[43] See Peter Haas, ed., *Knowledge, Power, and International Policy Coordination*, special issue of *International Organization*, Vol. 46, No. 1 (Winter 1992).

[44] The legal rational sources of bureaucratic power identified by Max Weber are also sources of autonomy and authority within intergovernmental organizations. See H. H. Gerth and C. Wright Mills, eds., *From Max Weber: Essays in Sociology* (New York: Oxford University Press, 1978).

and commitments; human rights agreements have facilitated the organization of pressure groups within the wider international community that operate to put their own pressure on governments to abide by the standards.[45] A similar transnational process can be seen in security institutions area, as well.[46] The institutional agreement provides an organizational and normative framework for the activation of domestic and transnational groups who monitor and lobby governments over compliance.

Institutional agreements can also have an impact on the continuity of state policy, to the extent that agreements prompt changes in the character of the domestic institutions that make policy. Institutional agreements can indirectly lock in policy orientations and commitments of states by promoting changes in the domestic governmental institutions, which in turn shape and constrain policy in the desired ways. Changes in domestic institutions—promoted by institutional agreement—might, for example, help to strengthen the pro-free-trade coalition at the expense of protectionist groups. Domestic structures mediate social groups and interests, shaping and constraining organizational capacities and access to policy making.[47] In various ways, institutional agreements can have an impact on state policy-making structures, reinforcing or locking states into particular policy patterns.[48]

---

[45] See Kathryn Sikkink, "Human Rights, Principled Issue-Networks and Sovereignty in Latin Ameica," *International Organization*, Vol. 47 (Summer 1993), pp. 411–41; Audie Klotz, *Norms in International Relations: The Struggle against Apartheid* (Ithaca: Cornell University Press, 1995); Andrew Moravcsik, "Explaining International Human Rights Regimes: Liberal Theory and Western Europe," *European Journal of International Relations*, Vol. 1 (June 1995), pp. 157–89; and Thomas Risse, Stephen C. Ropp, and Kathryn Sikkink, eds., *The Power of Human Rights: International Norms and Domestic Change* (New York: Cambridge University Press, 1999).

[46] Hans Muller, "The Internationalization of Principles, Norms, and Rules by Governments: The Case of Security Regimes," in Volker Rittberger with the assistance of Peter Mayer, ed., *Regime Theory and International Relations* (Oxford: Clarendon Press, 1993), pp. 361–88; and John Duffield, "International Regimes and Alliance Behavior: Explaining NATO Conventional Force Levels," *International Organization*, Vol. 46 (Autumn 1992), pp. 819–55.

[47] There is a large domestic structures literature that explores how state structures and political institutions have these sorts of impacts. See Peter Evans, et al., eds., *Bringing the State Back In* (New York: Cambridge University Press, 1985); Peter J. Katzenstein, ed., *Between Power and Plenty* (Madison: University of Wisconsin Press, 1978); Peter Hall, *Governing the Economy: The Politics of State Intervention in Britain and France* (New York: Oxford University Press, 1986); Peter Gourevitch, *Politics in Hard Times* (Ithaca: Cornell University Press, 1986); Peter Evans, *Embedded Autonomy: States and Industrial Transformation* (Princeton: Princeton University Press, 1995). For an overview, see Kathleen Thelen and Sven Steinmo, "Historical Institutionalism in Comparative Politics," in Steinmo, Thelen, and Frank Longstreth, eds., *Structuring Politics: Historical Institutionalism in Comparative Perspective* (New York: Cambridge University Press, 1992), pp. 1–32.

[48] For example, as I argue in Chapter Seven, the United States pursued the North American Free Trade Agreement (NAFTA) agreement with Mexico in part in an attempt to lock in

More generally, in agreeing to a constitutional order, states are making a mutual commitment to operate within a given set of institutions and rules—they are creating a political process that makes certain that the various states within the order will remain linked and engaged with each other. This creates greater certainty about the future, which in turn allows longer-term calculations and investments in deepening relations. If a state knows that relations with other states within the order will not break apart, incentives grow to invest in the relationship. Put more sharply, if two states know that competition between them will remain contained within an institutionalized political process and not lead to war or the threat of war, they will more readily agree to cooperate and engage in relations. Less secure states, worried about their autonomy and relative position, will tend to refrain from such joint investments and relations.[49] In this sense, the relative certainty of stable and continuous relations between states—made possible by the binding character of constitutional agreement—creates incentives to cooperate, and this in turn reinforces the constitutional agreement.[50]

Path Dependency and Increasing Returns to Institutions

An important way in which institutions take on binding characteristics occurs when adjacent institutions and groups become connected to the institution and dependent on it for their own functioning. Institutions can be-

---

liberal economic reform in Mexico. The prospective institutional agreement provides leverage before it is signed: Mexico needed to make particular policy and institutional reforms before it met the terms of NAFTA partnership. After its signing, NAFTA also reinforced liberal economic policy by strengthening the reform coalition and creating new vested economic interests in favor of the continuation of economic integration with the United States. Institutional agreements can both trigger and reinforce domestic institutions that in turn make more certain that particular policy orientations and commitments will last.

[49] Robert Powell argues that where the threat of war is absent, states are more likely to calculate their interests in terms of absolute gains. Constitutional commitments are, in effect, joint commitments to conduct relations without the threat or resort to war. See Powell, "Absolute and Relative Gains in International Relations Theory," *American Political Science Review*, Vol. 85, No. 4 (December 1991), pp. 1303–20.

[50] In this sense, institutional binding is like marriage: two individuals realize that their relationship will eventually generate conflict and discord, so they bind themselves in a legal framework, making it more difficult to dissolve the relationship when those inevitable moments arrive. As Jon Elster argues, "By raising the costs of separation and imposing legal delays, marriage makes it less likely that the spouses will give way to strong but temporary impulses to separate." Elster, "Introduction," in Elster and Slagstad, eds., *Constitutionalism and Democracy*, p. 8. Legal marriage agreements raise the expectation that the relationship will last, which changes the calculations of goals and increases the willingness to invest in the future, such as raising children and buying a home. In turn, these steps strengthen the bonds between the spouses, which in turn reinforce the marriage.

come embedded within the polity, which in turn makes institutional change more difficult. That is, more people and more of their activities are hooked into the institution and its operations. A wider array of individuals and groups, in more countries and more realms of activity, have a stake—or a vested interest—in the continuation of the institution. The costs of disruption or change in the institution grow over time. This means that "competing orders" or "alternative institutions" are at a disadvantage. The system is increasingly hard to replace.

An important reason why political order can have path-dependent characteristics is the phenomenon of "increasing returns" to institutions.[51] There are several aspects to increasing returns. First, large initial startup costs tend to exist in the creation of new institutions. Even when alternative institutions might be more efficient or accord more closely with the interests of powerful states, the gains for the new institutions must be overwhelmingly greater before they overcome the sunk costs of the existing institutions.[52] Second, there tend to be learning effects that are achieved in the operation of the existing institution that give it advantages over a new institution. Finally, institutions tend to create relations and commitments with other actors and institutions that serve to embed the institution and raise the costs of change. Taken together, as Douglass North concludes, "the interdependent web of an institutional matrix produces massive increasing returns."[53]

When institutions manifest increasing returns, it becomes very difficult for potential replacement institutions to compete and succeed. The logic is seen most clearly in regard to competing technologies. The history of the videocassette recorder is the classic example. Two formats, VHS and

[51] Both rational choice and sociological theories of institutions offer theories of institutional path dependency, and both emphasize the phenomenon of increasing returns. See Brian Arthur, "Competing Technologies, Increasing Returns, and Lock-in by Historical Events," *Economic Journal*, Vol. 99 (March 1989), pp. 116–31.

[52] On sunk costs, see Arthur L. Stinchcombe, *Constructing Social Theories* (New York: Harcourt, Brace and World, 1968), pp. 108–18. The phenomenon of sunk costs means that the maintenance of an international institution will be easier than building a new institution, even when the hypothetical new institution may more closely accord with state interests. As one study indicates, "the high costs of regime building help existing regimes to persist." Sean Lynn-Jones, "The Incidents at Sea Agreement," in Alexander L. George, Philip J. Dallin, and Alexander Dallin, eds., *U.S.-Soviet Security Cooperation: Achievement, Failures, Lessons* (Oxford: Oxford University Press, 1988), pp. 498–99.

[53] North, *Institutions, Institutional Change and Economic Performance* (New York: Cambridge University Press, 1990), p. 95. For discussions of path dependency arguments and their implications, see Stephen Krasner, "Approaches to the State: Conceptions and Historical Dynamics," *Comparative Politics*, Vol. 16 (January 1984); and Paul Pierson, "When Effect Becomes Cause: Policy Feedback and Political Change," *World Politics*, Vol. 45, No. 4 (July 1993), pp. 595–628. For a survey of the literature of path dependency, see Stephen K. Sanderson, *Social Evolutionism: A Critical History* (London: Basil Blackwell, 1990).

Beta, were introduced at roughly at the same time and initially had equal market share, but soon the VHS format, through luck and circumstances unrelated to efficiency, expanded its market share. Increasing returns on early gains tilted the competition toward VHS, allowing it to accumulate enough advantages to take over the market.[54] Even if Beta was ultimately a superior technology, a very small market advantage by VHS at an early and critical moment allowed it to lower its production costs, and the accumulation of connecting technologies and products that require compatibility made it increasingly hard for the losing technology to compete. The costs of switching to the other technology rises as production costs are lowered, learning effects accumulate, and the technology becomes embedded in a wider system of compatible and interdependent technologies.[55] Most important, once consumers made investments in the VHS system, they did not want to pay the price of discarding them in favor of an alternative, even if they might opt for another technology if there were no costs attached to making the switch.

The notion of increasing returns to institutions means that once a moment of institutional selection comes and goes, the cost of large-scale institutional change rises dramatically, even if potential institutions, when compared with existing ones, are more efficient and desirable.[56] In terms of postwar settlements, this means that, short of another major war or a global economic collapse, it is very difficult to create the type of historical breakpoint needed to replace the existing order. At the postwar juncture, the institutions proposed by the leading state are not compared with an existing set of institutions. The war has eliminated—at least to a considerable degree—the old order, so the postwar institutional offering is not competing with an entrenched rival. But after the postwar institutions are in place, this cost logic changes. At these later moments, rival institutional orders must now compete with a preexisting order, with all the sunk costs and vested interests that it manifests.[57]

[54] See W. Brian Arthur, "Positive Feedbacks in the Economy," *Scientific American* Vol. 262, No. 2 (February 1990), pp. 92–99. Reprinted in Arthur, *Increasing Returns and Path Dependence in the Economy* (Ann Arbor: University of Michigan Press, 1995), pp. 1–12.

[55] Arthur, "Competing Technologies, Increasing Returns, and Lock-In by Historical Small Events."

[56] This notion of breakpoint or critical juncture is not developed in the increasing returns literature, but it is implicit in the argument, and it is very important for understanding the path dependency of particular types of international order. For a survey of path-dependent and increasing-returns logic as it relates to political systems, see Paul Pierson, "Path Dependency, Increasing Returns, and the Study of Politics," unpublished paper, Harvard University, 1996.

[57] A particular set of postwar institutions might in fact be adaptable—capable of internal change and reform—and this will increase the cost advantage of the existing institutions in the face of potential rivals. The post-1945 Bretton Woods institutions, for example, evolved

According to this path-dependent logic, these postwar institution-building moments are attractive precisely because they are so rare. If properly taken advantage of, institutions can be established that ensure a flow of gains well into the future. The state knows that the resolution of institutional controversies will have lasting consequences, and therefore it allocates power assets to this purpose even at the expense of losing more immediate distributional conflicts.

Power Disparities and Democratic States

The willingness and ability of states to pursue institutional order-building strategies hinge on two major variables: the extent of power disparities after the war and the character of the states involved in the settlement. These variables are discussed in turn.

Power Disparities and Institutional Agreement

The greater the asymmetries of power, the more the rebuilding of order after the war will turn on the resolution of issues relating to domination, abandonment, legitimacy, and strategic restraint. Put differently, the more that power is concentrated in the hands of a single state, the more the problem of order involves issues of compliance and domination between unequal states, and the more acute will be the problem of overcoming the strategic fears of subordinate states. Where the postwar distribution of power is less concentrated and where the winning coalition of states is larger and more equally constituted, settlement agreements will necessarily emerge from wider negotiations. It will be harder for one state to impose its conception of order on the others, and the specific advantages that an institutional settlement provides in muting the implications of power asymmetries are less acutely felt.

The greater the power of the leading state, the more incentives and capacities it will have to build order around binding institutions. It will have a greater "windfall" of power to manage, and this intensifies the incentive it has to try to lock in long-term gains and lower the enforcement costs by making the order acceptable to weaker and secondary states.[58] Moreover,

---

considerably over the postwar period, responding to functional changes but also adapting to pressures from states to make them more congenial to their interests. Adaptations in the existing institutions make the attractions of a wholesale replacement of these institutions less compelling, which in turn reenforces the stability and continuity of the prevailing postwar institutional order.

[58] The shifting of power disparities is also important. The more that the leading state anticipates that its power advantages will decline—and the more rapidly it believes this will happen—the greater will be the appeal of a constitutional order over the pursuit of its inter-

the greater the power of the leading state, the more it will have opportunities to organize the postwar order according to its long-term interests and the more it will possess resources with which to bargain over institutional agreements. This is true in two respects. First, it is in a more advantaged position to forego some short-term gains in exchange for the institutional agreements. It can provide wartime subsidies, reconstruction aid, market access, and so forth, to its weaker partners in order to secure their cooperation. Second, it is also in a more favorable position to offer ongoing restraints on the exercise of its power in return for institutional agreements. The greater the power of the leading state, the more it has to offer lesser states in seeking their institutional cooperation and the lower the opportunity costs of doing so. Similarly, the greater the postwar power disparities, the more that weaker and secondary states will necessarily worry about domination and abandonment—and, as result, the greater their incentive to agree to lock themselves into a postwar order that ensures restraint and commitment by the leading state.

Defined in terms of gross military and economic capabilities, the United States was in a much stronger position in 1945 than it was in 1919 or than Britain was in 1815. These variations in power disparities are seen in Table 3–1, which provides comparisons of relative military expenditures and gross national product of the major states after the three major wars and after the Cold War. Power asymmetries were much sharper after 1945 than in the earlier cases. Power—understood as a composite of military and economic capabilities—was more concentrated in the hands of a single state. The United States emerged from World War II as the leading military power and it possessed nearly half of world economic production.[59] The United States did emerge from World War I with the leading economy—it was almost three times the size of Great Britain in domestic economic product—but its military capabilities were not substantially greater

---

ests through simple domination. The ability of state leaders to discern the actual character of the postwar power disparities and make judgments about future power trends—even among contemporary elites with modern analytic techniques—is inherently problematic. Real-time perceptions of the balance of power are inevitably different from post hoc descriptions. This makes predictions of state behavior based on gross power differentials difficult, and increases the importance of attention to how state leaders in specific historical circumstances perceive and act upon changing power realities. See William C. Wohlforth, *Elusive Balance: Power and Perceptions during the Cold War* (Ithaca: Cornell University Press, 1993); Aaron L. Friedberg, *The Weary Titan: Britain and the Experience of Relative Decline, 1895–1905* (Princeton: Princeton University Press, 1988); and Charles A. Kupchan, *The Vulnerability of Empire* (Ithaca: Cornell University Press, 1994). Over time, states have had better data at their disposal and can therefore more accurately assess their power trajectory. In the aftermath of wars, states are also in a better position to assess power disparities. As Geoffrey Blainey argues, war clarifies power relations. Blainey, *The Causes of War* (New York: Free Press, 1973).

[59] See Appendix Two for a fuller presentation of relevant military and economic data.

TABLE 3–1
Great Powers Indexed to Leading Postwar State

	Country and Percentage of Lead State Value						
Year	*Largest*		*2ⁿᵈLargest*		*3ʳᵈLargest*		*4ᵗʰLargest*	

Year	*Largest*		*2ⁿᵈLargest*		*3ʳᵈLargest*		*4ᵗʰLargest*	
Gross National Product								
1820	Russia	109	France	106	U.K.	100	Germany	47
1920	U.S.A.	100	U.K.	34	France	21	Germany	19
1945	U.S.A.	100	U.K.	20	Russia	20	Germany	12
1996	U.S.A.	100	Japan	60	Germany	31	France	20
Military Expenditures								
1816	U.K.	100	Germany	80	Russia	62	France	62
1920	U.S.A.	100	U.K.	89	Russia	71	Japan	27
1945	U.S.A.	100	U.K.	19	Russia	10	Japan	4
1996	U.S.A.	100	Russia	27	France	17	Japan	17

Source: See Appendix Two.

than those of the British. After 1815, Britain had the leading economy and exceeded the other great powers in military spending, but it remained a world naval power without a direct military presence on the continent.[60]

Differences in power disparities across the three cases are also determined by specific circumstances related to the end of the war. These elements include: the extent to which the old order was destroyed by the war, the decisiveness of the victory, and the degree to which the leading state was responsible for winning the war. The greater the breakdown of order, the greater the opportunities to recast the rules and principles of order. Where the breakdown is extensive, the postwar juncture is more path-dependent, and this situation provides incentives for the leading states to seek far-reaching and principled agreements on postwar order. In effect, the extent to which the leading state can in fact lock in a favorable postwar order is greater when the degree of breakdown in the old order is greater. Extensive breakdown also tends to eliminate the default option; it makes it harder to accept a nonagreement.

When the war ends with a decisive victory, the terms of the peace can be more extensive and ambitious; the defeat of the losing states is associated with the defeat of the old order, and the opportunities to usher in new rules and principles of order increase. When the war ends in an armistice or a

---

[60] See Paul Kennedy, *The Rise and Fall of the Great Powers: Economic Change and Military Conflict from 1500 to 2000* (New York: Random House, 1987), chapter four.

cease fire, it is more difficult for the winning states to impose a comprehensive settlement. The role of the leading postwar state in winning the war also has a bearing on its power after the war. Bargaining over postwar order tends to begin even before the fighting stops, and if the lead state is a decisive presence in ensuring victory it is in a stronger position to dominate the postwar proceedings.

These contextual aspects of power disparities tend to reinforce the variations noted earlier. Although the United States was not an early entrant into the World War II, by 1945 it was a leading military presence and played a critical role in ending the war in both Europe and Asia. Much as Britain did during the Napoleonic war, the United States used its resources during the war to orchestrate a definitive victory for the coalition states. The decision to seek unconditional surrender in the war, and the resulting occupation of the defeated states, also increased the power position of the United States. After 1918, the United States had found itself in a less commanding position. The war ended in a less decisive armistice, and the United States played a less decisive role in ending the war. During the Napoleonic wars, Britain was critical not only in ensuring victory but also in using its wartime resources—particularly financial subsidies—to hold the coalition together and gain agreement on alliance cooperation after the war. These differences in postwar power disparities and positioning are crucial in explaining variations in the capacities and incentives for postwar states to move toward an institutionalized postwar settlement.

Democracy and Institutional Agreement

Democracies are better able to create binding institutions and establish credible restraints and commitments than nondemocracies.[61] Several spe-

---

[61] As argued earlier, the problem with institutional binding strategies is that they leave states potentially exposed to the opportunistic actions of other states. The leading state, in placing limits on its use of power, must be confident that it will not be exploited by secondary states, and secondary states must be confident that they are not opening themselves to domination or abandonment by the leading state. For self-regarding states to agree to pursue their interests within binding institutions, they must convey to each other a credible sense of commitment. They must be certain that binding institutions actually do bind. They must reassure each other that they will not abandon their mutual restraint and exploit momentary advantages. Neorealists, of course, argue that such guarantees are never sufficient to go forward with far-reaching institutionalized cooperation. Under conditions of anarchy, neorealists assert, states will be reluctant to seek even mutually advantageous agreements if it leaves them vulnerable to cheating and or the relative gains of others. In a self-help system such as anarchy, states face huge obstacles to institutionalized cooperation because the interdependence and differentiation that comes with it are manifest within an anarchy as vulnerability. See Joseph M. Grieco, "Anarchy and the Limits of Cooperation: A Realist Critique of the Newest Liberal Institutionalism," *International Organization*, Vol. 42, No. 3 (Summer 1988), pp. 485–507.

TABLE 3–2
Democracy and Institutional Agreement

Characteristic	Implication
transparency	reduces surprises
	generates higher confidence information
decentralized policy	policy viscosity
process	opportunities for enforcement
open and decentralized	access and voice opportunities
system	transnational and transgovernmental
	connecting points

cific characteristics can be identified that allow democracies to more readily make agreements that reduce risks of domination and abandonment.[62] These characteristics are political transparency, accessibility, and policy viscosity, and they are summarized in Table 3–2.

Democracies have higher levels of political transparency than nondemocracies, which allows other states to make more exact determinations of the state's commitment to rules and agreements. Political transparency refers to the openness and visibility of the polity, and democracies have a variety of characteristics that promote such transparency, most crucial of which is the decentralization of power and decision making. Because decision making is dispersed, more people and a more elaborate process is involved. As a result, more of the business of politics must be conducted in the open. Reinforcing this situation are the norms and expectations of democratic politics. Elected officials are ultimately accountable to voters, and therefore the expectation is that the public will observe—if not directly participate in—policy making. Secrecy is seen to be the exception and not the norm. Finally, the competitive party system also generates information about the state's policy intentions and commitments. The vetting process of national elections increases the chances that leaders will be known entities who embrace well-hewn policy orientations. Political competition is a punishment-and-reward system that creates incentives for leaders to be open and accountable. The electoral system creates incentives for each party to expose inconsistencies and credibility gaps in the policy commitments of the other party.[63] Because of these competitive party dynamics

[62] For a survey of arguments in this area, see Kurt Taylor Gaubatz, "Democratic States and Commitment in International Relations," *International Organization*, Vol. 50, No. 1 (Winter 1996), pp. 109–39. See also Charles Lipson, "Reliable Partners: The 'Promising Advantage' of Democracies as an Explanation of Peace," Unpublished paper, University of Chicago, 1998.

[63] For a formal exploration of the relationship between external commitments and internal political costs, see James Fearon's work on domestic audience costs. The argument is that the

and the transparency of the decision-making process, other states are less subject to surprises than they are by nondemocracies, and this increases the confidence that others will have in the state's commitments.[64]

The openness and decentralization of democratic states also provides opportunities for other states to consult and make representations directly, thus increasing their willingness to make binding commitments.[65] The multiple points of access allow other states to make direct assessments of policy commitments and to lobby on behalf of their interests. The array of officials and offices that have a hand in policy are all potential access points. In some instances, elaborate consultative mechanisms may exist to facilitate consultation and representation; in others, it may be less direct and formal, with governments working through private representatives and agents.[66] Democratic polities provide opportunities for access by other states, which can increase levels of information about policy intentions and commitments, and it can also provide opportunities for foreign governments to press their interests within the policy-making process.[67] As a result, the credibility of commitments rise.

Finally, democratic states have greater institutional checks on abrupt policy shifts than nondemocratic states, and this "policy viscosity" serves to reduce policy surprises.[68] One type of check is simply that policy in a

---

signals that leaders send to other actors are more credible when those signals bear domestic political costs. See Fearon, "Domestic Political Audiences and the Escalation of International Disputes," *American Political Science Review*, Vol. 88 (September 1994), pp. 577–92.

[64] Other nations will be more willing to enter into an agreement that they know will be maintained. Referring to the openness of American democracy, Michael Mastanduno argues, "the transparency of the United States political system helps to increase the prospects for enduring international cooperation." Mastanduno, "The United States Political System and International Leadership: A 'Decidedly Inferior' Form of Government," in G. John Ikenberry, *American Foreign Policy: Theoretical Essays*, 2nd ed. (New York: HarperCollins, 1996), p. 343. See also Peter Cowhey, "Domestic Institutions and the Credibility of International Commitments: Japan and the United States," *International Organization*, Vol. 47, No. 2 (Spring 1993), pp. 299–326.

[65] In this sense, information about intentions and commitments flows in both directions. Democracies expose themselves more fully to other states than do nondemocracies, and their accessible institutions also allow them to absorb more information on the policies and motivations of other states.

[66] See Daniel Deudney and G. John Ikenberry, "The Nature and Sources of Liberal International Order," *Review of International Studies*, Vol. 25 (April 1999), pp. 179–96.

[67] When groups of democracies interact, their open, decentralized, and permeable characteristics facilitate more extensive interpenetration than when nondemocracies interact. In the study of interorganizational relationships, Neal Smelser has described this situation as "structural conductivity"—the structures of society that permit or even encourage organizations to form relationships. See Neil J. Smelser, *Theory of Collective Behavior* (New York: Free Press, 1962).

[68] This term is introduced in Daniel Deudney and G. John Ikenberry, "Liberal Competence: The Performance of Democracies in Great Power Balancing," unpublished paper, 1994.

decentralized pluralistic democracy must usually pass through a series of veto points. Policy making is essentially a process of coalition building, and this makes it less likely that one individual can command policy unilaterally and move it abruptly in ways that are threatening to others. Likewise, the competitive electoral process also exerts an ongoing pressure on the overall direction of policy. Successful leaders must build majority coalitions of voters. This creates an incentive to reflect the positions of the "median voter."[69] The structure of electoral politics ensures that the range of policies will be—at least over the long term—within the center of the political spectrum.

As a result, democracies are able to convey greater credibility in their commitments than nondemocracies. Their openness and transparency allows greater opportunities to determine the character and durability of policies. Their accessibility allows other governments not just to gather information but also to deliver information directly and actively participate at least on the fringes of policy making. The competitive party system also provides a mechanism that exerts a pull on policy, creating an ongoing incentive for policy to be situated in the center of the political spectrum. None of these factors guarantees that democratic polities will always make good on their commitments, but they do reduce the uncertainty that abrupt and untoward shifts in the policy will emerge.

If democracies have special capacities to establish binding institutional agreements, the postwar junctures have varied greatly in the degree to which the participating states were in fact democratic. The big divide was really between the twentieth-century settlements—in which the major parties to the postwar settlements were democratic—and the earlier settlements, which were basically between nondemocracies. Britain was an emerging constitutional democracy in the early nineteenth century. But the other major European states were mostly monarchical and autocratic. These differences are important in explaining variations in the ability of postwar states to move toward an institutionalized settlement.

The constitutional model of order building is an ideal type. Postwar states are most likely to seek an institutional bargain when democratic states face each other in highly asymmetrical power relations: that is, when a newly powerful state is most concerned with establishing an order that does not require a continuous power struggle and weaker states are most worried about domination and abandonment; and when the type of states that are party to the settlement are most able to establish institutions that are credible and binding. These circumstances are present to a greater or lesser extent in the 1815, 1919, and 1945 cases, but none fully conforms to the ideal typical features of the model. The 1815 and 1919 cases show some

---

[69] See Cowhey, "Elect Locally—Order Globally."

traces of the institutional order building logic but also its limits. The cases are examined to identify both the sources and constraints on institutional order building: the way specific features of postwar power disparities and the presence or absence of democratic states played a role in the ultimate outcome.[70] More than in 1815 and 1919, the 1945 settlement provided incentives and opportunities to move toward an institutional settlement. After the war, the rolling sequence of institutional bargains and compromises between the United States and the other industrial democracies unfolded, resulting in the most institutionalized order yet seen. The rise of the Cold War after 1947 had an obvious and important impact on the willingness and ability of the Western states to create and operate within binding institutions after World War II. For this reason, tracing the fate of these institutions after the Cold War is an important step in assessing the significance of the institutional model in explaining post-1945 order among the major industrial democracies.

[70] The historical cases are used to assess the explanatory capacity of the institutional model's hypotheses in three ways: through process tracing, each case is examined to see the impact of the major variables on the institutional strategy of the leading state and the character of the order that followed; through comparisons between the three major cases for variations in the major variables and outcomes; and through an examination of American policy and institutional relations among the major Western states after the Cold War. The sharp shifts in the international distribution of power after 1991—ending the Soviet threat and enhancing American preponderance—provides an opportunity to assess the claims about the institutional bases of the 1945 settlement.

Chapter Four

THE SETTLEMENT OF 1815

THE PEACE settlement that ended the Napoleonic wars in 1815 gave Europe the most elaborately organized political order yet. Led by Great Britain, the European states mounted a sustained effort to find a mutually agreeable, comprehensive, and stable order; this effort culminated in the celebrated Congress of Vienna. By most measures the order was, in fact, quite successful. War among the great powers ceased for forty years and an entire century would pass before the international order was again consumed by a general European war.[1]

The Vienna settlement departed from earlier postwar settlements in the way the leading state attempted to use institutions to manage relations among the great powers.[2] In the last years of the war and during the peace

---

[1] Scholars differ as to how long the concert system lasted. Some argue that it was in decline or ended in the early or mid-1820s. See Inis Claude, Jr., *Swords into Plowshares* (New York: Random House, 1956); F. H. Hinsley, *Power and the Pursuit of Peace* (Cambridge: Cambridge University Press, 1963); and Harold Nicolson, *The Congress of Vienna: A Study in Allied Unity: 1812–1822* (New York: Viking, 1961 edition). Others argue that it lasted until the Crimean war (1854–1856) or until World War I. See Paul W. Schroeder, *Austria, Great Britain, and the Crimean War: The Destruction of the European Concert* (Ithaca: Cornell University Press, 1972); Gordon A. Craig and Alexander L. George, *Force and Statecraft* (New York: Oxford University Press, 1983); and Kal J. Holsti, "Governance without Government: Polyarchy in Nineteenth-Century European International Politics," in James N. Rosenau and Ernst-Otto Czempiel, ed., *Governance without Government: Order and Change in World Politics* (New York: Cambridge University Press, 1992), pp. 30–57.

[2] Scholars have long debated the Vienna settlement's logic and significance, particularly the issue of whether the concert system constituted simply a modification and refinement of the balance of power or a much more fundamental departure from the balance. See the debate in the *American History Review* forum, centered around Paul W. Schroeder, "Did the Vienna Settlement Rest on a Balance of Power?" *American History Review*, Vol. 97, No. 3 (June 1992), pp. 683–706. The leading view of the Vienna settlement has been that it was fundamentally a reestablishment of the balance of power. As Edward Gulick argues: "When the time came to discuss preliminary plans for peace, the statesmen flew as straight as bees toward the hive of balance of power. The state system was to be restored; Prussia was to be increased in order to stabilize north-central Europe; and France was to be reduced to a size compatible with the secure independence of other states." Gulick, *Europe's Classical Balance of Power* (Ithaca: Cornell University Press, 1955), p. 121. The balance-of-power system after 1815 might not have been as unvarnished as in the eighteenth century, but its fundamentals were the same. Others have argued that the balance of power was refined and socialized in Vienna; the operation of balance was more self-conscious and rooted in a mutual recognition of the necessities and virtues of "equilibrium" among the European powers. See Henry Kissinger, *A World Restored:*

negotiations, Great Britain pursued an institutional strategy aimed at establishing formal processes of consultation and accommodation among the postwar great powers. These institutional proposals—in particular, the alliance and the congress system—were novel in the way they attempted to bind potentially rival states together. In 1818, the congress system was inaugurated with the Congress of Aix-la-Chapelle, the first conference ever held between states to regulate international relations in time of peace. The earlier settlements created limits and restrains on power through the reinforcement of state autonomy, the redistribution of territory and power capacities, and the counterbalancing of power. The Vienna settlement called upon these mechanisms as well, but it also made use of institutions that were designed to provide some measure of restraint on the autonomous and indiscriminate exercise of power by the major states.[3]

There were, however, sharp limits to the binding character of these institutions; the British proposal for specific security guarantees failed and, overall, the institutional arrangements were of dramatically less breadth and depth than those that were proposed or employed after 1919 and 1945. But traces of a constitutional settlement are evident, albeit weak, partial, and in some respects fleeting. The asymmetries of power did provide dilemmas and opportunities that shaped the way the major states negotiated the terms of postwar order. Moreover, Britain and the other major powers did pursue a strategy of mutual restraint, loosely tying each to the other in

---

Metternich, Castlereagh and the Problems of Peace, 1812–1822 (Boston: Houghton Mifflin, 1973). Others have gone still further and argued that the Vienna settlement constituted a more fundamental break with older forms of European balance-of-power politics. In this view, Vienna represented the rejection of the classical balance in favor of a quasi-institutionalized concert system of great-power cooperation. See Charles A. Kupchan and Clifford A. Kupchan, "Concerts, Collective Security, and the Future of Europe," *International Security*, Vol. 16, No. 1 (Summer 1991), pp. 114–61; Robert Jervis, "Security Regimes," *International Organization*, Vol. 36, No. 2 (Spring 1982), pp. 173–94; Jervis, "From Balance to Concert: A Study of International Security Cooperation," *World Politics*, Vol. 38, No. 1 (October 1985), pp. 58–79; Richard Elrod, "The Concert of Europe: A Fresh Look at an International System," *World Politics*, Vol. 28, No. 2 (January 1976), pp. 159–74; and Paul Gordon Lauren, "Crisis Prevention in Nineteenth-Century Diplomacy," in Alexander George, ed., *Managing U.S.-Soviet Rivalry: Problems of Crisis Prevention* (Boulder, Colo.: Westview, 1983), pp. 31–64. Building on this view, the historian Paul Schroeder has led a reconsideration of the sources of order in post-Napoleonic Europe that emphasizes the transformations in the institutions and practices of European security. In this view, the settlement did not rest only (or even fundamentally) on the balance of power but was built on a mix of power and institutional constraint arrangements. See Paul W. Schroeder, *The Transformation of European Politics, 1763–1848* (Oxford: Oxford University Press, 1994).

[3] As one scholar puts it, "the greatest significance of the Vienna settlement lies in the fact that it saw the creation of the first deliberately contrived international system rather than in the precise nature of its territorial dispositions." Richard Langhorne, "Reflections on the Significance of the Congress of Vienna," *Review of International Studies*, Vol. 12, No. 4 (October 1986), p. 314.

treaty and alliance so as to mitigate strategic rivalry and the return to great-power war. The postwar alliance exhibited characteristics of a *pactum de controhendo*, a pact of restraint. These mutually entangling alliance relations supplemented, and to some extent replaced, balance of power as the core logic of order among the great powers of the European state system.

What were the incentives and opportunities that lay behind Britain's institutional strategy, and what determined the extent of its success? The constitutional model is useful in several respects in identifying both the impulses behind and limits on Britain's proposed use of institutions and features of the order that followed. First, Britain did try to use its tempo-rary power advantages both during and after the war to lock in a favorable order, and it resorted to mechanisms of institutional binding to do so. It was willing to forego some opportunities to exploit its position during and after the war—particularly toward Holland and in the colonial world—so as to signal restraint and facilitate agreement on the wider and agreed-upon institutional arrangements for the management of postwar order. British policy also reflected the incentives that a leading state has to secure an order with a measure of legitimacy, and it was willing to place some modest limits on its power to achieve this end.[4]

Second, the disparities of postwar power and the character of the states involved in the settlement were critical in determining the limits to which an institutional bargain was possible or desired. British power advantages were most evident during the war itself—manifest in its military forces and financial resources—and it used this leverage to organize and maintain the alliance in a way that would last beyond the war. Without British leverage, the outcome of the war could have been very different—with far-reaching implications for postwar order. As late as February 1814, Tsar Alexander threatened to ignore the alliance and march into Paris, dethrone Napoleon, and impose a new government.[5] At the other extreme, Prince von Metter-nich of Austria threatened to pursue an early and separate peace with Na-poleon. Either way, the alliance would have broken up, and the reintegra-tion of postwar France would have been problematic, ushering in, as Viscount Castlereagh, the British foreign minister, warned in a letter to Tsar Alexander, a "lawless scramble for power."[6] Britain had the most ad-vanced economy and it was a global naval power, but it did not have territo-rial ambitions in Europe or military capabilities to dominate the continent.

---

[4] Britain does not appear to have given up much in the way of short-term gains in exchange for the institutional cooperation of the other European states. The institutional bargain was more specifically an agreement by Britain and the other major states to restrain the arbitrary use of power in territorial disputes, made credible by alliance and consultation mechanisms.

[5] Charles Webster, *The Congress of Vienna, 1814–1815* (reprint, New York: Barnes and Noble, 1963), p. 45. First published by the British Foreign Office, 1919.

[6] Quoted in Andreas Osiander, *The States System of Europe, 1640–1990* (Oxford: Clarendon Press, 1994), pp. 176–77.

As the preeminent state after the war, its threat to the other great powers was more one of abandonment than domination. These circumstances limited what Britain was willing and able to offer the other European states in exchange for institutional agreement.

Equally important, the autocratic character of the states involved in the settlement placed limits on how far institutional strategies could be used. The proposal for a general security guarantee, first suggested by Prime Minister William Pitt in 1805, foundered precisely on the inability of the European leaders to make such commitments. Tsar Alexander's highly personal and erratic foreign policy was most emblematic of this more general problem. As the only country with a parliamentary democracy, Britain gave voice to the view that a representative government had more difficulty but ultimately greater credibility in making treaty commitments. Tsar Alexander's later proposal for a Holy Alliance also reflected a search for sources of commitment and restraint not rooted in the balance of power—but also not rooted in binding institutional mechanisms.

The model is helpful in identifying the factors that were present and absent at the 1815 juncture, which both precipitated and limited the institutional bargain. It is less helpful in identifying the specific intellectual breakthrough that led Britain to seize on institutional mechanisms as a tool of order building. The breakthrough was in its appreciation of the potential role of ongoing consultative mechanisms as institutional devices to maintain order and manage potential adversaries. This new thinking served to expand the order-building options of Britain and the other European states. As one historian notes, "There could have been an overpowering wish to establish a new international system at both practical and emotional levels, but it would have had no result unless some mechanism could be found for achieving what was so deeply desired."[7] These ideas may be traced back to Pitt's famous State Paper of 1805, which conceived of a postwar order that bound potential adversaries together through alliance and treaty guarantees.

This reconsideration of institutional possibilities reflected an evolution of thinking about ways to stabilize and manage relations among the major powers, and it was also a search for practical arrangements to facilitate joint management of European order—to create, in effect, a sort of oligarchic system of management. These practical steps began simply with attempts, led by Britain, to renew the wartime alliance—the so-called Quadruple Alliance as it had been formed in the Treaty of Chaumont in March 1814. Britain insisted that the wartime alliance—and its mechanisms and guarantees—should survive the end of the war and remain in place to ensure management of the peace settlement. Institutional innovations were made in very practical ways.

[7] Langhorne, "Reflections on the Significance of the Congress of Vienna," p. 315.

The Strategic Setting

The coalition that defeated Napoleon was united by its resistance to French hegemony. But the war did not eliminate hegemony as a "problem of power" on the continent. Britain, which was most important and persistent in resisting France, emerged from the war as the preeminent global power, whereas Russia emerged as the leading power in Eastern Europe. The settlement was as much about how to organize European order around these leading states—and the new asymmetrical power relations they produced on the continent—as it was about thwarting French ambitions.

In the years between 1789 and 1812, French domination of continental Europe had steadily grown through annexation and conquest. By 1812, whatever ambiguities had existed about Napoleon's imperial ambitions gave way in a wave of further annexations, including most of northern Italy, all territories to the west of the Rhine, and substantial parts of the Low Countries. At its zenith, France commanded a European empire that stretched from the Atlantic to Poland and from the Baltic to the Mediterranean.[8] Behind France's expanding domain was the most formidable military in Europe, more than 600,000 strong in 1812, and a vast economic sphere of control organized around the Continental System. That system, originating in 1806, was both a campaign of economic warfare against Britain and a means to exercise control over the states of Europe.

Napoleon's invasion of Russia in June 1812 signaled the beginning of the French collapse. Russia and Sweden signed treaties with Britain. As Russia pursued Napoleon's armies across Europe, Prussia and eventually Austria joined the anti-Napoleonic coalition, and in 1813 and early 1814 they, along with Russia, fought bloody campaigns against the French. In mid-1813, the "last coalition" took shape, when Britain finally joined the eastern powers. In the autumn of 1813, the British took active leadership of the coalition, providing subsidies and direction to the other governments and leading the intra-allied negotiations over the terms of peace. The culmination of the British initiative was the Treaty of Chaumont in early 1814, which laid the foundation for victory, the terms of peace, and the structure of postwar security in Europe.[9] By early 1814, the war had turned decisively in favor of the allies. An armistice was signed in April, followed by the first Peace of Paris in May.

In a span of only two years, Europe experienced the most dramatic power transition it had yet seen. The collapse of the Napoleonic empire com-

---

[8] Schroeder argues that the zenith of Napoleon's empire was 1809, because all the subsequent annexations and campaigns served to undermine it. Schroeder, *The Transformation of European Politics*, p. 371.

[9] Ibid., p. 501.

pletely and abruptly altered the distribution of power, shifting and magnifying the position of Britain and Russia. In the aftermath of the war, British financial and naval strength and the military power at the disposal of the Russian tsar were critical realities underlying European diplomacy.[10] The war did not lead to the triumph of a single hegemonic state, but neither did it result in a simple pluralistic system of states—an image evoked in the balance-of-power view of the postwar settlement. In effect, two leading states at either end of the European continent emerged as the leading arbiters of the postwar settlement.

Britain was the leading global power in 1815, and for the first time in its history it exerted a commanding influence over the reconstruction of Europe.[11] Its leading position, as Paul Kennedy notes, was the result of a combination of achievements—naval mastery, financial credit, commercial expertise, alliance diplomacy, and an expanding colonial empire.[12] Behind British ascendancy was its economy, the most advanced in Europe. The actual size of Britain's economy, measured in terms of gross domestic product, was roughly equal to those of France and Russia after 1815.[13] But it was a more technologically advanced and productive economy that led the rest of Europe into a new phase of industrialization. Between 1760 and 1820, Britain was responsible for about two-thirds of Europe's growth in industrial production.[14] This rising British advantage is reflected in the changing relative shares of world manufacturing output (see Table 4–1). Britain's share doubled in the decades spanning the Napoleonic wars.

Britain's preeminent position, and its aid and subsidies that provided the basis for the successful war effort, was not lost on the other European states. "England," wrote Metternich's advisor, Friedrich von Gentz, "appeared in Vienna with all the glamour which she owed to her immense successes, to the eminent part which she had played in the Coalition, to her limitless influence, to a solid basis of prosperity and power such as no other country has acquired in our days—in fact to the respect and fear which she inspired and which affected her relations with all the other Governments. Profiting by this, England could have imposed her will on Europe."[15]

---

[10] See F. R. Bridge and Roger Bullen, *The Great Powers and the European State System, 1815–1914* (London: Longman, 1980), p. 7.

[11] Charles Webster, *Foreign Policy of Castlereagh, 1812–1815* (London: G. Bell and Sons, 1950), p. 3

[12] Paul Kennedy, *The Rise and Fall of the Great Powers: Economic Change and Military Conflict from 1500 to 2000* (New York: Random House, 1987), pp. 151–58.

[13] See Appendix Two.

[14] P. Bairoch, "International Industrialization Levels from 1750 to 1980," *Journal of European Economic History*, Vol. 11, No. 2 (Fall 1982), p. 291.

[15] Quoted in Nicolson, *The Congress of Vienna*, p. 128.

TABLE 4–1
Relative Shares of World Manufacturing Output, 1800–1860

	1800	1820	1860
Europe as a whole	28.1	34.2	53.2
United Kingdom	4.3	9.5	19.9
Habsburg Empire	3.2	3.2	4.2
France	4.2	5.2	7.9
German States/Germany	3.5	3.5	4.9
Russia	5.6	5.6	7.0
United States	0.8	2.4	7.2

Source: Paul Bairoch, "International Industrialization Levels from 1750 to 1980," *Journal of European Economic History*, Vol. 11, No. 2 (Fall 1982), p. 296.

Britain's power was both enhanced and limited by its detachment from specific territorial disputes on the continent. It did not have specific objectives within continental Europe. Beyond the establishment of a secure and independent Dutch state, Britain simply wanted a peaceful and stable Europe, which would require a variety of arrangements often summarized by British diplomats as "equilibrium." On the one hand, Britain's relative aloofness from the continent, coupled with its commanding naval and economic position, gave it both the incentives to think comprehensively and for the long term about postwar order and the ability to shape the coalition that would support its designs. On the other hand, it limited what Britain could or was willing to exchange in the way of restraints on its power for cooperation by the other European states.

Russia also had a looming position on the eastern edge of Europe. The tsar was able to claim that Russia was decisive in defeating Napoleon, and he was eager to present his visionary agenda for the future of Europe. By the beginning of the Vienna congress, Russia was the most powerful country on the continent. After the war and during the following decade, as Table 4–2 indicates, Russia had a standing military establishment nearly triple the size of any other great power. He was more constrained, however, than Britain. Alexander's fear was that Russia, as one analyst notes, "might be pushed to the periphery of the European system."[16] His goal was to make Russia a respected member and key player in European politics. Further limiting its options, Russia was also financially dependent on Britain for its war effort.

[16] Osiander, *The States System of Europe*, pp. 178–79.

TABLE 4–2
Military Personnel of the Great Powers, 1816–1830

	1816	1830
United Kingdom	255,000	140,000
France	132,000	259,000
Russia	800,000	826,000
Prussia/Germany	130,000	130,000
Habsburg Empire	220,000	273,000
United States	16,000	11,000

Source: Paul Kennedy, *The Rise and Fall of the Great Powers: Economic Change and Military Conflict from 1500 to 2000* (New York: Random House, 1987), p.154.

During and after the war, the European world was caught in a struggle between competing lead states with overlapping European continental positions. In Napoleon's hands, French hegemony had over-reached, and this invited counterbalancing, resistance, and collapse. The struggles of this era, as Paul Schroeder emphasizes, "were not a contest between the French Revolution and the old regime, or between expansionist France and the rest of Europe, or even between France and Britain as secular rivals, the tiger and the shark, but a conflict between three hegemonic powers as to which, or which combination of them, would control and exploit the countries in between."[17] The defeat of Napoleon was not the defeat of hegemony or domination on the continent; it only altered which states would be the leading powers and the conditions under which they would exercise their power.

Prussia and Austria were much weaker. With a population of fifteen million people and few resources, Prussia was only a nominal great power and barely survived the Napoleonic wars. Austria was in a slightly better position than Prussia but also paled in comparison to Russia and the British Empire. Russia had the largest population, territory, and standing army. Britain led the world in industry, commerce, finance, and overseas colonies.[18] These asymmetries in power capabilities were even more dramatic when the relative vulnerability of the states is considered. Britain and Russia were much less vulnerable to military aggrandizement than the other

[17] Schroeder, *The Political Transformation of Europe*, p. 309.

[18] These comparisons are stressed by Paul Schroeder, "Did the Vienna Settlement Rest on a Balance of Power?" pp. 686–90. Schroeder makes the strongest case in the historical literature that the post-Napoleonic period was dominated by British and Russian "pursuit of hegemony," although often under the guise of balance-of-power rhetoric.

continental power. Geographical remoteness strengthened their position. The failure of Napoleon in Russia was itself a ratification of this reality. As Schroeder argues, "Britain and Russia were so powerful and invulnerable that even a (highly unlikely) alliance of the three other powers against them would not seriously threaten the basic security of either, while such a (hypothetical) alliance would likewise not give France, Austria, and Prussia security comparable to that which Britain or Russia enjoyed on their own."[19]

The dominant position of Britain and Russia was acknowledged by their governments in 1805, when Tsar Alexander sent a representative to London to propose an Anglo-Russia alliance that would specify certain (somewhat vague) Europe-wide aims. The British government responded with its own proposal for a concert of powers in the aftermath of the Napoleonic wars, and it emphasized the special position that the two major powers occupied: "The insular situation and extensive resources of Great Britain, aided by its military exertions and naval superiority; and the immense power, the established Continental ascendancy and remote distance of Russia already give to the territories of the two Sovereigns a security against the attacks of France—even after all her acquisitions of influence, power, and dominion—which cannot be the lot of any other country. They have therefore no separate objects of their own in the arrangements which are in question, no personal interest in this Concert but that which grows out of the general interest and security of Europe, and is inseparably connected with it."[20] The other continental great powers would have rights and responsibilities as well, but the British argued that after a settlement was achieved, it should be placed under the special guarantee of Great Britain and Russia, who had "no separate objects of their own."[21] In effect, British and Russian governments were arguing that their two countries—powerful, invulnerable, and on the frontiers of Europe—had a special duty and opportunity to ensure the peace after the return of France to its historical position.

The three would-be leading European states each possessed a different array of strengths, assets, and liabilities, and each confronted the states of Europe with different threats and attractions. Russia threatened Poland and the Ottoman Empire. British commercial and naval supremacy made it as much a threat to the outer European states as Napoleon's Continental

---

[19] Ibid., p. 687.

[20] "Official Communication made to the Russian Ambassador at London," 19 January 1805. Text in Charles Webster, ed., *British Diplomacy, 1813–1815: Select Documents Dealing with the Reconstruction of Europe* (London: G. Bell and Sons, 1921), Appendix 1, p. 390.

[21] Ibid.

System.[22] The smaller states of Europe may have united behind Britain and Russia in defeating French hegemony, but as victors Britain and Russia faced the same dilemmas and perils that French hegemony had confronted: they would need to make their superordinate power acceptable to the other European states or be willing to use their power to coercively maintain their hold on the European system. The brutal and arbitrary character of Napoleonic hegemony made the asymmetries in European power obvious and potentially untenable. But the looming presence of British and Russian power was also a defining features of the war and the postwar situation. The smaller European states would need to reconcile themselves with British and Russian power at the same time that they cooperated with Britain and Russia in ending the war and making the peace.

Within this context of two powerful states on the edges of Europe, the central European countries maneuvered to protect themselves and ensure that neither major power dominated the continent. For Metternich and Austria this meant playing a sophisticated balancing game. Prussia as well was forced to look to the postwar distribution of power and alliances to protect its weak position in the middle of Europe. Metternich welcomed Russian military involvement, as it weakened Napoleon, but he also wanted France to remain sufficiently powerful to play its traditional role in maintaining a "just equilibrium." Balancing the power distribution was the essence of this intra-European process of stabilizing security relations after the war. But it was also a process that took place within a wider context of huge power asymmetries and looming regional hegemony.

If the postwar European states had been more equal in size, the postwar settlement might have simply reestablished an order built on the balance of power. But the preeminence of Britain and to a lesser extent Russia meant that order would also hinge on other mechanisms of restraint on these leading states. Talleyrand, the French diplomat, made this observation in Vienna: "If Europe were composed of States being so related to one another than the minimum of resisting power of the smallest were equal to the maximum of aggressive power of the greatest, then there would be a real equilibrium. But the situation of Europe is not, and will never be, such. The actual situation admits solely of an equilibrium which is artificial and precarious and which can only last so long as certain large States are animated by a spirit of moderation and justice which will preserve that equilibrium."[23] The problem of order building after Napoleon was finding ways to encourage moderation among states in highly asymmetrical relationships.

---

[22] Schroeder, *The Transformation of European Politics*, p. 309.
[23] Quoted in Nicolson, *The Congress of Europe*, p. 155.

British Thinking about Postwar Order

Britain responded to incentives to use the war and its aftermath to lock in a Europe-wide settlement. At various junctures and in several different ways, the British defined their interests in a more comprehensive and longer-term way than was necessary or inevitable. To be sure, the overriding British concern at this juncture was the destruction of French hegemony. But in the pursuit of this goal a wide variety of possibilities existed. Britain could have settled on simply securing its immediate goals in the war, such as the restoration of an independent Netherlands and the establishment of maritime rights that would ensure British naval supremacy. But the British sought a more far-reaching and elaborate settlement, even if this meant giving way or compromising on more immediate goals.

The thrust of British postwar order-building policy is consistent with the institutional model. British leaders did seek to capitalize on their momentary power advantages to lock in a favorable and durable order; they recognized that a durable order would best be secured through mutually satisfactory rules and institutions; and they offered some modest assurances of strategic restraint in order to gain agreement on institutions and processes that would bind the major states together and limit strategic rivalry. But there were also sharply defined limits on how far Britain would be willing to go in binding itself to a European order through security guarantees, and there were also severe limits on the ability of the other European states to make binding commitments as well.

Of all the states that opposed Napoleon, Britain was the most consistent in urging a comprehensive settlement that would set in place a durable and widely acceptable European order. Castlereagh spoke often about the virtues of a settlement based on "principle" and "principles," and argued that specific points of contention should give way to general agreement. "I wish to direct my main efforts to secure an equilibrium in Europe, to which object, as far as principle will permit, I wish to make all local points subordinate," Castlereagh wrote to Wellington during the Congress of Vienna.[24] Moreover, this view in favor of a comprehensive system of order, according to Castlereagh, was held as a conviction only by Britain. "Our misfortune is," Castlereagh wrote back to London, "that the powers all look to points instead of the general system of Europe."[25] Reflecting Britain's interest in a comprehensive settlement, Castlereagh talked frequently about the need

[24] Castlereagh to Wellington, 25 October 1814. Reprinted in Charles Webster, ed., *British Diplomacy, 1813–1815*, p. 217.
[25] Quoted in Osiander, *The States System of Europe*, p. 175.

for a "system" and for compromises to be made based upon what was "best for the general interest."[26]

During the war, the British goal of a comprehensive peace meant that the war itself must culminate in a decisive and united victory for the allies, although not necessarily with the removal of Napoleon. Initially, this meant making sure that Metternich brought Austria into the war on the allied side, and that it did not pursue a separate peace with Napoleon. As the allies moved toward victory, Britain also had to ensure that its allies did not break off the war and make a continental peace that excluded Britain. As Schroeder notes: "Castlereagh in particular realized that Britain could not force its allies to continue the war beyond their interests or capacities, but must instead persuade them that a defeat for Britain, which he conceded was possible, would ultimately be worse for them than for Britain itself."[27] This reinforced Britain's inclination to be generous and flexible with the peace terms. A general and moderate peace was the supreme goal, and the details were of less importance than agreement on an overall settlement.

Securing a Comprehensive Peace

Britain's expansive thinking was laid out in a cabinet memorandum written on the eve of Castlereagh's departure for the European continent.[28] The British terms for peace, Charles Webster notes, "were naturally dictated mainly by purely British interests, but these were brought into relation to the general scheme of reconstruction of the Continent, and it was clearly recognized that the one depended on the other."[29] The memorandum indicated that Castlereagh was to seek to establish a "clear and definite understanding with the Allies" on matters of "common interest" and, to ensure a united front, to also reach agreement on what the allies would discuss with France. The British argument was that if Britain could get its core interests secured (particularly, naval supremacy and security of Holland), it would agree to negotiate away some of its colonial possessions so as to gain general agreement. As the end of the war was in sight, British interests were clearly seen to be tied to the wider settlement of controversies over European order.

[26] Letter No. 1, Secret and Confidential, from Castlereagh (Paris) to Clancarty (Frankfurt), 5 November 1815. Quoted in Lauren, "Crisis Prevention in Nineteenth-Century Diplomacy," p. 32.

[27] Schroeder, *The Transformation of European Politics*, p. 475.

[28] Memorandum of Cabinet, 26 December 1813. Reprinted in Webster, ed., *British Diplomacy, 1813–1815*, pp. 123–28.

[29] Webster, *The Congress of Vienna*, p. 33.

Importantly, the British memorandum concluded by indicating that the alliance was not to end with the war, but rather should continue into the future and act as a coalition of mutual obligation to guard against a resurgent France. "The Treaty of Alliance," according to Castlereagh's instructions, "is not to terminate with the war, but to contain defensive engagements, with mutual obligations to support the Powers attacked by France, with a certain extent of stipulated succours."[30] As Webster reports, Castlereagh had "his own ideas as to a wider application of the ideas of 'alliance' and 'guarantee,' " but these ideas, which moved further in the direction of the postwar alliance as a *pactum de controhendo*, were not fully articulated at this juncture and they were subordinated to the goal of maintaining the alliance against France.[31]

British thinking about a comprehensive peace and an ongoing alliance dated back to 1805, during negotiations with Russia over alliance, but it was given more concrete articulation by Castlereagh in the fall of 1813 when Austria, at long last, joined the coalition. During this period, Castlereagh sought to give more coherence to British war aims and formulate instructions for British representatives in the field. "It was now," Webster notes, "that he first produced the scheme for an Alliance against France which should continue in peace as well as in war and give some unity to Europe in future danger."[32] Britain sought to place itself more squarely at the center of peace negotiations in an attempt to "wed the system of treaties between the individual Powers into one comprehensive instrument, which should place the coalition beyond the reach of dissolution by Napoleon's diplomacy."[33] These ideas again animated Castlereagh in late 1813, as he prepared for direct consultations with the continental allies.

During the war, the most important ways in which Britain sought to achieve a comprehensive postwar settlement was in its efforts to keep the coalition together and in using the wartime alliance as a mechanism to manage the peace. It was not inevitable that the European states who were together attempting to push France back within its borders would cooperate over the terms of the peace. It was far less certain that they would agree to construct a comprehensive set of arrangements to manage postwar order. The wartime coalition was disorganized and shifting, united by very little beyond a shared interest in resisting French hegemony. As Charles Webster writes, "Having driven Napoleon from Central Europe, they were in no sort of agreement as to how they would deal with the problems raised by his defeat."[34]

---

[30] Quoted ibid., p. 36.
[31] Ibid.
[32] Webster, *The Foreign Policy of Castlereagh, 1812–1815*, p. 160.
[33] Ibid.
[34] Webster, *The Congress of Vienna*, pp. 21–22.

Napoleon, in fact, had opportunities to break up the coalition during the war by exploiting temporary military advantages to agree to a cease-fire and purse a separate or limited peace agreement with neighboring states, such as Austria. In February 1814, Napoleon gave Foreign Minister Caulaincourt discretionary authority to negotiate a peace that gave France its "natural" borders. But after a series of unexpected French military victories, Napoleon canceled these instruments and insisted on holding on to more territory, including much of Italy. In this and other instances, Napoleon failed to exploit divisions among the allies, particularly Metternich's misgivings about a total British and Russian victory. Metternich was willing to accept a negotiated peace that allowed Napoleon to stay in power, whereas Castlereagh argued that a stable European peace depended on the end of Napoleonic rule.

Maintaining the Alliance

At various points during the war, Britain played a decisive role in keeping the coalition together through diplomatic initiatives and generous subsidies, and in shaping postwar agreements. In these various ways, the manner in which Britain calculated its interests is revealed. First, Britain sought to keep the coalition together in some minimal way and it used money and diplomacy to do so. By the end of 1813, the coalition was indeed breaking apart.[35] Metternich persuaded the tsar and the British to respond to an offer of negotiation by Napoleon. But afterward, Napoleon backed down and the war commenced again. The coalition partners had different interests, mostly dealing with territorial claims and ambitions. The possibility of a series of separate peace agreements between Napoleon and the other states was very real. Certainly, little agreement existed on how the war would end, and the possibilities included the outright defeat of the French armies, the overthrow of Napoleon, or some sort of cease-fire.

Britain was able to secure allied unity and keep the war going through subsidies and loans (or what Napoleon's defenders frequently referred to as "Pitt's gold"). In 1813, Britain concluded a treaty with Austria that included a subsidy of one million pounds to support a one-year military campaign. This was added to even more generous subsidies for Russia, Prussia, and Sweden. Contributions of money and arms were also given to Spain,

---

[35] As Webster argues: "It had neither military nor diplomatic unity. It had neither decided to overthrow Napoleon nor devised any method either of obtaining peace or of prosecuting war. The task of reconciling the differences of the Allies, of binding them closer together, of creating machinery by which they could act in unison against Napoleon, and of providing some plan by which Europe could be reorganized so as to obtain a period of stability after a generation of warfare, was largely the work of Great Britain, and more especially of her Minister of Foreign Affairs, Lord Castlereagh." Ibid., p. 29.

Portugal, and Sicily.[36] "The financial weapon was, indeed, what Castlereagh relied upon to secure his ends," Webster reports. "Castlereagh made it abundantly clear that future subsidies were to depend on the Allies agreeing to his terms."[37] The settlement of disputes among the allies over the terms of the war's end were intimately related to the provision and amount of British subsidies. Castlereagh had ideas about a comprehensive European settlement, but it was the prospect of British financial assistance that made them particularly appealing on the continent.[38]

The relationship between British subsidies and war aims was connected in another way. Because the British Parliament needed to approve financial allocations, Castlereagh was under some pressure to gain explicit assurances of the intentions of the continental powers before the Parliament was asked for financial support for the coming year.[39] Parliament wanted assurances that the allies would support British war aims and not pursue a separate peace that excluded Britain from the continent. In this way, parliamentary control of the British war subsidy had two effects of the peace process: it created added incentives for the allies to negotiate the postwar settlement early, even while the war was going on, and it gave Britain added bargaining power. It was not just that Britain had the financial capacity to orchestrate the war through aid and loans but that the conditions for assistance were more clear-cut and credible.[40]

Second, Castlereagh actively attempted to settle disputes between the allies, so as to prevent the breakup of the unified front. Most of these disputes were territorial. Castlereagh ventured into allied negotiations in January 1814, and the ministers for the Four Powers endorsed a set of agreements (the Langres Protocol) that recognized the specific interests of each of the allies but also stipulated that France would need to be returned to her natural borders.[41] It was also at this meeting that the ministers agreed to a postwar congress in Vienna. Although specific territorial deals were not settled at this point, principles of balance and compensation were used to indicate the manner in which settlements would be achieved.

---

[36] Paul Schroeder reports that these combined contributions and subsidies were more than Britain had given in all previous wars together, and Britain's own military costs exceeded its expenditures on all others. In relative terms, Britain's costs in money and lives in waging the Napoleonic wars were greater than those incurred during World War I. Schroeder, *The Transformation of European Politics*, pp. 485–86.

[37] Webster, *The Foreign Policy of Castlereagh, 1812–1815*, pp. 162–63.

[38] See Nicolson, *The Congress of Vienna*, pp. 58–59. The best discussion of British subsidy policy during the war is John M. Sherwig, *Guineas and Gunpowder: British Foreign Aid in the Wars with France, 1793–1815* (Cambridge: Harvard University Press, 1969).

[39] See Webster, *The Foreign Policy of Castlereagh, 1812–1815*, p. 162.

[40] As we shall see, the United States was in a similar position during World War II.

[41] See Webster, *The Congress of Vienna*, p. 43.

In the spring of 1814, the ongoing ambiguity over how the war was to end threatened the alliance again. After the French army had won some battles, Austria was ready for an armistice and Russia was beginning to consider this option. Castlereagh argued in March in a letter to Liverpool: "Nothing keeps either Power firm but the consciousness that without Britain the peace cannot be made. They have all been lowering their tone to me, but I have explicitly told them that if the Continent can and will make a peace with Bonapart upon a principle of authority, for such a peace Great Britain will make the greatest sacrifices. But if they neither will nor can, we must, for their sake as well as our own, rest in position against France."[42] Castlereagh tried to bolster the confidence of the other allies, and Britain made efforts to strengthen their military position. He also tried to allay their mutual suspicions.

Castlereagh was engaged in a delicate balancing act, and the character of the postwar peace hinged on his success. If Metternich's eagerness to end the war were to prevail and the war end too soon or in a series of separate peace agreements with France, Napoleon would remain in power within France's "natural" borders. This outcome would split the alliance. Allied disarray, combined with a rejuvenated France, would only lead to more great-power conflict and war. But if the war were too severe, with Alexander marching into Paris with a conquering army to impose his own peace terms, the alliance would also dissolve and the postwar settlement would again be marked by the competitive scramble for spoils and advantage. Castlereagh had to search for a compromise formula that avoided both these outcomes. To do so, Britain relied on its indispensable role in subsidizing the allied war effort and its aloofness for continental territorial disputes to end the war in a way that would ensure a satisfactory peace.

Locking in Postwar Agreements

Importantly, the British sought a treaty with the other allied partners to lock in the terms of the peace settlement. Castlereagh undertook the negotiation leading to the Quadruple Alliance as a way to achieve agreement among the allies over British interests, particularly the disposition of the Netherlands. But the treaty also secured broader order-building objectives: it bound the allies to pursue the war until settlement objectives were obtained, and it pledged the allies to defensive alliance after the war as insurance against a resurgent France.

The decisive moment came in the spring of 1814 with the signing of the Treaty of Chaumont.[43] Metternich reluctantly moved toward the other al-

---

[42] Quoted ibid., p. 49.
[43] Signed on 9 March 1814.

lies in the agreement over peace terms. France was to be limited to its "ancient" rather than "natural" frontiers, Italy and Germany would be independent intermediary states, and Belgium would be independent of France. As earlier, Napoleon's own stubborn insistence on an armistice based on more expansive borders undercut Metternich's desire for a quick end to the war. But Castlereagh was also able to resist the desires of Russia and Prussia, who were willing to risk a unified peace in favor of military victory and the installation of a new regime in France. Again, Castlereagh's goal was for allied unity over everything else. The Treaty of Chaumont bound the allies to their agreed-upon war aims, which included a confederated Germany, an Italy of independent states, an independent Switzerland, a free Spain under the Bourbon dynasty, and an enlarged Holland. But most consequentially, the treaty obligated the powers to continue the alliance for twenty years after the war ceased, and to agree to protect each other against a resurgent France.[44] This was the beginning of the Quadruple Alliance, an agreement to remain allies after the war and supervise political order on the continent.

The view that the treaty was to be integral to the construction and maintenance of postwar European order was acknowledged by Castlereagh, when he told his government that the treaty was intended "not only as a systematic pledge of preserving concert amongst the leading Powers, but a refuge under which all the minor States, especially along the Rhine, may look forward to find their security upon the return of peace relieved of the necessity of seeking a compromise with France."[45] It was to be an order, as Article 16 of the treaty indicated, that secured the "balance of power," which in its specific context meant a just and mutually agreeable distribution of territory, rights, and obligations.

Britain's critical role in orchestrating the treaty is difficult to overemphasize. The orientations of the other European powers all led in different directions and away from allied unity. The flexibility of the British position and Castlereagh's search for compromise among the allies were key to reaching agreement. But Britain's indispensable position in waging the war itself was decisive. As Schroeder notes, "In reassuring the allies that Britain would not cut off its subsidies or retire from the Continent and retain its colonial conquests, [Castlereagh] deftly reminded them of what Britain could do and how they could neither wage war or make peace without her."[46] The use of subsidies to gain agreement was critical. Subsidies had

---

[44] Webster, *British Diplomacy, 1813–1815*, pp. 138–61.

[45] Castlereagh to Liverpool, 10 March 1814. Quoted in Webster, *The Congress of Vienna*, p. 51.

[46] Schroeder, *The Transformation of European Politics*, p. 501.

earlier been made conditional on the separation of Holland from France. In the treaty, new subsidy arrangements were agreed to, enough to ensure support for another year of campaigns if necessary.[47] Agreement on Britain's terms came at a price. In money and men, Britain was to contribute twice as much as each continental power.[48]

In these various ways, Castlereagh and the British government were taking the long view of British interests. They sought to keep the alliance together because this was the only way that a general settlement could be achieved. To do this, the British had to use their resources to subsidize its partners, help settle disputes among the allies over territory and postwar goals, and articulate an acceptable set of terms for ending the war. The willingness of the British government to subordinate specific issues to the maintenance of allied unity was also a sign that they recognized that the end of the war was a rare and fleeting opportunity to shape interstate politics in Europe. Castlereagh and his government clearly wanted to get things settled in a way that would provide a durable and stable order well into the future.

Strategic Restraint

Britain's desire for a mutually acceptable settlement was also displayed in its restraint in the exercise of power, restraint that was aimed at encouraging the development of a set of mutual expectations about how disputes would be settled after the war. In these instances, Britain and the leaders of other states appear to have been sending a signal that in not aggrandizing their position, they were seeking similar conduct in others. These moments of restraint were part of a more general pattern of compromise and restraint in wartime allied relations, fostered most importantly by Britain.

In communications with the other European leaders, Castlereagh drew a tight connection between restraint and moderation on the one hand and a stable and mutually agreeable order on the other. A European "system" of order, Castlereagh argued, must necessarily be based on principle, moderation, and some measure of legal-institutional authority. In a letter to Tsar Alexander in October 1814 that dealt with the dispute over Poland, Castlereagh argued that the spirit of "forebearance, moderation, and generosity" alone could "secure to Europe the repose" that the tsar and the other leaders wanted.[49] In letters to other European leaders, the British foreign minister repeatedly made the argument that a just and durable set-

---

[47] Sherwig, *Guineas and Gunpowder*, chapter fourteen.
[48] Webster, *The Congress of Vienna*, pp. 50–51.
[49] 12 October 1814. Quoted in Osiander, *The States System of Europe*, pp. 176–77.

tlement could only emerge if the leading European states exercised moderation and refrained from self-aggrandizement.[50]

British restraint was manifest in their relations with the Dutch. British interest in an independent Dutch state was a primary strategic goal in the war, and in negotiations with its allies the British ensured that this was not in dispute. But the British did not push their interests in the Netherlands at the expense of an overall European settlement. Importantly, as Schroeder reports, they "did not try to make the United Netherlands simply a British satellite," even though this possibility was "real and potentially dangerous."[51] The Netherlands emerged from the Napoleonic wars extremely dependent on the British. "Yet the British allowed and encouraged the Netherlands to be an independent intermediary power, at the risk, as actually happened fairly quickly, that the Netherlands would develop political, commercial, and colonial policies contrary to British interests."[52] British willingness to forego more direct domination of the Netherlands was not very costly, but it was a way to signal strategic restraint to the other major states.

POSTWAR INSTITUTIONAL BINDING

Several different types of mutual restraint mechanisms were employed by Britain and the other great powers in their attempt to maintain stability in Europe after the war, by creating a series of mutually reinforcing institutional layers to European political order and moving it away from a simple balance-of-power system. Three mechanisms were most important. First, at the core of the settlement was the alliance itself, which the allies agreed would extend into peacetime. This was the mechanism that seemed to introduce some measure of restraint on power. Second, the congress system was also used as a process of institutional consultation among the great powers. It provided a mechanism for joint management of conflict and the adjudication of territorial disputes. Finally, there was a diffuse promulgation of norms and rules of European public law, which together were intended to gave the institutional, territorial, and great-power arrangements in Europe a certain sense of legal-based legitimacy and authority.

---

[50] The willingness to forego acquisition of Dutch colonies in order to establish a reputation for moderation among the continental European states also reflected strategic restraint. At Vienna, Castlereagh argued that he still felt doubts about the acquisition of Dutch colonies. "I am sure our reputation on the Continent as a feature of our strength, power and confidence is of more real value to us than any acquisition thus made." Quoted in Nicolson, *The Congress of Vienna*, p. 99.

[51] Schroeder, *The Transformation of European Politics*, p. 489.

[52] Ibid., p. 490.

Binding through Alliance

The most important institution of postwar order was the alliance itself. From the first, Britain saw the alliance as more than simply a vehicle for prosecuting the war against Napoleon. It was to survive the war and serve as a vehicle for managing the peace settlement. The British government was outspoken in arguing in favor of a European political order that went well beyond the old system of balance. Terms such as "balance" and "equilibrium" were used, but they embodied more legal-institutional ideas about the character and operation of European order than the older notion of balance of power.

British interest in a far-reaching European security agreement was signaled as early as 1805. In response to the Russian proposal for a Anglo-Russian alliance that was to have diffuse (and somewhat vague) European-wide goals,[53] Pitt responded in his famous memorandum of January 1805, proposing a concert of powers that would have three aims: rescue countries that were dominated by France, which would be returned to its former limits; provide security for those states whose territory was returned from the French empire; and form "a general agreement and Guarantee for the mutual protection and security of different powers, and for re-establishing a general system of public law in Europe."[54] Later in the paper, Pitt went on to elaborate this proposal for a system of mutual protection and security:

> Supposing the Efforts of the Allies to have been completely successful, and the two objects already discussed to have been obtained, His Majesty would nevertheless consider this Salutary Work as still imperfect, if the Restoration of Peace were not accompanied by the most effectual measures for giving Solidity and Permanence to the System which shall thus have been established. Much will undoubtedly be effected for the future Repose of Europe by these Territorial Arrangements, which will furnish a more effectual Barrier than has before existed against the Ambition of France. But in order to render this Security as complete as possible, it seems necessary, at the period of a general Pacification, to form a Treaty to which all the principal Powers of Europe should be Parties, by which their respective Rights and Possessions, as they then have been established, shall be fixed and recognized, and they should all

[53] Alexander proposed in 1804 that at the end of the war, "after having attached the nations to their governments by making these incapable of acting except in the greatest interest of their subjects," and European governments must "fix the relations of the states among each other on more precise rules, such as it will be in the interest of the nations to respect." The tsar's memorandum of 11 September 1804 is quoted in F. H. Hinsley, *Power and the Pursuit of Peace*, p. 193.

[54] "Official Communication made to the Russian Ambassador at London," 19 January 1805, in Webster, ed. *British Diplomacy, 1813–1815*, p. 390.

bind themselves mutually to protect and support each other, against any attempt to infringe them—It should reestablish a general and comprehensive system of Public Law in Europe, and provide, as far as possible, for repressing future attempts to disturb the general tranquillity, and above all, for restraining any projects of Aggrandizement and Ambition similar to those which have produced all the Calamities inflicted on Europe since the disastrous era of the French Revolution.[55]

The great powers would ensure that the territories of Europe, after the retreat of France, regained their "ancient rights." But territorial rights were not absolute, they could be compromised when they conflicted with the peace and security of Europe as a whole. The great powers themselves would determine when sovereignty and territorial rights were to dominate. Pitt anticipated agreement on the "rights and possessions" of the allied states of Europe, and these states would be bound together to protect and uphold the underlying settlement.[56]

This basic British view, that the alliance must continue beyond the war, was articulated again by Castlereagh in the fall of 1813, as Britain prepared to take a more active role on the continent. It was Castlereagh's Project of Alliance that carried forward Pitt's initial proposal for a continuation of the alliance after the war to ensure against French resurgence and to manage European political conflict. The defensive alliance would be the centerpiece of the settlement and all negotiations would be conducted by common consent of the allied powers.[57]

In seeking to continue the alliance after the war, the British were introducing an institutional innovation into the organization of European order.

---

[55] Ibid., p. 393. For a discussion of this 1805 memo and the eventual Concert of Europe, see Nicolson, *The Congress of Vienna*, pp. 54–57; and Rene Albrecht-Carrie, *The Concert of Europe, 1815–1914* (New York: Harper & Row, 1968), p. 28.

[56] There is some controversy among historians as to who precisely authored the famous 1805 dispatch that shaped Viscount Castlereagh's subsequent proposals for the congress system. Edward Ingram ascribes the intellectual and strategic origins of the plan to Lord Mulgrave, the newly appointed foreign secretary, who responded to Pitt's invitation on 14 December 1804 to his colleagues for suggestions about the goals for which a new coalition should fight. Musgrave's ideas on the territorial settlement and the reconstruction of the states of Europe found their way into the 1805 memorandum. See Ingram, *In Defence of British India: Great Britain in the Middle East, 1775–1842* (London: Frank Cass, 1984), pp. 103–14. On the question of how to devise a system of security against future aggression, Lord Grenville, another member of the cabinet, appears to have been influential, arguing as early as 1798 for a "union of the Great Powers" as a mechanism to insure the establishment of a general peace. See John M. Sherwig, "Lord Grenville's Plan for a Concert of Europe, 1797–1799," *Journal of Modern History*, Vol. 34, No. 3 (September 1962), pp. 284–93. Pitt himself, not possessed with grand strategic or political ideas, was a practical politician who in this period was reacting to powerful domestic pressures and attempting to deal with a difficult potential ally in Russia. Personal correspondence with Paul Schroeder, 30 April 1999.

[57] See Webster, *British Diplomacy, 1813–1815*, pp. 19–29.

Rather than balance against potential aggressors, Britain was seeking to use the alliance to bring these states into a mutually restraining partnership. The potential restraining role of alliances, discussed in Chapters Two and Three, is noted by Robert Osgood: "Next to accretion, the most prominent function of alliances has been to restrain and control allies, particularly in order to safeguard one ally against actions of another that might endanger its security or otherwise jeopardize its interests."[58] Likewise, Paul Schroeder argues that security alliances are often attractive to states for their mutually restraining effects, "restraining or controlling the actions of the partners in the alliance themselves."[59] The anticipation is that threats and security dilemmas will be dampened by locking the potential adversaries together in an institutionalized security pact.

The Quadruple Alliance served this purpose of mutual restraint, an idea proposed by Castlereagh and embodied in Article Six of the treaty. As Schroeder argues: "Not only the cataclysm of the previous quarter-century, but also the strains and problems of the final coalition against Napoleon in the period 1812–1814, the conflicts among the great powers that arose during the peace congress, and Napoleon's return from Elba—all combined to convince the great powers that it was vitally necessary for them to make a durable alliance of mutual cooperation and restraint."[60] The alliance provided a mechanism for the great powers to cooperate, but it also provided a way for them to keep watch on one another and, on occasion, influence and restrain one another. As Andreas Osiander argues, "they had to cooperate precisely *because* they could not trust one another."[61]

The Quadruple Alliance was at the center of a wider set of restraining pacts. In 1818, worry over great-power cooperation and allied restraint led to the expansion of the alliance to include France, creating a Quintuple Alliance.[62] The Holy Alliance of September 1815, proposed by Tsar Alexander as a sort of union of Christian monarchs and people, articulated a more abstract and diffuse commitment to great-power cooperation and mutual restraint. Although it did not contain any concrete security guarantees or obligations (Castlereagh thought is was "sublime mysticism and nonsense," and Metternich called it a "loud sounding nothing"), the Holy Alliance was used by both Russia and Austria over more than a decade as

[58] Robert E. Osgood, *Alliances and American Foreign Policy* (Baltimore: Johns Hopkins Press, 1968), p. 22.

[59] Schroeder, "Alliances, 1815–1945: Weapons of Power and Tools of Management," in Klaus Knorr, ed., *Historical Dimensions of National Security Problems* (Lawerence: Regents Press of Kansas, 1976), p. 230.

[60] Ibid., p. 231.

[61] Osiander, *The States System of Europe*, p. 234. Emphasis in original.

[62] See Gulick, *Europe's Classical Balance of Power*, and Webster, *The Foreign Policy of Castlereagh, 1815–1822*.

a vehicle to influence and restrain each other. Finally, the German Federation of 1815 was a defensive league that provided mutual security against a resurgent France. But it was also, as Schroeder argues, "a pact of restraint for controlling the German problem from within."[63] In particular, a Germany "united by a federal bond" provided a means to reconcile and mute the rival leadership claims of Austria and Prussia as well as providing a bulwark of stability and independence for the smaller and middle-sized states.[64] Although these alliances differed widely in their form and rationale, they all served as institutions of mutual restraint—creating common expectations about the future of relations among the alliance partners and mechanisms for mutual influence.

The strengthening of the "great power principle"—that the leading states of Europe constituted a special grouping with both rights and responsibilities—reinforced the operation of the post-Napoleonic pacts of moderation and restraint. During the war, the leaders of the allied states increasingly acknowledged that they would need to play a privileged role in overseeing and managing the postwar system. "Great changes," Webster argues, "were almost unconsciously being made in the principles of the European polity. The Allies claimed to represent not only themselves but all Europe, and they intended to settle all the main points by themselves."[65] As deliberations over security arrangements proceeded, the allied governments agreed that as a practical matter, they themselves would need to enforce or ensure compliance together. They, after all, were the states most capable of undoing the agreements and inflicting the most damage to the European order and to each other.[66] This special role for the four leading allied states was articulated in the first Peace of Paris. The treaty was signed by the Eight Powers (Austria, Britain, France, Portugal, Prussia, Russia, Spain, and Sweden) but in a secret article, the four "allied powers" agreed that they themselves would determine the disposition of territories ceded by France, even though these agreements would ultimately be presented to the congress for approval.[67] Great-power status differentiated the four leading states from the smaller states of Europe and reinforced their mutual alliance commitments to manage the order and, by so doing, manage each other.

---

[63] Schroeder, "Alliances, 1815–1945: Weapons of Power and Tools of Management," p. 232.

[64] Webster, *The Foreign Policy of Castlereagh, 1812–1815*, p. 207.

[65] Ibid., p. 206.

[66] The notion that order could best be maintained by the assertion of the rights and responsibilities of the Great Powers was not invented during the Napoleonic wars, but it was more clearly formulated in this period and integrated more fully into the agreements of the postwar settlement.

[67] See Osiander, *The States System of Europe*, pp. 232–39.

Institutionalized Consultation and Restraint

The agreement on continuous alliance consultations—at the heart of the 1815 settlement—was born during the talks that marked the last stage of the war. When representatives of the allied powers met between January 1814 and November 1815, they expected that Napoleon would sue for peace and settlement negotiations would begin. But Napoleon held out, and the allied representatives began a protracted period of consultations, dealing with an ongoing variety of wartime matters. "They were in effect involved in an international conference, and a lengthy one at that. There were of course awkwardnesses, but in general they found that the practice of regular meetings was effective in keeping the allies together and effective in handling the last days of Napoleon."[68] After three months of these consultations, Castlereagh announced that he was not going to discuss postwar arrangements except at meetings of the four ministers.[69]

This entirely new process of ongoing consultations began with the arrival of Castlereagh at allied headquarters in Basil on 18 January 1814. What Castlereagh and Metternich discovered, as one historian notes, was that "the only successful way to keep together was to be together, in close physical contact, and to rely more upon constant meeting than upon the ordinary courses of diplomacy."[70] Castlereagh was convinced that direct and ongoing discussions were necessary to overcome differences and maintain unity of the alliance. He emphasized early on "the importance of the new method of diplomacy that had grown out of the war, the frank and formal, though confidential, discussion of the most delicate problems between the principal statesmen. Only by that means, he thought could he solve the difficult questions of reconstruction, which had already begun to cause doubt and suspicion."[71] Later, during his stay at Basil, Castlereagh argued that the continuous deliberations did in fact help overcome differences. He noted that the allied states (which he called the "confederacy") was "exposed to prejudice and disunion from the want of some central council of deliberation, where the authorised Ministers of the respective Powers may discuss face to face the measures in progress, and prepare a result for the consideration of their respective sovereigns." Through this process, Castlereagh reported, "every individual question which they have

[68] Langhorne, "Reflections on the Significance of the Congress of Vienna," p. 318.

[69] Stadion reported to Metternich from Chatillon that "Lord Castlereagh "appeared decided . . . to treat of the objects which cause his return *only* in conferences of the four ministers." Webster, *The Foreign Policy of Castlereagh, 1812–1815*, pp. 212–13.

[70] Richard Langhorne, "The Development of International Conferences, 1648–1830," *Studies in History and Politics*, Vol. 2, No. 2 (1981/82), p. 77.

[71] Webster, *The Foreign Policy of Castlereagh, 1812–1815*, p. 199.

been called upon to deliberate has been decided, not only unanimously, but with cordial concurrence."[72]

It was this wartime process of consultation that produced the watershed Treaty of Chaumont. The allied consultations at this point had begun to give stronger shape and identity to the notion of a European grouping of great powers, a grouping that in some loose sense "represented" or "acted on behalf of" Europe. It was also the Treaty of Chaumont that formally ratified the notion that the allied powers would continue after the war to enforce the settlement and protect the peace. The treaty expressed the British view, first articulated by Pitt in 1805, that the allies must commit to "concert together . . . as the means best adapted to guarantee to Europe, and to themselves reciprocally, the continuance of the Peace."[73] Several weeks later, the first Peace of Paris called for the convening of a "General Congress" in Vienna to "regulate" the agreement that emerged from the peace treaty.[74]

The practice of great-power meetings was again spelled out in the renewal of the Quadruple Alliance, which was part of the second Peace of Paris, signed 20 November 1815.[75] Article Six of the alliance document stated that the peace agreement would be maintained through periodic conferences of the allied sovereigns or their ministers to ensure the execution of the treaty. In effect, there was to be continuous great-power management of European order.[76] The article gave a formal commitment by the allies to perpetuate the conference diplomacy that was started in the final phases of the war. This principle of permanent diplomacy by conference as a way to maintain the postwar order was, as one historian notes, "as near a constitution as the Concert of Europe was ever to get and it formalised the development of a new piece of machinery in the now complex and efficient factory of international relations."[77]

---

[72] Quoted ibid., p. 209.

[73] Article V of Treaty of Chaumont, 1 March 1814. See Edward Hertslet, *The Map of Europe by Treaty* (London, 1875), Vol. 3, pp. 2,043, 2,048.

[74] See Article 32 of the first Treaty of Paris, 30 March 1814. Ibid., Vol. 1, pp. 1–17.

[75] This was the Treaty of Defensive Alliance that was signed by the Four Powers on the same day that they signed the Second Peace of Paris. Text ibid., pp. 372–75.

[76] Article VI read: "To facilitate and to secure the execution of the present Treaty, and to consolidate the connections which at the moment so closely unite the Four Sovereigns for the happiness of the world, the High Contracting Parties have agreed to renew their meetings at fixed periods, either under the immediate auspices of the sovereigns themselves, or by their respective Ministers, for the purpose of consulting upon their common interests, and for the consideration of the measures which at each of these periods shall be considered the most salutory for the repose and prosperity of Nations, and for the maintenance of the Peace of Europe." Ibid., p. 375.

[77] Langhorne, "The Development of International Conferences, 1648–1830," p. 85.

The establishment of an ongoing conference to regulate affairs of common concern was a novel feature of the Vienna settlement. International conferences before the Congress of Vienna occurred only at the termination of war, and their purpose was primarily concerned with the establishment of peace. In the decades after the Vienna settlement, Europe saw the establishment of the practice of holding periodic conferences during peacetime for the consideration of matters of general interest to the governments of Europe. Initially, these conferences were primarily concerned with political and not legal issues, and a variety of general treaties emerged. The specific agreements are of less interest than the general framework of deliberations. One scholar notes that the Congress of Vienna, which began meeting in 1815, "took on to some extent the character of a legislative assembly, and the Final Act of that Congress was of great importance in the development of the public law of Europe."[78]

The function of this ongoing joint management mechanism, as it was expressed in the congress method, was recognized by the participants. Castlereagh, in a letter written from Aix-la-Chapelle in October 1818, noted the innovative importance of the ongoing consultations: "It is satisfactory to observe how little embarrassment and how much solid good grow out of these reunions, which sound so terrible at a distance. It really appears to me to be a new discovery in the European government, at once extinguishing the cobwebs with which diplomacy obscures the horizon, bringing the whole bearing of the system into its true light, and giving to the counsels of the Great Powers the efficiency and almost the simplicity of a single State."[79]

The most important function of the congress system was to establish a shared understanding of how the resolution of territorial disputes would take place. This understanding was that the great powers would have the right and responsibility to resolve territorial disputes; that territorial expansion by a great power would need to receive the acquiescence of the other great powers; and that this consultative process should operate so as to resolve conflicts short of war. The great powers would together in concert review and render judgments on alterations in international order, determining together what were acceptable and appropriate forms of change, and thereby circumscribing dangerous and revisionist state actions.[80]

[78] Fredrick Sherwood Dunn, "International Legislation," *Political Science Quarterly*, Vol. 42, No. 4 (December 1927), p. 578.

[79] Viscount Castlereagh, *Correspondence, Dispatches and Other Papers*, 12 vols., edited by his brother, the Marquess of Londonderry (London: John Murray, 1848–1853), Vol. 12, p. 54.

[80] The novel character of these restraining institutions was noted by Friedrich von Gentz in 1818. The system established in Vienna was "unheard of in the history of the world. The

There are several ways in which this consultation process served as a mechanism of power restraint. One was simply that, as a formal body of the great powers, it was able to articulate some shared expectations and standards of legitimacy about the organization of European political order. All state actions were not equally legitimate—and actions or territorial changes that were broadly acceptable would be easier to pursue and defend. Also, the consultation mechanism provided opportunities for the great powers to keep watch on each other and bring the foreign policies of the great powers into an arena for collective scrutiny. Overall, concert diplomacy acted as a mechanism to moderate and restrain the exercise of power by the major states primarily through the promulgation of norms of restraint and peer pressure. The purpose of the consultation process, according to Castlereagh, was "to group" the offending state, or as Metternich suggested, it was a "point of moral contact." As one analyst argues, "Instead of direct military confrontation, the principal means was moral suasion—an appeal to the collective responsibility of the great powers for European peace and stability, to the norm of what the other powers considered appropriate and legitimate behavior. In a sense, the Concert idea became the collective conscience of the European great powers, reminding each of its responsibilities and obligations in international politics."[81]

This mechanism was put to the test in the dispute over the disposition of Poland and Saxony, the most difficult of the postwar territorial conflicts. Russia sought a Poland under its domination, a threat made real by its occupation of the country. If Russia prevailed, than Prussia would need to be compensated with lands further west in Germany, which in turn would disrupt arrangements for setting up independent states on the frontier of France. Alexander appeared to be engaged in territorial aggrandizement, but he also envisaged a constitutional Poland under his rule, and these developments were very disturbing to other great powers, particularly Austria.[82] At the same time, Austria and Prussia were in conflict over the future of Germany and, in particular, the reorganization of Saxony, which Prussia

---

principle of equilibrium or, rather, counterweights formed by particular alliances—the principle which has governed, and too often troubled and engulfed, Europe for 3 centuries—has been succeeded by a principle of general union, uniting all the states by a federative bond under the direct of the 5 principal Powers." Europe, he argued, was reunited "under an areopagus of its own creation," with the great powers acting collectively to uphold the rights of states and protecting the peace. Quoted in F. H. Hinsley, *Power and the Pursuit of Peace*, p. 197.

[81] Elrod, "The Concert of Europe: A Fresh Look at an International System," p. 168.

[82] In rejecting Russian designs on Poland, Castlereagh argued that the new Russian frontier "would degrade the monarchs of Prussia and Austria in the eyes of their subjects and, whatever compensations they received elsewhere, leave them at the mercy of Russian military power. Russia, he even hinted, would have an influence over Europe to be compared with that of Napoleon." Webster, *The Foreign Policy of Castlereagh, 1812–1815*, p. 343.

sought to annex with support from Russia. Because of these complications, there was no possibility of a united opposition among the major powers to resist Russia in Poland.

Alexander sought to bring this claim on Poland to a resolution in late 1814 and requested a formal meeting of the allies. The conference proceeded to discuss Saxony, as well. Austria and England demanded that France be admitted to the conference, to which Prussia vehemently objected. All knew that the admission of Talleyrand would spell the end of Prussia's hopes for Saxony. Prussia also knew that Alexander was weakening, so it sought to force a settlement early. Webster writes that "Hardenberg intimated that Prussia could not afford to remain longer in a state of provisional occupation of Saxony, and that, if recognition of her rights was refused, she would consider it as tantamount to a declaration of war." Webster notes that this produced a strong response from Castlereagh: "I took the occasion to protest," Castlereagh wrote back to England, "in the strongest terms against this principle as a most alarming and unheard-of menace: that it should be competent for one Power to invade another, and by force compel a recognition which was founded upon no treaty."[83]

The threat of war quickly went away. Castlereagh did go ahead with a secret treaty that was defensive in character and meant to ensure against attack by Prussia. Metternich and Talleyrand accepted the draft, which was modeled on the Chaumont Treaty against France. The treaty did mean war if Prussia did not give way. Webster reports that in a few days, all threat of war disappeared.[84]

As this episode suggests, the allies were working out mutual understandings about what was acceptable and unacceptable state action. Castlereagh in particular was eager to establish the understanding that territorial disputes would be settled according to a process of compromise and reciprocity, informed by some general notion of fairness and legitimacy. As the war ended, the use of force to settle disputes among the allies was considered outside the bounds of the alliance—even if the war-weary powers were able or willing to resort to arms, which was generally not the case. The expectation was established that the settlement of disputes would be conducted in a more restrained and reciprocal manner.

LIMITS ON COMMITMENT AND RESTRAINT

The Vienna settlement was built around pacts of restraint—but they were sharply limited. The treaties spelled out a variety of mutual commitments to uphold certain principles of order and to operate according to certain

[83] Webster, *The Congress of Vienna*, pp. 132–33.
[84] Ibid., p. 134.

shared expectations. Almost all the territorial frontiers of Europe were in need of redrawing after the war, and the great powers agreed to settle these matters among themselves. They also agreed to ongoing consultations so as to maintain the general peace. But the institutional settlement fell short of specific commitments of mutual protection and enforcement.

These limits can be seen in the fate of the allied discussions of treaty guarantees. The idea of a guarantee was first advanced by Pitt in 1805. He argued that the postwar settlement should be given "solidity and permanence" by a "treaty to which all the principal powers of Europe should be parties, by which their respective rights and possessions, as they then have been established, shall be fixed and recognized: and they shall all bind themselves mutually to protect and support each other against any attempt to infringe them."[85] At this earlier time, Pitt envisaged that Britain and Russia would play a special role in enforcing the settlement, reflecting their large and relatively disinterested position in Europe.[86]

As the war ended, Castlereagh and the tsar again began to think in terms of a general guarantee. In conducting allied diplomacy in the winter and spring of 1815, Castlereagh laid the ground for a general guarantee. On 13 February, Gentz, who had acted as secretary of the Congress, drafted a declaration embodying the idea, and on the same day Castlereagh sent a circular letter to his ambassadors indicating that there was "every prospect of the Congress terminating with a general accord and Guarantee."[87] Among the allies, there was at least initial acceptance of the idea. Castlereagh, Metternich, and Talleyrand even suggested that the guarantee be extended to the Ottoman Empire (which was seen as a way to check Russian encroachments). The tsar agreed, provided that the allies helped mediate an end to long-standing Turkish-Russian disputes.[88] But among the four major allies, the view was shared that the postwar treaty would be accompanied by a guarantee of mutual protection. As one historian notes, "As the making of the settlement proceeded, there seemed to be a general assumption, most often alluded to by the Tsar, that the military alliance held always in reserve would be accompanied by a treaty of general guarantee. This would be attached to the settlement and would be signed by all parties as indicating their commitment to the maintenance of the public law in its new definition."[89]

---

[85] "Official Communication made to the Russian Ambassador at London," 19 January 1805, in Webster, ed., *British Diplomacy, 1813–1815*, pp. 389–94.

[86] Russia was first to propose a special security guarantee with Britain, and it was recognized in the treaty between Russia and Great Britain of 11 April 1805, although only in rather vague and general terms.

[87] Webster, *British Diplomacy, 1813–1815*, pp. 306–7.

[88] See discussion in Schroeder, *The Transformation of European Politics*, pp. 573–74.

[89] Langhorne, "Reflections on the Significance of the Congress of Vienna," p. 317.

The idea of a guarantee disappeared, however, in the midst of the confusion created by the return of Napoleon from Elba. It remains a mystery why this is so, but the reconsideration of Russia and Britain are certainly central to the explanation.[90] Tsar Alexander, who initially had championed the idea, underwent a Christian conversion and turned his attention in the last stages of the war to the construction of a Holy Alliance.[91] The tsar was still inspired by Castlereagh's original guarantee proposal of February 1814, but the Russian ruler now sought to move away from agreements grounded in public law toward promises that rulers would make among themselves based on a shared Christian faith. In effect, the Russian leader was shifting ground and arguing for a different type of guarantee—not traditional safeguards, guarantees, and alliances that bound states together with specific legal obligations, but to a more diffuse moral commitment that the leaders of Christian states would use shared religious principles to guide relations with their subjects and with each other.[92] Few diplomats in Europe accepted this view, but it effectively removed Russia as a supporter of a more formal treaty guarantee.

The British government was also rethinking the idea of a guarantee. One reason was the likely resistance within the House of Commons, which was generally isolationist and suspicious of European involvement.[93] The Parliament, wrote Lord Palmerston in 1841 about the general orientation of British foreign policy, was not inclined to "approve of an engagement which should bind England prospectively."[94] But the retreat of Russia was also a factor in British rethinking. Even if the British cabinet had been willing to accept a general treaty guarantee, there was ample reason for British leaders to be skeptical of the actual commitment of the other allied governments, not least Russia, to abide by such guarantees.

In the end, it appears that Britain could not summon the domestic support to make a general security guarantee, and the tsar came to believe in other mechanisms of restraint and enforcement. Britain was certainly the most able to extend such a guarantee if it were so inclined. It was the major proponent of a comprehensive and binding postwar settlement. The constitutional structures of the British government also meant that treaty commitments were grounded more deeply in the domestic political system and

---

[90] See Douglas Dakin, "The Congress of Vienna, 1814–15, and Its Antecedents," in Alan Sked, ed., *Europe's Balance of Power, 1815–1848* (New York: Barnes and Noble, 1979), pp. 30–31.

[91] The Holy Alliance was drawn up by Tsar Alexander and signed on 26 September 1815 by the Emperor Francis I and by Fredrick William III, and ultimately by all European rulers except for the king of England, the pope, and the sultan of Turkey.

[92] Langhorne, "The Development of International Conferences, 1648–1830," p. 85.

[93] See Langhorne, "Reflections on the Significance of the Congress of Vienna," p. 317.

[94] Quoted in Nicolson, *The Congress of Vienna*, p. 53.

the rule of law. They were therefore particularly authoritative and dependable as international commitments.[95] But the nascent democratic character (at least by early nineteenth-century standards) of the British government also imposed limits on what its diplomatic representatives could pledge or agree to.

This notion—that democratic states can make more credible treaty commitments and guarantees but also that commitments are more difficult for a democratic government to make (which is precisely why they are more credible)—was hinted at by Castlereagh during the war when a treaty of guarantee was discussed with Sweden. Castlereagh wrote to a colleague:

> It is almost impossible to make foreigners understand the delicacies and difficulties of our Parliamentary system. We can do much in support of foreign states (I believe no Power so much), but we must do it our own way. The continental Governments that have no account to render to a Parliament can commit themselves to guarantee possessions and never lay down arms till others are acquired, well knowing that they are amenable to no authority for the prudence of such engagements, and that when they become impracticable the engagements are dissolved either by circumstances or by mutual consent. They can also keep such engagements secret as long as it suits their convenience. In our system concealment is not practicable for any length of time, and when the stipulations are canvassed they are impeached upon every extreme case that ingenuity can suggest as falling within their possible operation.[96]

Castlereagh went on to note that it was not that Britain was incapable of giving guarantees—he admitted such guarantees had been given to Portugal and Sicily—but that they must emerge from a more complicated and demanding process of government decision making.

The Russian tsar, on the other hand, was largely his own man, and agreements would live or die by his personal word and convictions. As Tsar Alexander came to embrace a mystic Christian faith, his government's willingness to make legal-institutional commitments declined, and the underpinning of the settlement had to adjust as well. In Castlereagh's view, Russia was not a threat to the postwar settlement because of territorial greed and ambition but, as Schroeder observes, because of a "lack of prudence and consistency" and the "inability to decide what they [read Alexander] really wanted."[97] At Vienna, when the tsar described a Europe where Russia was as strong as the rest of the continent together, Castlereagh objected, insisting, as Schroeder notes, that "Alexander's character, however

---

[95] This argument is developed in Chapter Three.

[96] Castlereagh to Thornton, 10, 20 October 1812. Quoted in Webster, *The Foreign Policy of Castlereagh, 1812–1815*, p. 101.

[97] Schroeder, *The Transformation of European Politics*, p. 503.

noble, was not a sufficient guarantee against a potential abuse of Russia's power."[98]

The tsar's autocratic rule created the conditions for an arbitrary and idiosyncratic foreign policy, and it created limits on the willingness of the other European governments to make institutional agreements with Russia. Even the other autocratic states in Europe saw Russia as incapable of acting in a sufficiently responsible and predictable manner. Friedrich von Gentz, the Austrian adviser, said of the tsar, "None of the obstacles that restrain and thwart the other sovereigns—divided authority, constitutional forms, public opinion, etc.—exists for the Emperor of Russia. What he dreams of at night he can carry out in the morning."[99]

As a result, Castlereagh dropped the idea and the settlement process moved back to the renewal the Treaty of Chaumont (the Quadruple Alliance), which was reaffirmed at the same time that the allies signed the second Peace of Paris with France on 20 November 1815. Article Six of the Quadruple Alliance, which established the principle of a permanent process of great-power consultation, became the cornerstone of the postwar political order.

The failure of Pitt's idea for a general guarantee moved Castlereagh back in the direction of institutionalized consultations as the mechanism to manage order. The successful use of the great-power consultation process had made a favorable impression on Castlereagh. According to Webster, in making the second Peace of Paris, "Castlereagh had seen the idea of diplomacy by conference which he took with him on his first journey to the continent, justified again and again in the course of the last two years. The treaty of alliance, therefore, might be the means of making permanent a system which had been tested by experience, and thus securing peace by discussion and agreement instead of by the threat of armed force. This device had now become in his mind a far better instrument than Pitt's idea of guarantee, which he had advocated at Vienna."[100]

A process of permanent diplomacy by conference was to be the central mechanism for keeping order in Europe. The odd personal evolution of Tsar Alexander from radical constitutionalism to mystical pietism, together with the low credibility of the twice-restored French government, made an arrangement for a general guarantee impossible. The limits of authoritative and binding arrangements to enforce the peace through a treaty commitment to use force were reached. It was impossible to create such institutional arrangements with the existing states who would necessarily

[98] Ibid., p. 533.

[99] Friedrich von Gentz, "Considerations on the Political System in Europe" (1818), in Mack Walker, ed., *Metternich's Europe* (New York: Walker, 1968), p. 80.

[100] Webster, *The Foreign Policy of Castlereagh, 1812–1815*, pp. 480–81 and 497–99.

be party to the agreement, particularly Russia. The autocratic and fickle character of the Russian state, as embodied in its leader, doomed the creation of a stronger institutional settlement.

Boundaries, Packages, and Windows of Opportunity

Although the settlement did not have formal guarantees, it did create an institutionalized process with well-developed understandings and expectations about how conflict was to be regulated within Europe. Two other factors were important in giving shape to the settlement, both strengthening the commitments that it incorporated. One was the boundaries that existed around the settlement: it "fenced off" issues that could have made agreement impossible. The other was the way in which the pieces of the settlement were tied together: it "fenced in" agreements that by their interconnection strengthened the overall settlement.

The Vienna peace talks were successful partly because of what they left off the table. Britain refused from the start to have the European settlement take up the issue of its war in America or its maritime rule. The British did agree to have their colonial possessions brought into the settlement in the determination of compensations, but they were primarily a bargaining chip that the British could use to reach agreement on other issues. Russia was also able to separate the peace agreement from its involvements in Persia and the Ottoman Empire, where it continued to press its territorial claims. If the proposal for a general treaty guarantee had gone forward, and if it had been extended (as Castlereagh, Metternich, and Talleyrand proposed) to the Ottoman Empire, this would certainly have brought unresolved conflicts into the Vienna settlement.[101]

Britain and Russia were able to remain largely unrestricted as the world's leading powers in their non-European involvements. This had several consequences. Britain and Russia were not required to submit all their wider global interests to regulation and agreement by the continental European states, making agreement in Vienna more limited and acceptable to the participating states. But just as importantly, the splitting off of non-European issues spared the diplomats in Vienna consideration of wider international conflicts that could have doomed agreement. "The Vienna settlement," as Schroeder argues, "in settling European questions and ignoring extra-European ones, shielded Europe, fenced it off from extraneous quarrels. European states and others could continue to trade, expand, compete, and even wage war abroad, and did so."[102] By separating and shel-

---

[101] Ironically, the failure of a general guarantee had the effect of removing the thorny question of Russian influence in the Near East from the Vienna settlement.

[102] Schroeder, *The Transformation of European Politics*, p. 575.

tering European politics from wider global developments, agreement among the allied powers was made more delimited and stable.

Within the European settlement, however, everything became interconnected, reinforcing the overall authority of the settlement. The devising of a single treaty was critical in giving weight to the overall settlement; it signaled that a overall set of understandings and settlements was being created for the whole of Europe. Although there was no formal guarantee, "the incorporation of the whole settlement into a single grand treaty, signed by all the powers who thereby acquired a general responsibility for it in whole as well as in part," raised the costs of violation of the agreements.[103] Violation of one treaty threatened them all.

There was a logic at work. Individual states, in order to get what they wanted into the treaty, had to agree to the larger document. "By the procedure adopted," Webster notes, "each Power, in order to obtain from the Vienna Treaty the protection and guarantee of its own special interests, had to agree to the rest, however much it might object to any particular portion of it. As almost every State was affected by the treaty, the result was to place the Vienna settlement in a special position, which no other instrument has ever attained."[104] Precisely because the settlement was based on the incorporation of many specific agreements and compromises, it had the accumulated impact of linking individual gains to the general observation of the larger package. The effect was an implicit enforcement mechanism that operated to give stability and authority to the settlement.

Finally, this logic of a package of agreements that reinforced the whole settlement reflects the crucial character of the postwar settlement. Leaders realized that a rare opportunity had emerged to get their specific interests included in the larger settlement, and to do so would likely lock in their gains well into the future. The attraction of the congress mechanism is seen in the great rush of leaders to attend the Vienna gathering. Although the allied powers had earlier decided to reserve for themselves the right to make all the important determinations of the settlement, the congress mechanism was an open invitation for other would-be sovereigns and political claimants to have their rights and territories established.

When the allied powers announced their intention to convene a congress for the settlement of European affairs, the wider European constituencies saw this as a great hope. As Webster reports, "The dispossessed princes and potentates, who had been submerged in the great flood of the Revolution and Empire, saw, indeed, in the Congress an assembly which would restore their stolen 'rights,' while the Governments of the smaller States

---

[103] Langhorne, "The Development of International Conferences, 1648–1830," p. 84. See also Schroeder, *The Transformation of European Politics*, p. 573.

[104] Webster, *The Congress of Vienna*, p. 101.

looked to Europe to round off their possessions by giving them long-coveted cities and countries."[105] These hopes were in part based on a misconception. The great powers were not about to give an unwieldy congress of plenipotentiaries the authority to rewrite the map of Europe and articulate the terms of peace. The final settlement would have looked much as it did even if most of the officialdom that flocked to Vienna had not come at all. The great powers understood the congress to be essentially a way to put a legitimating stamp on the agreements and secret treaties that they worked out among themselves. But the wider European audience was correct that an important juncture had opened, and regardless of their eventual role in the proceedings, the consequences of the decisions would be long and widely felt.

Conclusion

The political order that emerged from the Vienna settlement combined elements of the old European logic of balance with new legal-institutional arrangements meant to manage and restrain power. Its most important departure from previous peace agreements was that it sought to cope with problems of menacing states and strategic rivalry by tying states together through treaty and a jointly managed security consultation process. It foreshadowed but fell short of the 1919 and 1945 settlements, which tackled a wider range of security, political, and functional problem areas, established semi-permanent multilateral institutions, and created more invasive agreements that extended further into the domestic polities of the participating states.

Britain's use of institutional strategies during and after the war and the mixed character of the resulting order are explicable in terms of the institutional order-building model. Movement toward an institutional settlement is a response to an incentive that emerges from the underlying circumstances of postwar power asymmetries. A newly powerful—and certainly newly hegemonic—state has incentives to seek agreement on rules and institutions to lock in a favorable postwar order and to use institutional arrangements to build legitimacy and conserve power. Britain, and to a lesser extent Russia, sought a comprehensive peace and were willing to participate in a power-restraining postwar alliance to achieve such a settlement. Evidence of this calculation is seen in the thinking of British leaders—Pitt, Wellington, and Castlereagh. Britain wanted a peace that would be stable and not require a great deal of direct British involvement. This meant that the settlement would need to be satisfactory to all the major

[105] Ibid., p. 73.

states of Europe and that there would need to be new institutional arrangements to make it work.[106]

British thinking and actions during and after the war suggest that they did respond to the opportunities and incentives that the war created to define their interests in longer-term ways, and saw institutional agreements as a means to do so. Securing agreement on a European-wide settlement was not inevitable. The allies were not united on war aims, and the possibility of separate settlements with Napoleon existed throughout the later stages of the war. Britain saw itself as critical in fostering a European-wide agreement, and it was willing to use its power advantages to ensure a general agreement. Britain and (to a lesser extent) its allies pursued various forms of strategic restraint so as to foster agreement on a mutually acceptable order.

Power disparities favoring Britain were evident during the war itself. As the world's leading commercial and financial power, Britain was in a position to subsidize the other states in the anti-Napoleonic coalition. This had several implications. First, it gave Britain the ability to keep the coalition together, allowing it to win the war and to use the alliance for its longer-term goals. It is almost impossible to think that the war would have ended as it did—with allied unity and a victory neither too severe nor too lenient—without Britain's substantial subsidies and continuous allied diplomacy. Second, the central role of Britain in bankrolling the war meant that it could tie loans and aid to agreement on postwar arrangements.[107] Operating within a parliamentary government, Castlereagh had incentives to persuade the allies to acquiesce in British war aims so as to ensure the flow of subsidy support. It was not just that Britain had the money to give allies, it was that the money was conditional on parliamentary approval. This gave British leaders both incentives and leverage to obtain early and favorable agreement by the allies to British postwar designs. Finally, British financial and military capabilities allowed it to lead the alliance and to use the alliance to lock in postwar commitments. The Treaty of Chaumont, where the major issues of the settlement and the continuation of the alliance were agreed to, was directly tied to the continuation of British war subsidies.

The outcome would have been very different if each of the states in the allied coalition had been equally capable and self-financed. It would have

---

[106] This British view about the attractions of a postwar order that would largely run itself is very similar to American thinking about post–World War II order.

[107] The similarities between Britain in 1813–1814 and the United States in 1942–1945 are striking. Both had the resources needed to win the war and lead the coalition. Each used aid to extract agreement well before the war ended on postwar rules and institutions. During the First World War, the United States eventually came to the aid of the European allies, but it did not play as decisive a role early on and was not therefore in a position to lock in agreement before the war ended.

been much more difficult to prosecute the war in a way that shaped the peace. With its leading role, Britain could use the coalition to do more than simply defeat Napoleon. Britain was also in a position to turn the coalition into an instrument of order creation. Castlereagh maximized his country's bargaining power by obtaining agreement on the broad outlines of the settlement while Britain was still indispensable in winning the war.

The specific institutional bargain that Britain pursued in building order does not, however, accord fully with the model. There is no clear evidence that Britain actually gave up substantial short-term gains in exchange for institutional agreement on the continent. Britain did make several gestures: it agreed not to exploit its position in the colonial world, and it relinquished any direct claims to Holland in the territorial settlement. But these were not really concessions. In fact, part of what made the settlement acceptable to Britain was that most of its non-European interests were left off the negotiating table. But these gestures of moderation do reflect a more general effort by Britain to signal a policy of postwar restraint. Its willingness to maintain the alliance and operate within the great-power consultation process were also, in effect, pledges of restraint offered in exchange for the participation and restraint of the other major states.

Likewise, the sharp limits on the commitments and guarantees that were established after the war are consistent with the institutional model. These limits were set in part by the types of governments that were party to the Vienna settlement. This could be seen most clearly in the fate of the proposal for a general guarantee. The British Parliament was reluctant to commit to such guarantees, a fact acknowledged when Castlereagh noted the higher standard that representative governments must insist on in making treaty guarantees. But the British reluctance also reflected the lack of credibility that the other governments could bring to such a guarantee. Certainly Russia was without the ability to establish guarantees that went beyond the promise of the tsar. Tsar Alexander's Holy Alliance assumed an entirely different basis on which to make international commitments; it effectively derailed the further institutionalization of the concert system. Power restraints where still manifest in institutions that tied states together, but the locking mechanism was organized around consultation diplomacy and great-power norms.

Chapter Five

THE SETTLEMENT OF 1919

OF ALL the great postwar settlements, the peace of 1919 has provoked the most study, controversy, and regret. The "failure" of the Versailles settlement has been the source of unending debate over the causes and implications of the lost peace, the limits of liberal internationalism, and the possibility of international order based on democracy, self-determination, and the rule of law. No peace settlement has been more frequently invoked in public and scholarly argument about the sources of peace and the lessons of history.

The peace settlement after World War I is striking in several respects: it involved the most explicit and public discussion of the principles and organization of postwar order yet seen; postwar leaders clashed over competing designs for postwar order—not unusual, except that the differences were deep ones concerning the basic logic of order; and the public and political parties in Europe and America were heavily engaged in inspiring or constraining war aims and postwar proposals, shaping and limiting the ability of American and European leaders to pursue their postwar order-building goals.

The United States emerged as the leading world power after the war, and it brought an ambitious institutional agenda aimed at binding democratic states together in a universal rule-based association. These institutional proposals were more sweeping than those that Britain brought to Vienna in 1815; they envisioned a worldwide organization of democracies—a League of Nations—operating according to more demanding rules and obligations. The great powers would still form the core of this democratic community, but power balancing would be replaced by more legal- and rule-based mechanisms of power management and dispute resolution.

The constitutional model is useful in several respects in identifying the logic that informed America's institutional strategy and the disputed postwar order that followed. First, the United States did try to use its momentary power advantages during and after the war to secure a postwar settlement that locked in a favorable order, and it attempted to use offers of restraint on and commitment of its own power to gain an institutional agreement with European states. An institutional agreement that would bind the great powers together, including Germany, and create principled commitments and mechanisms for the settlement of disputes was at the heart of Woodrow Wilson's proposal for a postwar league. The willingness of the United States to forego opportunities to exploit its position for short-term gains in order to facilitate agreement was a constant policy theme of the Wilson administration—seen initially in its "peace without victory" pronouncement—but specific sacrifices are difficult to identify. American concessions were more general: the administration signaled a willingness to restrain its own arbitrary exercise of power by operating within an institutionalized postwar order, and offered a diffuse security commitment to its European allies. These concessions were ultimately not sufficient in the view of the Europeans, even while the American Congress resisted them because they were too far-reaching. But this was the institutional bargain upon which the fate of the settlement hinged.

Second, the disparities of postwar power and the democratic character of the states involved in the settlement were important variables that shaped the incentives and limits on the institutional settlement. Postwar power asymmetries did favor the United States, providing it with resources and opportunities to lock in an institutional agreement. Wilson was very confident—in retrospect, overconfident—that American financial and commercial preponderance would bring the European leaders around to his position. Similarly, Britain and France did worry, at least to some degree, about American domination and abandonment, as evidenced by the British willingness to sign on to Wilson's league proposal and by the French proposal of a formal tripartite security treaty in exchange for its endorsement of the league. Both countries fashioned their postwar proposals with an eye toward binding the newly powerful United States to Europe.

Although gross power disparities favored the United States, the specific circumstances at the end of the war and Wilson's conduct of policy tended to undercut the American position. In contrast to Britain in 1815 and the United States in 1945, the United States entered the war very late and was not able to marshal its resources to gain allied agreement on postwar goals during the fighting, when it had its greatest leverage. In the late stages of the war, American leverage over the terms of settlements were not the resources it had to offer the Europeans but its threat to pursue an early and separate peace with Germany. But European fear of American abandonment and its worry about the Wilson administration's intrusiveness in European politics did make them receptive to an institutional bargain that included American offers of commitment and restraint.

In the 1919 settlement, the major victorious states were democratic for the first time in history, although the worldwide democratic revolution that Woodrow Wilson anticipated and understood as essential to a successful League of Nations—bringing supportive center-left coalitions to power in Europe—never occurred. Yet there was a presumption shared by each of the allied leaders that institutional agreements after the war would be best pursued between democracies. This was perhaps Wilson's most cherished conviction. The French proposal for a more traditional security alliance with Britain and the United States was also championed as a commitment possible only between constitutional democracies. The actual impact of democracy on the possibility of institutional agreement after the war was more mixed. The public outpouring of support in Europe for Wilson's peace plan pushed the allies toward some sort of compromise on a postwar league, but the pressures and resistance of party politics in Europe and the American Congress made agreement trickier and more demanding.

The model cannot account fully for the failure of the American government to ratify some version of the peace agreement. At a general level, the disparities of power and the democratic character of the states worked in favor of an institutional bargain—if not an ironclad security guarantee, at least a looser security commitment and institutional ties created through the League of Nations. It was Wilson's own highly personal and stubborn convictions about the coming world democratic revolution and sources of institutional commitments that were decisive in shaping the compromise at Versailles and dooming treaty ratification. Wilson's vision of a liberal postwar order hinged on the success of grand historical processes that would bring progressive and center-left coalitions to power and lead to a cooperative association of nations. The American president was less concerned with specific institutional mechanisms and commitments that could provide more practical and limited agreement between postwar governments.

THE STRATEGIC SETTING

When the war began in August 1914, few people expected it to become a world war, enveloping Europe in the mostly deadly conflict in its history. The social and economic destruction that the war left in its wake was unprecedented and unanticipated. It was not possible to foresee at its start that the war would sweep away the Hohenzollern, Romanov, Habsburg, and Ottoman dynasties, lead to the dismemberment or disintegration of the German, Russian, Austro-Hungarian, and Turkish empires, introduce the principle of self-determination, or prompt the establishment of the League of Nations. More than in 1815, the breakdown of the old order was nearly complete. The resulting political disintegration of most of Europe rendered uncertain the basic features of the post-1919 world.

The new postwar distribution of power left the United States as the preeminent state. Its ascendancy, repeating the British experience, was grounded in economic success. The United States had passed Britain in economic size and productivity in the late nineteenth century, but its lead continued to increase in the decades before and after 1919. Before the war, the United States already had an economy twice the size of Britain, but

TABLE 5–1
Relative Share of World Manufacturing Output, 1900–1938

	1900	1913	1928	1938
Britain	18.5	13.6	9.9	10.7
United States	23.6	32.0	39.3	31.4
Germany	13.2	14.8	11.6	12.7
France	6.8	6.1	6.0	4.4
Russia	8.8	8.2	5.3	9.0
Austria-Hungary	4.7	4.4	—	—
Italy	2.5	2.4	2.7	2.8

Source: Paul Bairoch, "International Industrialization Levels from 1750 to 1980," *Journal of European Economic History*, Vol. 11, No. 2 (Fall 1982), pp. 292, 299.

after the war it was nearly triple in size.[1] As Paul Kennedy notes, "The United States seemed to have all the economic advantages which some of the other powers possessed in part, but none of their disadvantages."[2] Population, agricultural production, raw materials, industrial capacity, and financial capital—in all these areas, the United States was unrivaled in size and efficiency. This rising economic dominance can be seen in the American share of world manufacturing production (see Table 5–1), which continued to grow in relative terms into the 1930s. America's geographical remoteness and its aloofness from European great-power politics meant that before the war its military capacity lagged behind economic advancement. The changing relative military capacity of the United States is reflected in its share of total great-power military expenditures before and after the war (see Table 5–2). As war broke out on the continent and after a decade of massive European military spending, United States military power was relatively insignificant. But its underlying economic dynamism allowed it quickly to match the Europeans once it was drawn into the war. By 1920, the United States was a leading military power, although its other power capacities—commercial, financial, and agricultural—continued to be a greater source of postwar preeminence.

During the war itself, the allies were dependent on the United States for financial assistance and war supplies. "The volume of American exports during the war was huge, and this brought about a radical change in the relative financial positions of the nations. At the end of hostilities London

[1] See Appendix Two.
[2] Paul Kennedy, *The Rise and Fall of the Great Powers: Economic Change and Military Conflict from 1500 to 2000* (New York: Random House, 1987), p. 243.

TABLE 5–2
Share of Total Great-Power Military Expenditures, 1910–1925

	1910	1915	1920	1925
United States	16.9	1.3	31.8	18.0
Great Britain	18.6	23.1	28.3	17.7
France	15.0	17.5	7.0	9.9
Germany	18.2	25.0	1.5	4.5
Hungary	7.0	10.0	—	—
Russia	18.8	22.5	22.7	44.2
Japan	5.6	0.5	8.6	5.5

Source: Calculated from data presented in Appendix Two.

would no longer be the cosmic banking center, and the American Treasury would control the finances of Europe. Its stock of Gold had almost doubled since 1914 and amounted to nearly half of the world supply. The British owed it several billions of dollars and in turn had loaned billions to Continental powers. . . . The American republic had risen to a position of power as Europe consumed itself."[3] This economic preeminence and its value to the allied war effort ensured that the United States would have a leading voice in the settlement.

Yet the power asymmetries were not entirely favorable to the United States. When the war ended, the United States did not have an overwhelming military presence on the continent, and the Germans were not forced into unconditional surrender. When the armistice was signed, ending the war, American expeditionary troops were still making their way to the front. Moreover, the allied powers were well aware that the way the war ended and the share of sacrifice in fighting the war would influence who would have a voice in the peace process.[4] The commander of American forces in Europe, General John J. Pershing, wrote to Secretary of War Newton Baker that "When the war ends, our position will be stronger if our army acting as such shall have played a distinct and definite part."[5] It was for this reason that Pershing opposed the armistice, hoping to be better positioned after the war.

[3] Arthur Walworth, *America's Moment, 1918: American Diplomacy at the End of World War I* (New York: Norton, 1977), p. 4.
[4] Great Britain suffered 900,000 battle deaths in the war and France 1.4 million, which together were forty-seven times as many as the United States.
[5] Quoted in David Kennedy, *Over Here: The First World War and American Society* (New York: Oxford University Press, 1980), p. 173.

President Wilson was apparently less concerned with this problem. As William Walworth notes, "[H]e was confident of the adequacy of the America's material power to command the acquiescence of the exhausted combatants of Europe."[6] Europe was bankrupt and war weary, and the United States would be vastly more powerful. As Wilson told Colonel House in July 1917, "When the war is over we can force them to our way of thinking, because by that time they [the allies] will, among other things, be financially in our hands."[7] Yet many Europeans believed that the United States had not paid the price to be the main architect of peace. As one historian notes, "It is a very narrow line that separated the disinterestedness of a spokesman for humanity from the presumption of an intruder who had come late into the conflict and, by the terrible accountancy of war, had bought his seat at the table at a discount."[8] Woodrow Wilson sought to lead the world toward a liberal postwar settlement, but to get his way he was relying more on the forces of history than the forces of war.

The European allies recognized their new dependence on the United States, and they were eager to keep America involved in Europe after the war in order to support the postwar economic recovery and stabilize great-power relations on the continent.[9] As a result, even though many European diplomats doubted Wilson's authority to speak for the allied states and were skeptical of his statements during the war about a "just and permanent settlement" and his view that (as he told European journalists in April 1918) "nobody had a right to get anything out of this war," they were careful not to resist totally. At least some of the European support for Wilson's peace plans was based less on intellectual agreement than on wanting not to lose American help in ending the war and rebuilding Europe. "They did not venture to speak publically in opposition to the general principles of the president," Walworth argues. "They kept in mind the vast power of the United States and their dependence on its economic strength."[10] Toward the end of the war, European leaders also appreciated the wide popular appeal of Wilson's message.

Although European leaders realized that they needed to work with the United States, they were also troubled by how it might choose to use its

[6] Walworth, *America's Moment, 1918*, p. 17.

[7] Quoted in Arthur S. Link, *Woodrow Wilson: Revolution, War, and Peace* (Arlington Heights, Ill.: Harlan Davidson, 1979), p. 80. For a discussion of America's financial leverage over postwar Europe, see William R. Keylor, "Versailles and International Diplomacy," in Manfred F. Boemeke, Gerald D. Feldman, and Elisabeth Glaser, eds., *The Treaty of Versailles: A Reassessment after 75 Years* (Cambridge: Cambridge University Press, 1998), pp. 477–78.

[8] H. G. Nicholas in Arthur S. Link et al., *Wilson's Diplomacy: An International Symposium* (Cambridge, Mass.: Schenkman, 1973), pp. 80–81.

[9] Lloyd E. Ambrosius, *Woodrow Wilson and the American Diplomatic Tradition: The Treaty Fight in Perspective* (Cambridge: Cambridge University Press, 1987), p. 34

[10] Arthur Walworth, *America's Moment, 1918*, p. 15.

newfound power. The British newspaper baron George Riddell told British Prime Minister David Lloyd George in December 1917 that "I don't trust the Americans. Naturally, they desire to make America the first nation in the world; they will have a huge mercantile fleet, which they have never had before; and they will have opened new markets all over the world, markets which they have been developing while we have been fighting."[11] This sentiment captured the "problem of power" as the war's end: new asymmetries of power were created by the violent upheaval, and the United States was in an extraordinary position to shape the peace settlement. In order to get the willing cooperation of the other states, however, it had to overcome fears of domination and abandonment.

AMERICAN WAR AIMS AND SETTLEMENT IDEAS

In the initial years of the war, the Wilson administration grappled with its policy toward Europe along two fronts: how to get involved in the war to help bring it to an end, in particular how to deal with Germany; and how to foster a postwar order that would ensure peace. Wilson's position on both these questions followed from a basic view about what had caused the war in Europe, namely, the old politics of military autocracy and power balancing. It was not the aggression of a single state but, importantly, the larger system that was to blame. It was for this reason both that the United States stood aloof from the war—neutral at the outset and eventually only a reluctant belligerent—and also why it offered the most radical and sweeping ideas for the peace settlement.

While the war in Europe was deadlocked in trench warfare during 1916, the United States maintained its neutrality and sought to mediate a settlement. In December of that year, Wilson asked the warring governments to state their terms for peace. But the British and French allies were suffering great losses at the hands of the Germans and were not willing to see the war end until German military power was destroyed. Victories on the battlefield later in 1916 only added to their resolve.[12] Allied war aims shifted and hardened. This intransigence only reinforced Wilson's view that the allies were themselves seeking conquest and domination and were therefore partly responsible for the war. The German government of Chancellor

[11] Quoted in Kennedy, *Over Here*, p. 194 n 5.

[12] As Link points out, "In the spring and summer of 1916, the Germans occupied Belgium, northern France, and most of eastern Europe and the Balkans. They would have held most of the trump cards at a peace conference. Therefore, the Allies were understandably reluctant to agree to an armistice without an ironclad promise from Wilson that the United States would have entered the war if the Germans refused to evacuate their conquered territories. Wilson never made, and could not constitutionally make, any such commitment." Link, *Woodrow Wilson: Revolution*, p. 50.

Theobald von Bethmann-Hollweg communicated interest in an American meditated settlement but did not spell out its terms for peace.

It was at this juncture in early 1917 that Wilson articulated the opening American view of an acceptable peace settlement; the president believed that if the United States did not push for an early peace agreement the country would inevitably be drawn into the war. On 22 January, Wilson addressed a joint session of Congress and made the case for a "peace without victory, a peace among equals." Wilson made it clear that the United States stood apart from Europe and was determined to shape the peace settlement. "The question upon which the whole future peace and policy of the world depends on this: Is the present war a struggle for a just and secure peace, or only for a new balance of power?"[13] Wilson called for the establishment of a League of Nations that would ensure the terms of the peace and provide for American involvement in the new order. In effect, Wilson presented a deal to the Europeans: The United States would commit itself to participation in an international peacekeeping league after the war if the Europeans agreed to a peace on America's terms.[14]

Wilson argued that the United States had a right to help shape the peace settlement. No peace could be permanent if it were based on the "balance of power" rather than a "community of power, not organized rivalries but an organized peace." Such a peace settlement, with "guarantees of a universal covenant," could not be ensured without participation of the New World. But the proposed American guarantee was very abstract. Wilson argued, with implicit reference to the Virginia Bill of Rights, that "No peace can last, or ought to last, which does not recognize and accept the principle that Governments derive all their just power from the consent of the governed, and that no right anywhere exists to hand people about from sovereignty to sovereignty as if they were property." The American guarantee was based on the premise that other countries would manifest American principles of democracy and popular sovereignty. The United States would join other countries in guaranteeing world peace, Wilson argued, because the peace would be consistent with the American tradition. In such an union of democracies, the nature of guarantees are different from commitments in the old world of balance of power politics, and in Wilson's view they were more acceptable to the American people. In the American president's words, "There is no entangling alliance in a concert of power."[15]

[13] Woodrow Wilson, address to the Senate, 22 January 1917, in Arthur S. Link, ed., *The Papers of Woodrow Wilson* (Princeton: Princeton University Press, 1966–), Vol. 40, p. 539.

[14] See David Fromkin, *In the Time of the Americans: The Generation that Changed America's Role in the World* (New York: Knopf, 1995), p. 106.

[15] Wilson, address to the Senate, 22 January 1917, in Link, ed., *The Papers of Woodrow Wilson*, Vol. 40, pp. 533–39.

When Wilson presented his ideas for a settlement in January 1917, the United States was still at peace. Two weeks earlier, Germany had secretly decided on a policy of unrestricted submarine warfare, and announced this to the world on 31 January. After this, Wilson severed relations with Germany, and he asked Congress for a declaration of war on 2 April. In the months that followed, Wilson continued to make speeches that advanced American ideas of a settlement. In the summer of 1917, Wilson emphasized that the United States had entered the war to fight German militarism, not the German people. This was his way of again arguing for a peace without victory, and making the point that peace would need to be based on a community of democratic countries. The enemy was not Germany, it was militarism and autocracy. In declaring war on Germany, Wilson said that the United States was going to fight "for the ultimate peace of the world, and for the liberation of its peoples, the German peoples included."[16] But unlike Wilson's earlier appeals, now he was asking, if not for victory over Germany, at least victory over German militarism.[17]

This shift in Wilson's position, identifying the German military state as the cause of war, opened the way for subsequent modifications in the American position. When the United States entered the war on the side of the allies, Germany did become the enemy. To rally public support, it was necessary to paint Germany and its "military masters" as evil. The distinction also allowed Wilson to justify his support for the stern punishment of Germany agreed to later on at the Paris conference, the implication being that it was not the German people who were the object of allied wrath but its antidemocratic military state.[18]

---

[16] Wilson, address to a Joint Session of Congress, 2 April 1917, in Link, ed., *Papers of Woodrow Wilson*, Vol. 41, p. 525.

[17] Wilson's emphasis on democratic reform as the chief force that would provide the basis for a new world order, and his specific attack on Germany, were wedded to Colonel House's more pragmatic view—held most strongly in the early stages of the war—that Germany should be salvaged so as to play a great-power role in a sort of yet-to-be-defined concert. It was this view that led House to suggest to Wilson that a distinction be made between the German rulers and the people. "In the event of war with Germany," House wrote the president at the height of the Luisitania crisis, "I would suggest an address to Congress placing blame of this fearful conflict upon the Kaiser and his military entourage and I would exonerate the great body of German citizenship stating that we were fighting for their deliverance as well as the deliverance of Europe." House to Wilson, 3 June 1915. Quoted in Lloyd Gardner, "The United States, the German Peril and a Revolutionary World: The Inconsistencies of World Order and National Self-Determination," in Hans-Jürgen Schroder, ed., *Confrontation and Cooperation: Germany and the United States in the Era of World War I, 1900–1924* (Oxford: Berg, 1993), pp. 272.

[18] In effect, Wilson was arguing that Germany could only have a peace on generous terms if it got rid of its "military masters," repudiate conquest, and withdraw from conquered territory. Whether Germany was to get a generous peace depended on choices made by Germany, particularly by the extent they reformed their political institutions, and the American (and allied) view of whether constitutional democracy had really in fact taken hold.

As the United States became more involved in the war, the importance of democratic government to the success of a postwar peace was increasingly stressed by Wilson. In his response to the pope's appeal for peace in August 1917, Wilson again made the distinction between the German people and its government, and linked it to postwar commitments and guarantees: "We cannot take the word of the present rulers of Germany as a guarantee of anything that is to endure, unless explicitly supported by such conclusive evidence of the will and purpose of the German people themselves. . . . Without such guarantees treaties of settlement, agreements for disarmament, covenants to set up arbitration in the place of force, territorial adjustments, reconstitutions of small nations, if made with the German government, no man, no nation, could now depend on."[19] Wilson was concerned with establishing the conditions for postwar assurances and commitments, and in his view it was democratic government that provided the necessary conditions.[20]

The stakes in the debate over postwar goals rose again in the last months of 1917, after another dramatic turn of events: the Bolshevik revolution, the Treaty of Brest-Litovsk, and the departure of Russia from the war. If Wilson was appealing to the people of Europe over the heads of their leaders, he was now joined in doing so by Lenin and the Bolsheviks. After coming to power, the new Russian government published previously secret treaties between tsarist Russia and the allies that detailed the agreements over how the spoils of war were to be divided among them. This seemed to confirm Bolshevik claims that the war was imperialist in origin. Like Wilson, Lenin sought to galvanize the support of European opinion, particularly among liberals, trade unions, and socialists, around a peace plan that would end the war and, in turn, lead a movement toward the transformation of European politics. The Bolsheviks had appropriated Wilson's call for a new diplomacy, and he needed to respond.[21] His administration took up the challenge and formulated a public presentation of its own war aims: a speech that announced the celebrated Fourteen Points.[22] The statement included goals that Wilson had previously articulated and, at the end

---

[19] Wilson, reply to the peace appeal of the pope, 27 August 1917, in Link, ed., *Papers of Woodrow Wilson*, Vol. 44, p. 57. On Walter Lippmann's influence on this speech and on Wilson's argument that only democracies are fit partners for peace, see Fromkin, *In the Time of the Americans*, pp. 133–34.

[20] H.W.V. Temperley, *A History of the Peace Conference of Paris* (London: Oxford University Press, 1920), Vol. 1, p. 187.

[21] Thomas J. Knock, *To End All Wars: Woodrow Wilson and the Quest for a New World Order* (New York: Oxford University Press, 1992), p. 142.

[22] This speech proved to be Wilson's most important statement of war aims. See Woodrow Wilson, address to a Joint Session of Congress, 8 January 1918, in Link, ed., *Papers of Woodrow Wilson*, Vol. 45, p. 538.

of the speech, Wilson presented his final aim: the establishment of a "general association of nations" that would guarantee the independence and territorial integrity of all countries. With this speech, Wilson began a battle of ideas with Lenin and other rival peacemakers. Wilson's goal was to persuade the people of Europe that American principles, not Bolshevik ones, provided the most enlightened basis for a new postwar order.

By the end of the war, the Wilson administration's ideas for peace had been given full public voice. Wilson proposed to construct a union of democratic states, organized around a new peacekeeping institution, the League of Nations, although Wilson was still not specific on what the league would do and the extent of its political and security guarantees and obligations. The basic liberal vision embraced by Wilson was articulated most concisely in a speech on 4 July 1918, when he outlined his Four Objectives for the peace settlement: "What we seek is the reign of law, based upon the consent of the governed, and sustained by the organized opinion of mankind."[23] If peace was to endure, as one historian summarizes Wilson's position, "the world must be regenerated as a commonwealth of independent nations composed of free citizens able to choose their own governments."[24]

Thus Wilson presented a case for a new international organization to supervise and guarantee the peaceful settlement of disputes and reinforce democratic government worldwide, most critically in Europe. But Wilson's assumption of democratic change was what everything else rested on. It was Wilson's view of the European war that imperialism, perpetuated by militarism and autocracy, was the root cause. The war, therefore, must overturn these atavistic regimes. The struggle was between democracy and autocracy.[25]

By 1918, Wilson's unifying idea was clear: the war was to inaugurate a democratic revolution not only in the Old World but worldwide. Temperley summarized this essential Wilsonian view about the postwar order: "America and Europe were not only to be one in sympathy but to be bound together by a charter of freedom which would show that there was to be no difference between American principles and those of mankind."[26] Wilson's view was that the rest of the world was coming to embrace American

[23] Wilson, address at Mount Vernon, 4 July 1918, in Link, ed., *Papers of Woodrow Wilson*, Vol. 48, p. 517.

[24] Temperley, *A History of the Peace Conference of Paris*, Vol. 1, p. 196.

[25] Wilson told American teachers in June 1918, for example, that the United States was a "practitioner of the new creed of mankind" and Germany was the "most consistent practitioner of the old." The war, he said, was a "battle to determine whether the new democracy or the old autocracy shall govern the world." Wilson, message to teachers, 28 June 1918, in Link, ed., *Papers of Woodrow Wilson*, Vol. 48, pp. 455–56.

[26] Temperley, *A History of the Peace Conference of Paris*, Vol 1, p. 197.

principles, and this would overcome all the great postwar problems, including how to guarantee the peace and how to overcome European fears of
American domination and abandonment.[27]

BRITISH AND FRENCH WAR AIMS

At the beginning, British war aims were modest and defensive, but they
soon grew more ambitious in the goals of defeating Germany and shaping
the postwar settlement. The gradual expansion of British objectives in the
war had several causes. It was partly a reflection of the effort by leaders to
appeal to the British people and justify the sacrifice of war. It was also
driven by an effort, particularly in December 1916 and in 1917, to appeal
to Wilson and stave off the early peace negotiations that Wilson sought
with Germany. In addition, there were genuine liberal internationalists surrounding Lloyd George. Although the emphasis and extent of these internationalist goals differed from those of Wilson, there were at least some
within the British War Cabinet who were interested in constructing a new
pattern of international relations and building a postwar peacekeeping
league that went beyond the reconstruction of the European balance.

Various positions existed in Britain on the war and war aims. The Liberal
party was in power, a party "where the tradition was still peace and quiet."[28]
Even the Liberal-Imperialists were increasingly concerned with preservation of the empire rather than new expansionist ventures. Within the party
there were the old-style Gladstonian Liberals who were devoted to the
economy, and newer radicals who were preoccupied with bolstering social
welfare. These factions also feared that war might sweep the Conservatives
back into power, as the party most associated with the military.[29]

---

[27] It was this expected democratic revolution in Europe that allowed Wilson to reconcile
American isolationism from the Old World and his vision of a postwar collective security
system. In a speech in Manchester during his tour of Europe, Wilson explained: "You know
that the United States has always felt from the beginning of her history that she must keep
herself separate from any kind of connection with European politics, and I want to say frankly
to you that she is not now interested in European politics. But she is interested in the partnership of right between America and Europe. If the future had nothing for us but a new attempt
to keep the world at a right poise by a balance of power, the United States would take no
interest, because she will join no combination of power which is not the combination of all
of us. . . . Therefore it seems to me that in the settlement that is just ahead of us something
more delicate and difficult than was ever attempted before is to be accomplished, a genuine
concert of mind and of purpose." Quoted in Ambrosius, *Woodrow Wilson and the American
Diplomatic Tradition*, p. 54.

[28] Lawrence W. Martin, *Peace without Victory: Woodrow Wilson and the British Liberals* (New
Haven: Yale University Press, 1958), p. 22. See also Thomas Jones, *Lloyd George* (Cambridge:
Harvard University Press, 1951).

[29] For a survey of British war aims and domestic positions on the peace settlement, see
Erik Goldstein, *Winning the Peace: British Diplomatic Strategy, Peace Planning, and the Paris
Peace Conference, 1916–1920* (Oxford: Oxford University Press, 1991).

The Cabinet's decision to enter the war was triggered by the German invasion of Belgium. This act of aggression, which violated traditional British policy to protect the independence of the Low Countries, won over most members of government. The growth of German power also made necessary the support of a strong France. These considerations led to the announcement on 3 August 1914 by Foreign Minister Sir Edward Grey that Britain would oppose any German attempt to attack French channel ports.[30] As such, the initial British justification for going to war was quite limited.

In late 1916, the Germans and Americans appeared to be looking for early negotiations over peace. Wilson's peace initiative in late 1916 irritated the British because it drew few distinctions between German and Allied responsibility for the war and their war aims. This worried the British and French governments: halting the war without defeating Germany risked the return of conflict in the near future. The British held discussions with the French in late December and decided to respond to Wilson in a way that would appeal to American opinion: they would support the goals of a postwar league but they also insisted on a satisfactory territorial and military settlement.[31] The new British foreign secretary, Arthur Balfour, also sent a supplemental note to the American administration, again with the goal of staving off immediate negotiations with the Germans over peace. The note sought to identify the array of British war aims: insistence on redrawing the map on national lines as a prerequiste to the establishment of an international organization; discrediting German leaders and the establishment of democracy in Germany; and a general appeal to Anglo-American liberalism, pledging devotion to the international reforms favored by the "best thinkers of the New and Old Worlds."[32]

By early 1917, the British and the French were attempting to articulate their war aims with sufficient breadth as to appease Wilson and thereby derail early peace negotiations. Nonetheless, British thinking on the terms of peace was uncertain and conflicted. As Martin notes, "Although the exchanges with Wilson had gone some way to clarify Britain's war aims, there was still plenty of confusion and vagueness."[33] Some in the Imperial War Cabinet wanted Britain to fight to the end so as to destroy German power, while others were willing to accept a negotiated settlement. There were some who were inspired by Wilson's call for a League of Nations that

---

[30] Martin, *Peace without Victory*, p. 23.

[31] See George Curry, "Woodrow Wilson, Jan Smuts, and the Versailles Settlement," *American Historical Review*, Vol. 66 (July 1961), p. 972.

[32] Martin, *Peace without Victory*, p. 41. The note was sent 13 January 1917.

[33] Martin, *Peace without Victory*, p. 42.

would guarantee the peace, and others who wanted only to reconstitute the postwar balance of power.[34]

The collective ambivalence of the British government was captured in a memorandum drawn up for Lloyd George by General Smuts that reflected the recent meetings of the Imperial Cabinet. Part of the report favored the destruction of German's colonial empire, including the detachment of the Turkish territory that was a potential threat to British colonies in Asia. But another part of the report advanced the Wilsonian view that democracy among the great powers was necessary to ensure postwar peace, arguing that public opinion was an important force shaping the settlement, which required the justification of British war aims in moral terms.[35] Lloyd George himself had made the argument to the War Cabinet in March 1917 that the democratization of Europe was the only way to ensure against future wars. "Liberty," he said, "is the sure guarantee of peace and good will amongst the peoples of the world. Free nations are not eager to make war."[36] But others in the cabinet were inclined simply to reinforce Britain's postwar position as the only protection against future conflict.

Just as the Russian revolution had prompted the Wilson administration to emphasize the principled character of America's postwar goals, so too it led Lloyd George to emphasize the idealist features of British war aims. In January 1918, only days before Wilson's Fourteen Points speech, Lloyd George attempted to provide a coherent statement of British war aims. Claiming to speak for the nation and empire, George said that the British were not fighting to dismember Germany or destroy the Imperial Constitution of Germany, although he claimed that the adoption of democratic institutions in Germany would make a negotiated peace easier. Like Wilson, Lloyd George stated that "the consent of the governed must be the basis of any territorial settlement in this war."[37] The territorial settlement in Eastern Europe must be based on self-determination, he argued, and the disposition of German colonies would need to wait for the peace conference, although the wishes of the inhabitants themselves should control their ultimate disposition. He argued that reparations must be provided, but he rejected the demand for war indemnities or "shifting the cost of warlike operations from one belligerent to another." Concluding, Lloyd George stated what he regarded as the three conditions necessary for a

[34] As Temperley notes, "Of none of the Entente Powers were the war-aims less clearly defined than in the case of Great Britain. Even on subjects of capital importance their statesmen did not always seem agreed." Temperely, *A History of the Peace Conference of Paris*, Vol. 1, p. 189.

[35] Martin, *Peace without Victory*, pp. 44–45.

[36] Lloyd George, quoted ibid., p. 43.

[37] Lloyd George speech, 5 January 1918, reprinted in David Lloyd George, *War Memoirs of David Lloyd George* (Boston: Little, Brown, 1936), Vol. 5, Appendix B, pp. 63–73.

lasting peace: the reestablishment of the sanctity of treaties; a territorial settlement based on the right of self-determination; and the creation of some international organization "to limit the burden or armaments and diminish the probability of war."[38]

Lloyd George's statement of war aims was the most systematic and authoritative statement by a European leader before the armistice. He supported the idea of a League of Nations, but it was tepid support. In this, Lloyd George was attempting to find a middle ground between Wilson, who saw it as the capstone of the entire peace, and the French view, which was made clear by its new Premier, Georges Clemenceau. The latter declared in November 1917 that his goal was military victory before the League of Nations, that the new organization was not essential to the war, and that he opposed German membership after the war because her signature was worthless.[39]

Wilson and Lloyd George did share a variety of ideas about the terms of peace. Indeed, Wilson's conception of a new international organization was at least partly inspired by liberal ideas that were first articulated and embraced by British liberals. They shared a suspicion of special interests and had a faith in democratic control of foreign policy. They both believed in the rational settlement of conflicts. They both were anti-imperialists and agreed that imperialism sprang from autarchy and militarism.[40]

Lloyd George and Wilson differed, however, on their views toward the German government, and this in turn revealed deeper differences. The British leader argued that he was eager to see the Germans adopt a democratic constitutions, and that this would provide encouraging evidence that the impulse toward military domination was gone and a peace settlement was within reach. "But after all this is a question for the German people to decide," Lloyd George concluded.[41] Wilson, on the other hand, embraced a much more far-reaching view of the necessity of change in Germany. The German military autocracy was fundamentally illegitimate and must be swept away in the course of war. The British were interested in destroying militarism, but Wilson wanted to destroy autocracy or at least render it insignificant. Wilson's postwar designs depended on constitutional reform in Germany and a wider democratic watershed in Europe. The British leader welcomed such developments—they would facilitate a peace agreement—but the postwar order would need to be a more traditional one.

[38] Ibid.

[39] See Temperley, *A History of the Peace Conference of Paris*, Vol. 1, p. 192.

[40] Martin, *Peace without Victory*, p. 21. See also Curry, "Woodrow Wilson, Jan Smuts, and the Versailles Settlement."

[41] Lloyd George speech, 5 January 1918.

French war aims were less elaborate than British and American positions, but they were no less clear.[42] The French government led by Clemenceau, more than any other allied government, was resolved to restore the European balance of power and take advantage of every opportunity to place France in a position of unassailable military superiority over Germany. Toward this end, Clemenceau sought to break apart German territory, occupy strategic border areas, ensure German disarmament, and impose heavy reparations.[43]

The French view of the postwar world was dominated by the overriding concern for security against Germany. German armies had twice, within fifty years, invaded France, exposing its weak position in the face of German militarism.[44] The importance placed upon creating a new balance of power in Europe depended to a large degree on the perception of the future security threat from Germany. The French government was convinced that even with the eventual defeat of Germany, they were faced with a relentless power that had an undiminished desire for domination. For this reason, the aim of the war was obvious: to destroy German power. The elaboration of safeguards against Germany should precede any experiment in reconciliation.[45]

France's single-minded concern with overcoming the problem of German power after the war entailed pursuing a combination of strategies, not always consistent. These strategies were threefold.[46] The most overt was to diminish German power directly through territorial dismemberment, reparations, and disarmament. The possible development of democracy in Germany was not seen as a solution. Clemenceau rejected Wilson's distinction between the German military autocracy and the German people. The goal must be radical weakening of the German economy and a "federalization" of the German state. Lloyd George reported a remark made by Cle-

---

[42] For a useful overview of differences between French and American policies, see David Stevenson, "French War Aims and the American Challenge," *Historical Journal*, Vol. 22, No. 4 (1979), pp. 877–94.

[43] Clemenceau and other French officials were determined to organize a coalition of powerful states, as Arnold Wolfers put it, committed to "holding the lid down on the boiling kettle of European unrest and dissatisfaction, not in a strategy, espoused by the British for pragmatic reasons, and Wilson for philosophical ones, that called for a removal of the causes of revolt in order to eliminate the chances of an explosion." Wolfers, *Britain and France between the Two Wars* (Hamden, Conn.: Archon Books, 1963), p. 5.

[44] Paul Birdsall, *Versailles Twenty Years After* (London: George Allen & Unwin, 1941), p. 196.

[45] W. M. Jordan, *Great Britain, France and the German Problem: 1918–1939* (London: Oxford University Press, 1943), pp. 6–7.

[46] For a good discussion of the complexity of French strategies, see Marc Trachtenberg, "Versailles after Sixty years," *Journal of Contemporary History*, Vol. 17, No. 3 (July 1982), pp. 498–99.

menceau in March 1919 that reflected the French position, "that the more separate and independent republics were established in Germany, the better he would be pleased."[47]

A second strategy involved some measure of conciliation and political engagement of postwar Germany. The French leader did not emphasize this strategy or think it sufficient, but he did have at least some interest in participating in a peacekeeping institution that would supervise the territorial settlement and deal with reparations and other postwar issues. Wilson met with Clemenceau in Paris on 15 December 1918 for a series of meetings. At the third encounter, Wilson raised the League of Nations proposal, and Clemenceau voiced some skepticism of its workability but also said that it was a worthy endeavor.[48] At the very least it would need to be supplemented by France's own military defense. It was a secondary strategy at best, and it might actually divert attention away from the proper steps necessary for French security.

The final strategy was the containment of German power through alliance and the aggregation of allied power. Clemenceau remained resolute in his belief that a balance of power was necessary to protect France after the war. As the French leader argued in late 1918 in a famous speech to the Chamber of Deputies:

> I was saying that there was this old method of solid and well-defined frontiers, armaments, and what is called the balance of power. . . . This system today seems to be condemned by very high authorities. Yet I would say that if this balance, which has been spontaneously produced by the war, had existed earlier; if, for example, England, America, France, and Italy had agreed in saying that whoever attacked one of them was attacking the whole world, the war would not have taken place. . . . So there was this old system of alliances, which I am not for giving up—I can tell you this openly—and my dominant thought in going to the conference is that nothing must occur which shall separate in the post-war period the four powers which have come together in the war. For this entente, I shall make every sacrifice.[49]

Although Clemenceau was single-minded about weakening the German state and creating a balance of power to counter German aggression, he remained open to various strategies of doing so.[50] In an important signal

[47] Lloyd George, quoted in Birdsall, *Versailles Twenty Years After*, p. 29.

[48] See Knock, *To End All Wars*, p. 198.

[49] Clemenceau, speech in the Chamber of Deputies, 29 December 1918, quoted in Jordan, *Great Britain, France and the German Problem*, p. 37.

[50] On the flexibility of French postwar goals and Clemenceau's willingness to compromise on many of France's demands in exchange for an Anglo-American security guarantee, see David Stevenson, "French War Aims and Peace Planning," in Boemeke, Feldman, and Glaser, eds., *The Treaty of Versailles*, pp. 87–109.

of the possible ways in which the French government might pursue its German strategy, Clemenceau proposed in 1919 that the League of Nations be turned into a more traditional alliance of French, British, and American forces, functioning with an international army and a general staff.[51] Such an alliance would ensure ongoing allied domination of Germany, which was precisely its appeal to France. Wilson, of course, resisted this idea, not least because it would be politically impossible to commit the United States to abridge the war-declaring power of Congress and move it to an international body. As Thomas Bailey notes, "Wilson was amply warned by his advisers—and this must have been evident to him without such advice—that a treaty providing for an international police force would not have a ghost of a chance in the Senate."[52]

Hence the objectives of the allied leaders toward Germany sharply diverged. France desired a sufficient weakening of the German state to create a new balance of power strongly in its favor. The British were torn between the establishment of balance on the continent and movement toward a more concert-based order, drawing on formal institutional agreements and a league of nations. The dominant American goal was the triumph of constitutional democracy in Germany and across Europe, which would ensure peace, a reasonable but unambiguous punishment of Germany, and the creation of a new community of nations organized around liberal principles and practices.

Armistice, Reparations, and the German Question

When the allies assembled in Paris on 12 January 1919, very little of the peace settlement had been agreed to in advance.[53] Almost all of the major questions of the settlement remained to be negotiated: reparations, German disarmament, territorial questions, and the League of Nations. Only when the war came to a close were the consequences of allies fighting the same war for different reasons so rudely apparent. Wilson's bargaining position reached its zenith in October 1918 as he negotiated with Germany—and with his allies—on the terms of the armistice requested by Germany. After this juncture, Wilson's leverage with the allies declined and his domestic position also weakened, whereas British and French elec-

---

[51] See Knock, *To End All Wars*, pp. 221–22; and Ambrosius, *Woodrow Wilson and the American Diplomatic Tradition*, pp. 72–77.

[52] Thomas A. Bailey, *Woodrow Wilson and the Lost Peace* (New York: Macmillan, 1944), pp. 179–84.

[53] This, of course, is in stark contrast to 1815 and 1945, when Britain and the United States, respectively, used their dominant wartime position to gain early agreement on common war aims and settlement goals.

tions prior to the peace conference strengthened their hands.[54] The absence of credible democratic reform in Germany only made Wilson's efforts at gaining a moderate peace and securing his longer-term settlement goals more difficult.

The German government asked Wilson for an armistice based on the peace terms announced by Wilson in speeches on January 8 (the Fourteen Points address) and September 27. This sparked the first serious discussion among the allies about how to end the war and the future of Germany, and it exposed the perils of allies fighting the same war with different goals. Wilson's position was simple: if Germany became a constitutional democracy and acted on behalf of the German people, a settlement short of unconditional surrender was acceptable. French and British leaders sought to hold out for clear-cut guarantees and commitments by Germany to disarm, and pushed for agreement among the allies about postwar territorial issues on the German border. American politicians were also pressing for a hard line on ending the war, many wanting unconditional surrender. Wilson was caught between his statements about a moderate and fair peace and these mounting pressures. In an exchange of notes with the German government, Wilson sought additional assurances that he was dealing with "the veritable representatives of the German people who have been assured of a genuine constitutional standing." If, on the other hand, he was still dealing with the military autocrats, the United States "must demand not peace negotiations, but surrender."[55]

In the midst of domestic elections in late October 1918, Wilson found himself drawn into negotiations with Lloyd George and Clemenceau over the terms of the armistice with Germany. The American leader wanted agreement on the terms of a settlement before a collapse of the German military gave the allies an opportunity to take the peace settlement into their own hands. Colonel House met with the British and French leaders in Paris for a series of contentious meetings. When the allies threatened to reject Wilson's Fourteen Points as the basis of the peace with Germany, House warned that the United States might seek a separate peace. Lloyd George objected to Wilson's "freedom of the sea" commitment, arguing that the British could not give up control of the seas. The French, following the advice of Marshal Foch, the French commander of allied and associated forces, proposed specific postwar reductions in German military armaments and called for the occupation of the Rhineland. Premier Clemenceau also insisted on broadly understood "reparations for damages," arguing that Germany must provide compensations "for all damages done to the

[54] Bailey, *Woodrow Wilson and the Lost Peace*, pp. 67–70.
[55] Quoted in Knock, *To End All Wars*, p. 175.

civilian population of the Allies and their property by the aggression of Germany by land, by sea and from the air."

Surprisingly, Colonel House acknowledged these allied desires, and a pre-armistice agreement was reached. The British and French leaders agreed that the eventual peace settlement with Germany would be based on Wilson's Fourteen Points. But this was only possible with critical American concessions to the British on freedom of the seas and to the French on armaments, border security along the Rhine, and sweeping reparations.[56] House sent a message to Wilson on 4 November reporting his "great diplomatic victory." But it was a victory only at the expense of giving the allies, particularly the French, a military and territorial stranglehold on postwar Germany that Wilson had previously opposed.

The agreement between House and the British and French leaders was a watershed in shaping the postwar peace. Each side thought it had gained the advantage. House and Wilson came away from the agreement believing that, although they gave some ground on the treatment of Germany, they had achieved a great success: the Fourteen Points would be the basis of the peace. Lloyd George and Clemenceau also thought they had cleverly gotten their prized war aims—and only at the expense of acceptance of very vague statements of principle. Historians still debate the terms and consequences of the pre-armistice agreement.[57]

When Wilson rose before Congress to announce the agreement on an armistice, the terms of a peace settlement had taken a much more punitive turn. Germany had agreed to severe conditions: confiscation of military armaments, occupied territory along the Rhine, compensation for civilian war damages. The allies had insisted on all but unconditional surrender, and Wilson had agreed to the terms, as had the new German government. Wilson was nevertheless determined to go to Paris to defend his settlement ideals.[58]

Representatives of twenty-seven countries gathered in Paris for the peace conference in January 1919. It began with great solemnity and fanfare—a diplomatic gathering that even eclipsed the Congress of Vienna in scope and importance. But the meetings were really a continuation of the

---

[56] Ibid., pp. 181–83.

[57] Some argue that Wilson won acceptance of the Fourteen Points, but only by conceding basic terms that would ultimately haunt Wilson and prevent the realization of his agenda. See Klaus Schwabe, *Woodrow Wilson, Revolutionary Germany, and Peacemaking, 1918–1919* (Chapel Hil: University of North Carolina Press, 1985); and Inga Floto, *Colonel House in Paris: A Study in American Policy at Paris, 1919* (Copenhagen: Universitetsforlaget I Aurhus, 1973; reprinted by Princeton: Princeton University Press, 1980). See also essays in Boemeke, Feldman, and Glaser, eds., *The Treaty of Versailles.*

[58] Wilson, an annual message on the State of the Union, 2 December 1918, in Link, ed., *Papers of Woodrow Wilson,* Vol. 53, p. 285.

process instituted at the allied conferences that led up to the pre-armistice agreement: Clemenceau, Lloyd George, House, and Italy's Orlando settled essential points before they were submitted to the Supreme War Council.[59]

In the first weeks of the conference, Wilson dominated the discussions and succeeded in making agreement of the postwar League of Nations a necessary prelude to the settling of territorial and political questions that were being examined by the various commissions of experts. During the second phase of the peace conference, when Wilson returned to the United States on 14 February, the commissions did more work on territorial, economic, and technical issues. When Wilson returned to Paris on 14 March, until the Treaty of Versailles was finished and presented to the German delegation on 7 May, the three leaders made their most important decisions.

Seen from the American view, the basic struggle was between Wilson, who sought to organize the overall settlement and infuse it with the liberal principles articulated by the American president, and the other major powers, who sought to make good on their own territorial and security goals and commitments to each other. What unfolded was a series of compromises that left the principles severely in doubt. On territorial questions, the question concerned how to dispose of German colonial territories in Africa, the Pacific area, and the Far East, all of which had been seized by allied forces. Wilson sought to ensure that fate of these territories be determined with impartiality and some measure of self-determination, eventually involving the creation of a mandate system administered by the new League of Nations. The governments in Paris tendered a multitude of territorial claims. Britain wished to keep the territories it had gained from Germany in Africa and the Pacific. Japan sought control of German territories in the Shantung province of China and former German islands north of the equator. In a response that reflected the basic logic of the territorial controversies, in order to secure Japanese assent to the treaty, and therefore to the League, Wilson reluctantly accepted Japanese claims on Shantung, even though it violated the principle of self-determination.[60]

French postwar security was the overriding focus of the Paris conference. Wilson's promise of a democratic Germany was not sufficient to alter Clemenceau's ambitions, which under a plan devised by Marshal Foch, included the recovery of Alsace-Lorraine, the occupation of the western border of the Rhine, and the dismemberment of western parts of Germany into smaller autonomous republics. Wilson steadfastly opposed this plan, which went beyond the terms of the pre-armistice agreement. In a dramatic

---

[59] Bailey, *Woodrow Wilson and the Lost Peace*, pp. 137–38.

[60] Ibid., pp. 163–78, 276–85; and Ambrosius, *Woodrow Wilson and the American Diplomatic Tradition*, p. 121.

138 CHAPTER FIVE

showdown, the only alternative to the complete breakdown of the peace conference was compromise. In the end, France pulled back from its demands for German dismemberment and permanent occupation of the Rhineland. In return, Britain and the United States agreed to permit a fifteen-year occupation of the Rhine, the permanent demilitarization of the west bank of the Rhine, and sweeping German disarmament, and they pledged their countries for a limited period to defend France if it were attacked by Germany.[61] Wilson had no intension of pushing for ratification of this tripartite treaty in the American senate, but agreeing to it in Paris was sufficient to get a compromise with France at a difficult moment.[62]

The bitterest debates of the Paris conference were on the issue of reparations and indemnities. French and British leaders, under pressure from domestic public opinion, pushed for terms that went well beyond the pre-armistice agreement. The earlier understanding was that Germany would only be responsible for civilian damages, but in Paris it was demanded that Germany should be liable for the entire costs of the war to the allied peoples and for some of the costs incurred by their governments. Wilson made substantial concessions when faced by these demands. He agreed that Germany should bear the costs of disability pensions to allied veterans and their families, as part of German responsibility for civilian damages. He conceded that France had the right to occupy the Rhineland if Germany failed to make good on its reparations obligations and control of the Saar Valley as compensation for the destruction within France caused by retreating German forces. France wanted permanent control of the Saar. Wilson struggled to a compromise allowing for a fifteen-year occupation, followed by a plebiscite that would determine its future political rule.[63]

---

[61] Bailey, *Woodrow Wilson and the Lost Peace*, pp. 229–31. On the British view of this proposed tripartite agreement, see Michael L. Dockrill and J. Douglas Gould, *Peace without Promise: Britain and the Peace Conferences, 1919–23* (London: Batsford, 1981), p. 38.

[62] There was an important escape clause in the two separate bilateral treaties with France. If one country failed to ratify its treaty, the other treaty would also not go into force. In the United States, the treaty was not even reported out of the Senate Foreign Relations Committee. For accounts of the American and British guarantees to France, see Ambrosius, *Woodrow Wilson and the American Diplomatic Tradition*, esp. pp. 108–13; Melvyn P. Leffler, *The Elusive Quest: America's Pursuit of European Stability and French Security, 1919–1933* (Chapel Hill: University of North Carolina Press, 1979), pp. 3–18; Anthony Lentin, "Several Types of Ambiguity: Lloyd George and the Paris Peace Conference," *Diplomacy and Statecraft*, Vol. 6 (March 1995), pp. 223–51; and Anthony Lentin, "The Treaty That Never Was: Lloyd George and the Abortive Anglo-French Alliance of 1919," in Judith Loades, ed., *The Life and Times of David Lloyd George* (Bangor, Gwynedd: Headstart History, 1991); William R. Keylor, "The Rise and Demise of the Franco-American Guarantee Pact, 1919–1921," *Proceedings of the Annual Meeting of the Western Society of French History*, Vol. 15 (1988), pp. 367–77.

[63] Link, *Woodrow Wilson: Revolution, War, and Peace*, pp. 89–91.

Finally, the leaders in Paris easily agreed to Article 231 of the treaty and its sweeping provisions: "The Allied and Associated Governments affirm and Germany accepts the responsibility of Germany and her allies for causing all the loss and damage to which the Allied and Associated Governments and their nationals have been subjected as a consequence of the war imposed upon them by the aggression of Germany and her allies." This clause did not require Germany to accept "war guilt," strictly speaking, only to accept responsibility for damages done by the war. But it did become a symbol of the way in which the peace was agreed to and imposed on Germany, leaving it alone with responsibility for the war.

In each of these instances, Wilson resisted where he could and conceded where he had to in order to achieve agreement on his prize element of the treaty, the League of Nations. His goal was to put the League at the center of the peace treaty and weave it into the entire settlement. Wilson's insistence that the treaty agreement come at the beginning of the peace conference reflected this view. He did not want to let the allied governments achieve their territorial and political goals and simply walk away from the league proposal at the end. As an integral part of the settlement, Wilson anticipated that the league could play a role in redressing the mistakes and mistreatments that found their way into the treaty.

COMMITMENT, RESTRAINT, AND THE LEAGUE

The League of Nations, in Wilson's view, was a vehicle to lock European states into a new type of order. It was the key to the entire settlement: an institution that would ensure peaceful settlements of disputes and reinforce democratic governance. Wilson's hope of including Germany in the league was based explicitly on the anticipated binding and restraining function of the postwar institution. Germany could be better monitored and controlled if it were inside the league.[64] For others, particularly the French, the league was either of little consequence or a diversion from the more serious questions of postwar security arrangements. European leaders did want a peace settlement that tied the United States to Europe in a more traditional security relationship. The British used their support for the league as a way to foster closer security ties, whereas the French sought a much more explicit bargain: support for the league in exchange for an American and British security guarantee.

Wilson wanted to transform European politics without getting too involved in actually working with or protecting Europe. The United States would take advantage of the ongoing democratic revolution to establish

[64] See Ambrosius, *Woodrow Wilson and the American Diplomatic Tradition*, p. 133.

institutions that would bind the democracies together and ensure a congenial world order well into the future. The momentary power advantages that the United States had after the war reinforced Wilson's ambition to use the war to usher in a new liberal diplomacy. In the midst of the armistice negotiations in October 1918, Wilson told a senator who was urging that the United States seek Germany's unconditional surrender, "I am thinking now only of putting the U.S. into a position of strength and justice. I am now playing for 100 years hence."[65] Wilson was responding to the incentives provided by the postwar juncture to secure long-term gains. This logic was more compelling to Wilson than any particular territorial or material gains that might be achieved in the short run—and the League of Nations was the mechanism to lock in these gains.[66]

The binding impact of the League, according to Wilson, would grow over time. If the leading democracies could act together to establish the new institution, traditional security commitments or territorial guarantees would be unnecessary. European leaders thought otherwise and attempted to lure the United States into an ongoing commitment. After the United States came into the war, some British officials appealed to Wilson to articulate specific plans for a postwar peacekeeping organization and to indicate America's role in it. Other British officials hesitated to support the League of Nations at a later stage because they did not believe that the American Senate would ratify the treaty. The French were eager for an even more direct and binding commitment, proposing a tripartite alliance between the major allied powers.[67] Even if European leaders were not overwhelmed by American military power or its role during the war, they did worry about the stability and dependability of America in Europe.

Wilson was the first head of state to endorse the idea of a postwar peacekeeping organization, but his support was vague and he did not press

[65] Quoted in Knock, *To End All Wars*, p. 172. Earlier, before the United States got into the European war, Wilson made a similar point. In a conversation with Ida Tarbell in 1916, Wilson said that "I have tried to look at this war ten years ahead, to be a historian at the same time I was an actor. A hundred years from now it will not be the bloody details that the world will think of in this war: it will be the causes behind it, the readjustments which it will force." Quoted in Link, *Woodrow Wilson: Revolution, War, and Peace*, p. 2.

[66] A major difference between American supporters and opponents of the League of Nations was their assessment of whether the United States would dominate the new organization. Iowa Senator Albert B. Cummins noted that "The President of the United States believes that this compact should be made because he is sincerely of the opinion that the United States can and will control the league of nations and may use it for the government of the earth in the welfare of the people of the earth." Quoted in Ambrosius, *Woodrow Wilson and the American Diplomatic Tradition*, p. 93.

[67] Capturing this sentiment at the Paris peace conference, Clemenceau, in an interview with the Associated Press, appealed to the American people "to renounce their traditional aloofness." Quoted in Ambrosius, *Woodrow Wilson and the American Diplomatic Tradition*, p. 75.

his administration to work out the details of the league plan.[68] British officials, on the other hand, were eager to get Wilson's support for the league
concept, and they took it upon themselves to develop concrete institutional
plans.[69] Only as the Paris peace conference neared did Wilson attempt to
articulate an American set of ideas. The vagueness of the American support
for the league reflected a more general uncertainty—felt by officials in
Britain and France—about America's postwar commitment to European
security.

The first steps to push for a postwar league were taken by British Foreign
Minister Grey, who passed a message to Wilson through unofficial channels in November 1914 that he hoped that the United States would enter
into some sort of postwar organization to ensure the peace. In a later letter,
Grey conveyed a similar message through the British ambassador to Washington, Cecil Spring Rice: "An agreement between the Great Powers at
the end of this war with the object of mutual security and preservation of
the peace in the future might have stability if the United States would
become a party to it and were prepared to join in repressing by force whoever broke the Treaty."[70] In August 1915, Grey sent a message to Colonel
House, again making the case for a postwar league and sketching some of
its basic principles. The refusal to hold a conference to adjudicate disputes
was, in Grey's view, a "fatal step" that brought on the war. What is needed
is "some League of Nations that could be relied on to insist that disputes
between two nations must be settled by arbitration, mediation or conference of others. International law hitherto has had no sanction. The lesson
of this law is that the Powers must bind themselves to give it a sanction."[71]

In the autumn of 1915, House devised a plan by which the United States
and Britain would join together in pressing for a peace settlement mediated
by Wilson. Grey responded by saying that the British would agree to coop-

[68] Lord Robert Cecil, who was Britain's leading architect of British policy toward the
League of Nations at the Paris conference, wrote in his conference diary about the authorship
of the League proposal: "It is almost entirely Smuts and Phillimore combined, with practically
no ideas in it so that his [Wilson's] scheme [for the League was] largely the production of
others." 22 January 1919. Quoted in Andrew Williams, *Failed Imagination? New World Orders
of the Twentieth Century* (Manchester: Manchester University Press, 1998), p. 54.

[69] For a discussion of the origins of Wilson's League of Nations ideas, see Ambrosius,
Woodrow Wilson and the American Diplomatic Tradition, pp. 15–50. See also Edward H. Buehrig,
Woodrow Wilson and the Balance of Power (Bloomington: Indiana University Press, 1955), chap-
ter six; and Herbert G. Nicholas, "Woodrow Wilson and Collective Security," in Link, ed.,
Woodrow Wilson and a Revolutionary World, 1913–1921, pp. 174–89.

[70] Quoted in Leon E. Boothe, "Anglo-American Pro-League Groups and Wilson 1915–
18," *Mid-America*, Vol. 51 (April 1969), p. 93.

[71] Grey to House, 10 August 1915, quoted in Peter Raffo, "The Anglo-American Preliminary Negotiations for a League of Nations," *Journal of Contemporary History*, Vol. 9 (October
1974), p. 155.

erate only if the United States agreed to join a postwar international organization to achieve disarmament, freedom of the seas, and the preservation
of the peace through united actions.[72] Gray's response reflected the British
view that the United States needed to be brought into the management of a
postwar peace on as enduring and consistent basis as possible. The postwar
league, in the British view, would serve this purpose.

Colonel House exchanged messages with Grey and indicated that President Wilson was thinking along the same lines as the British but that the
American side did not yet have a specific plan. In the meantime, a group
of unofficial British internationalists, organized around former ambassador
to the United States Lord James Bryce began discussing and promoting
the idea of a postwar league. They urged American internationalists to take
the lead in the effort. On both sides of the Atlantic, associations such as
the Leagues to Enforce the Peace in the United States and the League of
Nations Society in Britain worked to muster public opinion in favor of a
postwar association of states.[73]

After the United States entered the war, British officials continued to
appeal privately to the Wilson administration to come forward with more
concrete plans for a postwar peace organization. Wilson's only major public statement about his ideas came in his Fourteen Points speech in January
1918. In correspondence with Colonel House in September 1917, Assistant
Foreign Secretary Lord Robert Cecil urged the United States to begin
planning and in February 1918 indicated to House that the British would
go forward with a commission to study specific proposals. Wilson was still
not moved. In a private message, Wilson said: "Frankly, I do not feel that
it is wise to discuss the formal constitution of a league to enforce peace. The
principle is easy to adhere to, but the moment questions of organization are
taken up all sorts of jealousies come to the front which ought not to be
added to other matters of delicacy."[74] Wilson sought to postpone the debate
on the league and therefore discouraged preparations and planning. The
most he would do was refer the matter to a study group lead by House—
which became known as the Inquiry—that mostly focused on ascertaining
what allied governments were likely to demand at the approaching peace
conference. Wilson still did not want to provoke a national debate on the
league idea.

The British moved ahead in spelling out specific features of the league.
In March 1918 a interim report by the British planning group, the so-
called Phillimore Committee, indicated the key features. These included

[72] See Link, *Woodrow Wilson: Revolution, War, and Peace*, p. 36.

[73] Ambrosius, *Woodrow Wilson and the American Diplomatic Tradition*, pp. 40–41. See also
Williams, *Failed Imagination?* pp. 20–26.

[74] Quoted in Boothe, "Anglo-American Pro-League Groups and Wilson," p. 101.

the principles of arbitration and league conciliation in the event of disputes between nations, sanctions against covenant-breaking states, and a statutory three months cooling-off period after the recommendation of the league.[75] In its survey of past concert and congress systems, a central argument of the Phillimore report was that such schemes could only work with democratic states, and that "although the spread of *democratic* nationalism seemed to have paved the way to success," militarist and absolutist states remained stumbling blocks to a postwar league.[76]

It was only in the summer of 1918, when the British government was ready to publish the results of the Phillimore Committee, that Wilson became more actively involved in the details. The president requested House to rewrite the British report, adding American thinking to the ideas, and it was the resulting document that became the basis for the American proposals at the peace conference. When Wilson sailed for Europe in December 1918, he had become the champion of the League of Nations idea, but the specific plans and commitments that such a new body would entail were still ambiguous, and the domestic political debate that would have clarified the limits and possibilities of American involvements and obligations in postwar Europe had not yet taken place.[77]

The British government was further ahead in developing a proposal, drawing on the schemes of Lord Robert Cecil, now head of the League of Nations section of the British delegation to Paris, and an influential draft of a league charter by Jan Smuts, the South African diplomat who was a member of the Imperial War cabinet.[78] Skepticism within the British government remained over the workings of the League of Nations, but most officials saw it as a way to draw the United States into more active involvement in Europe.[79] A postwar institution would establish specific American commitments and guarantees.

Wilson and Clemenceau met in Paris on 15 December 1918 for a series of meetings. At the third encounter, Wilson raised the League of Nations proposal, and Clemenceau voiced skepticism about its workability but also said it was a worthy endeavor. Later, Clemenceau was pressed by pro-Wil-

[75] This report is reprinted in Ray Stannard Baker, *Woodrow Wilson and World Settlement* (Garden City, N.Y.: Doubleday, Page, 1922), Vol. 3, pp. 67–73.

[76] Quoted in Williams, *Failed Imagination?*, p. 30.

[77] Ambrosius, *Woodrow Wilson and the American Diplomatic Tradition*, pp. 43–44.

[78] Smuts's pamphlet, *The League of Nations: A Practical Suggestion*, was written in late November 1918, and influenced Wilson considerably in the final drafting of the league treaty. See Ambrosius, *Woodrow Wilson and the American Diplomatic Tradition*, pp. 56–57; and George Curry, "Woodrow Wilson, Jan Smuts, and the Versailles Settlement."

[79] Louis Botha, South African member of British War Cabinet, reflected this view: "Our object must be to bind Britain and America together. That will make for the peace of the world." Comments to Lord Riddell. See *Lord Riddell's Intimate Diary of the Peace Conference and After* (London: Victor Gollancz, 1933), entry for 22 December 1918, p. 5.

son socialists in the Chamber of Deputies to clarify his position on the League and the settlement and to answer criticisms that his own government had no peace program of its own. Clemenceau said that "There is an old system which appears to be discredited today, but to which . . . I am still faithful." It was a system of alliances, he said, that will guide him at the upcoming conference. His basic position was that French security required the sharp and permanent reduction in Germany military power.[80]

Wilson thought he had more of an ally in the British than the French. But Lloyd George and his coalition also had a mixed position. Reflecting the enormous domestic support for the league, they were willing to support the league concept, but Lloyd George also campaigned for severe treatment of the Germans. There was a "well organized national consensus," as Knock argues, on the league. The two major league organizations merged in October 1918 to form the League of Nations Union with Lloyd George and Balfour as honorary presidents. But in the December 1918 election, many of the national British politicians who supported the league (including Arthur Henderson, the leader of British Labour) fell victim, and Lloyd George shifted his emphasis toward the popular view that the peace settlement should extract large indemnities from Germany and prosecute the Kaiser.[81] In a review of British policy by the Imperial War Cabinet in advance of the Paris conference, the British leaders were inclined to support Wilson on the League of Nations but press their claims for substantial reparations. Lloyd George spoke for the majority in arguing that if they supported Wilson on the league, he could be brought around to agreement, "though possibility under protest, to the things to which we attached importance."[82]

SECURITY COMMITMENTS TO EUROPE

Wilson's vision of the League of Nations was of an association of democracies that would provide mechanisms for conflict resolution and mutual security obligations. Members of the league would make commitments to each other to guarantee the peaceful settlement of territorial disputes and work collectively to oppose states that did otherwise. But the underlying commitment at the heart of the league's collective security structure could not simultaneously reassure two divergent constituencies: the guarantees were too vague and uncertain to satisfy French concerns about its security,

[80] Knock, *To End All Wars*, p. 198.
[81] Ibid., p. 199.
[82] The Imperial War Cabinet met on 30 and 31 December 1918. Lloyd George is quoted in ibid., p. 201.

but also too ambitious and entangling to reassure American politicians that their country's own independence and sovereignty were not threatened.

At the Paris conference, two proposals for postwar security organizations were discussed. One was advanced by the French: an alliance of the allied states, with an international army and a combined general staff. This would be an alliance of the victors. It would entail an ambitious supranational organization that would provide almost absolute security guarantees. For the French it would ensure permanent military superiority regardless of what happened to Germany after the war.[83] The proposal would bind the United States to Europe, and its French and British allies together in explicit security commitments and an elaborate intergovernmental organization. This was a far-reaching proposal that went well beyond a traditional alliance, in many ways resembling the later NATO alliance.[84]

The other proposal was Wilson's league, which would invite membership of all the states, regardless of their role in the war. It would be a looser association of countries, without a formal supranational organization, but with an elaborate set of explicit obligations and expectations and a variety of enforcement mechanisms. It would be a concert of power, its effective functioning depending on the leadership of the major states. The covenant of the league bound its members to an alliance of nonaggression, and it created machinery for international cooperation in a variety of areas and for the prevention of war. At the heart of the league was the famous Article 10: "The members of the League undertake to respect and preserve as against external aggression the territorial integrity and existing political independence of all Members of the League. In case of any such aggression or in case of any threat or danger of such aggression the Council shall advise upon the means by which this obligation shall be fulfilled."[85]

The league was to include a parliament, in which all members would be represented, and an executive council, in which the great powers would dominate. In addition, there would be a separate and independent judicial branch—a permanent court of international justice—a secretariat, and various commissions with responsibility to oversee specific treaties or to foster cooperation in social and economic areas. As Wilson presented the proposal in Paris, the league was to be a "living thing" that would provide "a definite guarantee of peace."[86]

It is also important to note what the league was not. It did not obligate its members to uphold specific territorial guarantees or entail automatic commitments by its members to the use of force. It elaborated agreements

[83] See ibid., pp. 221–22; and Link, *Woodrow Wilson: Revolution, War, and Peace*, pp. 98–99.
[84] Ambrosius, *Woodrow Wilson and the American Diplomatic Tradition*, pp. 75–77.
[85] Article 10, Covenant of the League of Nations.
[86] Quoted in Link, *Woodrow Wilson: Revolution, War and Peace*, p. 99.

on the use of sanctions to enforce territorial boundaries and spelled out principles that member nations were to pledge to uphold. But it did not make hard and fast legal commitments to specific courses of action. The United States, if it had joined, was not obligating itself to any specific military commitments.[87] Wilson understood this. Several times during the debate over the league, Wilson acknowledged that any stronger charter would not be passed by the United States Senate.[88] On several occasions Wilson argued that the binding character of the league would need to grow over time, reflecting a gradual deepening of commitments by countries to a set of commonly embraced postwar principles. To insist on unambiguous legal commitments at the outset would not be politically possible.

At the same time, Wilson resisted the efforts of others, including Secretary of State Robert Lansing and Lloyd George, to water down the commitments, such as they were. Lansing argued that compulsory arbitration and collective security threatened to undermine the Monroe Doctrine, the war-making powers of the Congress, and the American tradition of no entangling alliances. He sought to replace Wilson's "positive guaranty" with a "negative covenant" that would simply involve pledges by members to not violate each other's territory and political independence.[89] Wilson resisted this move. At the Paris conference, Lloyd George, surprising many who thought he had backed the existing versions of the league's charter, sought to minimize the "paper obligations" of the league, seeking instead a more informal organization of the great powers. By moving closer to the French position, Lloyd George may have simply been seeking more concessions by Wilson—which did in fact occur. But Wilson was caught in a dilemma: he needed to give the league some teeth in order to make it matter as the organizer of the postwar order, but not too many teeth, because it would loose the support of the allies and the American Senate.

It seems clear that Wilson wanted a league with sufficient guarantees of response to aggression as to deter such aggression in the first place. The goal was to make the obligations as compelling as possible, but to leave the commitment to the collective use of force to resist aggression just short of

[87] This was explained clearly by Wilson's delegate to the League of Nations preparatory meetings, Raymond B. Fosdick, in a statement to the *New York Times* on 8 February 1920: "Under the Covenant, the United States will always be a member of the Council. Under the Covenant, too, the decisions of the Council have to be unanimous in all matters that relate to peace or war or the method by which the judgment of the world is put into effect. The United States has an absolute veto power on any move or motion it does not like. At any time it can stop anything that it does not agree with." in Fosdick, *Letters on the League of Nations* (Princeton: Princeton University Press, 1966), p. 117.

[88] Ambrosius, *Woodrow Wilson and the American Diplomatic Tradition*, p. 45.

[89] See Knock, *To End All Wars*, p. 205; and Ambrosius, *Woodrow Wilson and the American Diplomatic Tradition*, pp. 59–63.

binding or absolute.[90] As Wilson indicated later during the Senate debate on the treaty, the decision on the sanctioning of force to resist aggression would reside within the Council of the league, and the United States would be a permanent member of this body, and therefore would always be able to veto any proposals to use force.

This question of whether and how to draw the line on a binding commitment to use American military force pursuant to league obligations was clearly posed by the French plan for a postwar military alliance. Wilson resisted the French plan because it would be an alliance against the losers in the war. But he also resisted it because he was aware—and wary—of the ironclad commitment that such an alliance would entail. He realized that it would not be possible to bring the American Congress or people along on such a commitment. With the League of Nations, Wilson sought to draw the line as close to a guarantee as possible.[91]

Wilson's underlying notion was his belief that legal and moral institutions are not easily imposed on society, domestic or international. Institutional constraints and obligations must grow and evolve. This is what Wilson had in mind when he argued in Paris that the league was a "living thing." It must take root and slowly become part of the set of obligations and expectations that states would eventually assume.[92]

This view of international institutions and law had a parallel in Wilson's view of democracy and the domestic rule of law. In his earlier work on American government, Wilson argued that "democracy is, of course, wrongly conceived when treated as merely a body of doctrine. It is a stage of development. It is not created by aspirations or by new faith; it is built

---

[90] Ambrosius, *Woodrow Wilson and the American Diplomatic Tradition*, pp. 45–47.

[91] Wilson understood that the United States would need to accept some institutionalized restraints and commitments on its power in order to get European participation. His view was captured by a commentary on the league written by the American delegate Raymond Fosdick in November 1919: "If we ask reservations which we may not intend to use, we have no right to expect the world to bind itself in the same lighthearted way. . . . To one who has been closely associated with the situation in England and France, it is extremely doubtful if the foreign governments will agree to be bound by them. They will not knowingly sit down to a game in which the cards are stacked against them, or in which the United States is allowed to hold several aces up its sleeve. They will not willingly consent to enter a compact where one of the parties asks them to agree that it will not assume any responsibilities except such as from time to time it may choose." Memorandum prepared by Fosdick, Arthur Sweetser, and Manley Hudson, 1 November 1919, in Fosdick, *Letters on the League of Nations*, pp. 48–51.

[92] This view was shared by advisers around the American president who were involved in postwar planning. See Lawrence E. Gelfand, *The Inquiry: American Preparations for Peace, 1917–1919* (New Haven: Yale University Press, 1963), p. 308. It was also consistent with prevailing legalist views of international relations. See Francis Anthony Boyle, *Foundations of World Order: The Legalist Approach to International Relations, 1898–1922* (Durham: Duke University Press, 1999).

up by slow habit."[93] Similarly, in conversations with the French ambassador to Washington in March 1917, he spoke of the gradual process by which international law and obligations must develop. As Arthur Link argues, Wilson believed that the League of Nations would not come into full force immediately: "It would have to develop slowly. It would be necessary to begin with a universal entente, with the mutual obligation to submit international disputes to a conference of countries not directly involved. Perhaps that would, little by little, create precedents which would break the habit of the recourse to arms."[94] If democracy within countries required a maturation process, as Wilson thought it did, so too did the development of law and rights between nations.[95] As Wilson indicated in a note to Colonel House in March 1918, "the League must grow and not be made."[96]

It was this view about the developmental processes of democracy, international law, and the proposed League of Nations that allowed Wilson to take the position he did on international commitments. Wilson had a clear view that Article 10 of the League of Nations did not entail a ironclad and automatic commitment to use the American military to uphold territorial guarantees. He did not think that ratification of the Versailles Treaty and the League Covenant meant that congressional authority over the use of the armed forces was being transferred to an international body. But he did think that over time, as the League of Nations became increasingly a part of the machinery and political architecture of international politics, the American government would come to honor the expectations and obligations of the community of democracies.

THE FAILURE OF DOMESTIC SUPPORT

When Wilson took the United States into the war, he had the support of most Americans. Even his Republican critics in Congress pushed for American involvement, and most were for the pursuit of a decisive victory. Wilson did not face an isolationist public. He did face a congressional opposition skeptical of his collective security ideas and the loftiest formulations of his "peace without victory" pronouncements. He also faced a congressional opposition that was itself divided over how the United States

[93] Quoted in Link, *Woodrow Wilson: Revolution, War, and Peace*, p. 5.

[94] Conversation with French Ambassador Jean Jules Jusserand, 7 March 1917. Reported in Link, *Woodrow Wilson: Revolution, War and Peace*, pp. 75–76.

[95] For a discussion of Wilson's developmental view of international law, see Thomas J. Knock, "Kennan versus Wilson," in John Milton Cooper, Jr., and Charles E. Neu, eds., *The Wilson Era: Essays in Honor of Arthur S. Link* (Arlington Heights, Ill.: Harlan Davidson, 1991), pp. 313–14.

[96] Wilson to Edward M. House, March 22, 1918, in Link, ed., *The Papers of Woodrow Wilson*, Vol. 47, p. 105.

should get involved in building postwar order. Some were isolationists, but a majority held a range of views that favored the pursuit of an internationalist postwar policy. The ultimate failure of Wilson's agenda—the defeat of the Versailles Treaty in the Senate—was not a triumph of isolationism but a failure to find a compromise within the internationalist camps. This was a failure of lost opportunities and not an inevitable outcome of divergent interests.[97]

During 1917, the Republicans matched Wilson in pushing the United States into the war. Indeed, the two former Republican presidents, William Howard Taft and Theodore Roosevelt, both argued for decisive victories, and Roosevelt thought that peace on the terms of the Fourteen Points was "too soft." Wilson had the support of the League to Enforce the Peace, headed largely by moderate Republicans including Taft, which called for active American involvement in the postwar peace. Indeed, before the general elections of 1918, the American people would have found it difficult to differentiate the parties in terms of their views of the war.

It was at this juncture that Wilson introduced partisanship into the debate over the peace settlement. With the end of the war in sight, he campaigned for the return of Democrats to the Congress so that he could be unhampered in the approaching negotiations. This created a party division over Wilson's peace plans, when in reality the division of opinion was much more fragmented, even within the Republican opposition.[98] The result was that, as Arno Mayer observes, "the domestic foundations of Wilsonianism had contracted still further."[99]

The election resulted in a clear majority for the Republicans in the Senate and House, which would meet after 4 March 1919 to consider the treaty. Wilson had unwittingly reunited the Republican party. Roosevelt, presuming to speak for the newly victorious Republican party, announced to the world after the elections: "Our allies and our enemies, and Mr. Wilson himself, should understand that Mr. Wilson has no authority whatever to speak for the American people at this time. His leadership has been emphatically repudiated by them."[100] Compounding the domestic political

[97] For an overview of the treaty debate, see Ambrosius, *Woodrow Wilson and the American Diplomatic Tradition*.

[98] As Bailey argues, after Wilson's partisan move, "The Republicans could now say that they had loyally supported the war, which they had; that they had sent their boys to France, which they had; that it had been an American war, which it had. But now it was going to be a Democratic peace." Bailey, *Woodrow Wilson and the Lost Peace*, pp. 60–61. See also Kennedy, *Over Here*, pp. 231–45; and Seward W. Livermore, *Woodrow Wilson and the War Congress, 1916–18* (Seattle: University of Washington Press, 1966), pp. 105–247.

[99] Arno J. Mayer, *Politics and Diplomacy of Peacemaking: Containment and Counterrevolution at Versailles, 1918–1919* (New York: Alfred A. Knopf, 1967), pp. 55–62.

[100] Quoted in Samuel Flagg Bemis, *A Diplomatic History of the United States*, revised edition (New York: Henry Holt, 1942), p. 631.

problem, the administration did not see fit to include any prominent Republicans in the delegation that Wilson led to the Paris conference. Yet Wilson's view was that he could still win over both the Europeans and the American Senate.

Before the end of the war, Wilson's peace proposals, articulated for the first time in January 1917, triggered a domestic debate and revealed multiple points of view. The supporters of Wilson's settlement ideas—a league tied to "peace without victory"—were few among established American politicians. Those that criticized Wilson tended to fall into three categories.[101] One group, led by William Jennings Bryan, was isolationist; politicians in this group liked Wilson's attack of militarist European leaders but opposed American membership in the League of Nations. This group of politicians were most notably Midwestern, including Republican Senator William E. Borah of Idaho. They opposed any settlement that might involve a continuing responsibility for American military involvement in Europe.

A second group, led by Theodore Roosevelt, were in favor of a league—indeed, Roosevelt had proposed the league concept in 1905—but wanted it to take the form of a more traditional alliance of like-thinking great powers. This was also an idea proposed by Wilson advisor Edward House on the eve of the European war: an alliance of Germany, Great Britain, and the United States, perhaps joined by France or Japan. The reservation that Roosevelt and Senator Henry Cabot Lodge had about Wilson's proposed League of Nations was that it committed the United States to military intervention around the world—an obligation that the American people would ultimately not honor. As David Fromkin notes, "This, believed Lodge and TR, would be dishonorable. It was a long-standing theme in the thought of both men that Americans never should sign a treaty—never should make promises—they were unlikely to keep."[102]

A third group, led by former President Taft, favored a league but was against the "peace without victory" terms. Taft and others in this group gave public support to Wilson's call for new postwar peacekeeping machinery. What they opposed was the absence of a definitive victory and the linking of the League of Nations to the peace settlement itself. But regardless of how the war ended, this group was willing to vote in favor of the treaty and the covenant.[103]

---

[101] For a good survey of these groups, see Fromkin, *In the Time of the Americans*, pp. 107–8.

[102] Ibid., p. 108.

[103] In March 1919, after the Senate opposition to the covenant was building, Wilson gave a passionate speech at the Metropolitan Opera House in New York in defense of the league idea. On the same evening, Taft also spoke and continued to support inclusion of the League of Nations in the peace treaty, but also called for modest reservations. See Knock, *To End All Wars*, pp. 241–44.

Rather than splitting off the isolationists and building a pro-league coalition around moderate and internationalist Republicans, Wilson succeeded in making the debate one between his league supporters and traditionalists. His liberal postwar agenda became the subject of abuse—labeled as socialist, utopian, idealist, and dangerous. At the same time, Wilson was in a headlong process of compromise with the allies on reparations and territory, which disillusioned Wilson's pro-league supporters.

While negotiations in Paris continued in March 1919, Senator Lodge, who was Wilson's greatest critic and chairman of the Senate Foreign Relations Committee, rallied thirty-seven senators to sign a statement that declared the League of Nations, "in the form it is now proposed at the peace conference," to be unacceptable. Isolationists also began to mount a fierce rhetorical attack on the covenant. After consultations with Taft and other Republicans supporters of the League, Wilson modified some aspects of the proposal. Rights were provided for member states to withdraw from the league after giving due notice, domestic issues were exempted from the league's jurisdiction, colonial mandates could be refused by member states, and the Monroe Doctrine was accorded formal recognition.[104]

By the time Wilson returned to the United States, he was confident that the treaty was capable of passing the Senate, and he was disinclined to compromise any further. Support for the covenant was widespread: thirty-two state legislatures, thirty-three governors, and the overwhelming majority of newspaper editors endorsed it.[105] In the meantime, a series of reservations had been advanced in the Senate, and Wilson was determined to oppose them. Opposition to the covenant also continued to mount. Isolationists—the so-called "irreconcilables"—led by Senator Borah, attacked the treaty, arguing that it would entangle the United States in endless bloody European wars.

But isolationists were a minority. The real struggle was between internationalists who favored the sort of collective security organization that Wilson proposed and internationalists who favored a more limited American commitment to Europe and the potential use of force. The critical issue in the Senate among the nonisolationists was Article 10 of the treaty. Article 10 guaranteed the political independence and territorial integrity of every member nation. Other articles in the covenant established machinery for the arbitration of territorial disputes and indicated that an act of war against one member would be an act of war against all. Under this situation, the league was to respond automatically with an economic embargo and decide within the Council what military measures should be used to repel the aggression.

[104] Bailey, *Woodrow Wilson and the Lost Peace*, pp. 205–6, 214–18.
[105] On national support for the league in 1919, see ibid., pp. 203–5.

The debate in the Senate was ultimately about this commitment. What was the character of the commitment, would such a system of collective security work, and should the United States make such a commitment by becoming a member? The decisive opposition came from politicians who were opposed to obliging the United States to this collective security system. There was a clear majority of Senators who favored other aspects of the league: arbitration, a world court to oversee international law, and agreements on disarmament. The critical question was whether the United States should go one step further and make a commitment that entailed the possible use of American military forces to guarantee the territorial integrity and political independence of member states around the world.

Some opponents worried about the abridgement of American sovereignty, others worried that it was a system that would simply defend the territorial and political status quo, and others warned that it would not allow the United States to discriminate between its vital interests and the wider sweep of the League of Nations commitments. The critical point in the debate was about the binding character of the American security commitment to the collective security organization. The moderate Republican view, represented by Lodge, was that they would accept most of the activities and obligations of the League but insisted on reserving for the Senate the basic decision concerning the degree of participation in league responses to specific cases of aggression. These objections to the league were ultimately put in the form of reservations—fourteen in all—to the treaty. The most important was Reservation 2, which stated that the United States assumed no obligations to preserve the territorial integrity and political independence of any other country, unless Congress made a specific decision to assume such an obligation.

Wilson defended Article 10 in public speeches around the country. His argument was that the commitment by member countries to uphold the territorial integrity and political independence of its members "speaks for the conscience of the world."[106] If one member state engaged in aggression against another, the dispute was to go automatically to arbitration, and if war would nonetheless ensue, the other member states would automatically implement an economic embargo. Wilson's view was that such a threat of sanctions would make war utterly unlikely. But war might still occur. If it were a major war such as just experienced in Europe, Wilson said, it was true that the United States would not remain neutral. But if it is a minor

[106] Wilson, address in Reno, 22 September 1919, in Link, ed., *Papers of Woodrow Wilson*, Vol. 63, p. 428.

war far removed from the Western Hemisphere, the United States need not get involved.[107]

Wilson's resistance to the resolution, however, was as much about the political message it sent the world as the technical question of the terms of American commitment to the covenant. Indeed, Wilson conceded that there really were no binding legal obligations to go to war to fulfill the terms of league membership. The covenant did in fact reserve the right of the United States to make the final decision for war. In the case of all disputes where the United States was not a direct party, the decision on the use of force would come before the Council, where the United States would have a veto over the decision. As a result, as Wilson argued, there was absolutely no possibility that the United States could be forced to use military force against its will.[108]

In an attempt to find a compromise, a Democratic senator—Gilbert Hitchcock—introduced reservations that simply clarified the American understanding of Article 10. Senator Lodge succeeded in organizing the defeat of these "friendly" reservations and introduced his own, including the reservation that Wilson thought effectively killed the American obligation to the treaty. Wilson was faced with a decision: to accept the Lodge reservations and gain Senate approval of the treaty or reject the reservations. His choice was based on the view that Lodge's reservation on Article 10 amounted to nullification of the covenant. He rallied the Democrats to defeat the Lodge reservations. The Senate was left with a choice of either

[107] Wilson resisted the Senate reservation to Article 10, arguing that it would destroy the foundation of collective security. What the Republican reservation proposed, Wilson said in a speech in Cheyenne, was "that we make no general promise, but leave the nations associated with us to guess in each instance what we were going to consider ourselves bound to do and what we were not going to consider ourselves bound to do. It is as if you said, 'We will not join the League definitely, but we will join it occasionally. We will not promise anything, but from time to time we may cooperate. We will not assume any obligations. . . .' This reservation proposes that we should not acknowledge any moral obligation in the matter; that we should stand off and say, 'We will see, from time to time; consult us when you get into trouble, and then we will have a debate, and after two or three months we will tell you what we are going to do.' The thing is unworthy and ridiculous, and I want to say distinctly that, as I read this, it would change the entire meaning of the Treaty and exempt the United States from all responsibilities for the preservation of the peace. It means the rejection of the Treaty, my fellow countrymen, nothing less." Quoted in Link, *Woodrow Wilson: Revolution, War and Peace*, pp. 119–20.

[108] Former President Taft acknowledged this view in a letter to Raymond Fosdick in early 1920. Taft said, "I don't think the reservations are going to make a great deal of difference." In his own handwriting at the end of the letter, Taft went on to say, "But that is no reason why we should not make the reservations as soft as we can." In Fosdick, *Letters on the League of Nations*, p. 93.

outright approval or rejection of the treaty. Unable to split the moderate internationalist Republicans from the irreconcilables, the Senate defeated the treaty by a vote of fifty-three to thirty-eight.

But given Wilson's own view of the contingent and qualified character of the obligation to use force, it is not obvious why the Lodge reservation—while not a constructive part of Wilson's agenda—needed to be a treaty killer. Wilson agreed with Lodge on the technical issue: the United States did in fact reserve the right to make its own choice, according to its constitutional authority, on the use of military force abroad. The Lodge reservation deflated the moral authority that Wilson could wield after the war in the building of the League of Nations, but it did not necessary alter the underlying terms of America's membership in the league. Knock notes the careful position that Wilson had on the American commitment to the League of Nations: "Wilson did set out his position many times in correspondence. And its contents do not conform to the picture of unlimited military commitments and entanglements in European politics which his contemporary opponents painted for the start and for which realists have often taken him to task. To the contrary, they demonstrate an awareness of the limitations that the Constitution might impose upon American participation in international military actions."[109]

The dilemma that Wilson faced in crafting a settlement around the League of Nations was in providing European governments with enough of a commitment to their security to ensure their participation in the postwar liberal order, and not too much to raise the resistance of the American Congress. Wilson apparently failed on both counts. But failure on the second count—with Congress—was not inevitable. Lodge's reservations were politically objectionable to Wilson but they were not a fundamental revision of the treaty.[110] Wilson's inability to provide the commitments necessary to Europe were built into the structure of American politics and the specific security imperatives felt in Europe. But short of specific security guarantees and a tripartite alliance, a settlement was possible that would bring the Europeans and the United States into a loose security institution. France would still need to pursue other security measures, but a League of Nations with American participation could have been orchestrated and it

[109] Knock, "Kennan versus Wilson," p. 314.

[110] Capturing the lost opportunities in the Senate handling of the peace treaty, Fosdick notes in a letter to a League of Nations official in Europe, "In all this business we have been shadowed by a double tragedy: first, the attitude of Senator Lodge and his bloc who have seen the League only as a God-given opportunity to crush the President; and second, the illness of Wilson which has robbed us of leadership at a time when we needed it most. The League here in the United States might have survived one or the other tragedy, but it is questionable in my mind whether it can survive both." Letter to Sir Eric Drummond, 10 January 1920, in Fosdick, *Letters on the League of Nations*, p. 95.

could have paved the way for subsequent commitments and guarantees not initially seen as necessary by Wilson or possible by the United States Senate.

WILSON'S FAILED DEMOCRATIC REVOLUTION

Wilson's optimism that his bold peace plan would work was premised on the belief that the Europeans were in the midst of a democratic revolution. The war itself was a war to democratize the world, and the peace settlement would push this movement further. With the assumption that Europe and the wider world would embrace American democratic principles, Wilson could pass over otherwise thorny issues of the postwar settlement. When Wilson set off for Europe to negotiate the peace in December 1918, it was still possible for him to be optimistic about the direction of political change in Europe. But, in retrospect, it was a democratic high tide rather than a gathering flood.

Wilson's goal was to orchestrate a democratic movement in Europe and in the process encourage public opinion (what he called the "organized opinion of mankind") to press the allied governments to support his postwar settlement goals.[111] But although the public, particularly in Britain, did show considerable enthusiasm for Wilson's program, political leaders were far less receptive. This was partly because the military success in 1918 confirmed the stability of incumbent conservative coalitions in Britain and France, thereby preventing the sort of domestic political upheaval that might have led to new coalitions committed to Wilson's program. But just as importantly, because of continuing American reluctance to use its power fully for internationalist goals, Wilson's program was not backed up by offers of economic and military assistance that might have made his settlement ideas more attractive and credible. However appealing the peace plans might have been to war-weary Europeans, the absence of political incentives and security guarantees dampened their appeal among European political leaders.

Wilson went to Europe in December 1918 to win over European opinion to his position on the peace settlement, and he articulated its liberal principles: open diplomacy, disarmament by all powers, freedom of the seas, removal of trade barriers, self-determination for minorities, restraint on reparations imposed on Germany, and the formation of a League of Nations to enforce the peace. The president sought to win European acceptance of these terms more by moral and ideological appeal than by the exercise of American power or diplomatic tact. He used the media as well

---

[111] See Link, *Woodrow Wilson: Revolution, War, and Peace*, p. 13.

as personal tours to launch a crusade that would appeal to the moral in-
stincts of Europe's masses and prompt them to reject the injustices of the
old diplomacy.[112] Wilson was attempting to speak directly to Europe's conscience and to instill a new conception of world order. As one historian
stated, "President Wilson applied the idea of international social control
to American foreign relations, promoting collective security to restrain national egoism."[113]

Liberal principles were gaining support in Europe throughout 1917 and
1918, partly as a result of events in Russia. The Russian Revolution gave
momentum to leftist parties in Europe and caused intellectual ferment
across the political spectrum. The Bolshevik peace plan, issued soon after
the provisional government was formed in Petrograd, was boldly progressive and placed pressure on the Allies for a substantive response.[114] Radicals
in Britain were also clamoring for more moderate war aims and a liberal
postwar order.[115]

Even before the armistice and Wilson's trip to Europe, the American
president had been monitoring the prospects for liberal and social democratic political coalitions on the continent. Earlier in 1918, Colonel House
sent the journalist Ray Stannard Baker to report on the prospects for favorable political change in Europe. It was House's view that the best hope for
European cooperation with Wilson's postwar goals was for liberal and social democratic governments to came to power. It was important, therefore,
to encourage and work with these liberal elements.[116] Baker reported from
Europe in the summer of 1918, urging the same thing. The allied governments only paid lip service to Wilson's program; it was Labor, most Liberals, and the radicals who supported his settlement ideas, and Wilson's peace
goals were tied to the fortunes of these growing liberal and progressive
groups.[117]

---

[112] Mayer, *Politics and Diplomacy of Peacemaking*, p. 368.

[113] Lloyd Ambrosius, *Woodrow Wilson and the American Diplomatic Tradition*, p. 2.

[114] The April 1917 statement included the following passage: "The purpose of free Russia
[was] not domination over peoples, nor spoilation of their national possessions, nor the violent occupation of foreign territories, but the establishment of a permanent peace on the basis
of self-determination of peoples. The Russian people [were] not aiming to increase their
power abroad at the expense of other people; they [had] no aim to enslave or oppress anybody." Quoted in Arno J. Mayer, *Political Origins of the New Diplomacy, 1917–1918* (New
Haven: Yale University Press, 1959), p. 75.

[115] Martin, *Peace without Victory*, chapter three.

[116] Quoted in Inga Floto, "Woodrow Wilson: War Aims, Peace Strategy, and the European
Left," in Link, ed., *Woodrow Wilson and a Revolutionary World*, p. 132.

[117] In a letter dated 28 May 1918, Baker wrote to State Department official Frank L. Polk:
"We should be careful not to rely, save upon the military side, upon either Lloyd-George or
Clemenceau governments, nor upon the forces back of them, for they are more or less bound
by secret understandings and special interests with which we have nothing to do, and which

Wilson's postwar strategy was built on this optimistic view: the war would leave the United States in a commanding economic and military position to set the terms of the peace, while an exhausted and bankrupt Europe would move leftward from conservative and nationalist governments toward liberal and social democratic governments. Woodrow Wilson was in an unusual position to rally these rising left-moving democratic forces, and they in turn would ensure the success of Wilson's peace aims.[118] These expectations—that the United States would be in a commanding power position, that European politics would continue to move leftward after the war, and that Wilson's appeals to the masses over the heads of European leaders could translate into real political change—were all proven elusive in the months before and after the war ended.

Nonetheless, the extent to which Wilson had established himself as the champion of liberal peace and democracy among the French and British public became evident during the president's trip to Europe in December 1918. In France, Wilson was greeted by throngs of supporters and given a hero's welcome by trade unions and parties on the left. His reception in Britain was similar. Even the conservative *Times* of London commented that "we are all idealists now in international affairs, and we look to Wilson to help us realize these ideals and to reconstruct out of the welter a better and fairer world."[119] In Rome, Milan, and other cities around Europe, Wilson was treated as a savior. As Knock argues, "These unprecedented demonstrations transcended mere pageantry. Indeed, they were an articulate expression of mass political opinion—and one, significantly, set in motion by the liberal, labor, and socialist movements within the Allied countries."[120]

With the extraordinary outpouring of public support during his trip, it is easy to see why Wilson was so optimistic about an unfolding democratic revolution in Europe. In returning to the United States after a later trip to

---

would embarrass, if not defeat, the whole great constructive plan we have in mind for a democratic settlement at the close of the war. . . . Either government is likely at any time to go to smash before a gust of popular feeling. Indeed, I have met a number of true liberals here who, while they have no faith in Lloyd-George, are backing up the Lloyd-George government quite consciously as a war instrument and are prepared, the moment a chance of peace comes, to demand a more democratic government." Papers of Ray Stannard Baker, Library of Congress.

[118] This view was expressed by Baker in a letter to Polk dated 10 August 1918: "The great source of Mr. Wilson's strength is that while each governing group over here can command a part of its own people, Mr. Wilson in so far as his policy is disinterested and democratic, can command large and powerful groups in all the nations. They can never get real unity, because each has a separate policy, while he can. Therefore, we must never let these democratic forces in England and France get away from us." Papers of Ray Stannard Baker, Library of Congress.

[119] London *Times*, quoted in Mayer, *Politics and Diplomacy of Peacemaking*, p. 188.

[120] Knock, *To End All Wars*, p. 195.

Europe in September 1919, Wilson still had great expectations: "I discovered that what we called American principles had penetrated to the heart and understanding not only of the great peoples of Europe, but to the hearts and understandings of the great men who were representing the peoples of Europe. . . . I can fancy those men of the first generation that so thoughtfully set his great Government up, the generation of Washington, Hamilton, Jefferson, and the Adamses—I can fancy their looking on with a sort of enraptured amazement that the American spirit should have made conquest of the world."[121]

The prosecution of the war clearly had a profound impact on the political and intellectual climate in Britain and France. The resurgence of the left and the rising popularity of Wilson's war aims early in 1918 were associated not only with growing disaffection with the war but also with fear that the dissolution of the eastern front which followed the Brest-Litovsk Treaty would give Germany overwhelming military superiority in the West.[122] These developments made American participation in the war more necessary, and European political leaders were eager for the United States to become engaged. British and French government officials were careful not to criticize Wilson's ideas while the war continued. Yet European public opinion was not rising to Wilson's appeal simply to secure American assistance. The wave of popular support for Wilson emerged in 1918, well after the United States had entered the war. Furthermore, neither the British nor the French governments simply bent to Wilson's goals. Lloyd George remained ambivalent about Wilson's vision of a new diplomacy; Clemenceau remained one of Wilson's more formidable foes throughout 1918 and 1919. Wilson succeeded in appealing to the people of Europe on moral and ideological grounds, rather than through the exercise of American power.

In Wilson's travels around Europe prior to the Paris peace conference, the public welcome and support was unprecedented for a visiting head of state. But the question remained, as Thomas Knock poses it: "Still, it was not clear, practically speaking, how the adoration of the masses could be converted into tangible political leverage, and not only with respect to the League of Nations."[123] The great appeal of Wilson in Europe did not sit well with the European leaders who stood by and watched the public embrace the American president.

This was Wilson's problem: his peace ideas appealed to British and French public opinion but they gained little support among European gov-

---

[121] Wilson speech, 6 September 1919, quoted in Temperley, *A History of the Peace Conference of Paris*, Vol. 1, p. 197.

[122] Mayer, *Political Origins of the New Diplomacy*, p. 311.

[123] Knock, *To End All Wars*, p. 197.

ernment leaders. The swell of popular support for Wilson in Europe did not translate into a change of the leader's views of the peace settlement or a change in the ruling coalitions in Britain or France. At the end of 1917, the conservative forces, initially strengthened by the outbreak of the war, still maintained firmly in control of the war cabinets in both countries. In fact, according to Arno Mayer, between 1914 and 1917, "the forces, of order achieved a position of power to which they had aspired only in their most daring dreams before the war,"[124] Steeped in the practices and assumptions of the old diplomacy, war policy was characterized by secret negotiations, plans for territorial annexations, and hopes for total defeat of Germany.

During 1918, however, conservative control of the war cabinets, particularly in Britain, eroded considerably. The Russian Revolution and the political crisis of 1917–1918 led to the formation of a strong center/left coalition in both Britain and France. In Britain, growing popular support for the radical cause forced Labourites to move to the left. To maintain control of the government, Lloyd George had to incorporate liberal war aims into official policy.[125] In other words, the shift in popular views of the war and British goals had an impact on the tone and emphasis of British war goals. A similar shift did not occur in France, precisely because a center/left coalition was not strong enough to threaten Clemenceau's position.

After the defeat of Germany, the political pendulum in Britain again swung to the right, given a strong push by the nationalist and patriotic sentiment stimulated by victory. The waning of support for the liberal peace program corresponded with the strengthening of the right in the wake of military victory. Lloyd George accordingly paid increasing attention to the Conservatives and their preferences for the shape of the negotiated peace.[126] The center/left coalition eroded and the left grew fragmented, leading to the dissolution of the locus of political activism and idealism that Wilson had tapped to win support of the Fourteen Points. Wilson's call for a liberal peace had by no means been rejected, but those still committed to his peace goals were unable to wield effective political power.

With opportunities for political advancement closed off by the resurgence of the right, Wilson's peace program had little to offer European government leaders. The United States did not have the material resources to create incentives for these elites to move in the directions Wilson desired. Nor, given the apparent reluctance of the American Senate to endorse the full measure of Wilson's plans, were the commitments that the

---

[124] Mayer, *Political Origins of the New Diplomacy*, p. 14.
[125] Martin, *Peace without Victory*, pp. 132–34 and 148–54.
[126] Ibid., p. 192.

United States was willing to make to Europe either substantial or credible. Wilson's call for the reduction of war reparations, the disarmament of the victors as well as the vanquished, and the adoption of liberal trade ideas did not offer European government elites an attractive basis to maintain their rule. Without more substantial exercise of American power through the wielding of postwar aid and security guarantees, there was little to induce European leaders to undertake what would constitute a revolution in their conception of the international order. Wilson did leave an indelible mark on the European left. Especially in Britain during the 1930s, notions of collective security and disarmament had a profound effect on foreign-policy.[127] Yet in the absence of political change in the coalitions that governed in Britain and France, Wilson's popular appeals were not able to be transformed into enduring political change.

Conclusion

The constitutional model identifies incentives that informed American order building after the war and the logic of the failed institutional bargain. The United States did pursue an institutional order-building strategy after the war. Newly preeminent, it responded to incentives and opportunities to reach an institutional bargain that would lock others states into a congenial international order. This was at the heart of Wilson's liberal program: to create a stable and legitimate postwar order organized around democratic countries that operate within liberal institutions and uphold collective security. The postwar juncture was seen by Wilson as a momentary opportunity to put in place a settlement that might persist for decades. This opportunity—and his own personal moral vision—led Wilson to articulate a long-term American interest that would be secured through the establishment of institutionalized relationships among the democracies. Wilson did not offer specific concessions on short-term gains in seeking agreement with European leaders, but he did offer more diffuse gestures of restraint.

The asymmetries of power after the war also led Britain and France to worry about American domination and abandonment, and they actively courted a formal security tie. The British used their own support of the League of Nations as a mechanism to shape the American commitment, whereas the French pursued a more formal security alliance. The French were more concerned with resurgent German military power than with overt American domination, but they and the British were eager to reduce the uncertainties of rising American power by binding it to Europe.

---

[127] Michael Howard, *The Continental Commitment* (London: Temple Smith, 1972), pp. 110 ff.

But why did an institutional bargain fail? Reasons can be identified that lie both inside and outside the constitutional model. If a formal security alliance between the United States and Europe was the only way to build a stable and cooperative order among these countries after the war, a focus on stubborn and divergent great-power interests is perhaps sufficient to explain the outcome. France certainly wanted a more traditional and binding security guarantee than the United States was willing or able to provide. Variations in the distribution of power or the presence or absence of democratic states are less useful in explaining the failure of this alliance agreement.

But another outcome that failed was a more modest institutional agreement that tied the United States to Europe less directly through the League of Nations, perhaps supplemented by other specific inducements and commitments. This would have been an institutional settlement that would have tied the major states together more closely than did the 1815 settlement, but that was less formally binding than the security ties that emerged between the United States and Europe after World War II. It was doomed less by conflicting great-power interests and more by more specific circumstances related to the American exercise of power after the war and personal convictions of Wilson.

The preeminence of American power did not translate into usable leverage in the waning moments of the war or in Paris during the negotiations. Britain in 1815 and the United States in 1945 more fully exploited their leadership of the wartime alliance to lock in agreement on postwar arrangements. The "associate" position of the United States in the alliance also made it a less credible as a leader of the peace settlement. Even if the United States had played a more commanding role in the war, it is not clear that Wilson would have used that power effectively to coopt the allies into a common agreement on war aims and settlement terms. But without such power, Wilson was left to rely on moral persuasion and the cultivation of European public opinion.

Behind the inability of the United States to bind itself to its European allies were factors that had to do with Wilson himself. Wilson's opposition to Senator Lodge's reservations, particularly the one concerning Article 10 of the covenant, had more to do with the spirit of America's commitment to Europe than it was a technical dispute over the nature of the obligation. Wilson saw the reservation as undercutting the political underpinnings of commitment which he understood to be the elemental source of international law and institutional binding. This is true, even if Wilson acknowledged that technically the United States, as a member of the League of Nations Council, would always be able to veto the use of military force and therefore would retain the authority on such decisions.

Wilson's actions also hinged on a basic assumption about an expected worldwide democratic revolution. When Wilson presented his Fourteen Points in January 1918, it looked as if the tide of European politics was moving in a liberal and social democratic direction. The revolution in Russia seemed to confirm the democratic revolution that was sweeping the major industrial societies. The dramatic outpouring of genuine popular support that greeted Wilson in his triumphant visits to London, Paris, Rome, and Milan on the eve of the peace conference also reinforced this sense that a world democratic upsurge would empower his negotiating position. Governments with center-left governments would emerge and sign on to Wilson's vision. But the high tide of revolutionary ferment was reached in early 1918, and the direction was decidedly conservative as the war came to an end.

Wilson hitched his liberal peace program to the great forces of war and social change that he saw unfolding around him. Although these forces worked in his favor in 1918, they worked against him in 1919 and after. The war brought the United States to a new position of power, but the way the war ended and Wilson's lost opportunities left the United States unable to dictate the terms of the peace. Wilson's own conceptions of commitment and global historical change undercut an institutional agreement that was within his reach.

Chapter Six

THE SETTLEMENT OF 1945

THE SETTLEMENT that followed the Second World War was both the most fragmented and most far-reaching of any postwar settlement in history. This was the first major war in history that did not end with a single comprehensive peace settlement. Peace treaties were not concluded with the major axis powers, Japan and Germany. The Charter of the United Nations, unlike the Covenant of the League of Nations, was not attached to the peace settlement.[1] And yet, in the years between 1944 and 1951, the United States and its allies brought about history's most sweeping reorganization of international order.

World War II actually culminated in two major settlements. One was between the United States and the Soviet Union and their respective allies, and it took the form of Cold War bipolarity. The other was among the Western industrial countries and Japan, which resulted in a dense set of new security, economic, and political institutions, almost all involving the United States. The two settlements were interrelated. The Cold War reinforced cohesion among the advanced industrial democracies, and the breakdown of relations with the Soviet Union beginning in 1947 (and intensifying after 1950) was critical in shaping the character and extent of the American security commitment to Europe. Marshall Plan aid and alliance guarantees, undertaken by the United States to stabilize and reassure postwar Europe, were made politically acceptable because of the growing fears of Soviet communism. But although the Cold War reinforced Western order, the two settlements nonetheless had distinct origins and logics. One was the most militarized settlement in history, and the other was the most institutionalized.

Among the Western industrial countries, the settlement was particularly striking in its extensive use of multilateral institutions to organize a wide range of postwar relations, including the use of alliances to bind the United States and its European partners together. Between 1944 and 1951, the United States and the other advanced industrial democracies engaged in a flurry of institution building. The resulting institutionalization of postwar order was vastly greater in scope than in the past, dealing with issues of economic stabilization, trade, finance, and monetary relations as well as

---

[1] John W. Wheeler-Bennett and Anthony Nicholls, *The Semblance of Peace: The Political Settlement after the Second World War* (London: St. Martin's, 1972).

political and security relations among the postwar allies. The result was a "layer cake" of regional and global, multilateral and bilateral institutions. Whereas after World War I the United States sought to build a single universal institution with authority across all the realms of interstate relations, the United States and its partners after World War II created a diversified array of institutions, many of them organized more narrowly around the Western industrial democracies and the Atlantic region.

As in the past, leaders at this settlement brought with them lessons and reactions from earlier settlements. In 1919, leaders in Paris remembered Vienna. In 1945, the diplomats and politicians who negotiated an end to the war were even more burdened with this sense of the repetition of history. The war had been a continuation of the previous war. Many of these leaders had been young participants in the 1919 settlement and had formed strong views about its failings.[2] This time, the United States was in a much more commanding position—its opportunities to shape the postwar order were vastly greater—but the way it exercised its power and its official thinking about order building had also changed.

To a greater degree than in 1815 and 1919, the leading and secondary states had incentives and capacities to move toward a constitutional order. The United States emerged from the war with formidable capabilities to make institutional bargains with other states, and the sharp asymmetries of power heightened the incentives that the European governments had to make agreements that would establish restraints and commitments on the exercise of American power. The United States sought to take advantage of the postwar juncture to lock in a set of institutions that would serve its interests well into the future and, in return, it offered—in most instances quite reluctantly—to restrain and commit itself by operating within an array of postwar economic, political, and security institutions. United States policy also reflected the incentives that a leading state has in establishing a postwar order that is at least minimally legitimate, and it consistently compromised on institutional agreements with the Europeans to achieve this end.

The democratic character of the states involved also facilitated institutional agreement. European and American leaders argued quite explicitly that their willingness to establish binding ties with each other hinged on their shared democratic institutions. Democracy was both an end and a means. Western leaders repeatedly justified their unprecedented institutional commitments as necessary for the protection of common democratic values. But they also argued that such commitments were particularly cred-

---

[2] This is the theme of David Fromkin, *In the Time of the Americans: The Generation That Changed America's Role in the World* (New York: Alfred A. Knopf, 1995).

ible and effective because they were established between democracies. Moreover, the decentralized and pluralistic character of the United States government—which rendered it relatively transparent and open to influence—also served to reassure European leaders that the exercise of American power would be less arbitrary and unpredictable than that of an authoritarian regime. This made it easier and less risky to establish institutional ties, as well.

The initial American postwar goal—articulated first by Roosevelt in the 1941 Atlantic Charter—was to lock the democracies into an open, multilateral economic order jointly managed through new institutional mechanisms. The British imperial preference system—as much as German or Japanese regional blocs or a closed Soviet Union—was in conflict with such an order, and the United States used its leverage to push the British and continental Europeans toward an open postwar system. American officials advanced a wide array of order-building ideas, variously emphasizing free trade, global institutions, Atlantic community, geopolitical openness, and European integration. The specific formulation of the American liberal international goal evolved as the war ended and circumstances—such as European economic weakness, German reconstruction, and the Soviet threat—unfolded. The United States accepted compromise agreements in order to get European participation in postwar multilateral institutions. European weakness more than its outright resistance limited American postwar liberal multilateral goals, and soon after the war European integration and reconstruction became the critical component of securing a wider open multilateral order.

Throughout the postwar period, European leaders were more concerned with American abandonment than with domination, and they consistently pressed for a formal and permanent American security commitment. Until early 1948, the official American view was that the greatest threat to Europe was its own internal economic and political disarray, and the best way to insure a stable postwar order was a thriving and unified European "third force." The evolving American security commitment to Europe ultimately hinged on the question of Germany. The reconstruction of western Germany, seen by American officials as essential to the economic revival of Europe, also created a potential security threat within Europe, particularly for the French. At each stage of America's unfolding security commitment to Europe—the Marshall Plan, the Vandenberg Resolution, the North Atlantic Treaty, the integrated military command, and the stationing of ground troops within NATO—the United States sought to reconcile the reconstruction and reintegration of western Germany with European security. At each stage, the United States sought to overcome fears of renewed German aggression by binding its western zones to a wider Europe. At each stage, British and French officials insisted that such a solution was acceptable only if the United States also bound itself to Europe. Lord Ismay's famous words—that NATO was created to "keep the Russians out, the Germans down, and the Americans in"—captures the multifaceted ways in which binding security ties were employed to establish commitment and restraint.

The United States was able to overcome incentives that European and other states might have to resist or balance against that power. The emerging Cold War—and the perceived Soviet threat—did reinforce cooperation among the Western democracies, but it did not create it. Even before the European perceived a direct military threat from the Soviet Union, they actively cultivated a postwar American security commitment.[3] The open character of American hegemony, the extensive reciprocity between the United States and its partners, the absence of hegemonic coercion, and binding institutional relations all provided elements of reassurance and legitimacy despite the huge asymmetries of power.

America's partners were less fearful of domination or abandonment because they were reciprocally integrated into security alliances and multilateral economic institutions that limited the unaccountable exercise of power and created transgovernmental political processes for insuring ongoing commitments and resolving conflict. In the case of security guarantees, the United States moved toward a fixed and absolute commitment only with great reluctance, which was never fully resolved until the late 1950s. But the Europeans were able to work the emerging Atlantic system to extract American commitments. The open American polity provided points of access and "voice opportunities," which in turn provided opportunities for the allies to become directly involved in making alliance policy. The array of binding institutions connected to democratic states provided the basis for both commitment and restraint.

---

[3] The emergence of the Cold War and the fear of the spread of communism in Western Europe heightened American political stakes on the continent and made it both more necessary and easier for the United States to make a binding security commitment. But the American agenda of locking Europe and the wider world into an open liberal order, and the European agenda of establishing restraints and commitments on American power, preceded the Cold War. Indeed, after the Cold War began the Europeans may have found a solution to the problem of American abandonment, but they also increasingly felt the potential problem of American domination—that is, Europeans developed new fears that the United States might use Europe as a battlefield to settle its differences with the Soviet Union. Both before and after the Cold War, problems of restraint and commitment among highly unequal powers infused the relationship between America and Europe. It is difficult, nonetheless, to untangle completely which incentives were dominant during the rolling sequence of postwar institutional bargains. Beyond attention to timing and process tracing, assessment of the relative importance of the Cold War to institutional cooperation is helped by an examination of these relations after the Cold War. This is the purpose of Chapter Seven.

The Strategic Setting

The strategic situation that the United States and its allies faced after the war was a close fit to the stylized problem of order sketched in Chapter Three. The United States emerged from the war unusually powerful in relation to the European great powers and Japan. America's allies and the defeated axis states were battered and diminished by the war, whereas the United States grew more powerful through mobilization and war.[4] The American government was more centralized and capable, and the economy and military were unprecedented in their power and still on an upward swing.[5] In addition, the war itself had ratified the destruction of the old order of the 1930s, eliminated the alternative regional hegemonic ambitions of Germany and Japan, and diminished the viability of the British imperial order.

The huge disparity of power between the United States and the other great powers was the fundamental strategic reality after the war. The United States had roughly half of world economic production, a world-dominant military, leadership in advanced technologies, and surpluses of petroleum and food production.[6] The rising economic dominance of the United States is reflected in the relative economic size of the postwar great powers. In 1945, Britain and the Soviet Union were the closest economic rivals—each with roughly one-fifth the size of the American economy. This asymmetry in economic size lessened marginally as the Soviet Union and European states recovered from war, but American preeminence continued.[7] The American share of world industrial production indicated in Table 6–1 also reveals this basic economic preponderance. A similar disparity existed in military power, as seen in the relative share of military expenditures among the great powers (see Table 6–2). The United States ended the war with an unprecedented lead in military capability, which in turn declined somewhat after the Soviet Union recovered and the Cold War began. American relative military capability in relation to Western Europe, however, remained preponderant during the postwar decades.

[4] Great Britain, for example, lost about one-quarter of its national wealth and became the world's largest debtor nation, while in the United States the war pulled the country out of the depression, and the gross national product almost doubled.

[5] For a discussion of the ways in which World War II strengthened the American state and modernized its society and economy, see Michael S. Sherry, *In the Shadow of War: The United States since the 1930s* (New Haven: Yale University Press, 1995).

[6] For an overview of these hegemonic capabilities, see Stephen Krasner, "American Policy and Global Economic Stability," in William P. Avery and David P. Rapkin, eds., *America in a Changing World Political Economy* (New York: Longman, 1982).

[7] See Appendix Two.

TABLE 6–1
Relative Share of World Manufacturing Output, 1940–1955

	1938	1953	1963	1973
Britain	10.7	8.4	6.4	4.9
United States	31.4	44.7	35.1	33.0
Germany	12.7	5.9	6.4	5.9
France	4.4	3.2	3.8	3.5
Russia	9.0	10.7	14.2	14.4
Italy	2.8	2.3	2.9	2.9
Japan	5.2	2.9	5.1	8.8

Source: Paul Bairoch, "International Industrialization Levels from 1750 to 1980," *Journal of European Economic History*, Vol. 11, No. 2 (Fall 1982), p. 304.

TABLE 6–2
Share of Total Great-Power Military Expenditures, 1940–1955

	1940	1945	1950	1955
United States	3.6	74.5	42.9	52.4
Great Britian	21.4	14.1	7.0	5.6
France	12.3	1.0	4.4	3.8
Germany	45.6	—	—	—
Russia	13.2	7.1	45.7	38.2
Japan	4.0	3.3	—	—

Source: Calculated from data presented in Appendix Two.

This American postwar preeminence was recognized by observers at the time. "The U.S. was in the position today where Britain was at the end of the Napoleonic wars," noted British Foreign Minister Ernest Bevin in June 1947.[8] The British scholar, Harold Laski, also writing in 1947, captured the same sense of overarching American power: "Today literally hundreds of millions of Europeans and Asiatics know that both the quality and the rhythm of their lives depend upon decisions made in Washington. On the wisdom of those decisions hangs the fate of the next generation."[9]

[8] "The Chargé in the United Kingdom [Gallman] to the Secretary of State," 16 June 1947, *Foreign Relations of the United States*, 1947, Vol. 3, pp. 254–55. All the volumes of *Foreign Relations of the United States* are published by the U.S. Government Printing Office, Washington, D.C.

[9] Harold J. Laski, "America—1947, *Nation*, Vol. 165 (December 13, 1947), p. 641.

American foreign policy officials also understood that this extraordinary asymmetry in power was a defining feature of the postwar situation. George Kennan, in a major State Department review of American foreign policy in 1948, pointed to the new reality: "We have about 50% of the world's wealth but only 6.3% of its population. . . . Our real task in the coming period is to devise a pattern of relationships which will permit us to maintain this position of disparity without positive detriment to our national security."[10] The United States found itself in a rare position. It had power *and* choices.

Moreover, unlike the end of the First World War, the victory by the allies was complete. Unconditional surrender and postwar occupation of the defeated powers was an absolute condition for ending the war with Germany and Japan.[11] As early as April 1942, a subcommittee in the State Department that was set up to study postwar security problems concluded that war in Europe had reignited a second time only because Germany had not been driven to absolute defeat in 1918. The German people had been led to believe that they had been tricked into accepting a punative peace agreement even though the German military had not been beaten on the battlefield. The committee concluded that "On the assumption that the victory of the United Nations will be conclusive, unconditional surrender rather than an armistice should be sought from the principal enemy states."[12] Roosevelt immediately adopted the goal of unconditional surrender and, at the allied conference in Casablanca in January 1943, the allies agreed to this resolution of the war.[13] In both Europe and the Pacific, this was in fact how the war ended.

The United States was also more indispensable in bringing the war to a close than it was in the previous war. It did not suffer the highest human or material costs of war, but its resources and technology were vital for winning.[14] Its political leadership was more critical than it had been during World War I. The role of military assistance to Britain and Russia also provided a mechanism for the United States to gain agreement with Britain and the other allies over war aims and settlement goals. The United States could play a role not unlike Castlereagh's Britain during the Napoleonic

[10] "Memorandum by the Director of the Policy Planning Staff [Kennan] to the Secretary of State and Under Secretary of State [Lovett]," 24 February 1948, *Foreign Relations of the United States*, 1948, Vol. 1, p. 524.

[11] On the way lessons of the past war influenced American thinking in fighting and ending World War II, see Fromkin, *In the Time of the Americans*.

[12] Quoted in Wheeler-Bennett and Nicholls, *The Semblance of Peace*, p. 56.

[13] See Herbert Feis, *Churchill, Roosevelt, Stalin* (Princeton: Princeton University Press, 1957), pp. 108–13.

[14] America lost 400,000 soldiers in the war, whereas the Soviet Union suffered roughly 20 million killed.

war: its economic and military capabilities allowed its leaders to shape the coalition, influence when and how the war ended, and lock in commitments to the postwar order while it was still in an advantaged position. The American use of the 1941 Lend-Lease agreement with Britain was perhaps the most explicit instance of the use of wartime assistance to extract concessions over postwar European policies.

The United States also paralleled Britain in 1815 and the United States in 1919 in its position as the outlying great power within the system. Removed from both Europe and Asia, the United States was able to conceive of security relations more broadly and with an eye to the long term. The United States had the most secure fall-back options, and therefore its proposals were less constrained by considerations of power balance and the security dilemma. The United States had also been in this position after the First World War, but in 1945, the United States was in a more commanding position: it was stronger and more indispensable, the war resulted in a more thorough breakdown of order, and the defeat of the enemy was more decisive.

These are the conditions that defined the problem of order after the war: new and huge power asymmetries, a completely defeated enemy, an old international order in ruins, and an uncertain future. The United States was in an unprecedented position to shape world politics. But America's commanding power also intensified the fears of domination and abandonment felt by weaker states. It is here that the character of the United States itself—as an open and reluctant hegemonic power with distinctive ideas about political order—and the array of proposed postwar institutions facilitated agreement on a settlement organized around binding institutions.

Two Post-War Settlements

World War II produced two postwar settlements. One was a reaction to deteriorating relations with the Soviet Union, and it culminated in the "containment order." It was a settlement based on the balance of power, nuclear deterrence, and political and ideological competition. The other settlement was a reaction to the economic rivalry and political turmoil of the 1930s and the resulting world war, and it culminated in a wide range of new institutions and relations among the Western industrial democracies and Japan. This settlement was built around economic openness, political reciprocity, and multilateral management of an American-led liberal political order.[15]

---

[15] The argument that there were two distinct postwar settlements is made in G. John Ikenberry, "The Myth of Post-Cold War Chaos," *Foreign Affairs*, Vol. 75, No. 3 (May/June 1996), pp. 79–91.

The two settlements had distinct political visions and intellectual rationales, and at key moments the American president gave voice to each. On 12 March 1947, President Truman gave his celebrated speech before Congress announcing aid to Greece and Turkey, and wrapped it in a new American commitment to support the cause of freedom around the world. The Truman Doctrine speech was a founding moment of the "containment order"; it rallied the American people to a new great struggle, this one against the perils of world domination by Soviet communism. A "fateful hour" had arrived, Truman told the American people. The people of the world "must choose between two alternate ways of life." If the United States failed in its leadership, Truman declared, "we may endanger the peace of the world."[16]

It is forgotten, however, that six days before this historic declaration, Truman gave an equally sweeping speech at Baylor University. On this occasion, Truman spoke of the lessons the world must learn from the disasters of the 1930s. "As each battle of the economic war of the thirties was fought, the inevitable tragic result became more and more apparent. From the tariff policy of Hawley and Smoot, the world went on to Ottawa and the system of imperial preferences, from Ottawa to the kind of elaborate and detailed restrictions adopted by Nazi Germany." Truman reaffirmed American commitment to "economic peace," which would involve tariff reductions and rules and institutions of trade and investment. In the settlement of economic differences, "the interests of all will be considered, and a fair and just solution will be found." Conflicts would be captured and domesticated in an iron cage of multilateral rules, standards, safeguards, and dispute resolution procedures. According to Truman, "this is the way of a civilized community."[17]

The "containment order" is well known in the popular imagination. It is celebrated in our historical accounts of the early years after World War II, when American officials struggled to make sense of Soviet military power and geopolitical intentions. In these early years, a few "wise men" fashioned a coherent and reasoned response to the global challenge of So-

---

[16] Truman, "Address to Joint Session of Congress on Aid to Greece and Turkey," 12 March 1947. *Public Papers of the Presidents of the United States: Harry S. Truman, January 1 to December 31, 1947* (Washington, D.C.: United States Government Printing Office, 1963), pp. 176–80. For historical accounts of this foreign policy turning point, see Dean G. Acheson, *Present at the Creation: My Years at the State Department* (New York: W. W. Norton, 1969); Howard Jones, *"A New Kind of War": America's Global Strategy and the Truman Doctrine in Greece* (New York: Oxford University Press, 1989). On whether the Truman Doctrine was a Cold War watershed, see John Lewis Gaddis, "Was the Truman Doctrine a Real Turning Point?" *Foreign Affairs*, Vol. 52 (January 1974), pp. 386–92.

[17] Truman, "Address on Foreign Economic Policy," Baylor University, Waco, Texas, 6 March 1947. *Public Papers of the Presidents: Truman, 1947*, pp. 167–72.

172

viet communism.[18] The doctrine of containment that emerged was the core concept that gave clarity and purpose to several decades of American foreign policy.[19] In the decades that followed, sprawling bureaucratic and military organizations were built on the containment orientation. The bipolar division of the world, nuclear weapons of growing size and sophistication, the ongoing clash of two expansive ideologies—all these circumstances gave life to and reinforced the centrality of the "containment order."[20]

By comparison, the ideas and policies of the Western order were more diffuse and wide-ranging. It was less obvious that the intra-Western agenda was a "grand strategy" designed to advance American security interests. As a result, during the Cold War it was inevitable that this agenda would be seen as secondary, a preoccupation of economists and American business. The policies and institutions that supported free trade and economic openness among the advanced industrial societies were quintessentially the stuff of "low politics." But this is a historical misconception. The Western settlement was built on varied and sophisticated ideas about American security interests, the causes of war and depression, and the proper and desirable foundations of postwar political order. Indeed, although the "containment order" overshadowed it, the ideas behind order among the Western industrial countries were more deeply rooted in the American experience and a thoroughgoing understanding of history, economics, and the sources of political order.

The most basic conviction behind American thinking about postwar order in the West was that the closed autarkic regions that had contributed to world depression and split the world into competing blocs before the war must be broken up and replaced by an open and nondiscriminatory

---

[18] For a popular account of the "founding fathers" of the containment order, see Walter Isaacson and Evan Thomas, *The Wise Men: Six Friends and the World They Made* (New York: Simon and Schuster, 1986).

[19] The seminal role of George Kennan as architect of containment policy is stressed in John Lewis Gaddis, *Strategies of Containment: A Critical Appraisal of Postwar American National Security Policy* (New York: Oxford University Press, 1984). More recently, Melvyn P. Leffler has argued that many American officials and experts from across the foreign and defense establishment independently began to embrace containment thinking. See Leffler, *A Preponderance of Power: National Security, the Truman Administration, and the Cold War* (Stanford: Stanford University Press, 1992). On Kennan's changing views of containment, see Kennan, *American Diplomacy, 1925–50* (Chicago: University of Chicago Press, 1951); Kennan, *Memoirs, 1925–50* (Boston: Little, Brown, 1967); and the interview with Kennan in "X-Plus 25," *Foreign Policy*, Vol. 7 (Summer 1972), pp. 3–53. On the bureaucratic politics of containment policy within the State Department, see Robert L. Messer, "Paths Not Taken: The United States Department of State and Alternatives to Containment, 1945–1946," *Diplomatic History*, Vol. 1, No. 4 (Fall 1977), pp. 297–319.

[20] For excellent historical accounts of this emerging containment order, see Marc Trachtenberg, *A Constructed Peace: The Making of the European Settlement, 1945–1963* (Princeton: Princeton University Press, 1999); and Leffler, *A Preponderance of Power*.

world economic system. Peace and security were impossible in a world of closed and exclusive economic regions. The challengers to liberal multilateralism occupied almost every corner of the advanced industrial world. Germany and Japan, of course, were the most overt and hostile challengers. Each had pursued a dangerous pathway into the modern industrial age that combined authoritarian capitalism with military dictatorship and coercive regional autarky. But the British Commonwealth and its imperial preference system was also a challenge to liberal multilateral order.[21] The hastily drafted Atlantic Charter was an American effort to insure that Britain signed onto its liberal democratic war aims.[22] The joint statement of principles affirmed free trade, equal access for countries to the raw materials of the world, and international collaboration in the economic field so as to advance labor standards, employment security, and social welfare. Roosevelt and Churchill were intent on telling the world that they had learned the lessons of the interwar years—and those lessons were fundamentally about the proper organization of the Western world economy. It was not just America's enemies, but also its friends, that had to be reformed and integrated.[23]

Roosevelt wanted to use the Atlantic Charter as a way to extract from the British a pledge not to use the war for purposes of territorial or economic imperialism. In doing so, he was attempting at least in part to prevent a repetition of what he strongly felt hurt peace efforts after World War I: allied intrigues and secret understandings pursued without American knowledge, which had the effect of undermining Wilson's Fourteen Points. But Roosevelt was also seeking agreement with Britain on war aims at a early moment when the United States was in a strong position. This too

---

[21] For arguments that the great mid-century struggle was between a open capitalist order and various regional, autarkic challengers, see Bruce Cumings, "The Seventy Years' Crisis: Trilateralism and the New World Order," *World Policy Journal*, Vol. 3, No. 2 (Spring 1991); and Charles Maier, "The Two Postwar Eras and the Conditions for Stability in Twentieth-Century Western Europe," in Maier, *In Search of Stability: Explorations in Historical Political Economy* (New York: Cambridge University Press, 1987), pp. 153–84. A similar sweeping historical argument—described as a struggle between "liberal" and "collectivist" alternatives—is made in Robert Skidelsky, *The World after Communism* (London: Macmillan, 1995).

[22] Churchill insisted that the charter did not mandate the dismantlement of the British Empire and its system of trade preferences, and only the last-minute sidestepping of this controversial issue insured agreement. See Lloyd C. Gardner, "The Atlantic Charter: Idea and Reality, 1942–1945," in Douglas Brinkley and David R. Facey-Crowther, eds., *The Atlantic Charter* (London: Macmillan, 1994), pp. 45–81.

[23] For accounts of the Atlantic Charter meeting, see Winston Churchill, *The Grand Alliance* (Boston: Houghton Mifflin, 1950), pp. 385–400; Sumner Welles, *Where Are We Heading?* (London: Harper and Brothers, 1947); Robert Sherwood, *Roosevelt and Hopkins: An Intimate History* (New York: Harper, 1948); and Theodore A. Wilson, *The First Summit: Roosevelt and Churchill at Placentia Bay, 1941* (Boston: Houghton Mifflin, 1969).

was a lesson that Roosevelt and other American officials had learned from Wilson's experience.[24]

Roosevelt's aim with the Atlantic Charter was to begin the process of locking the European democracies into an open and managed postwar order. Roosevelt shared the view of many officials in the State Department, later echoed by Truman, that economic closure and discrimination were the fundamental cause of political conflict and instability in the 1930s and eventually of the war—and that an open and stable economic order was essential to ensure postwar peace.[25] This was a widely shared view. John Foster Dulles, a prominent Republican foreign policy expert, applauded the Atlantic Charter and its emphasis on a postwar world that allowed for "growth without imperialism," supported by "an international body dedicated to the general welfare" and the establishment of "procedures within each country" that ensured movement toward economic openness.[26] During the 1944 election, the Republican party's committee on postwar foreign policy reaffirmed its commitment to a "stabilized interdependent world," and urged United States participation after the war in cooperation with other states to prevent military aggression, expand international trade, and secure monetary and economic stability.[27]

The containment order, of course, was not planned or even fully antici-pated during the war, although Churchill and other British and American officials began to have their doubts about the Soviet Union's postwar intentions even then. Roosevelt, however, remained convinced until his death in March 1945 that he could handle Stalin and pave the way toward a postwar order where the United States and the Soviet Union engaged in cooperative management of global interstate relations.[28] As Wheeler-Ben-nett and Nicholls note, "From the earliest period of the war, when neither the Soviet Union nor the United States was a belligerent, he had visualized an American-Soviet partnership for peace in the then uncertain shaping of the post-war world. When later they become comrades in arms, this con-

[24] Wheeler-Bennett and Nicholls, *The Semblance of Peace*, p. 37.

[25] Roosevelt's view was summarized in a memo to Morris L. Ernst in March 1943: "We were wrong in 1920. We believe in international co-operation and the principles of the Atlan-tic Charter and the Four Freedoms. We propose to back those who show the most diligence and interest in carrying them out." Roosevelt to Morris L. Ernst, 8 March 1943, in *F.D.R.: His Personal Letters, 1928–1945* (New York: Duell, Sloan and Pearce, 1950), p. 1,407.

[26] John Foster Dulles, "Peace without Platitudes," *Fortune*, Vol. 25, No. 1 (January 1942) pp. 42–43.

[27] See Andrew Williams, *Failed Imagination? New World Orders of the Twentieth Century* (Manchester: Manchester University Press, 1998), pp. 98–100.

[28] For the view that FDR was already anticipating a postwar break with Russia, see Robert Dalleck, *Franklin D. Roosevelt and American Foreign Policy, 1932–1945* (New York: Oxford University Press), p. 476.

cept increased rather than diminished. Russia and America were to be cast in the role of two super-policemen, supervising East and West, under the aegis of the United Nations. . . . President Roosevelt was immutably convinced that he, and he alone, could bring about this unlikely miracle."[29]

In a series of allied summits—Teheran in 1943 and Yalta and Potsdam in 1945—the allied leaders attempted to coordinate their military operations and negotiate on the terms of the settlement, including territorial issues, the treatment of Germany, and the shape of a postwar international peacekeeping organization. Roosevelt's goal up until Yalta was to maneuver the allied victors into a great-power peacekeeping organization. Britain and China would join Russia and the United States, and they would enforce the peace on the basis of regional responsibilities.[30] FDR's idea rested on the ability to maintain cooperation among the great powers. This became an immediate casualty of the end of the war. As the world war turned into Cold War, the two postwar settlements began to take shape. Yet even as the prospects of cooperation with the Soviet Union faded, the American agenda of promoting stable economic openness—enshrined in the Atlantic Charter—remained at the center of postwar order building. After 1947, it was an agenda pursued more narrowly among the Western democracies, and involved more direct American involvement and elaborate institutional strategies.

COMPETING AMERICAN VISIONS OF POSTWAR ORDER

During and immediately after the war, American officials and policy experts advanced and debated a wide range of ideas about postwar order. As the war ended, some of these ideas found their way into policy and others disappeared. Domestic opposition, European weakness and resistance, and rising tensions with the Soviet Union all exerted an impact on the viability of particular grand designs. The result was a sort of "rolling process" whereby different policy ideas gained ascendancy and lost support, and different coalitions of policy thinkers and bureaucrats formed and reformed around postwar policies. In the end, the United States embraced a postwar policy orientation committed to economic openness and pluralistic democracy among the Western great powers and Japan, reinforced by a range of international and regional institutions across the areas of economic and security relations. The shifts in American policy reveal the ways in which the United States attempted to foster both a postwar order that would lock the other major industrial states into an open order and also

[29] Wheeler-Bennett and Nicholls, *The Semblance of Peace*, p. 296.

[30] See John Lamberton Harper, *American Visions of Europe: Franklin D. Roosevelt, George F. Kennan and Dean G. Acheson* (New York: Cambridge University Press, 1994), chapter three.

one that was mutually acceptable to them. This involved agreeing to insert itself into elaborate intergovernmental institutions and relationships, including a binding security commitment.

Groups advocating six kinds of grand design competed for primacy as the United States grappled with postwar order. One group of advocates articulated ambitious ideas and plans for what might be called "global governance." These were proposals that supported the creation of governing institutions that would be supranational and universal. Some proposals were advanced by scientists and other activists who sought international control of atomic weapons and new global security institutions.[31] Others were seeking new forms of global governance to deal with industrial modernism and rising economic interdependence. Nation-states, they believed, were no longer capable of dealing with the technological and economic scale and scope of the modern world. Peace and prosperity could only be ensured by the creation of a global political order where governments shared sovereignty with some sort of new world state.[32] Prominent "one worlders" such as Albert Einstein, Cord Meyer, Norman Cousins, and Emery Reeves, put forward passionately felt hopes and visions of a great leap forward toward world government.[33] These groups and ideas existed mostly outside of the American government, remaining peripheral to the actual politics and planning of the postwar settlement, although the founding of the United Nations was seen by some as a partial achievement.

A second school of postwar thought was concerned with the creation of an open trading system. The most forceful advocates of this position came from the Department of State and its secretary, Cordell Hull. Throughout the Roosevelt presidency, Hull and other State Department officials consistently held the conviction that an open international trading system was central to American economic and security interests and was also fundamental to the maintenance of peace. Hull believed that bilateralism and economic blocs of the 1930s, practiced by Germany and Japan but also Britain, were the root cause of the instability of the period and the onset

[31] See Alice K. Smith, *A Peril and a Hope: The Scientists' Movement in America, 1945–47* (Chicago: University of Chicago Press, 1965).

[32] A variety of popular books were published in the mid-1940s that sketched indictments of the nation-state and visions of new global governance. See, for example, Wendell L. Willkie, *One World* (New York: Simon and Schuster, 1947); Emery Reeves, *The Anatomy of Peace* (New York: Harper and Row, 1945); Cord Meyer, Jr., *Peace or Anarchy* (Boston: Little, Brown, 1947); and Harris Wofford, Jr., *It's Up to Us: Federal World Government in Our Time* (New York: Harcourt, Brace, 1946).

[33] For an overview of these ideas and personalities, see Welsey T. Wooley, *Alternatives to Anarchy: American Supranationism since World War II* (Bloomington: University of Indiana Press, 1988).

of war.[34] Charged with responsibility for commercial policy, the State Department championed tariff reduction agreements, most prominently in the 1934 Reciprocal Trade Agreement Act and the 1938 U.S.-British trade agreement. Trade officials at the State Department saw liberal trade as a core American interest that reached back to the Open Door policy of the 1890s.[35] In the early years of the war, this liberal economic vision dominated initial American thinking about the future world order and became the initial opening position as the United States engaged Britain over the postwar settlement. As America emerged from the war with the largest and most competitive economy, an open economic order would serve its interests. An open system was also seen as an essential element of a stable world political order; it would discourage ruinous economic competition and protectionism that was a source of depression and war. But just as importantly, this vision of openness—a sort of "economic one worldism"—would lead to an international order in which American "hands on" management would be modest. The system would, in effect, govern itself.

A third American position on postwar order was primarily concerned with creating political order among the democracies of the North Atlantic region. The vision was of a community or union between the United States, Britain, and the wider Atlantic world. Ideas of an Atlantic union can be traced to the turn of the century and a few British and American statesmen and thinkers, such as Secretary of State John Hay, the British ambassador to Washington Lord Bryce, the American ambassador to London Walter Hines Page, Admiral Alfred T. Mahan, and writer Henry Adams. These writers and political figures all grasped the unusual character and significance of Anglo-American comity, and they embraced a vision of closer transatlantic ties.[36] These ideas were repeatedly articulated over the follow-

[34] As Secretary Hull argued, "unhampered trade dovetailed with peace; high tariffs, trade barriers, and unfair economic competition, with war." Hull, *The Memoirs of Cordell Hull* (New York: Macmillan, 1948), Vol. 1, p. 81.

[35] Herbert Feis, the State Department's economic advisor, noted the continuity of the department's position when he argued during the war that "the extension of the Open Door remains a sound American aim." See Feis, "Economics and Peace," *Foreign Policy Reports*, Vol. 30, No. 2 (April 1944), pp. 14–19. On the State Department's commitment to a postwar open trading system, see Lloyd Gardner, *Economic Aspects of New Deal Diplomacy* (Madison: University of Wisconsin Press, 1964); Richard Gardner, *Sterling-Dollar Diplomacy: The Origins and the Prospects of Our International Economic Order* (New York: McGraw Hill, 1969); and Alfred E. Eckes, Jr., *Opening America's Market: U.S. Foreign Policy since 1776* (Chapel Hill: University of North Carolina Press, 1995), chapter five.

[36] See James Robert Huntley, *Uniting the Democracies: Institutions of the Emerging Atlantic-Pacific System* (New York: New York University Press, 1980), p. 4. For discussion of the historical and intellectual foundations of the Atlantic system, see Forrest Davis, *The Atlantic System: The Story of Anglo-American Control of the Seas* (New York: Reynal and Hitchcock, 1941); Robert Strausz-Hupe, James E. Dougherty, and William R. Kintner, *Building the Atlantic*

ing decades. During World War II, Walter Lippmann gave voice to this view, that the "Atlantic Ocean is not the frontier between Europe and the Americas. It is the inland sea of a community of nations allied with one another by geography, history, and vital necessity."[37]

Various experiences and interests fed into the Atlantic idea. One was strategic and articulated during and after the two world wars. Suspicious of Woodrow Wilson's League of Nations proposal, French Premier Georges Clemenceau proposed in 1919 an alliance between France, Britain, and the United States—an alliance only among what he called "constitutional" countries.[38] The failure of the League of Nations reaffirmed in the minds of many Americans and Europeans the virtues of a less universal security community that encompassed the North Atlantic area. Others focused on the protection of the shared democratic values that united the Atlantic world. These ideas were most famously expressed in Clarence Streit's 1939 book, *Union Now: The Proposal for Inter-Democracy Federal Union*.[39] Concerned with the rise of fascism and militarism and the fragility of the Western democracies in the wake of a failed League of Nations, Streit proposed a federal union of the North Atlantic democracies.[40] In the years that followed, a fledgling Atlantic Union movement came to life. An Atlantic Union Committee was organized after the war, and prominent Americans called for the creation of various sorts of Atlantic organizations and structures.[41] American and European officials were willing to endorse principles

---

World (New York: Harper and Row, 1963); and Harold van B. Cleveland, *The Atlantic Idea and Its European Rivals* (New York: McGraw-Hill, 1966).

[37] Walter Lippmann, *U.S. Foreign Policy: Shield of the Republic* (Boston: Little, Brown, 1943), p. 83. It is thought that this was the first appearance in print of the term "Atlantic Community." For a discussion see Ronald Steel, *Walter Lippmann and the American Century* (Boston: Little, Brown, 1980), pp. 404–8.

[38] As noted in Chapter Five, the French proposal was to transform the League of Nations into a North Atlantic treaty organization—a union complete with an international army and a general staff. See Thomas J. Knock, *To End All Wars: Woodrow Wilson and the Quest for a New World Order* (New York: Oxford University Press, 1992), pp. 221–22.

[39] Streit, *Union Now: The Proposal for Inter-Democracy Federal Union* (New York: Harper and Brothers, 1939).

[40] It would be a "union of these few peoples in a great federal republic built on and for the thing they share most, their common democratic principle of government for the sake of individual freedom." Ibid., p. 4.

[41] The most ambitious plans of Atlantic Union, which attracted some of the same supporters as the world federalists, were widely debated during and after the war, but faded soon thereafter. The Atlantic Union committee survived and culminated in an eminent citizens' meeting in Paris in 1962. This gathering issued a "Declaration of Paris," which called for the drafting of blueprints for a true Atlantic Community. But American and European governments failed to respond. See Huntley, *Uniting the Democracies*, pp. 9–10; and Wooley, *Alternatives to Anarchy*, chapters five and six.

of Atlantic community and unity—most explicitly in the 1941 Atlantic Charter—but they were less interested in supranational organization.[42]

A fourth position on postwar order was animated more directly by considerations of American geopolitical interests and the Eurasian rimlands. This is where American strategic thinkers began their debates in the 1930s, as they witnessed the collapse of the world economy and the emergence of German and Japanese regional blocs. The question these thinkers pondered was whether the United States could remain as a great industrial power within the confines of the Western Hemisphere. What were the minimum geographical requirements for the country's economic and military viability? For all practical purposes, this question was answered by the time the United States entered the war. An American hemispheric bloc would not be sufficient; the United States must have security of markets and raw materials in Asia and Europe. The culmination of this debate and the most forceful statement of the new consensus was presented in Nicholas John Spykman's *America's Strategy in World Politics*.[43] If the rimlands of Europe and Asia became dominated by one or several hostile imperial powers, the security implications for the United States would be catastrophic. To remain a great power, the United States could not allow itself "merely to be a buffer state between the mighty empires of Germany and Japan."[44] It must seek openness, access, and balance in Europe and Asia. A similar conclusion was reached by experts involved in a Council on Foreign Relations study group, whose concern was the necessary size of the "grand area"—that is, the core world regions on which the United States depended for economic viability.[45]

[42] Although the supranational ideas of the Atlantic Union movement were largely ignored, they did inspire thinking about European Union. In 1940, Emmanuel Monick, a financial attaché in the French embassy in London, was struck by Streit's Atlantic Union ideas and proposed the idea of a French-British indissolvable union to Jean Monnet—an idea that was later presented to the French cabinet. See Huntley, *Uniting the Democracies*, p. 11. See also Jean Monnet, *Memoirs*, English translation (Garden City, N.Y.: Doubleday, 1978), pp. 17–35.

[43] Spykman, *America's Strategy in World Politics: The United States and the Balance of Power* (New York: Harcourt, Brace, 1942). See also a shorter book published after Spykman's death, *The Geography of the Peace* (New York: Harcourt, Brace, 1944). Others making similar arguments include William T. R. Fox, *The Super-Powers: The United States, Britain, and the Soviet Union—Their Responsibility for Peace* (New York: Harcourt, Brace, 1944), and Robert Strausz-Hupe, *The Balance of Tomorrow: Power and Foreign Policy in the United States* (Philadelphia: University of Pennsylvania Press, 1945).

[44] Spykman, *America's Strategy in World Politics*, p. 195.

[45] See Council on Foreign Relations, "Methods of Economic Collaboration: The Role of the Grand Area in American Foreign Economic Policy," in *Studies of American Interests in the War and Peace*, 24 July 1941, E–B34 (New York: Council on Foreign Relations). For a history of the CFR postwar planning studies, see Carlo Maria Santoro, *Diffidence and Ambition: The*

This view that America must have access to Asian and European markets and resources—and must therefore not let a prospective adversary control the Eurasian landmass—was also embraced by postwar defense planners. As the war was coming to an end, defense officials began to see that America's security interests required the building of an elaborate system of forward bases in Asia and Europe. Hemispheric defense would be inadequate.[46] Defense officials also saw access to Asian and European raw materials—and the prevention of their control by a prospective enemy— as an American security interest. The historian Melvin Leffler notes that "Stimson, Patterson, McCloy, and Assistant Secretary Howard C. Peterson agreed with Forrestal that long-term American prosperity required open markets, unhindered access to raw materials, and the rehabilitation of much—if not all—of Eurasia along liberal capitalist lines."[47] Indeed, the base systems were partly justified in terms of their impact on access to raw materials and the denial for such resources to an adversary. Some defense studies went further, and argued that postwar threats to Eurasian access and openness were more social and economic than military. It was economic turmoil and political upheaval that were the real threats to American security, as they invited the subversion of liberal democratic societies and Western-oriented governments. A CIA study concluded in mid-1947: "The greatest danger to the security of the United States is the possibility of economic collapse in Western Europe and the consequent accession to power of Communist elements."[48] Access to resources and markets, socioeconomic stability, political pluralism, and American security interests were all tied together.

A fifth view of postwar order also was concerned with encouraging political and economic unity in Western Europe—a "third force." This view emerged as a strategic option as wartime cooperation with the Soviet Union began to break down after the war. In 1946 and 1947, the world increasingly began to look as if it would become bipolar. "One world" designs for peace and economic order became less relevant.[49] As officials in

---

Intellectual Sources of U.S. Foreign Policy (Boulder, Colo.: Westview, 1992); and Williams, *Failed Imagination?*, pp. 92–95.

[46] See Melvyn P. Leffler, "The American Conception of National Security and the Beginning of the Cold War, 1945–48," *American Historical Review*, Vol. 89, No. 2 (April 1984), pp. 349–56. See also his *A Preponderance of Power*, chapter two.

[47] Leffler, "The American Conception of National Security," p. 358.

[48] CIA, "Review of the World Situation as It Relates to the Security of the United States," September 26, 1947. Quoted in Leffler, "The American Conception of National Security," p. 364.

[49] Burton Berry, a career Foreign Service officer, noted in 1947 that it was time to "drop the pretense of one world." Quoted in John Lewis Gaddis, "Spheres of Influence: The United States and Europe, 1945–1949," in Gaddis, *The Long Peace: Inquiries into the History of the Cold War* (New York: Oxford University Press, 1987), p. 57.

the State Department began to rethink relations with Western Europe and the Soviet Union, a new policy emphasis emerged, one concerned with the establishment of a strong and economically integrated Europe. The idea was to encourage a multipolar postwar system, with Europe as a relatively independent center of power, in which Germany was integrated into a wider unified Europe.

This new policy was advanced by several groups within the State Department. The emphasis on building centers of power in Europe was a view George Kennan had long held, and it was articulated most consistently by his Policy Planning staff. "It should be the cardinal point of our policy," Kennan argued in October 1947, "to see to it that other elements of independent power are developed on the Eurasian land mass as rapidly as possible in order to take off our shoulders some of the burden of 'bi-polarity.' "[50] Kennan's staff presented its first recommendations to Secretary of State George Marshall on 23 May 1947. Their emphasis was not on the direct threat of Soviet activities in Western Europe but on the war-ravaged economic, political, and social institutions of Europe that made communist inroads possible. An American effort to aid Europe "should be directed not to combatting communism as such, but to the restoration of the economic health and vigor of European society."[51] In a later memorandum, the Policy Planning staff argued that the program should take the form of a multilateral clearing system to lead to the reduction of tariffs and trade barriers and eventually to take the form of a European Customs Union.[52] Moreover, the Policy Planning staff argued that the initiatives and responsibility for the program should come from the Europeans themselves. This group clearly envisaged a united and economically integrated Europe standing on its own apart from the Soviet sphere and the United States. "By insisting

[50] Kennan to Cecil B. Lyon, 13 October 1947, Policy Planning Staff Records. Quoted in Gaddis, "Spheres of Influence," p. 58. In Kennan's view, the arguments in favor of a multipolar—rather than bipolar—order were several. Multiple power centers were more likely to endure over the long term than the centers of power in a bipolar system, and this was important because containment would need to be a protracted exercise, and the willingness of the American people to sustain American leadership of a bipolar balance was uncertain. Moreover, a multipolar order was more likely to protect the values and institutions of the Western countries; it played to the strength of these countries. See John Lewis Gaddis, *Strategies of Containment*, esp. p. 42. See also Steve Weber, "Shaping the Postwar Balance of Power: Multilateralism in NATO," in John G. Ruggie, ed., *Multilateralism Matters: The Theory and Praxis of an Institutional Form* (New York: Columbia University Press, 1993), pp. 240–42.

[51] "The Director of the Policy Planning Staff [Kennan] to the Under Secretary of State [Acheson]," 23 May 1947, *Foreign Relations of the United States*, 1947, Vol. 3, p. 225. Kennan quotes the memorandum in his memoirs. George Kennan, *Memoirs: 1925–1950* (Boston: Little, Brown, 1967), p. 336.

[52] Ernst H. Van Der Beugel, *From Marshall Plan to Atlantic Partnership* (Amsterdam: Elsevier, 1966), p. 43.

on a joint approach," Kennan later wrote, "we hope to force the Europeans to think like Europeans, and not like nationalists, in this approach to the economic problems of the continent."[53]

A unified Europe was also seen by American officials as the best mechanism for containing the revival of German militarism. Kennan held this view, arguing in a 1949 paper that "we see no answer to German problem within sovereign national framework. Continuation of historical process within this framework will almost inevitably lead to repetition of post-Versailles sequence of developments. . . . Only answer is some form of European union which would give young Germans wider horizon."[54] As early as 1947, John Foster Dulles was arguing that economic unification of Europe would generate "economic forces operating upon Germans" that were "centrifugal and not centripetal"—"natural forces which will turn the inhabitants of Germany's state toward their outer neighbors" in a cooperative direction. Through an integrated European economy, including the internationalization of the Ruhr valley, Germany "could not again make war even if it wanted to."[55] Likewise, the American high commissioner for Germany, John McCloy, argued that a "united Europe" would be an "imaginative and creative policy" that would "link Western Germany more firmly into the West and make the Germans believe their destiny lies this way."[56] If Germany was to be bound to Europe, Europe itself would need to be sufficiently unified and integrated to serve as an anchor.

Encouraging European unity also appealed to State Department officials who were working directly on European recovery. In their view, the best way to get Europe back on its feet was through encouraging a strong and economically integrated Europe. The goal was also to increase the Western orientation of European leaders and to prevent a drift to the Left or the Right. This could be done not just by ensuring economic recovery but also by creating political objectives to fill the postwar ideological and moral

---

[53] Kennan, *Memoirs: 1925–1950*, p. 337. In a summary of his views at the time, "Mr. Kennan pointed out the necessity of European acknowledgement of responsibility and parentage in the plan to prevent the certain attempts of powerful elements to place the entire burden on the U.S. and to discredit it and us by blaming the U.S. for all failures." "Summary of Discussion on Problems of Relief, Rehabilitation and Reconstruction of Europe," 29 May 1947, *Foreign Relations of the United States*, 1947, Vol. 3, p. 235.

[54] "Question of European Union," Policy Planning staff paper quoted in Klaus Schwabe, "The United States and European Integration: 1947–1957," in Clemens Wurm, ed., *Western Europe and Germany, 1945–1960* (New York: Oxford University Press, 1995), p. 133.

[55] Ronald W. Pruessen, *John Foster Dulles: The Road to Power* (New York: Free Press, 1982), chapter 12.

[56] Thomas A. Schwartz, *America's Germany: John J. McCloy and the Federal Republic of Germany* (Cambridge: Harvard University Press, 1991), p. 95. See "A Summary Record of a Meeting of Ambassadors at Rome," 22–24 March 1950, *Foreign Relations of the United States*, 1950, Vol. 3, p. 817.

vacuum. As one May 1947 document argued, "the only possible ideological content of such a program was European unity."[57] Other officials who were concerned primarily with a postwar open trading system were alarmed by the economic distress in Europe and saw American aid and European unity as necessary steps to bring Western Europe back into a stable and open system.[58] These views helped push the Truman administration to announce the Marshall Plan of massive American aid. The plan itself would be administered in a way to promote European unity.[59] The idea of a united Europe was to provide the ideological bulwark for European political and economic construction. But disputes between the British and French over the extensiveness of supranational political authority and economic integration as well as European unwillingness to establish an independent security order left the early proposals for a European "third force" unfulfilled.

A final postwar view was of a full-blown Western alliance aimed at the bipolar balancing of the Soviet Union. By 1947, the world was beginning to look very different from the way most officials had envisaged in their postwar planning.[60] Although many American officials foresaw a decline of Allied unity after the war, few anticipated (much less desired) a hostile bipolar standoff and a formal and permanent American security alliance with Western Europe. This strategy emerged reluctantly in response to the Soviet takeover of Eastern Europe and the persistent efforts of Europe-

[57] Quoted in Beugel, *From Marshall Plan to Atlantic Partnership*, p. 45.

[58] See "The European Situation," Memorandum by the Under Secretary of State for Economic Affairs, *Foreign Relations of the United States*, 1947, Vol. 3, pp. 230–32. For a discussion, see Richard Holt, *The Reluctant Superpower: A History of America's Global Economic Reach* (New York: Kodansha International, 1995), pp. 126–31.

[59] For the argument that European cooperation and unity—perhaps even an "economic federation"—was an integral part of the European Recovery Program, see "Summary of Discussion on Problems on Relief, Rehabilitation and Reconstruction of Europe," 29 May 1947, *Foreign Relations of the United States*, 1947, Vol. 3, p. 235. See also Michael Hogan, "European Integration and the Marshall Plan," in Stanley Hoffman and Charles Maier, eds., *The Marshall Plan: A Retrospective* (Boulder, Col.: Westview, 1984); Hogan, *The Marshall Plan: America, Britain, and the Reconstruction of Western Europe, 1947–1952* (New York: Cambridge University Press, 1987); and Armin Rappaport, "The United States and European Integration: The First Phase," *Diplomatic History*, Vol. 5 (Spring 1981), pp. 121–49.

[60] Reflecting this circumstance, State Department official Charles Bohlen wrote in August 1947: "The United States is confronted with a condition in the world which is at direct variance with the assumption upon which, during and directly after the war, major United States policies were predicted. Instead of unity among the great powers—both political and economic—after the war, there is complete disunity between the Soviet Union and the satellites on one side and the rest of the world on the other. There are, in short, two worlds instead of one. Faced with this disagreeable fact, however much we may deplore it, the United States in the interest of its own well-being and security and those of the free non-Soviet world must reexamine its major policy objectives." "Memorandum by the Consular of the Department of State [Bohlen]," 30 August 1947, *Foreign Relations of the United States*, 1947, Vol. 1, pp. 763–64.

ans to draw the United States into an ongoing European defense commitment. European reluctance to become an independent "third force" was reinforced by threatening developments in the East, such as the February 1948 Czechoslovak coup. American policy continued to be one of reaction and reluctance as Europeans sought a closer security relationship with the United States.[61] It was not until the Berlin crisis in June 1948 that American officials began to favor some sort of loose defense association with Western Europe. The Western Union formally requested negotiations with the United States on a North Atlantic treaty in October 1948.

This wide range of views makes it clear that the architects of the postwar settlement were trying to build more than one type of order. Several conclusions follow. First, there was a range of order-building ideas that predated the rise of bipolarity and containment. This helps explain the "layer cake" of institutions that eventually emerged. In fact, it is remarkable how late and reluctant the United States was in organizing its foreign policy around a global balance of power. As late as 1947, the State Department's Policy Planning staff did not see the Soviet Union as a direct security threat to Europe or the United States—nor did they see "communist activities as the root of the difficulties in western Europe." The crisis in Europe was fundamentally a result of the "disruptive effects of the war" on the economic, political, and social structures of Europe.[62]

Second, the ideas that were advanced and debated before the breakdown of relations with the Soviet Union dealt primarily with the reconstructions of relations within the West, particularly among the Atlantic countries. Some postwar designs were more universal, such as those concerning free trade and global governance, but they also were to be anchored in a deepened set of relations and institutions among the Western democracies. Other ideas, such as the geopolitical arguments about access to the Eurasian rimlands, saw the stability and integration of the liberal capitalist world in essentially instrumental terms. But the goals and policies would have the same result. Likewise, many of those who eventually supported NATO and containment did so not simply to build an alliance against the Soviet Union but also because these initiatives would feed back into the Western liberal democratic order.

[61] Some officials in the Truman administration, such as Director of the Office of European Affairs, John D. Hickerson, were urging military cooperation with Western Europe. See "Memorandum by the Director of the Office of European Affairs [Hickerson] to the Secretary of State,19 January 1948, *Foreign Relations of the United States*, 1948, Vol. 3, p. 6–7. Others, such as George Kennan, resisted the idea of military union, arguing that it would be destructive of the administration's goal of European unity. See "Memorandum by the Director of the Policy Planning Staff [Kennan] to the Secretary of State," 20 January 1948, *Foreign Relations of the United States*, 1948, Vol. 3, pp. 7–8. See also Kennan, *Memoirs: 1925–1950*, pp. 397–406.

[62] "The Director of the Policy Planning Staff [Kennan] to the Under Secretary of State [Acheson]," 23 May 1947, *Foreign Relations of the United States*, 1947, Vol. 3, p. 224–45.

Third, even many of the advocates of containment and the preservation of the European balance were also concerned with safeguarding and strengthening liberal democratic institutions in the West. One virtue that Kennan saw in a multipolar postwar order was that it would help to protect the liberal character of American politics and institutions. Kennan worried that if a bipolar order emerged, the United States might find itself trying to impose political institutions on other states within its sphere, and that would eventually threaten its domestic institutions.[63] The encouragement of dispersed authority and power centers abroad would reinforce pluralism at home.[64]

Despite their different aims, most of the many designs for postwar order converged on the centrality of establishing an open and plural Western order. To some this was an end in itself, and to others in was a means to wider goals—goals of global multilateral governance on the one hand or bipolar balance on the other. Each grand design needed a stable and open core of industrial democracies. American officials maneuvered to lock in such an order, but to do so in a way that would be acceptable to the Europeans. To do this entailed a reluctant American movement toward a more managed economic order and a more formal and binding security commitment.

FROM FREE TRADE TO MANAGED OPENNESS

After the United States joined the war, State Department postwar planners focused most intently on economic relations and articulated an overriding goal: the reestablishment of a multilateral system of free trade. But American policy evolved from the Atlantic Charter to the Bretton Woods conference and then to the actual postwar arrangements, as the United States maneuvered to find agreement with Britain and other European countries and cope with unfolding economic and political disarray. The Europeans were less interested in securing an open postwar economy than in providing safeguards and protections against postwar economic dislocations and unemployment. The United States eventually moved toward a compromise settlement. Rather than a simple system of free trade, the industrial countries would establish a managed order organized around a set of multilateral institutions and a "social bargain" that sought to balance openness with domestic welfare and stability.

---

[63] See discussion of a Kennan speech at the Naval War College in October 1948 in Gaddis, *Strategies of Containment*, pp. 43–44. See also Weber, "Shaping the Postwar Balance of Power," p. 241.

[64] Kennan also worried that a permanent military alliance with Europe would turn the United States into a dominating imperial power that would provoke resistance by the Europeans and the American public. See David Calleo, *Beyond American Hegemony: The Future of the*

American official thinking was that economic openness, which would ideally take the form of a system of nondiscriminatory trade and investment, was an essential element of a stable and peaceful world political order. One argument was simply that openness was necessary for sustained economic growth, which in turn was a precondition of peace. "Prosperous neighbors are the best neighbors," remarked Treasury official Harry Dexter White.[65] This was a reflection of the Cobdenite philosophy: that trade protection and tariffs were linked to political conflict and, ultimately, war. The more general argument was made by State Department officials under the sway of Cordell Hull, who saw a postwar world of blocs—and even less self-contained spheres of influence—as inconsistent with political stability. As such, State Department officials were as concerned with British aims in the European postwar settlement as with Soviet foreign policy. In July 1945, a State Department document warned that a spheres-of-influence settlement in Europe would "represent power politics pure and simple, with all the concomitant disadvantages. . . . Our primary objective should be to remove the *causes* which make nations feel that such spheres are necessary to build their security, rather than to assist one country to build up strength against another."[66]

But American officials were also convinced that the country's economic and security interests demanded economic openness; it was an essential element of political pluralism and the dispersion of power in Asia and Europe. Military planners were increasingly of this view as the war was coming to an end. The American embassy in Paris reported in 1944 that "General Eisenhower . . . does not believe that it would be in our interests to have the continent of Europe dominated by a single power, for then we would have a super-powerful Europe, a somewhat shaken British Empire and ourselves."[67] Such a view was also held in regard to Asia.[68]

American Alliance (New York: Basic Books, 1987), pp 28–39; and John Lewis Gaddis, *We Now Know: Rethinking Cold War History* (New York: Oxford University Press, 1997), p. 200.

[65] Eckes, *A Search for Solvency*, p. 52.

[66] Potsdam Briefing Paper, "British Plans for a Western European Bloc," 4 July 1945, *Foreign Relations of the United States: The Conference of Berlin (The Potsdam Conference)*, 1945, Vol. 1, pp. 262–63. For a discussion of American opposition to a spheres of influence settlement, see John Lewis Gaddis, "Spheres of Influence: The United States and Europe, 1945–1949"; and Trachtenberg, *A Constructed Peace*, chapter one.

[67] "The American Representative to the French Committee of National Liberation at Paris (Caffery) to the Secretary of State," 20 October 1944, *Foreign Relations of the United States*, 1944, Vol. 3, p. 743. See John Lewis Gaddis, "The Insecurities of Victory: The United States and the Perception of the Soviet Threat after World War II," in Michael J. Lacey, ed., *The Truman Presidency* (New York: Cambridge University Press, 1989), pp. 240–41.

[68] See Bruce Cumings, "Japan's Position in the World System," in Andrew Gordon, ed., *Postwar Japan as History* (Berkeley and Los Angeles: University of California Press, 1993), pp. 34–63.

The idea of open markets was something that liberal visionaries and hard-nosed geopolitical strategists could agree upon. It united American postwar planners, and it was the seminal idea that informed the work of the 1944 Bretton Woods conference on postwar economic cooperation.[69] In his farewell remarks to the conference, Secretary of the Treasury Henry Morgenthau asserted that the agreements reached marked the end of economic nationalism, by which he meant not that countries would give up pursuit of their national interest but that trade blocs and economic spheres of influence would not be the vehicles for doing so.

American ideas for a multilateral free trade order had few enthusiastic proponents in Britain or continental Europe. As David Watt has pointed out, "Whatever the underlying realities of power, Britain and France started from the assumption that their own pre-war spheres of influence would be maintained or restored to them. . . . These ambitions did not fit in very easily to a framework of American tutelage or dominance."[70] Beyond the desire to retain their imperial holdings, the Europeans also worried about postwar depression and the protection of their fragile economies. This made them weary of America's stark proposals for an open world trading system and favor instead a more regulated and compensatory system.[71]

In Britain, the debate over the postwar economic order centered on the future of the imperial preference system, and the political establishment was divided.[72] The core of the Conservative party favored the maintenance of empire; the Ottawa preference system was part of these special relations. "A section of the Conservative Party," E. F. Penrose points out, "valued the system of preferential duties on Empire goods as a force making for solidarity within the British Commonwealth of Nations."[73] Other conservatives, including Churchill, were more sympathetic to free trade and sup-

[69] This argument is made in Robert A. Pollard, *Economic Security and the Origins of the Cold War, 1945–1950* (New York: Columbia University Press, 1985).

[70] David Watt, "Perceptions of the United States in Europe, 1945–83," in Lawrence Freedman, ed., *The Troubled Alliance: Atlantic Relations in the 1980s* (New York: St. Martin's, 1983), pp. 29–30.

[71] On Anglo-American disagreements over the nature of the postwar order, see Randall Bennett Woods, *A Changing of the Guard: Anglo-American Relations, 1941–1946* (Chapel Hill: University of North Carolina Press, 1990). The strongest claims about American and European differences over postwar political economy are made by Fred Block, *The Origins of International Economic Disorder* (Berkeley and Los Angeles: University of California Press, 1977), pp. 70–122.

[72] On the general schools of thought among British foreign policy elites, see D. Cameron Watt, *Succeeding John Bull: America in Britain's Pace, 1900–1975* (Cambridge: Cambridge University Press, 1984), pp. 16–17.

[73] E. F. Penrose, *Economic Planning for the Peace* (Princeton: Princeton University Press, 1953), p. 19.

ported the preference system primarily to maintain unity within the conservative coalition. Labor politicians were more inclined to favor the preference system as a way to protect Britain's employment and balance of payments after the war, particularly if the international economy fell into recession. Turning away from multilateral open trade would mean relying on trade restriction and currency controls, perhaps splitting the world into blocs, but the British economy would be protected from the worst ills of trade competition and deflation. Still other officials realized that the imperial preference system and bilateral trade were not sustainable over the long term but wanted to use the Ottawa agreement to strike a better bargain with the United States.[74]

British and American differences came into focus in the summer of 1941, when the celebrated economist John Maynard Keynes, working for the British Treasury, traveled to Washington, D.C., to begin negotiations over postwar economic plans. These negotiations were triggered by disagreements over Article 7 of the Lend-Lease agreement, which set forth the terms for postwar settlement of mutual aid obligations. The article stipulated that neither country would seek to restrict trade, and both would take measures to reduce trade barriers and eliminate preferential duties. American politicians wanted to make sure, after helping to ensure Britain's survival, that its businesses would not be shut out of British commonwealth markets. State Department officials presented their ideas on postwar free trade, and Keynes resisted. As the State Department reports: "He said that he did not see how the British could make such a commitment in good faith, that it would require an imperial conference and that it saddled upon the future an ironclad formula from the Nineteenth Century. He said that it contemplated the impossible and hopeless task of returning to a gold standard where international trade was controlled by mechanical monetary devices and which had proved completely futile."[75] The discussions revealed sharply different views on the virtues of an open trading system. The State Department saw it as an absolute necessity and a matter of principle, while Keynes and his colleagues considered it an attempt to rebuild what they considered a harmful and long out-of-date laissez-faire trade system—or what Keynes called "the lunatic proposals of Mr. Hull."[76]

Movement toward a compromise came only later, after Keynes shifted to negotiations with American Treasury officials over postwar monetary order

[74] This was the position of most officials at the British Foreign Office and the Treasury. See the Foreign Office report "Note on Post-War Anglo-American Economic Relations," 15 October 1941 (Kew, Great Britain: Public Records Office, Foreign Office Files, Political Correspondence), FO371/28907.

[75] "Memorandum of Understanding, by the Assistant Secretary of State [Acheson]," July 28, 1941, *Foreign Relations of the United States*, 1941, Vol. 3, pp. 11–12.

[76] R. F. Harrod, *The Life of John Maynard Keynes* (London: Macmillan, 1951), p. 512.

and discovered a more tractable set of issues.[77] Keynes came to the view that perhaps an agreement could be reached with the United States for a monetary order that would be expansionary—an order that could keep the trading system open but safeguard against depression.[78] What followed was a flurry of monetary planning in both Britain and the United States, with Harry Dexter White leading American planning. Both British and American plans sought to eliminate exchange controls and restrictive financial practices, and to provide rules for alterations in rates of exchange. The Keynes plan was more ambitious, and included provisions for a new international currency and obligations on surplus countries to mobilize credit to correct maladjustments. The White plan restricted the obligations of creditor countries and proposed more modest resources for the purpose of responding to payment crises.[79] The two plans provided the framework of negotiations throughout 1943 and up to the Bretton Woods conference in July 1944. Many of the compromises were in the direction of the American plan, most importantly in the limitation on creditor country liability; but the plans shared a vision of managed open economic order that would attempt to give governments the tools and resources to manage imbalances without resort to deflationary and high-unemployment policies.

The agreement between British and American monetary planners was particularly important because it served to transcend the stalemate over the postwar trade system. Once agreement was reached in this area, the State Department found its old-style trade proposals of secondary significance in the emerging postwar settlement. The "embedded liberal" ideas of the Anglo-American deal on monetary order paved the way for broader agreement on postwar relations among the industrial countries.[80]

The new Anglo-American monetary agreement also had a political resonance within the wider circles of British and American politics. The Bretton Woods agreements allowed political leaders to envisage a postwar economic order in which multiple and otherwise competing political

---

[77] This argument is made in G. John Ikenberry, "Creating Yesterday's New World Order: Keynesian 'New Thinking' and the Anglo-American Postwar Settlement," in Judith Goldstein and Robert O. Keohane, eds., *Ideas and Foreign Policy: Beliefs, Institutions, and Political Change* (Ithaca: Cornell University Press, 1993), pp. 57–86.

[78] Eckes, *Search for Solvency*, p. 65.

[79] The White plan is published in "Memorandum by the Secretary of the Treasury [Morgenthau] to President Roosevelt," 15 May 1942, *Foreign Relations of the United States, 1942*, Vol. 1, pp. 171–90.

[80] For a discussion of "embedded liberalism," see John G. Ruggie, "International Regimes, Transactions, and Change: Embedded Liberalism in the Postwar Economic Order," in Stephen D. Krasner, ed., *International Regimes* (Ithaca: Cornell University Press, 1983); and John G. Ruggie, "Embedded Liberalism Revisited: Institutions and Progress in International Economic Relations," in Emanuel Adler and Beverly Crawford, eds., *Progress in Postwar International Relations* (New York: Columbia University Press, 1991).

objectives could be combined. The alternatives of the past—of the nine-teenth century and of the interwar period—suggested options that were too politically stark. Outside the narrow transatlantic community of econo-mists and policy experts, politicians were looking for options that could steer a middle course.

This search for a middle course between bilateralism and laissez-faire was clearly on the minds of the British. In a conversation with John Foster Dulles (at the time a corporation lawyer in New York), Ambassador Lord Halifax cabled the British Foreign Office in October 1942:

> The most interesting point on the economic side of the discussion was Mr. Dulles' exposition of the Cordell Hull School of free trade, and the place which it had in the plans of the Administration. I said to him that I thought that we did not clearly understand what the significance of the Hull policies was. There was a feeling in some quarters here that we were faced with two alternatives, either we must revert to a completely 19th century system of laissez-faire, or else we must safeguard our balance of payments position by developing a bilat-eral system of trade with those countries whose natural markets we were. It seemed to me that neither of these courses would work, the first was clearly impossible, the second might be disastrous. I asked Mr. Dulles whether there might be some middle course which would take account of our special diffi-culties and which at the same time would satisfy Mr. Cordell Hull on the ques-tion of discrimination, preferences, etc.[81]

The Bretton Woods agreements were important because they served as a basis for building broader coalitions around a relatively open and managed order. It was a middle path that generated support from both the conserva-tive free traders and the new enthusiasts of economic planning. It was agreed that just lowering barriers to trade and capital movements was not enough. The leading industrial states must actively supervise and govern the system. Institutions, rules, and active involvement of governments were necessary. One lesson came from the 1930s: the fear of economic conta-gion, where unwise or untoward policies pursued by one country threat-ened the stability of others. As Roosevelt said at the opening of the Bretton Woods conference, "the economic health of every country is a proper mat-ter of concern to all its neighbors, near and far."[82] But the settlement also provided governments with the ability to deliver on the new promises of the welfare state, pursuing expansionary macroeconomic policies and pro-tecting social welfare.

---

[81] Dispatch from Ambassador Halifax to the Foreign Office, 21(?) October 1942, FO371/31513.

[82] Roosevelt, "Opening Message to the Bretton Woods Conference," 1 July 1944. Quoted in the *New York Times*, 2 July 1944, p. 14.

More generally, the emphasis on creating an order that provided economic stability and security was, as seen earlier, a central objective of American planners, whose main concern was with postwar security and a European "third force." Liberal free traders came to this view by recognizing the new necessity of a managed capitalist order that was organized in such a way as to give governments the ability to pursue economic growth and stability. Security officials came to this view by recognizing that the greatest security threats to Europe (and indirectly the United States) came from inside these societies, through economic crisis and political disarray.[83]

In seeking agreement over postwar economic relations, the United States moved in the direction of Britain and the Europeans. The British were instrumental in seeking out the parts of the American government that were most congenial with their aims. The result was a system that was more or less open, provided institutions to manage this openness, but also offered enough loopholes to allow governments to protect their weak economies.[84] The United States gained its agreement and the European gained commitments, mechanisms, and obligations institutionalized in the postwar order.

FROM "THIRD FORCE" TO SECURITY COMMITMENT

In 1947 and the following years, the United States appeared to hold the military and economic power needed to shape the terms of European reconstruction. With a monopoly on the atomic bomb, a massive (although demobilizing) standing army, and an industrial economy enlarged by the war, the United States appeared to have all the elements of hegemonic power. Moreover, the United States had what Europeans needed most: American dollars. "More and more as weeks succeed weeks," the *Economist* noted in May 1947, "the whole of European life is being overshadowed

---

[83] For a discussion of the domestic pressures for a stable postwar economy, see Robert Griffith, "Forging America's Postwar Order: Domestic Politics and Political Economy in the Age of Truman," in Michael J. Lacey, ed., *The Truman Presidency*, pp. 57–88. On the wide appeal of growth-oriented policies and institutions, and their role in facilitated agreement within the West, see Charles Maier, "The Politics of Productivity," in Peter J. Katzenstein, ed., *Between Power and Plenty: The Foreign Economic Policies of Advanced Industrial States* (Madison: University of Wisconsin Press, 1978). On the concern of defense officials in fostering economic security and stability in postwar Europe, see Melvyn P. Leffler, "The American Conception of National Security and the Beginnings of the Cold War, 1945–48."

[84] The eventual agreement on trade relations also had these features. As a British official noted in discussions over trade arrangements, "there must be in the international settlement which we are now devising sufficient escape clauses, let-outs, special arrangements, call them what you will, which will enable those countries which are adopting internal measures for full employment to protect themselves." Quoted in Richard Gardner, *Sterling-Dollar Diplomacy*, p. 277.

by the great dollar shortage. The margin between recovery and collapse throughout Western Europe is dependent at this moment upon massive imports from the U.S."[85]

It is all the more striking, therefore, how successful European governments were at blunting and redirecting American policy toward Europe. This resistance by Europe to the construction of a European third force had several sources and differed from country to country. Each sought to use American power—to make it predictable, to establish ongoing commitments—for its own national purposes. The same considerations that led to the rejection of a full-blown united Europe prompted these same governments to encourage a direct American political and security commitment to Europe.

The British were the most resistant to a united Europe, but reacted positively to the larger political objectives of Marshall Plan aid. A secret Cabinet session in March 1948 concluded that Britain "should use United States aid to gain time, but our ultimate aim should be to attain a position in which the countries of western Europe could be independent both of the United States and the Soviet Union."[86] Yet as a practical matter, the British resisted significant steps in that direction. In a meeting of American ambassadors in Europe in October 1949, Ambassador David Bruce argued: "We have been too tender with Britain since the war: she has been the constant stumbling block in the economic organization of Europe."[87]

The British were eager to maintain their special relationship with the United States. They feared that it would be undermined by the emergence of a confederation with European states. Moreover, the political and economic burdens of sustaining a European center of power would only further strain the British Commonwealth system. As with several of the other European countries, the British also feared the eventual dominance of Germany or even Russia in a unified Europe. These considerations implied the need for more, not less, American involvement in postwar Europe, particularly in the form of the NATO security relationship. As David Calleo notes: "NATO seemed an ideal solution. With American commanders and forces taking primary responsibility for European ground defense, no question would remain about America's willingness to come to Europe's aid. Britain would reserve for itself those military and naval commands needed to retain control over its own national defense."[88] Indeed, in 1952 the British sought to reduce the role of the Organization for European

[85] "Dollars for Europe?" *Economist*, 31 May 1947, p. 833.

[86] Quoted in Gaddis, "Spheres of Influence," p. 66.

[87] "Summary Record of a Meeting of United States Ambassadors at Paris," 21–22 October 1949, *Foreign Relations of the United States*, 1949, Vol. 4, p. 492. See Leffler, *Preponderance of Power*, p. 320.

[88] Calleo, *Beyond American Hegemony*, p. 35.

Economic Cooperation and transfer its functions to NATO—a clear attempt to build the Atlantic relationship at the expense of European unity.[89]

British officials were more concerned with preventing a return by the United States to an isolationist position than with an overbearing American hegemonic presence in Europe. "The fear was not of American expansionism," Gaddis notes, "but of American isolationism, and much time was spent considering how such expansionist tendencies could be reinforced."[90] Just as they had during World War I, the British and other Europeans gave encouraging responses to American ideas about postwar security cooperation and peacekeeping, as two historians argue, "if only because it would bind the United States to participate in world affairs as she had omitted to do in the years between the wars."[91] It is no surprise, therefore, that in encouraging the United States to lead a security protectorate of Europe, the British began to stress the seriousness of the Soviet threat in Europe. In January 1948, British Foreign Minister Ernest Bevin warned Washington of "the further encroachment of the Soviet tide" and the need to "reinforce the physical barriers which still guard Western civilization."[92]

The French also actively courted an American security guarantee. To be sure, many French were sympathetic to the goal of a more unified Europe. Integration was useful in fostering French influence across Europe, and a political and economic union would also allow France to have some influence over the revival of the German economy as well as tie Germany to a larger regional framework.[93] But the French insisted that the rehabilitation of western Germany would only be acceptable within a security framework that involved the United States. An American security tie, even more than a unified Europe, was needed to contain both the Germans and the Soviets. As in the British case, an American security guarantee would also free up some resources, otherwise tied to European defense, that could be used for preserving the remains of its colonial empire.[94] Connected to Europe, the United States would be more predictable and its resources more available.

Throughout the postwar years, European pressure for a durable American security tie was connected to the problem of postwar Germany. In

[89] Beloff, *The United States and the Unity of Europe*, p. 69.

[90] Gaddis, "The Emerging Post-Revisionist Synthesis on the Origins of the Cold War," *Diplomatic History*, Vol. 7, No. 3 (Summer 1983), pp. 171–90.

[91] Wheeler-Bennett and Nicholls, *The Semblance of Peace*, p. 89.

[92] "Summary of a Memorandum Representing Mr. Bevin's Views on the Formation of a Western Union," enclosed in Inverchapel to Marshall, 13 January 1948, *Foreign Relations of the United States*, 1948, Vol. 3, pp. 4–6.

[93] See Charles Maier, "Supranational Concepts and National Continuity in the Framework of the Marshall Plan," in Stanley Hoffman and Charles Maier, eds., *The Marshall Plan: A Retrospective* (Boulder, Colo.: Westview, 1984), pp. 29–37.

[94] Calleo, *Beyond American Hegemony*, p. 35. See also Michael M. Harrison, *The Reluctant Ally: France and Atlantic Security* (Baltimore: Johns Hopkins University Press, 1981).

frequent meetings of foreign ministers during 1946 and 1947, American and British officials were unable to bridge differences with the Soviet Union over the joint management of occupied Germany.[95] At the same time, the economic weakness in western Europe made the rebuilding and reintegration of western Germany—particularly the industrial and coal-rich Ruhr region—into Europe increasingly important to the economic revival and political stability of Europe.[96] Such a move was resisted, however, most vigorously by the French, who felt threatened by the possible resurgence in German power. By the London foreign ministers' meeting in December 1947, the breakdown of a unified approach to postwar Germany was complete, and the issue between the Americans and Europeans was turning to precisely how western Germany was to fit within the larger Western order. American officials took the lead in seeking the reintegration of the western German zones.[97] But at each step along the way, France and Britain attempted to exchange their acquiescence on western German reconstruction for a binding American security commitment. France initially tried to tie its agreement to merge its occupation zone with the other zones to American security guarantees. The European worry, not entirely unjustified, was that the United States sought to encourage a unified and integrated Europe as a prelude to its own withdrawal from direct occupation or security ties. The glimmerings of a bargain began to emerge: the Europeans would agree to the rehabilitation and reintegration of western Germany in exchange for an American security treaty.

In late 1947, European efforts intensified to draw the United States into a security relationship. British Foreign Minister Bevin outlined his ideas on military cooperation to Secretary of State Marshall in December 1947. A regional European organization centered around Britain, France, and the Benelux countries would be linked to the other Western European countries and to the United States. Marshall signaled his interest in the plan but later indicated that the United States could not presently make

[95] On the breakdown of four-power talks over Germany and the fateful shift in American policy in favor of integration of the western German zones into Western Europe, see Trachtenberg, *A Constructed Peace*, chapter two.

[96] On the centrality of European economic recovery to political stability, and the importance of German economic revival to European economic recovery, see "Memorandum by the Under Secretary of State for Economic Affairs [Clayton]," 27 May 1947, and "Summary of Discussion on Problems of Relief, Rehabilitation and Reconstruction of Europe," 29 May 1947, *Foreign Relations of the United States*, 1947, Vol. 3, pp. 230–32, 234–36.

[97] Kennan argued that the French and other Europeans should be brought "to an enlightened understanding of the necessities of the German situation; to the acknowledgement of their responsibility for integrating western Germany into western Europe, and to a detailed agreement with us as to how this shall be done. To this effort we must expect to give, as well as to receive, concessions." "Resume of World Situation," 6 November 1997, *Foreign Relations of the United States*, 1947, Vol. 1, p. 774–75.

any commitments.[98] Importantly, in discussions with Secretary of State Marshall, Bevin did not argue that a security treaty with the United States was needed to protect Europe from the Soviet Union; a security guarantee was needed to protect western Europe from the possible revival of German aggression.[99]

Bevin renewed his call for a Western union in a January 1948 speech to the House of Commons, which advocated "uniting by trade, social, cultural and all other contacts those nations of Europe and the world who are ready and able to cooperate."[100] In conversations with the State Department, Bevin argued that European defense efforts would not be possible without American assistance. "The treaties that are being proposed cannot be fully effective nor be relied upon when a crisis arises unless there is assurance of American support for the defense of Western Europe."[101] The French also sought to draw the United States into playing a military role in Western Europe. Foreign Minister Georges Bidault called upon the United States "to strengthen in the political field, and as soon as possible in the military one, the collaboration between the old and the new worlds, both so jointly responsible for the preservation of the only truly valuable civilization."[102]

Some officials in the Truman administration, such as the director of the Office of European Affairs, John D. Hickerson, were urging military cooperation with Western Europe.[103] Others, most notably George Kennan, resisted the idea of a military union, arguing that it would be destructive of the administration's goal of European unity.[104] The official position of

[98] "Memorandum of Conversation by the British Foreign Office," undated, *Foreign Relations of the United States*, 1947, Vol. 3, pp. 818–19. See also Geir Lundestad, *American, Scandinavia, and the Cold War, 1945–1949* (New York: Columbia University Press, 1980), pp. 171–72.

[99] "British Memorandum of Conversation," *Foreign Relations of the United States*, 1947, Vol. 2, pp. 815–22.

[100] Quoted in John Baylis, "Britain and the Formation of NATO," in Joseph Smith, ed., *The Origins of NATO* (Exeter: University of Exeter Press, 1990), p. 11.

[101] "The British Ambassador [Inverchapel] to the Under Secretary of State [Lovett]," *Foreign Relations of the United States*, 1948, Vol. 3, p. 14. In his memoir, British Prime Minister C. R. Attlee referred to the making of the Brussels treaty and the Atlantic Pact as "the work of Bevin." Attlee, *As It Happened* (London: Heinemann, 1954), p. 171. See also Escott Reid, *Time of Fear and Hope: The Making of the North Atlantic Treaty, 1947–1949* (Toronto: McClelland and Stewart, 1977).

[102] Quoted in Lundestad, "Empire by Invitation? The United States and Western Europe, 1945–1952," *Journal of Peace Research*, Vol. 23 (September 1986), p. 270.

[103] "Memorandum by the Director of the Office of European Affairs [Hickerson] to the Secretary of State," 19 January 1948, *Foreign Relations of the United States*, 1948, Vol. 3, pp. 6–7.

[104] "Memorandum by the Director of the Policy Planning Staff [Kennan] to the Secretary of State," 20 January 1948, *Foreign Relations of the United States*, 1948, Vol. 3, pp. 7–8. See also Kennan, *Memoirs, 1925–1950*, pp. 397–406.

the Truman administration during this period was ambiguous: it was sympathetic to European concerns but reluctant to make a commitment. After repeated British attempts to obtain an American pledge of support, Under Secretary of State Robert Lovett informed the British ambassador that the Europeans themselves must proceed with discussions on European military cooperation. Only afterward would the United States consider its relationship to these initiatives.[105] The British, undeterred, continued to insist on American participation in plans for Western European defense.

The result was a quickening of European security preparations and an appeal for American involvement. Belgium, France, Luxembourg, the Netherlands, and Britain concluded negotiations on the Brussels Pact in March 1948 but also anticipated a defense association with the United States. Indeed, they agreed that the United States would need to take the lead in balancing the Soviet Union. It was not until the Czech coup, on 12 March 1948, that the United States formally agreed to engage in joint talks with the West Europeans on an Atlantic security system. American willingness to move toward an Atlantic treaty hinged on the importance of western Germany. There was no alternative to some sort of American treaty commitment if the revival of western Germany was to be accomplished without threatening France and if European integration was to go forward.

In the negotiations that followed, the French and British pressed for a formal, treaty-based commitment, and the United States conceded only enough to keep the Europeans moving toward economic and security cooperation and the acceptance of western German rehabilitation and reintegration. American declarations of "association" with European security efforts—such as the June 1948 Vandenberg Resolution—and agreement to prolong the occupation period were early efforts by the United States to reassure France and Britain without making specific security promises. Even once the United States decided—as it did in last months of 1948—that ongoing American security assistance to Europe would be necessary, it sought some ambiguity as to the specific defense commitment.[106] The final language of Article 5 of the treaty was a compromise that attempted to both provide a security guarantee and reserve the right of the American government—and the Senate—to determine its specific meaning.[107]

---

[105] "The Under Secretary of State [Lovett] to the British Ambassador [Inverchapel]," 2 February 1948, *Foreign Relations of the United States*, 1948, Vol. 3, pp. 17–18.

[106] See Ireland, *Creating the Entangling Alliance*, pp. 100–12.

[107] The NATO agreement signed in April 1949 pledged the new partners to close political and economic collaboration, and "to develop their individual and collective capacity to resist armed attack." The most important part of the agreement was Article 5: an "armed attack against one or more of them . . . shall be considered an attack against them all." Each party would then "individually and in concert with the other Parties [take] such action as it deems

The North Atlantic Pact was not understood by most American officials in 1949 as an automatic or permanent security guarantee. Its purpose was to lend support to European steps to build stronger economic, political, and security ties within Europe itself.[108] In this sense, the NATO agreement was a continuation of the Marshall Plan strategy: to extend assistance to Europe in order to improve the chances that Europe would succeed in reviving and integrating itself. Even the strongest advocates within the Truman administration of a security treaty with Europe understood that European unity was a necessary component of an Atlantic security pact, and many anticipated that once a confident and unified Europe emerged, the Atlantic alliance would recede in importance or even lapse.[109] Nowhere in the negotiations over the treaty was there an intention to create a large transatlantic NATO bureaucracy or an integrated military establishment headed by an American general.

Binding security ties took a major step forward after 1950. As the Cold War worsened—most dramatically with the Korean War and the advent of the Soviet bomb—and the practical necessity of Western military rearmament arose, pressure intensified for the rehabilitation of western Germany. The political stakes also were raised. Now the issues under discussion were German rearmament and the restoration of its political sovereignty. As in the initial postwar years, European acquiescence in the strengthening of western Germany hinged on American willingness to commit itself to European security. This would entail a more formal, far-reaching, and integrated role of the American military in the organization of European security. The solution to German rearmament and statehood was its further integration in European economic institutions and the Atlantic alliance. A powerful and independent Germany, able to balance between East and West, was unacceptable to the United States and to the other western governments.[110] This triggered complex and protracted negotiations that ultimately created an integrated European military force within NATO and legal agreements over the character and limits on West German sovereignty.[111] But the transformation of Germany's status within the western

---

necessary, including the use of armed force." The Senate ratified the treaty by a 82–to–13 vote, and protected its freedom of action by declaring that the constitutional relationship—and in particular the Senate's power to declare war—had not be altered by the agreement. See Timothy P. Ireland, *Creating the Entangling Alliance* (Westport, Conn.: Greenwood, 1981).

[108] See "Statement on the North Atlantic Pact, Department of State," 20 March 1949, *Foreign Relations of the United States*, 1949, Vol. 4, pp. 240–41.

[109] This point is made in Peter Foot, "America and the Origins of the Atlantic Alliance: A Reappraisal," in Smith, ed., *The Origins of NATO*, pp. 82–94.

[110] Tractenberg, *A Constructed Peace*, chapter four.

[111] A treaty governing the relationship between the new German state and Britain, France, and the United States was signed in 1952, and specified ongoing "rights and responsibilities" of the three powers. "Convention on Relations between the Three Powers and the Federal

system could only be accomplished with a watershed expansion of the American security role in Europe.

A reciprocal process of security binding lay at the heart of the emerging Western order. John McCloy identified the "fundamental principle" of American policy in the early 1950s: that "whatever German contribution to defense is made may only take the form of a force which is an integral part of a larger international organization. . . . There is no real solution of the German problem inside Germany alone. There is a solution inside the European-Atlantic-World Community."[112] The rearmament of western Germany would be accomplished with elaborate institutional restraints that would enmesh the German military within alliance structures. But to make an integrated military system work, the United States had to preside over it in order to reassure hesitant Europeans. France and Britain were eager to establish an integrated military system—with an American NATO commander and American troops stationed on the continent—but they feared German rearmament. Negotiations culminated in May 1952, with the signing of the European Defense Community treaty, which created an integrated European military force—an agreement only possible by embedding it within NATO and by assurance of America's "permanent association" within NATO.[113] It took two additional years to work out the complex and interrelated agreements and declarations—the so-called Paris Accords—that together provided the political structure that bound Germany, the United States, and Europe together.[114]

Throughout the early postwar period, the Europeans were more worried about American abandonment than domination. Their interest in building a postwar alliance was driven to a substantial degree by a desire to ensure stable and continuous American involvement. The United States was more interested, at least initially, in the development of a European "third force"

Republic of Germany, May 26, 1952, as modified by the Paris Accords of October 1954," reprinted in Department of State, *Documents on Germany, 1944–1985* (Washington, D.C.: Department of State, 1986), pp. 425–30. See also Paul B. Stares, *Allied Rights and Legal Constraints on German Military Power* (Washington, D.C.: Brookings Institution, 1990).

[112] Quoted in Schwartz, *America's Germany*, p. 228. For a similar view by Secretary of State Acheson, see "The Secretary of State [Acheson] to the Embassy in France," 29 November 1950, *Foreign Relations of the United States*, 1950, Vol. 3, p. 497.

[113] Reflecting the complexity of EDC negotiations, the treaty that was finally signed in May 1952 contained 132 articles and various protocols—in comparison to NATO's 14 articles. See Ronald W. Pruessen, "Cold War Threats and America's Commitment to the European Defense Community: One Corner of a Triangle," *Journal of European Integration History*, Vol. 2, No. 1 (1996), pp. 60–61; Saki Dockrill, "Cooperation and Suspicion: The United States' Alliance Diplomacy for the Security of Western Europe, 1953–54," *Diplomacy and Statecraft*, Vol. 5, No. 1 (March 1994), pp. 138–82; and Ernest R. May, "The American Commitment to Germany, 1949–55," *Diplomatic History*, Vol. 13 (Fall 1989), pp. 431–60.

[114] See Trachtenberg, *A Constructed Peace*, chapter four.

that would allow the Europeans to muster their own defense. NATO was partly a structure designed to reintegrate Germany into the Western system. This in turn was supported by many officials because it also served to counter Soviet power, but American policy was more ambitious than simply managing the emerging bipolar order—it also sought to reconstruct and reintegrate Germany as a liberal capitalist country, thereby locking in a stable and open order among the industrial democracies. It was both a means and an end.[115] The rise of tensions with the Soviet Union helped move the United States toward a more formal security commitment, but it was the Europeans who lead the effort by seeking to make American power more predictable, useful, and institutionalized.

LIMITING THE RETURNS TO POWER

In moving away for its original postwar economic and security goals, the United States was effectively engaging in strategic restraint, thereby reassuring its would-be European and Asian partners that participation in the American postwar order would not entail coercive domination. In other words, the United States gained the acquiesce of secondary states by accepting limits on the exercise of its own hegemonic power. At the heart of the American postwar order was an ongoing trade-off: the United States would agree to operate within an institutionalized political process and, in return, its partners agree would be willing participants.

There are a variety of ways in which the United States and its prospective partners were able to overcome constraints and create reassurances and credible commitments. The reluctant character of American hegemony, rooted in its legacy of isolationism and exceptionalism, lowered the fears of imperial-style domination. The "penetrated" character of American hegemony provided opportunities for voice and reciprocity in hegemonic relations. Likewise, the use of "institutional binding" as a mechanism to mutually constrain the hegemon and secondary states also provided the means to reassure America's partners that it would not abandon or dominate. Reassurance and commitment followed from American structure and policy. The structural circumstances that America presented the world were relatively straightforward: a big and open democracy, easily engaged and accessible to foreign governments and official representations. American policy and its self-conscious interest in fostering a postwar settlement that would be embraced as legitimate were also important. Together these elements

---

[115] Mary N. Hampton, "NATO at the Creation: U.S. Foreign Policy, West Germany and the Wilsonian Impulse," *Security Studies*, Vol. 4, No. 3 (Spring 1995), pp. 610–56; and Hampton, *The Wilsonian Impulse: U.S. Foreign Policy, the Alliance, and German Unification* (Westport, Conn.: Praeger, 1996).

produced the type of strategic restraint necessary to achieve agreement. The postwar order was established in a way that served to limit the returns to power.

Reluctant Hegemony

The shifts in American postwar economic and security positions, noted earlier, show the limits of American hegemony and the way in which the United States sought to make that hegemony acceptable to the Europeans. The United States did use its power to get the Europeans and Japanese to integrate and operate within an open postwar system.[116] But the United States was not eager to manage directly the system or coerce other states within it. It was willing to modify its position in order to get agreement. It reluctantly took on greater security commitments to gain overall acquiescence by the Europeans in a postwar order. European (and later Japanese) willingness to participate within the order was due in part to the generally reluctant posture of American foreign policy.

The reluctance of American hegemony can be seen in its early proposals for a system of free trade. In addition to its specific economic and political merits, a free-trade order had another attraction for the United States: it allowed it to be internationalist without making specific postwar security commitments. A liberal multilateral economic order would allow the United States to project its own ideals onto a world where depression and war had clearly demonstrated the bankruptcy of European ideas of spheres of influence and economic nationalism. If the United States could no longer isolate itself from the affairs of Europe, it would need to alter the terms of internationalist politics. Only on this basis would congressional and public opinion allow the United States to play an internationalist role. An open system of free trade, once established, would be self-regulating

---

[116] To be sure, the United States did attempt to use its material resources to pressure and induce Britain and the other industrial democracies to abandon bilateral and regional preferential agreements and accept the principles of a postwar economy organized around a nondiscriminatory system of trade and payments. The 1946 British Loan deal was perhaps the most overt effort by the Truman administration to tie American postwar aid to specific policy concessions by allied governments. This was the failed Anglo-American Financial Agreement, which obliged the British to make sterling convertible in exchange for American assistance. See Richard Gardner, *Sterling-Dollar Diplomacy*; and Alfred E. Eckes, Jr., *A Search for Solvency*. The United States knew it held a commanding position and sought to use its power to give the postwar order a distinctive shape. The huge disparity in American and European power was not immediately or fully appreciated in either Washington or European capitals at the war's end. Many of the most important adjustments in American policy, such as the delay of currency convertiblity and the increase in direct American assistance, were caused by a growing realization of the underlying economic and security weakness of Britain and continental Europe. See Leffler, *A Preponderance of Power*, chapter one.

and would not require direct American involvement in Europe. For an American public eager to see its troops return home, ideals and prudence reinforced this initial American view of postwar order.

The attraction of an open liberal economic system was that it could run itself. The United States could have it both ways: it could ensure that the postwar order was congenial to American economic and political interests, but it would also allow the United States to not get too involved overseas. In many ways, it was the same attraction that Wilson had for the League of Nations' collective security system: if all the major countries agreed to basic principles of democracy and joint security, the system would largely run automatically. In both periods, American reluctance actively to manage interstate relations allayed some European fears of American domination, but it raised worries about abandonment. After 1945, the United States did find ways to allay these worries, as well.

Early postwar efforts by the United States to aid Europe were also pursued in part to help foster the conditions in Europe that would allow the United States to withdraw eventually. This idea was explicit in the thinking of officials such as George Kennan, and it lay behind the notion of creating a European "third force" and the American championing of European integration. The Marshall Plan was to last just four years, after which the Europeans would be on their own. This view was expressed by Paul Hoffman, the Marshall Plan's first administrator: "the idea is to get Europe on its feet and off our backs."[117] When the NATO treaty was signed in 1949, it was also seen by many America officials as a transitional agreement that would provide encouragement and support for Europeans as they developed more unified economic, political, and security institutions.

This pattern of American policy toward Europe reflected a more general American orientation as the war came to an end. It wanted a world order that would advance American interests, but it was not eager to organize and run that order. It is in this sense that the United States was a reluctant superpower.[118] This general characteristic was not lost on Europeans who, rather than resisting the encroachments of the United States, actively "invited" American involvement.[119] To the extent that the United States could convey the sense that they did not seek to dominate the Europeans, it gave

---

[117] Quoted in Peter Foot, "America and the Origins of the Atlantic Alliance," p. 83.

[118] See Holt, *The Reluctant Superpower*.

[119] This argument has been developed most systematically by the historian Geir Lundestad. See his, "Empire by Invitation?," pp. 263–77; Lundestad, *The American "Empire" and Other Studies of US Foreign Policy in Contemporary Perspective* (New York: Oxford University Press, 1990); and Lundestad, " 'Empire by Invitation' in the American Century," *Diplomatic History*, Vol. 23, No. 2 (Spring 1999), pp. 189–217. See also David Reynolds, "America's Europe, Europe's America: Image, Influence, and Interaction, 1933–1958," *Diplomatic History*, Vol. 20 (Fall 1996); and Gaddis, *We Now Know*, chapter two, pp. 651–66.

greater credibility to America's proposals for a constitutional settlement. It provided some reassurance that the United States would operate within limits and not use its overwhelming power simply to dominate.

Beyond the reluctance of American hegemony, there was also a self-conscious effort by administration officials to infuse the postwar system with a sense of legitimacy and reciprocal consent. When American officials began to organize Marshall Plan aid for Europe, for example, there was a strong desire to have the Europeans embrace American aid and plans as their own, thus enhancing the legitimacy of the overall postwar settlement. At a May 1947 meeting, George Kennan argued that it was important to have "European acknowledgement of responsibility and parentage in the plan to prevent the certain attempts of powerful elements to place the entire burden on the United States and to discredit it and us by blaming the United State for all failures." Similarly, State Department official Charles Bohlen argued that United States policy should not be seen as an attempt "to force 'the American way' on Europe."[120] The United States wanted to create an order that conformed to its liberal democratic principles, but this could only be done if other governments embraced such a system as their own.

An important reason why American officials were preoccupied with the legitimacy of the postwar Western order was that this was seen as a necessary precondition of European political stability, economic growth, and centrist governing regimes. The United States spent little of its hegemonic power trying to coerce and induce other governments to buy into American rules and institutions. It spent much more time and resources trying to create the conditions under which postwar European governments and publics would remain moderate and pro-Western. Truman administration officials sought to encourage moderate political parties and governing coalitions in Europe. At the State Department, Charles Bohlen argued in 1946 that "It is definitely in the interest of the United States to see that the present left movement throughout the world, which we should recognize and even support, develops in the direction of democratic as against totalitarian systems."[121] Most American officials supported the Marshall Plan for precisely this reason. They hoped to create a socioeconomic environment in Europe that would be congenial to the emergence and dominance of moderate and centrist governments.

What emerged was a Western postwar order organized around liberal democratic policies and institutions. It was hegemonic in the sense that it was centered around the United States and reflected American-styled po-

---

[120] "Summary of Discussion on Problems of Relief, Rehabilitation and Reconstruction of Europe," 29 May 1947, *Foreign Relations of the United States*, 1947, Vol. 3, p. 235.

[121] Quoted in Gaddis, "Dividing Adversaries," in Gaddis, *The Long Peace*, p. 150.

litical mechanisms and organizing principles. It was a liberal order in that it was legitimate and marked by reciprocal interactions. Europeans were able to reconstruct and integrate their societies and economies in ways that were congenial to American hegemony but that also gave them room to experiment with their own autonomous and semi-independent political systems. Postwar Europe was in part organized by American hegemony, but it also used it for its own political ends.[122]

Democracy and Open Hegemony

A second way that the United States projected reassurance was structural. The open and decentralized character of the American political system provided opportunities for other states to exercise their "voice" in the operation of the American hegemonic order, thereby reassuring these states that their interests could be actively advanced and processes of conflict resolution would exist. In this sense, the American postwar order was an open or penetrated hegemony, an extended system that blurred domestic and international politics as it created an elaborate transnational and trans-governmental political system with the United States at its center.[123]

There are several ways in which America's open hegemony served to reinforce the credibility of the United States' commitment to operating within an institutionalized political order. The first is simply the transparency of the system, which reduced surprises and allayed worries by partners that the United States might make abrupt changes in policy. This transparency comes from the fact that policy making in a large, decentralized democracy involves many players and an extended and relatively visible political process. The open and competitive process may produce mixed and ambiguous policies at times, but the transparency of the process at least allows other states to make more accurate calculations about the likely direction of American foreign policy. This lowers levels of uncertainty and provides a measure of reassurance which, everything else being equal, provides greater opportunities to cooperate.

Another way in which the penetrated hegemonic order provided reassurances to partners was in the way that it allowed participation of outsiders and an Atlantic policy-making process that facilitated compromise and agreement. This extension of the American democratic system outward to Europe is noted by John Lewis Gaddis: "Having attained their authority

---

[122] This argument is made by Charles Maier, "Alliance and Autonomy: European Identity and U.S. Foreign Policy Objectives in the Truman Years," in Lacey, ed., *The Truman Presidency*, pp. 273–98.

[123] This argument is made in Daniel Deudney and G. John Ikenberry, "The Nature and Sources of Liberal International Order," *Review of International Studies*, Vol. 25 (Spring 1999), pp. 179–96.

through democratic processes, its [America's] leaders were experienced—
as their counterparts in Moscow were not—in the arts of persuasion, negotiation and compromise. . . . [T]he habits of democracy had served the nation well during World War II: its strategists had assumed that their ideas
would have to reflect the interests and capabilities of allies; it was also
possible for allies to advance proposals of their own and have them taken
seriously. That same pattern of mutual accommodation persisted after the
war."[124] On an wide range of postwar issues—occupation zone management, the Greece and Turkey crisis, and responses to the 1947 economic
crisis in Europe—the Europeans, particularly the British, were critical in
shaping American policy. Despite the sharp inequalities in power, political
influence flowed in both directions across the Atlantic.[125]

The fragmented and penetrated American system allowed and invited
the growth of a wide network of transnational and transgovernmental relations with Europe, Japan, and other parts of the world. The United States
became the primary site for the pulling and hauling of trans-Atlantic and
trans-Pacific politics.[126] Although this access to the American political process was not fully reciprocated abroad, the openness and democratic processes of the American political system assured other states that they would
have routine access to the decision-making processes of the United States.
Transnational processes—extensions of domestic democratic politics—
were readily constructed that facilitated bargaining and compromise.

The negotiations between the United States and Britain over postwar
economic arrangements during and just after the war are illustrative of the
larger pattern. The United States had a diversity of bureaucratic groups
that advanced positions on trade and monetary policy. British officials were
able to maneuver around their conflicts with the State Department over
postwar trade policy by finding more congenial partners at the Treasury
Department. In the years that followed, an intensive set of transgovernmental negotiations took place that culminated in the Bretton Woods
agreements. As indicated earlier, the British successfully moved the Ameri-

---

[124] Gaddis, *We Now Know*, p. 43.

[125] See David Reynolds, "Great Britain," in Reynolds, ed., *The Origins of the Cold War in Europe: International Perspectives* (New Haven: Yale University Press, 1994), pp. 80–83.

[126] For the transnational political process channeled through the Atlantic security institu-
tions, see Thomas Risse-Kappen, *Cooperation among Democracies: The European Influence on U.S. Foreign Policy* (Princeton: Princeton University Press, 1995). On the consensual and reciprocal style of U.S.-European relations within NATO, see Lawrence S. Kaplan, *The United States and NATO: The Formative Years* (Lexington: University Press of Kentucky, 1984). On the U.S.-Japanese side, see Peter J. Katzenstein and Yutaka Tsujinaka, "'Bullying,' 'Buying,' and 'Binding': U.S.-Japanese Transnational Relations and Domestic Structures," in Risse-Kappen, ed., *Bringing Transnational Relations Back In: Non-State Actors, Domestic Structures, and International Institutions* (Cambridge: Cambridge University Press, 1997) pp. 79–111.

can position on postwar economic order toward the embrace of a more managed open system that provided governments with tools for economic stabilization and expansionary options for macroeconomic imbalances.[127] The multiple governmental access points and decentralized character of American governmental decision making allowed the British to play a more influential role than might otherwise be possible in a more unitary and closed system.[128]

Taken together, the acceptability of American hegemony was facilitated by the ability of the Europeans and Japanese to maneuver within it. The British found this to be so, as Charles Maier notes: "Within the American 'hegemony' Britain preserved as much of her Commonwealth position, her shielding of her balance of payments, as possible. She also played what might be terms the 'Polybian' strategy, attempting to become the Greeks to America's Roman empire, wagering on the 'special relationship' to prolong their influence and status."[129] But in various ways, America's other partners could also find special avenues of access and convenience in the postwar order that made American power more useful and predictable. America's partners faced a leading postwar state that was relatively open and accessible. This allowed them to calculate that they would not be dominated and, indeed, that they could better achieve their interests by participating in the postwar order than resisting it.

Binding Institutions

Restraint and reassurance were also established through postwar institutions themselves, which together locked in open, multilateral policy orientations and bound the major Western states together. United States and Europe each attempted to lock the other party into specific postwar institutional commitments. They accomplished this in part by agreeing in turn to operate within those institutions as well, even if sometimes reluctantly. Governments ordinarily seek to preserve their options, to cooperate with other states but to leave open the option of disengaging. What the United

---

[127] The role of transgovernmental experts and coalitions in the formation of the Bretton Woods agreements is detailed in G. John Ikenberry, "A World Economy Restored: Expert Consensus and the Anglo-American Post-War Settlement," *International Organization*, Vol. 46 (Winter 1991/92), pp. 289–321.

[128] Open and decentralized American political institutions provided opportunities for allies and other states to influence the shape and direction, at least to some extent. Geir Lundestad argues: "Often they did this was success, and although the basic decision tended to reflect America's own concerns, the foreigners could, as a minimum, influence the scope and timing of the decision." Lundestad, *The American "Empire*," p. 56.

[129] Maier, "Supranational Concepts and National Continuity in the Framework of the Marshall Plan," p. 34. See also Gaddis, *We Now Know*, chapter two.

States and the other Western states did after the war was exactly the opposite: they built long-term economic, political, and security commitments that were difficult to retract. The emerging Cold War provided an impetus for the most formal and elaborate binding

The most complex and consequential binding institutions were security alliances. These aggregated power to counter the threat of Soviet communism, but they were also institutions that were intended to stabilize and manage power relations among the partner states. The NATO alliance provided a mechanism for the rehabilitation and reintegration of western Germany, an instrument of what has been called "dual containment."[130] But it also locked in America's reluctant security commitment to Europe and tied the European states together, reinforcing their movement toward regional integration. In this way, the NATO alliance operated along with other postwar institutions as a multifaceted instrument of "quadruple containment."

The most consistent British and French objective during and after the war was to bind the United States to Europe. The evolution in American policy, from the goal of a European "third force" to acceptance of an ongoing security commitment within NATO, was a story of American reluctance and European persistence. The European search for an American security tie was not simply a response to the rise of the Soviet threat. As early as 1943, Winston Churchill proposed a "Supreme World Council" (composed of the United States, Britain, Russia, and perhaps China) and regional councils for Europe, the Western Hemisphere, and the Pacific. In an attempt to institutionalize an American link to Europe, Churchill suggested that the United States would be represented in the European Regional Council, in addition to its role in its own hemisphere. Reflecting American ambivalence about a postwar commitment to Europe, one historian notes, "Roosevelt feared Churchill's council as a device for tying the United States down in Europe."[131]

During and after the war, Britain and France sought to bind the United States to Europe in order to make American power more predictable, accessible, and usable. The NATO alliance was particularly useful as an institution that made the exercise of American power more certain and less arbitrary. Despite the vast differences in the size and military power of the various alliance partners, NATO enshrined the principles of equality of

---

[130] For a discussion of "dual containment," see Schwartz, *America's Germany*. Wolfram P. Hanrieder has also referred to American policy in this period as "double containment: the containment of the Soviet Union at arm's length, and of West Germany with an embrace." *Germany, America, Europe: Forty Years of German Foreign Policy* (New Haven: Yale University Press, 1989), p. 6.

[131] Harper, *American Visions of Europe*, p. 96.

status, nondiscrimination, and multilateralism.[132] The United States was the clear leader of NATO. But the mutual understandings and institutional mechanisms of the alliance would reduce the implications of these asymmetries of power in its actual operation.

The security alliance also served to reduce European fears of resurgent and unbridled German military power. The strategy of tying Germany to Western Europe was consistently championed by George Kennan. "In the long run there can be only three possibilities for the future of western and central Europe. One is German domination. Another is Russian domination. The third is a federated Europe, into which the parts of Germany are absorbed but in which the influence of the other countries is sufficient to hold Germany in her place. If there is no real European federation and if Germany is restored as a strong and independent country, we must expect another attempt at German domination."[133] Two years later, Kennan was again arguing that "without federation there is no adequate framework within which adequately to handle the German problem."[134]

The idea was to rebuild Germany's economic and military capabilities within European and Atlantic institutions. This binding strategy was widely embraced at the time by American officials. Secretary of State Marshall made the point in early 1948: "Unless Western Germany during coming year is effectively associated with Western European nations, first through economic arrangements, and ultimately perhaps in some political way, there is a real danger that whole of Germany will be drawn into the eastern orbit with dire consequences for all of us."[135] When Secretary of State Dean Acheson went to the Senate to answer questions about the NATO treaty, Senator Claude Pepper posed the question: "The Atlantic Treaty has given these Western European nations some confidence against a resurgent Germany as well as Russia?" Acheson replied: "Yes. It works in all directions."[136] As Cold War tensions made western German rearmament increasingly necessary, the elaborateness of alliance restraints on German power also grew, reflected in the complicated negotiations over an inte-

---

[132] See Weber, "Shaping the Postwar Balance of Power: Multilateralism in NATO."

[133] "Report of the Policy Planning Staff," 24 February 1948, *Foreign Relations of the United States*, 1948, Vol. 1, Part 2, p. 515. For a discussion of Kennan's thinking, see Harper, *American Visions of Europe*, chapter five.

[134] "Minutes of the Seventh Meeting of the Policy Planning Staff," 24 January 1950, *Foreign Relations of the United States*, 1950, Vol. 3, p. 620.

[135] "Minutes of the Sixth Meeting of the United States-United Kingdom-Canada Security Conversations, Held at Washington," 1 April 1948, *Foreign Relations of the United States*, 1948, Vol. 3, p. 71.

[136] Quoted in Lloyd C. Gardner, *A Covenant with Power: American and World Order from Wilson to Reagan* (New York: Oxford University Press, 1984), p. 100.

grated military command and the legal agreements that accompanied the restoration of German sovereign.[137]

If NATO bound both western Germany and the United States to Europe, it also reinforced British and French commitment to an open and united Europe. The United States was intent not only on the rehabilitation and reintegration of Germany; it also wanted to reorient Europe itself. In an echo of Wilson's critique of the "old politics" of Europe after World War I, American officials after 1945 emphasized the need for reform of nationalist and imperialist tendencies. It was generally thought that the best way to do so was to encourage integration.[138] Regional integration would not only make Germany safe for Europe, it would also make Europe safe for the world. The Marshall Plan reflected this American thinking, as did Truman administration support for the Brussels Pact, the European Defense Community, and the Schuman Plan. In the negotiations over the NATO treaty in 1948, American officials made clear to the Europeans that a security commitment hinged on European movement toward integration. One State Department official remarked that the United States would not "rebuild a fire-trap."[139] The American goal was, as Dean Acheson put it in reference to the EDC, "to reverse incipient divisive nationalist trends on the continent."[140] American congressional support for the Marshall Plan was also premised, at least in part, on not just transferring American dollars to Europe but also on encouraging integrative political institutions and habits.[141]

---

[137] The objective of binding the allies together through an integrated NATO military organization was acknowledged—and celebrated—by Secretary of State John Foster Dulles in a statement to the North Atlantic Council in 1953: "Fourteen nations have here found the habit of working together. Our Annual Review is an institution which is unique in the history of alliances. Never before in peacetime have sovereign nations opened the top secret documents of their ministries of defence to the scrutiny of other countries, no matter how closely they were allied. Never before have nations taken recommendations from an international body concerning the length of military service, balance of forces between military services and other equally delicate problems, and, what is even more revolutionary, accepted these recommendations, often in the face of contrary domestic political consultations. . . . Again we are breaking new ground by the creation of a group of public servants who owe their allegiance not to any one of our fourteen member countries but to all of us collectively." "Statement by the Secretary of State to the North Atlantic Council," *Foreign Relations of the United States*, 1952–1954, Vol. 5, pp. 464–65.

[138] See Harper, *American Visions of Europe*; and Hogan, *The Marshall Plan*.

[139] "Minutes of the Fourth Meeting of the Washington Exploratory Talks on Security," 8 July 1948, *Foreign Relations of the United States*, 1948, Vol. 3, pp. 163–69.

[140] "The Secretary of State to the Embassy in France," 19 October 1949, *Foreign Relations of the United States*, 1949, Vol. 4, p. 471.

[141] See Beugel, *From Marshall Plan to Atlantic Partnership*; and Geir Lundestad, *"Empire" by Integration: The United States and European Integration, 1945–1997* (New York: Oxford University Press, 1998).

When Marshall Plan aid was provided to Europe, beginning in 1948, the American government insisted that the Europeans themselves organize to jointly allocate the funds. This gave rise to the Organization for European Economic Cooperation (OEEC), which was the institutional forerunner of the European Community.[142] This body eventually became responsible for European-wide supervision of economic reconstruction, and it began to involve the Europeans in discussion of joint economic management. As one American official recalls, the OEEC "instituted one of the major innovations of postwar international cooperation, the systematic country review, in which the responsible national authorities are cross-examined by a group of their peers togther with a high-quality international staff. In those reviews, questions are raised which in prewar days would have been considered a gross and unacceptable foreign interference in domestic affairs."[143] The United States encouraged European integration as a bulwark against intra-European conflict even as it somewhat more reluctantly agreed to institutionalize its own security commitment to Europe.

The various elements of the settlement among the Atlantic countries fit together. The Marshall Plan and NATO were part of a larger institutional package. As Lloyd Gardner argues: "Each formed part of a whole. Together they were designed to 'mold the military character' of the Atlantic nations, prevent the balkanization of European defense systems, create an internal market large enough to sustain capitalism in Western Europe, and lock in Germany on the Western side of the Iron Curtain."[144] NATO was a security alliance, but it was also embraced as a device to help organize political and economic relations within the Atlantic area. As Mary Hampton argues, the Atlantic alliance was championed by those concerned with a Western balance against Soviet power but also but those who were seeking the "construction of a trans-Atlantic community of nations."[145] American officials were looking for ways to find a solution to the Franco-German antagonism that had fueled three great wars in less than a century. These impulses toward the reintegration of Germany and the political and economic unification of Western Europe shaped America's postwar goals in Europe and ultimately helped push the United States toward accepting the NATO commitment. As John Foster Dulles stated, the main emphasis of the At-

---

[142] The OEEC was launched on 5 June 1948. See Michael Hogan, *The Marshall Plan: America, Britain, and the Reconstruction of Western Europe, 1947–52* (New York: Cambridge University Press, 1987).

[143] Remarks by Amb. Lincoln Gordon in, David Ellwood, ed., *The Marshall Plan Forty Years After: Lessons for the International System Today* (Bologna: Bologna Center of the John Hopkins University, School of Advances International Studies, 1988), pp. 48–49.

[144] Gardner, *A Covenant with Power*, p. 81.

[145] Hampton, "NATO at the Creation," p. 611. See also Hampton, *The Wilsonian Impulse*.

lantic alliance was "on cooperation *for* something rather than merely *against* something."[146]

American strategic restraint after the war left the Europeans more worried about abandonment than domination, and they actively sought American institutionalized commitments to Europe. The American polity's transparency and permeability fostered an "extended" political order that reached outward to the other industrial democracies. Multiple layers of economic, political, and security institutions bound these countries together, reinforcing the credibility of their mutual commitments. The dramatic asymmetries of postwar power were rendered more acceptable as a result.

Conclusion

The order created after World War II among the advanced industrial countries was distinctive and unprecedented. More than the early postwar orders, it had—and continues to have—constitutional characteristics. The Western industrial order was characterized by multilayered institutions and alliances, open and penetrated domestic orders, and reciprocal and largely legitimate mechanisms for dispute resolution and joint decision making. It was marked by wide disparities in power—after the war, the United States stood in an unparalleled superordinate position is relation to Europe and Japan. But despite these power differentials, a mutually agreeable order was devised after the war and is still largely in place today.

Several specific arguments emerge from the record of post-World War II order building. First, the United States did seek to use its position as the leading postwar state to lock the other industrial powers into a particular type of international order organized around economic and political openness. These ideas, articulated first in the Atlantic Charter, remained in play even as the specific circumstances of order building changed unexpectedly in the years that followed. It would not be a world of closed blocs, national capitalism, or rival imperial orders. What changed with the rise of the Cold War were the shrinkage in the amount of the world that would be organized according to this logic and the types of institutional strategies that were pursued in order to secure such an order.

Second, America's broad postwar goals predated the rise of the Cold War and drew upon a wide array of complementary ideas about political, economic, and security order. State Department officials who advanced notions of an open world economy were reinforced by defense planners who linked American security interests to market and resource access to Asian and European regions. State Department planners, such as George

---

[146] Quoted in Hampton, "NATO at the Creation," p. 625.

Kennan, who were primarily concerned with rebuilding the economic and political infrastructure of Western Europe made common cause with other officials who were concerned with encouraging the emergence of continental European governments committed to an open and integrated Western order. This convergence on liberal democratic order was facilitated by the reluctance of the Truman administration to pursue more far-reaching options such as simple free trade or world government. An institutionalized and managed Western order that centered on openness and democracy was an appealing objective for some, and an indispensable means to an end for others. What the United States sought to lock in after 1945 was more ambitious and multifaceted than any goals after 1815 or even 1919. The persistence of this agenda was reinforced by the diversity of policy advocates who differed on many matters but by and large converged on the importance of open and multilateral relations among the major industrial democracies.

Third, the United States pursued these goals by agreeing to lock itself in to a highly institutionalized postwar order. In a sense, the United States "purchased" European agreement by conceding more favorable terms to them, agreeing to a massive aid program, and reluctantly accepting binding security guarantees. The evolution of American policy on postwar trade and monetary arrangements reflects this willingness to compromise to get European acquiescence, giving a better deal in the short run in order to get an institutional settlement that secured America's long-term interests. The Marshall Plan aid was even more explicit in this sort of trade-off: the United States transferred massive financial resources to Europe but with specific understandings that the European states would move toward greater political and economic unification. The American security commitments that followed—in 1949 with the NATO treaty and the later intensification of security ties—were also reluctantly extended in exchange for European commitments to greater regional security cooperation and a willingness to reintegrate and rearm western Germany.

Fourth, the political organization of postwar relations among the industrial democracies was driven by this process of mutual and reciprocal binding. The United States consistently sought to remain as unencumbered as possible after the war. This goal helps explain the appeal of the State Department's free-trade agenda and the later ideas of a European "third force." At the same time, American officials pursued a remarkably sophisticated agenda aimed at binding the Europeans together and tying western Germany into a more unified and integrated Europe. At first this agenda was driven by the demands of postwar economic renewal and the need for some solution to the German problem, imperatives that existed independently of the worsening of relations with the Soviet Union—although the Cold War did raise the stakes and sped the process. But at each stage in this process, European officials insisted that the binding together of Europe was only acceptable if the United States itself made binding commitments to them, as well. At each stage, the United States conceded only as much commitment as was needed to keep the Europeans on their path toward integration and reconstruction. Restraint, reassurance, and commitment were the price the United States had to pay in order to achieve its order-building goals in Europe and more widely.

The Europeans engaged in a similar trade-off: they agreed to steps toward European integration and accepted western Germany back into Europe, in part because in exchange they got a more institutionally restrained and connected postwar America. As suggested in the model of constitutional order building, the weaker and secondary states locked themselves in to a postwar order, but in return they received a favorable short-term return on their power and secured—at least to some extent—institutional arrangements that made the leading state more predictable, restrained, and accessible. The full measure of this binding of American power to Europe occurred relatively late after the war—only after 1950 and in response to a heightening of the Soviet threat—with the integration of NATO forces and the permanent stationing of American troops in Europe. This institutionalization of Atlantic security relations provided reassurances to Europe by making the exercise of American power more certain and predictable and by creating voice opportunity mechanisms.

Fifth, the institutional strategies that were employed after the war were critical in giving shape to the order among the industrial democracies and overcoming the insecurities otherwise inherent in highly asymmetrical power relations. The rise of the Soviet Union reinforced Western solidarity, but that solidarity was imagined and acted upon before Cold War hostilities broke out. Indeed, the shifts in thinking among American postwar planners—from the weakly institutionalized free-trade vision to the hands-on and managed Western economic, political, and security system— was driven more by the growing perception of European weakness after 1945 than by the threat of Soviet power.[147] In a meeting of American ambassadors in Paris in the summer of 1949, John J. McCloy, the high commissioner for Germany, argued that perhaps too much emphasis had been given to "the increase of Russian power in the world and too little thought to the enormously important factor that is the collapse of the British Empire."[148] The postwar relations among the Western countries were im-

---

[147] This is a theme in Leffler, "The American Conception of National Security and the Beginning of the Cold War, 1945–48," and Leffler, *A Preponderance of Power.*

[148] "Summary Record of a Meeting of United States Ambassadors at Paris," 21–22 October 1949, *Foreign Relations of the United States,* 1949, Vol. 4, p. 485.

portantly driven by efforts to solve their common problems and create safety nets in the service of an open and stable order.

Sixth, the goals behind Western liberal order were partly shaped by the manifold lessons and experiences that stimulated these ideas. It is sometimes argued that what differentiated the "successful" settlement after 1945 from the "unsuccessful" settlement after 1919 is that it was based on more "realist" understandings of power and order. Roosevelt, for example, was sensitive to considerations of power. His notion of the "Four Policemen" was a self-conscious effort to build a postwar settlement around a great-power collective security organization.[149] But the actual postwar settlement reflected a more mixed set of lessons and calculations. "Realist" lessons from the League of Nations debacle of the 1920s were combined with "liberal" lessons from the regional imperialism and mercantilist conflict of the 1930s. The United States did show more willingness to use its military victory and occupation after 1945 to implement its postwar aims in Germany and Japan. But those aims, nonetheless, were manifestly liberal in character.

Finally, there was an explicit presumption among American and European officials that binding postwar institutions—NATO in particular, but the other multilateral institutions as well—would only operate effectively to provide restraints and assurances if the participating states were democratic. British Foreign Minister Bevin's appeal to Secretary of State Marshall in December 1948, that the Atlantic countries should act to create a "spiritual federation of the west," implied that it was the commonality of democracy that ultimately was the basis for security cooperation. Later, when the allies deliberated over the manner in which western Germany would be integrated into the West, John McCloy argued that Germany would need to be a "willing participant" and eventually a "full partner" with the other countries in the emerging "concert of democratic powers."[150] A democratic Germany would be necessary to ensure its full participation in a noncoercive and legitimate Western order. Likewise, when Germany negotiated the return of its sovereignty in 1954, it had an incentive to embrace its new democratic institutions—recognizing that the western allies could only be relied upon to defend Germany if it embraced democratic values.[151] Democracy was both an end and a means. Western officials justi-

---

[149] Architects of the United Nations reflected this concern for power realities in their plans for permanent Great Power membership in the Security Council. For a discussion of FDR's "realist" departures from Wilsonian internationalism, see Dallek, *Franklin D. Roosevelt and American Foreign Policy, 1932–1945*; and Robert A. Divine, *Second Chance: The Triumph of Internationalism in America during World War II* (New York: Atheneum, 1967).

[150] Quoted in Trachtenberg, *A Constructed Peace*, p. 106.

[151] Ibid., p. 144.

fied the unprecedented degree of institutional cooperation and integration as necessary, in the words of John Foster Dulles, to "safeguard the freedom, common heritage and civilization of our people," but it was precisely because these countries were democratic that their governments could make these binding commitments.[152]

In these various ways, the huge asymmetries of power were rendered acceptable to America's partners, both because of the binding institutions that were employed and because of the structural features of the American polity. American officials went out of their way to reassure postwar partners and to cultivate a sense of legitimacy in the alliance and economic institutions they were creating. But in a larger sense, the United States was "doomed to reassure." Even if it did not actively seek to find agreement of mutually acceptable postwar rules and institutions, the operation of a large, pluralistic, and penetrated polity tended to produce those same results. The open system facilitated the collaborative search by American and British economists to find a Keynesian "middle ground" in the postwar economic order. The open American polity created opportunities for allies to lobby actively and engage American officials and influence the policy process. The institutions and alliances that were created were rendered more credible because they were based on treaties ratified by a democratic state, which means that they were commitments that would be difficult to overturn. If the United States would have been as powerful as it was after 1945, but not a democracy willing to employ a range of international institutions to bind itself to other states, it is difficult to envision its postwar partners willingly buying into such a postwar order.

---

[152] "Statement of the Secretary of State to the North Atlantic Council," *Foreign Relations of the United States*, 1952–54, Vol. 5, p. 461.

Chapter Seven

AFTER THE COLD WAR

THE END of the Cold War has evoked comparisons with 1815, 1919, and 1945. The fall of the Berlin Wall in 1989 and the collapse of the Soviet Union two years later brought to a sudden end four decades of superpower conflict. The old bipolar international order disappeared, and a new distribution of power took shape. The United States and its allies claimed victory, while the Soviet Union and its allies either slipped into oblivion or political and economic disarray. In the search for historical comparisons and lessons, scholars have good reasons to look back at earlier postwar settlements.[1]

But the end of the Cold War was also different. The destruction of societies and political regimes resulted from the collapse of the Soviet empire and not from the violence of war. Armies did not march across borders and occupy territory. In the years that followed in the end of the Cold War, more than a few Russians remarked—only half jokingly—that reform and reconstruction in the former Soviet Union would have been more successful if Russia had actually been invaded and defeated by the West; the United States and its allies might have been more generous in extending assistance. The Cold War ended "not with military victory, demobilization, and celebration but with the unexpected capitulation of the other side without a shot being fired."[2]

Only part of the post-World War II order—the bipolar order—was destroyed by the dramatic events of 1989–1991. The order among the democratic industrial powers was still intact. Indeed, many American and European observers were quick to argue that the Soviet collapse amounted to a triumph of Western institutions and policies. After past great wars, the old

---

[1] For discussions of the end of the Cold War as a postwar juncture, see K. J. Holsti, "The Post-Cold War 'Settlement' in Comparative Perspective," in Douglas T. Stuart and Stephen F. Szabo, eds., *Discord and Collaboration in a New Europe: Essays in Honor of Arnold Wolfers* (Washington, D.C.: Foreign Policy Institute, Johns Hopkins University, 1994), pp. 37–69; John Gerard Ruggie, "Third Try at World Order? America and Multilateralism after the Cold War," *Political Science Quarterly*, Vol. 109, No. 4 (1994), pp. 553–70; Ronald Steel, "Prologue: 1919–1945–1989," in Manfred F. Boemeke, Gerald D. Feldman, and Elisabeth Glaser, eds., *The Treaty of Versailles: A Reassessment after 75 Years* (New York: Cambridge University Press, 1998), pp. 21–34; and John Lewis Gaddis, "History, Grand Strategy and NATO Enlargement," *Survival*, Vol. 40, No. 1 (Spring 1998), pp. 145–51.

[2] Robert Hutchings, *American Diplomacy and the End of the Cold War: An Insider's Account of U.S. Policy in Europe, 1989–1992* (Baltimore: Johns Hopkins University Press, 1997), p. 343.

international order tended to be destroyed and discredited, and the way opened for sweeping negotiations over the basic rules and principles of postwar order. After 1989–1991, Western leaders were more likely to argue that the international order was working quite well. Western policy toward the Soviet Union had been vindicated, and the organization of relations among the industrial democracies remained stable and cooperative. The end of the Cold War might best be seen as the result of a fateful decision by Gorbachev in the late 1980s, as the Soviet system faltered around him, to seek accommodation and cautious integration with the West. The result was the collapse of one part of the postwar order and the continuing stability of the other.

The breakup of the Soviet Union and the end of bipolarity constituted a sudden shift in the international distribution of power. New asymmetries of power were exposed. The Soviet Union (and later Russia) faced a more powerful group of Western states, whereas Europe and Japan faced a more powerful America. At the close of the 1990s, the power asymmetries were again very sharp, with the United States in a preeminent position. Three general policy patterns can be identified as the major states responded to these changing power relations:

> The Soviet Union, experiencing an sharp decline in its power, pursued an accommodating foreign policy toward the West and acquiesced in the unification of Germany and the adsorption of its former East German ally into the Western alliance.
>
> The United States responded to its favorable shift in power by seeking expansion or creation of a variety of security and economic institutions—such as NATO, the North American Free Trade Agreement (NAFTA), the Asia Pacific Economic Cooperation (APEC), and the World Trade Organization (WTO)—as a way, at least in part, to lock other states into democratic and market orientations.
>
> The United States and the other industrial democracies, amidst the shifting power distributions during the 1990s, maintained and expanded cooperative relations. Despite the increasingly sharp and unprecedented asymmetries of power favoring the United States, major states did not seek to distance themselves from or balance against the United States.

Each of these trends is useful in assessing the institutional logic of Western order after the Cold War.[3] First, the deterioration of the Soviet's position in

---

[3] Post-Cold War patterns of order are important in assessing the book's central hypothesis. Chapter Six argued that an institutional bargain between the United States and Europe was pursued at least partially independently of the rise of Cold War tensions, even though the Cold War was a dominant catalyst for a binding American security commitment to Europe. Because both the institutional model and balance-of-power theory predict similar cooperative

the late-1980s—its weakening economy and declining control over Eastern Europe—could have triggered a variety of Soviet responses, including a more aggressive foreign policy, military mobilization, and coercion of its Warsaw Pact allies. Soviet President Mikhail Gorbachev, however, moved sharply in the opposite direction, pursuing accommodation and "new thinking." As will be discussed later, there is some evidence that this reorientation of foreign policy was rendered less risky to Soviet leaders because of the relatively benign configuration of Western power. Moscow could agree to let its Eastern European allies choose their own path of economic and political reform rather than threaten intervention—even as the Soviet Union's overall power position was declining—because it did not fear encroachment from the West.

The unification of Germany—and the absorption of East Germany into NATO—confronted the Soviets with the same dilemma, with even higher stakes. But again the Western countries were able to reassure the Soviets, particularly to the extent that the newly united Germany would be bound to European and Atlantic institutions. West Germany elicited acceptance of its goal of rapid unification, with the prospect of rising German power on the continent, by agreeing to remain bound to NATO and the European Community. Western institutions became a vehicle to overcome insecurities that followed the shifting European asymmetries of power after the Cold War.

Second, the pattern of American foreign policy after the Cold War is also at least partially consistent with the institutional logic of order building. American economic and military power increased during the 1990s, relative to both Russia and the other industrial democracies, and again the United States was faced with choices about how to use its power. Across a variety of economic and security areas, the United States pursued an expansive agenda of institution building: enlargement of NATO and the creation of NAFTA, APEC, and the WTO. These steps are largely consistent with the expectations of the model.

Finally, the durability of the post-1945 settlement among these Western powers and Japan can be assessed in the light of the end of the Cold War. Despite sharp shifts in the international distribution of power, the Western

---

outcomes during the post-1947 period among the Western industrial democracies, the pattern of relations after the disappearance of the external threat becomes particularly helpful in determining the underlying logic. If the institutional bargain persists after the end of the Cold War—that is, alliances are reaffirmed and expanded and conflict between these countries does not arise—this is confirming evidence for the institutional model. If the United States, reemerging after the Cold War as a preeminent power, pursues an institutional strategy similar to the one it pursued after 1945, this also is confirming evidence for the model. If the Soviet Union at the end of the Cold War acknowledges the power restraining functions of NATO and other Western institutions, this also provides useful evidence concerning the logic of the postwar order.

order has remained relatively stable. This is at least partly due to the institutional logic of the original settlement. By the end of the 1990s, the United States possessed unrivaled military and economic power, but the other major states have not actively sought to move away from or balance against American power. Nor has the level of conflict between the United States and its allies increased since the end of the Cold War. On the contrary, the scope and density of intergovernmental relations between the industrial democracies has actually expanded. The logic and stability of the Western order—crystallized in the late 1940s—is still evident today.

WESTERN ORDER AND THE SOVIET COLLAPSE

The collapse of the Soviet Union was mainly the result of internal contradictions and failures of the Soviet system. But the specific way in which Gorbachev and other Soviet leaders responded to these domestic problems was at least partly shaped by the external environment, including the United States and its Western allies.[4] It was not inevitable that the Soviet Union would respond as it did in the late 1980s with domestic liberalization and foreign policy accommodation. After coming to power in early 1985, Gorbachev began to pursue policies of *glasnost* (openness) and *perestroika* (economic restructuring) that soon resulted in greater political openness but also in an intensification of economic troubles. Domestic reform was matched by Gorbachev's "new thinking" in foreign policy, whereby the Soviet leader advanced a series of far-reaching arms reduction proposals and articulated a vision of greater global cooperation.[5] These Soviet initiatives surprised the outside world. At earlier moments of economic and political crises in tsarist and Soviet history, the response was more typically the opposite: greater domestic repression and a more aggressive foreign policy.[6]

A turning point in Soviet policy was Gorbachev's famous speech before the United Nations General Assembly in December 1988, in which he announced a unilateral reduction of five hundred thousand Soviet troops, with close to half coming from Eastern Europe and the western parts of

[4] This section draws on Daniel Deudney and G. John Ikenberry, "The International Sources of Soviet Change," *International Security*, Vol. 16, No. 3 (Winter 1991/92), pp. 74–118; Deudney and Ikenberry, "Soviet Reform and the End of the Cold War: Explaining Large-Scale Historical Change," *Review of International Studies*, Vol. 17 (Summer 1991), pp. 225–50; and Deudney and Ikenberry, "Who Won the Cold War?" *Foreign Policy*, No. 87 (Summer 1992), pp. 123–38.

[5] See Mikhail Gorbachev, *Perestroika: New Thinking for Our Country and the World* (New York: Harper & Row, 1987).

[6] See Helmut Sonnenfeldt and William G. Hyland, "Soviet Perspectives on Security," *Adelphi Papers*, No. 150 (Spring 1979), pp. 1–24.

the Soviet Union.[7] By this sweeping reduction in Soviet forces, Gorbachev was proposing an end to the sharp military division of Europe that lay at the heart of the Cold War. But he was also signaling a new Soviet tolerance of political change within Eastern Europe itself, declaring that the "use of force" cannot be and should not be an "instrument of foreign policy," and that "freedom of choice" was a universal principle that applied to both capitalist and socialist systems. This statement amounted to a de facto renunciation of the Brezhnev Doctrine, which had declared it a Soviet right and responsibility to intervene in Eastern Europe to safeguard socialism. Gorbachev was declaring an end to the Cold War and signaling to countries such as Poland and Hungary that the Soviet Union would not stand in the way of political change.[8]

Why was Gorbachev willing to undertake this risky unilateral move to end the Cold War through accommodation, steep arms deductions, and a hands-off policy in Eastern Europe? There are many reasons, of course, but the overall institutional character of the Western order—the United States and its European allies—presented a relatively benign face to the Soviet Union during its time of troubles. The Western democracies together formed a grouping of countries that made it very difficult for them individually or collectively to exploit or dominate the Soviet Union as it contemplated the transformation of its posture toward the outside world. As Russian Foreign Minister Andrei Kozyrev noted subsequently, the Western countries are pluralistic democracies and this "practically rules out the pursuance of an aggressive foreign policy."[9]

A cluster of institutional characteristics made the Western order fundamentally a defensive aggregation of power as it confronted the Soviet crisis. The pluralistic and democratic character of the countries that formed the Atlantic alliance, the multiple and often conflicting positions toward the Soviet Union that existed within and among these countries, and transnational and domestic opposition movements toward hard-line policies all worked to soften the face that the Soviet Union saw as it looked westward. The alliance itself, with its norms of unanimity, made an aggressive policy

---

[7] In the year preceding this speech, Gorbachev pursued a series of accommodating initiatives. In December 1987, Gorbachev made his first visit to the United States for a summit meeting with President Reagan and signed a treaty that eliminated nuclear weapons carried by intermediate-range missiles. In February 1988, Gorbachev announced that the Soviet Union would withdraw its forces from Afghanistan. In June 1988, Soviet regulations were changed to make in easier for Soviet citizens to travel abroad. In July 1988, Shevardnadze convened a conference of Soviet diplomats to promulgate a policy based on common human values.

[8] Don Oberdorfer, *The Turn: From the Cold War to the New Era* (New York: Simon and Schuster, 1991).

[9] See Andrei Kozyrev, "Partnership or Cold Peace?" *Foreign Policy*, No. 99 (Summer 1995), pp. 3–14.

by one country difficult to pursue. These aspects of Western order all served to make Gorbachev's historic gamble less risky. The threats to Soviet security lay closer to home.

There is a widely shared view that the Cold War ended by Soviet capitulation to the steady Western policy of containment and, in the 1980s, to the Reagan administration's dramatic military buildup.[10] By this analysis, Reagan's newly vigorous military posture and ideological offensive doomed the Soviets. In fact, the Reagan administration, the United States, and the Western world all presented much more complex and often contradictory positions. Reagan was surrounded by hard-liners who wanted to push the Western military advantage, but other officials and Reagan himself entertained more ambivalent views, particularly on issues of nuclear weapons. Reagan's willingness to consider far-reaching nuclear arms reductions was indicated at the November 1985 Geneva summit, and even more dramatically at the Reykjavik summit in October 1986. Nuclear hard-liners in the administration worked to disavow Reagan's views, but Reagan did provide Gorbachev with the signal that radical initiatives might be reciprocated rather than exploited.[11]

In addition to the ambivalence of Reagan himself, the hard-line position of the Reagan administration was undercut by several other factors. One was that the aggressive talk in the early years of the administration had fueled a large peace movement in the United States and Western Europe in the 1980s, a movement that put considerable pressure on Western governments to pursue far-reaching arms control proposals. That mobilization of Western public opinion created a political climate in which the rhetoric of the early Reagan administration was a political liability. By the American presidential election in 1984, the administration embraced arms control goals that it had previously spurned.[12] This new policy line culminated in a speech to the UN General Assembly in September 1984. To the Soviet leaders who Reagan had previously called "the focus of evil in the modern world," the American president now made a new appeal: "For the sake of

[10] For popular versions of this view, see Peter Schweizer, *Victory: The Reagan Administration's Secret Strategy That Hastened the Collapse of the Soviet Union* (New York: Atlantic Monthly Press, 1994); and Jay Winik, *On the Brink: The Dramatic, Behind-the-Scenes Saga of the Reagan Era and the Men and Women Who Won the Cold War* (New York: Simon and Schuster, 1996).

[11] The argument that the arms control diplomacy of the Reagan years was successful because Secretary of State George Schultz and others sidestepped the hard-liners around Reagan is made in Oberdorfer, *The Turn*. Raymond Garthoff argues that the Geneva summit of 1985 marked the point when Secretary Shultz was able to bring Reagan fully around to his strategy of diplomatic reengagement of the Soviet Union. See Raymond L. Garthoff, *The Great Transition: American-Soviet Relations and the End of the Cold War* (Washington, D.C.: Brookings Institution, 1994), p. 247.

[12] Garthoff, *The Great Transition*, chapter four.

a peaceful world ... let us approach each other with ten-fold trust and thousand-fold affection."[13]

In Western Europe, the arms control movement was even more vocal, putting pressure on the Reagan administration to be more forthcoming or risk a split in the alliance. The Western political system as a whole exhibited a sort of counterbalancing dynamic. Hard-line policies in the United States stimulated a more vocal arms control and disarmament movement which, in turn, had the effect of softening the intensity of the original hard-line position.[14]

The Reagan administration's tough policies were also undercut by powerful Western interests that favored East-West economic ties. In the early months of Reagan's administration, the grain embargo imposed by President Jimmy Carter after the 1979 Soviet invasion of Afghanistan was lifted in order to keep the Republican party's promises to Midwestern farmers. And despite strenuous opposition by the Reagan administration, the NATO allies pushed ahead with a natural gas pipeline linking the Soviet Union with Western Europe. That a project creating substantial economic interdependence could proceed during the worst period of Soviet-American relations in the 1980s demonstrated the failure of the Reagan administration to present an unambiguous Western hard line toward the Soviet Union.

When the Bush administration came to office, the diversity of views among advisers and agencies on how to respond to Gorbachev continued. Some in the administration wanted to see more concrete evidence that Gorbachev's "new thinking" was real and credible. But the dominant view was that Gorbachev should be encouraged by giving him tangible signs of reciprocation. Likewise, the diversity of views within the alliance—ranging from British skepticism to French ambivalence to German enthusiasm— worked to weaken a tough response to the Soviet Union. The dominant view was reflected in a cable to Washington from Jack Matlock, the American ambassador to the Soviet Union in 1989: "We have an historic opportunity to test the degree the Soviet Union is willing to move into a new relationship with the rest of the world, and to strengthen those tendencies in the Soviet Union to 'civilianize' the economy and 'pluralize' the society."[15] The Bush administration sought to channel the rapidly unfolding

[13] "United Nations: Address before the 39th Session of the General Assembly," 24 September 1984, *Weekly Compilation of Presidential Documents*, (Washington, D.C.: Office of the Federal Register), Vol. 20, No. 38 (1 October 1984), p. 1,359.

[14] Matthew Evangelista argues that Western transnational scientific and scholarly groups were an important source of policy ideas and political support for Soviet officials who were pursuing reform agendas in foreign and military policy. See Evangelista, *Unarmed Forces: The Transnational Movement to End the Cold War* (Ithaca: Cornell University Press, 1999).

[15] Quoted in Hutchings, *American Diplomacy and the End of the Cold War*, p. 33.

political changes in the Soviet Union and Eastern Europe in the direction of peaceful integration and democratic reform. The unexpected nature of the change coming out of Moscow and the goal of maintaining allied unity in its face reinforced the reactive and benign character of American policy.

Overall, the Soviet view of the Western order in the 1980s was not unlike the European view of American hegemony after 1945. The West represented an overwhelming concentration of power, but the actual exercise of that power was sufficiently constrained and institutionalized and the possibilities of reassurance sufficiently available that cautious cooperation rather than outright power balancing was possible. A single, consistent, and unambiguous hard-line policy was structurally impossible to sustain within the Western order.

German Unification and Soviet Acquiescence

A remarkable aspect of the end of the Cold War was how quickly Germany was reunited and how little this historic development was resisted by the Soviet Union. Less than a year after the Berlin Wall fell in November 1989, a treaty was signed that formally united the German Democratic Republic (GDR) with the Federal Republic. Just months before, most American and European observers thought that German unification was still only a distant possibility. Surprisingly, although the Soviet Union initially preferred other outcomes, it ultimately acquiesced in these unsettling developments. The Soviet Union conceded not only the integration of their former ally into West Germany but also that the newly united Germany would remain fully a part of the Western alliance and European Community. The balance between East and West shifted abruptly in favor of the West, but this did not trigger a new Cold War crisis; instead, Germany was quickly and quietly unified.

The formal step in Germany unification almost escaped notice. On 12 September 1990, the four allied victors in World War II met in Moscow to sign the Treaty of the Final Settlement, restoring full sovereignty to a united Germany and relinquishing their "rights and obligations" to Berlin and Germany.[16] Two weeks before the German settlement, at a summit between President George Bush and Soviet President Gorbachev in Helsinki, the issue of Germany unification was not even on the agenda.[17]

---

[16] "Treaty on the Final Settlement with Respect to Germany, Signed in Moscow on September 12, 1990," reprinted in Paul B. Stares, *Allied Rights and Legal Constraints on German Military Power* (Washington, D.C.: Brookings Institution, 1990), pp. 155–60.

[17] Philip Zelikow and Condoleezza Rice, *Germany Unified and Europe Transformed: A Study in Statecraft* (Cambridge: Harvard University Press, 1995), pp. 1–2. For other accounts of the negotiations over German unification, see Alexander Moens, "American Diplomacy and German Unification," *Survival*, Vol. 33, No. 6 (November/December 1991), pp. 531–45;

Negotiations leading to the unification of Germany in late 1989 and 1990 reveal the way in which the Western leaders were able to use Western institutions to signal restraint and provide reassurances to the Soviet Union as it faced the loss of the GDR. It was necessary to convince the Soviets that a newly unified Germany would not gravely threaten their security. West German Chancellor Kohl played a pivotal role in signaling to the Soviet Union—and also to Germany's European allies—that a united Germany would remain bound to NATO and integrated within the European Community. The wider Western system also operated to reassure Gorbachev: from a Soviet viewpoint, British and French leaders operated as a moderating voice in the unification process. As a result, the overall Western policy toward Moscow was more conciliatory than confrontational. The Soviets were also deeply involved in the complex negotiations over German unification, creating voice opportunities that made the final settlement more acceptable to them.

The issue of German unification emerged in late 1989 with the fall of the Berlin Wall and the intensification of political crisis in East Germany. The flow of refugees out of the GDR into Hungary and the appearance of opposition groups suddenly revealed the impotence of the Erich Honecker regime in East Berlin. The country was also in financial crisis, burdened by a $26.5 billion debt to the West and a large current account deficit. Despite these unsettling developments, Soviet policy remained quite passive. In a visit to East Berlin in October 1989, Gorbachev encouraged reform in the GDR but refrained from involvement in internal decisions about how to deal with unrest. His view was that domestic reform together with assistance from the West would allow East Germany to launch itself on the Polish or Hungarian path of change. Increased integration between East and West was inevitable and desirable: it would not jeopardize socialism or the GDR's ability to survive.[18] After the Berlin Wall fell, this view became untenable.

Chancellor Helmut Kohl responded to the East German crisis by pressing the issue of German unification, unsettling not only Gorbachev but

---

Robert D. Blackwill, "German Unification and American Diplomacy," *Aussenpolitik*, Vol. 45, No. 3 (1994), pp. 211–25; Stephen F. Szabo, *The Diplomacy of German Unification* (New York: St. Martin's, 1992); Elizabeth Pond, *Beyond the Wall: Germany's Road to Unification* (Washington, D.C.; Brookings Institution, 1993); Michael R. Beschloss and Strobe Talbott, *At the Highest Levels: The Inside Story of the End of the Cold War* (Boston: Little, Brown, 1993); George Bush and Brent Scowcraft, *A World Transformed* (New York: Knopf, 1998); James A. Baker, *The Politics of Diplomacy: Revolution, War and Peace, 1989–1992* (New York: G. P. Putnam's Sons, 1995); and Hans-Dietrich Genscher, *Rebuilding a House Divided: A Memoir by the Architect of Germany's Reunification* (New York: Broadway Books, 1998).

[18] Mikhail Gorbachev, *Memoirs* (New York: Doubleday, 1995), pp. 523–27. Zelikow and Rice, *Germany United and Europe Transformed*, p. 92.

also British and French leaders. In an important speech to the Bundestag on 28 November Kohl outlined a ten-point program for German unification. The German leader called for a staged process: the expansion of travel, exchange, and economic assistance between the two German states, followed by free elections in the East and movement toward "confederative structures," eventually culminating in a single federal Germany. Kohl argued that this transformation of inter-German relations should take place within a larger European process that would allow for "an organic development which takes into consideration the interests of all parties concerned and guarantees a peace order in Europe."[19] The speech did not explicitly mention Germany's commitment to NATO, but in a message to President Bush after his speech, Kohl reaffirmed West Germany's "unwavering loyalty" to NATO.[20]

The broad thrust of German policy was to reassure its neighbors—both East and West—that a unified and inevitably more powerful Germany would be deeply enmeshed in wider regional institutions.[21] Foreign Minister Hans-Dietrich Genscher articulated this basic German view in a January 1990 speech: "We want to place the process of German unification in the context of EC [European Community] integration, of the CSCE [Conference on Security in Europe] process, the West-East partnership for stability, the construction of the common European house and the creation of a peaceful European order from the Atlantic to the Urals."[22] Genscher and other German leaders did not always mention NATO in these statements, which worried American officials in the early months of the unification debate, but the basic message was clear: to gain agreement on unification, Germany was prepared to further bind itself to its neighbors.

The United States sought to reassure Gorbachev that Soviet security was not at risk in the unfolding developments but also to offer support to Kohl as he tried to allay the worries of other European leaders.[23] In September 1989, when Prime Minister Margaret Thatcher visited Moscow, Bush sent along a note to Gorbachev stressing that change in Eastern Europe should not be taken as a threat to the Soviet Union.[24] At a summit of

[19] Quoted in Zelikow and Rice, *Germany Unified and Europe Transformed*, p. 120.

[20] Quoted ibid., p. 122.

[21] On Chancellor Kohl's ambition of tying Germany to Europe and the Atlantic alliance so as to reassure neighboring countries, see Elizabeth Pond, *The Rebirth of Europe* (Washington, D.C.: Brookings Institution, 1999), pp. 39–40.

[22] "German Unity within the European Framework," speech by Foreign Minister Hans-Dietrich Genscher at a conference at the Tutzing Protestant Academy, 31 January 1990. Quoted in Hutchins, *American Diplomacy and the End of the Cold War*, p. 120. See also Genscher, *Rebuilding a House Divided*, pp. 335–38.

[23] Hutchins, *American Diplomacy and the End of the Cold War*, p. 100.

[24] Zelikow and Rice, *Germany Unified and Europe Transformed*, p. 73.

Soviet and American leaders in Malta in early December, Bush indicated to Gorbachev that the United States had not tried to exploit developments in Eastern Europe. Bush said that the United States has "not responded with flamboyance and arrogance. . . . I have conducted myself in ways not to complicate your life. That's why I have not jumped up and down on the Berlin Wall."[25] Soon afterward, at a meeting of NATO leaders in Brussels, Bush again stressed that it was important that Gorbachev not feel cornered.

While attempting to reassure Moscow, the United States was also trying to rally allied support for Kohl's plan for unification. This entailed extracting assurances from West Germany and stressing the wider institutional structures within which change should occur. The overriding American goal throughout these months was to ensure that a unified Germany would remain firmly embedded in the Atlantic alliance. During late 1989, the United States began to articulate a policy that linked German unification to assurances about Germany's continued commitment to European and Atlantic institutions. President Bush presented this view as American policy at the NATO meeting in Brussels on 4 December and later stated it in public: "unification should occur in the context of Germany's continued commitment to NATO and an increasingly integrated European Community, and with due regard for the legal role and responsibilities of the Allied powers."[26] The American president argued that NATO should remain the guarantor of stability in Europe, and to this end the United States remained committed to European security and the stationing of ground forces in Europe. In effect, German unification would be rendered acceptable to its neighbors by the same means that a revived West Germany was rendered acceptable after World War II: Germany would be embedded in wider Euro-Atlantic institutions. The NATO alliance and European economic integration would bind Germany to Europe, and the United States would ensure agreement by adding its own security commitment.[27]

Reassurance of this sort was necessary. Prime Minister Thatcher of Britain was the most reluctant to see German unification move quickly. Her

[25] Quoted ibid., p. 127.

[26] Bush, President's News Conference in Brussels, 4 December 1989, in *Public Papers of President George Bush, 1989* (Washington, D.C.: Government Printing Office, 1990), Vol. 2, p. 1,648.

[27] In a December 1989 speech in Berlin, Secretary of State Baker emphasized the larger institutions that must evolve to support a united Germany: NATO must play a wider political role on the continent and develop ties to the East; the European Community should move forward with greater political as well as economic integration; and the Conference on Security and Cooperation in Europe (CSCE), as an institution that encompassed East and West, should play a greater role in developing common standards on human rights and processes of consultation. Address of Secretary of State Baker, "A New Europe, a New Atlanticism: Architecture for a New Era," Berlin Press Club, 11 December 1989, State Department transcript.

view was that the quickening pace of developments in Eastern Europe must not get out of hand and threaten Soviet security. In a letter to Bush she argued: "We must demonstrate that we do not intend to exploit the situation to the detriment of the Soviet Union's security interests. This will involve continuing to make plain our view that the future of the Warsaw Pact, like that of NATO, is a matter for its members to decide without interference from outside; and that German reunification is not a matter to be addressed at present."[28] At a meeting with Bush at Camp David on 24 November 1989, Thatcher reiterated her view that German unification would destabilize Europe, spell the end of Gorbachev, and doom the prospects for democracy in Eastern Europe.[29]

French President François Mitterrand was also cautious about German unification, but his emphasis was on the need to deepen European integration and West Germany's ties to the European Community.[30] In a letter to President Bush on 27 November 1989, Mitterrand argued that "Each of our governments is very aware of the role that the EC can and must play in the definition of a new European equilibrium, as soon as the EC has reinforced its own cohesion."[31] Soon thereafter, in a meeting with Genscher, Mitterrand again linked German unification to progress toward a more integrated European union. Later, at a summit with Gorbachev in Kiev, Mitterrand heard the Soviet leader warn that on the day that Germany is unified, "a Soviet marshal will be sitting in my chair." Mitterrand indicated that he thought Kohl was moving too fast, but his main message was that inter-German relations must be dealt with as part of an all-European process.[32] In a meeting between Mitterrand and Bush on St. Martin in the Caribbean on 16 December, the French leader again affirmed his view that German unification must be linked to developments in NATO and the European Community. Arms control, EC integration, European monetary union, and American cooperation with Europe must all be addressed together in order to create a new Europe in which German unification would be a part. "Otherwise," warned Mitterrand, "we will be back in 1913 and we could lose everything."[33]

This linkage was on display at the Strasbourg meeting of EC leaders on 8 December. Mitterrand was able to gain Kohl's support for convening an intergovernmental meeting to amend the EC's Treaty of Rome in order to prepare the way for a new treaty of economic and political union. In return,

---

[28] Quoted in Zelikow and Rice, *Germany Unified and Europe Transformed*, p. 115.

[29] See Margaret Thatcher, *The Downing Street Years* (New York: HarperCollins 1993), p. 794; and Bush and Scowcroft, *A World Transformed*, pp. 192–93.

[30] On Mitterrand's initial inclination to seek delay in German unification, see Pond, *Beyond the Wall*.

[31] Quoted in Zelikow and Rice, *Germany Unified and Europe Transformed*, p. 116.

[32] Ibid., p. 137.

[33] Bush and Scowcroft, *A World Transformed*, p. 201.

the EC leaders adopted a statement that endorsed German unification within the context of wider European developments.[34] The linkage was explicit. Again in March 1990, after Kohl articulated an accelerated plan for unification, he also signaled Germany's readiness to embark on ambitious steps toward greater European integration, including a willingness to begin negotiations on the terms of European political union. A formal proposal to this effect was prepared by the French and German governments and presented to the EC in April. Kohl was already a supporter of greater European integration, but the willingness of the German leader to move quickly with an ambitious plan for European monetary and political union was tied to his own agenda for German unity.[35]

As East Germany continued to weaken and momentum toward unification grew, Soviet policy became more actively oriented toward blocking or at least slowing down the process. Gorbachev proposed that a meeting of the ambassadors of the Four Powers—Britain, the United States, France, and the Soviet Union—meet to agree on the future of East and West Germany. Gorbachev was aware of the uneasiness of British and French leaders and hoped that they and he might make common cause in forestalling a quick move toward unification. American officials worried that a Four Power gathering might lead to efforts by the Soviets to exchange their consent on unification for the neutralization of Germany or other abridgments on German sovereignty and its role in NATO—a worry that persisted in American government circles until agreement was finally reached. They also wanted to avoid the appearance that a settlement was being imposed by the World War II victors, a move that would be an echo of the disputed Versailles settlement.[36] The Kohl government, which was deeply offended by the idea of turning over to others the question of German unification, also resisted the convening of the Four Power mechanism.

In late 1989, Gorbachev's view of unification was straightforward. The end of World War II had resulted in a "historical reality" that had been acknowledged and formalized by both the East and the West, most recently in the 1975 Helsinki Accords. The reality was that there were two German states, and both were members of the United Nations and as such sovereign states. "This is the decision of history," Gorbachev argued.[37] This was an

---

[34] Zelikow and Rice, *Germany Unified and Europe Transformed*, p. 138.

[35] Hutchins, *American Diplomacy and the End of the Cold War*, p. 118. See also Pond, *The Rebirth of Europe*, pp. 42–47; and Peter J. Katzenstein, "United Germany in an Integrated Europe," in Katzenstein, ed, *Tamed Power: Germany in Europe* (Ithaca: Cornell University Press, 1997), pp. 1–2.

[36] See Baker, *The Politics of Diplomacy*, p. 196–97.

[37] Gorbachev, Remarks of the President and Soviet Chairman Mikhail Gorbachev and a Question-and-Answer Session with Reporters in Malta, 3 December 1989, in *Public Papers of President George Bush, 1989*, Vol. 2, p. 1,633. For a discussion of Gorbachev's evolving thinking, see Oberdorfer, *The Turn*, pp. 383–86.

appeal for the maintenance of the status quo. At the same time, Gorbachev gave some support during these months to proposals coming out of East Berlin for a confederation or "treaty community" between the two German states. The search was for some formulation that could allow some intermediate solution short of unification. Later, when unification became a fait accompli, Gorbachev insisted that a united Germany could not remain within NATO. Unification was possible, but Germany must be neutral and its military power limited. On Germany remaining in NATO after unification, Gorbachev told the press in Moscow on 6 March 1990: "It is absolutely out of the question."

Getting the Soviets to accept a united Germany in NATO was the goal of American diplomacy in the spring of 1990. The dilemma for the United States was to try to keep the Soviets involved in the negotiation process but not allow them to move negotiations into a forum that would let them raise the option of German neutrality. If the question of German unification were settled through Four Power talks, the Soviets could hold agreement on unification hostage to Western concessions on Germany's role in NATO. American officials recalled Stalin's 1952 offer of a unified but neutral Germany, but they also worried about lesser infringements on German sovereignty.[38] One response to this problem was the proposal for a "Two plus Four" process: the two German states would settle the question of unification directly, after the East Germans had held free elections, while the four World War II powers would "bless" this outcome and seek agreement with East and West Germany over the external elements of unification. This framework was eventually adopted at a joint meeting of NATO and Warsaw Pact ministers in Ottawa in February 1990.[39]

The United States also worked with its allies to allay Soviet fears that a united Germany might be a security threat. Soviet worries of this sort varied from meeting to meeting during the winter of 1989–1990. At a meeting in Moscow with Secretary of State James A. Baker III in February 1990, Gorbachev indicated that the Soviets did not worry about a united Germany: "Well, for us and for you, regardless of our differences, there is nothing terrifying in the prospect of a unified Germany."[40] At other moments, Gorbachev or Foreign Minister Eduard Shevardnadze were less sanguine. At an important internal Kremlin policy meeting in January 1990, there are indications that views differed widely. Some of Gorbachev's advisors, such as Anatoly Chernyayev, thought that a united Germany in NATO was not a threat—quite the contrary, it was a source of some reassurance, particularly as Kohl linked German unification to an "all-

---

[38] Hutchins, *American Diplomacy and the End of the Cold War*, pp. 107–8.

[39] Baker, *The Politics of Diplomacy*, p. 208–16.

[40] Quoted ibid., p. 205. See also Gorbachev, *Memoirs*, pp. 528–29.

European process." Others, such as Valentin Falin, thought it was wrong to accept the absorption of East Germany into West Germany and NATO so fatalistically. Gorbachev at this stage was still opposed to a united Germany's membership in the Western alliance.[41]

Aside from involving the Soviets in the Two plus Four process, the United States sought to persuade Gorbachev that a neutral united Germany would be more dangerous than one tied to NATO. This argument was advanced by Baker in talks with Shevardnadze in Moscow in February 1990. The Soviets by this time understood that unification was a fait accompli; it was now a question of a united Germany's external affiliations. Shevardnadze argued that a united Germany might eventually become militaristic and threaten the Soviet Union, hence their proposal for a disarmed and neutral Germany. Baker turned the argument around and posed the question to Gorbachev: "Assuming unification takes place, what would you prefer: a united Germany outside NATO and completely autonomous, without American forces stationed on its territory, or a united Germany that maintains its ties with NATO, but with the guarantee that NATO jurisdiction or troops would not extend east of the current line?"[42] Baker's argument in Moscow was that embedding German military power in Western institutions was preferable to neutrality, even to the Soviets.

Gorbachev notes in his memoir that the second part of Baker's statement eventually formed the basis for a compromise over Germany's military-political status. This was so even though at the time of the Moscow meeting the Soviet leader was unprepared to accept the proposal. Gorbachev recalls that "I too believed that we needed a 'safety net' which would protect us and the rest of Europe from any 'surprises' from the Germans. However, unlike the Americans, I thought that these security mechanisms should be provided not by NATO but by new structures created within a pan-European framework."[43] The opening for compromise dealt with the specific guarantees that might be attached to unification about the size and configuration of NATO and German forces.

The idea that guarantees might accompany Four Power agreement on unification was raised by the West German leaders, as well. To the surprise of many Western officials, Genscher raised the idea of limitations of NATO forces within the territory of the former GDR in a January 1990 speech.[44] In his Camp David meeting with Bush the next month, Kohl argued that NATO forces would not be able to be stationed in the former

[41] Zelikow and Rice, *Germany Unified and Europe Transformed*, pp. 161–64. See Gorbachev, *Memoirs*, p. 528.

[42] Quoted in Gorbachev, *Memoirs*, p. 529.

[43] Ibid. On Baker's report of the meeting, see Baker, *The Politics of Diplomacy*, pp. 234–35.

[44] Hutchins, *American Diplomacy and the End of the Cold War*, pp. 111–12. See also Zelikow and Rice, *Germany United and Europe Transformed*, pp. 253, 180–81.

East Germany.[45] This idea was eventually folded into a larger set of proposals that were assembled by Western officials in an effort to gain Soviet agreement on German membership in NATO. Rather than threaten the Soviets, the Atlantic alliance could be part of the wider institutional "safety net" that Gorbachev was seeking.

In May 1990 the United States was still seeking Soviet agreement on Germany within NATO. Baker took with him to Moscow what was called the "nine assurances"—a package of incentives prepared for use in the Two plus Four talks. The steps that the West would be willing to take to meet Soviet security concerns included assurances that unification would be accompanied by new conventional and nuclear arms limitation agreements, a German reaffirmation not to possess or produce nuclear, chemical, or biological weapons, agreement that NATO troops would not be stationed in the former territory of the GDR, and a promise that NATO would undertake to revise its strategy and its posture within a transformed Europe.[46] Most of these nine assurances had been presented to the Soviets during the previous few months, but the repackaging of them was itself part of the process of changing Soviet thinking.[47] In German meetings with the Soviets during this period, they presented their own package of reassurances that dealt with force levels and territorial limitations as well as promises of economic assistance.

The turning point came in May 1990, during Gorbachev's visit to Washington. Although he initially proposed that a united Germany must belong to both NATO and the Warsaw Pact, the Soviet leader conceded on this visit that all countries had the right to choose their own alliances.[48] In agreeing to this principle, Gorbachev was effectively agreeing that Germany had a right to stay within NATO. The Four Powers could not dictate German alliance membership. In agreeing to this principle and allowing the Germans themselves to decide, the dispute over German membership in NATO was on the way to resolution.[49]

The Soviet leader heard American officials again make the argument that binding Germany to NATO was the most effective security strategy for all parties concerned. Bush told Gorbachev that "It appears to me that

[45] Baker, *The Politics of Diplomacy*, p. 233.

[46] Ibid., pp. 250–51. The nine-point "incentive" package, which was prepared by State Department Counselor Robert Zoellick, is reprinted in Zelikow and Rice, *Germany United and Europe Transformed*, pp. 263–64.

[47] Interview, Robert B. Zoellick, 28 May 1999.

[48] Baker had a similar exchange with Gorbachev in Moscow two weeks before this exchange. See Baker, *The Politics of Diplomacy*, pp. 251–52.

[49] American officials involved in the process identify this admission by Gorbachev as the turning point. See ibid., pp. 253–54; and Zelikow and Rice, *Germany United and Europe Transformed*, pp. 277–80; Hutchins, *American Diplomacy and the End of the Cold War*, pp. 131–35.

our approach to Germany, i.e. seeing it as a close friend, is more pragmatic and constructive . . . all of us in the West agree that the main danger lies in excluding Germany from the community of democratic nations."[50] The Soviet Union was again being asked to see NATO—and Germany's role in it—as a security institution that could reduce Soviet worries rather than aggravate them. The American promise to recast NATO's mission was meant to make the alliance all the more acceptable.

At the July 1990 NATO summit in London that followed the Soviet-American talks, the alliance members agreed on a package of reforms that signaled a shift in its posture. Gorbachev had advocated even before the collapse of East Germany in November 1989 that the two alliances should evolve toward political organizations. The declaration on NATO reform that was agreed to at the London summit moved in this direction and incorporated elements that were meant to reassure the Soviets. These included an invitation to the Soviet Union and Warsaw Pact countries to establish permanent liaison missions to NATO, which was formalized the following year in the North Atlantic Cooperation Council and later the Partnership for Peace consultative process. The allies also promised to reorganize and downsize their forces and rely increasingly on multinational troop units, knitting German forces more tightly to the wider NATO command structure.[51] In a message to Gorbachev after the NATO summit, Bush reported that "As you read the NATO declaration, I want you to know that it was written with you importantly in mind, and I made that point strongly to my colleagues in London."[52]

Shevardnadze observed later that the decision made in London to alter NATO's mission and forces was a decisive step in allowing the Soviets to accept the terms of the German settlement. "In my circumstances, it was especially important to see some encouraging response from 'the other side' [the West]. Otherwise, we would be in an untenable position. When the news came out about the NATO session in London, I knew there had been a response."[53] The Two plus Four process had allowed the Soviets a voice opportunity, an opportunity to press the Western governments to step up the process of NATO transformation.

This episode provides evidence of the larger pattern: Western governments had the ability to reassure Soviet leaders that they would not exploit Soviet troubles, and that German integration within Western security and economic institutions would provide an effective guard against the resur-

[50] Quoted in Gorbachev, *Memoirs*, p. 533.
[51] Baker, *The Politics of Diplomacy*, pp. 258–59; and Bush and Scowcroft, *A World Transformed*, pp. 292–95.
[52] Quoted in Bush and Scowcroft, *A World Transformed*, p. 295.
[53] Shevardnadze, *The Future Belongs to Freedom*, p. 141.

gence of German power. The Soviets had come around to accepting a
NATO solution to the problem of German military power. In the view of
one of Gorbachev's advisors, Anatoly Chernyayev, as Zelikow and Rice
report, "Gorbachev himself had decided that he no longer feared NATO,
and no longer really believed that German membership in NATO posed a
real threat to the USSR."[54]

The willingness of the Soviet leaders to accept a unified Germany within
NATO was partly linked to the way the alliance bound the United States
to Europe. In various talks with American officials, both Gorbachev and
Shevardnadze indicated that they wanted a continuation of the American
troop presence in Germany. They eventually came to see NATO as a necessary vehicle to ensure this commitment. At the Malta summit with Bush
in December 1989, Gorbachev surprised the Americans by making the
unsolicited point that he saw the continued presence of American troops
in Europe as a source of stability, thus indicating the beginning of Soviet
thinking about how German unification would impinge on Soviet security.[55] Shevardnadze told Baker at a March 1990 meeting in Namibia that
part of the Soviet worry about Germany in NATO was that the United
States might withdraw from Germany. "You have to consider what is going
to happen tomorrow. Say we left East Germany. It could well be that you
would still be in Germany, and we would have no problems with that. But
what if you would have to withdraw also?" Baker responded that only a
functioning NATO alliance could guarantee an American military presence in Europe and only German membership in NATO could ensure the
continuation of the alliance.[56] The Soviets came to recognize that if the
United States was to be bound to Europe, Germany would need to be
bound to NATO.[57]

Soviet acceptance of a unified Germany within NATO required a revision of its view of the Western threat. NATO had to be seen as a fundamen-

---

[54] Zelikow and Rice, *Germany United and Europe Transformed*, p. 332.

[55] See Hutchins, *American Diplomacy and the End of the Cold War*, pp. 103–4; and Oberdorfer, *The Turn*, p. 381.

[56] Baker, *The Politics of Diplomacy*, p. 238. Bush and Gorbachev engaged in a very similar
exchange during their May 1990 summit in Washington. Gorbachev said that it was not in
the Soviet interest to see an American "withdrawal" from Europe, and Bush argued that
without Germany in NATO, the alliance would be jeopardized and with it the American
presence in Europe. This exchange is reported in Gorbachev, *Memoirs*, p. 533.

[57] More generally within the Soviet foreign policy establishment, some officials saw security benefits in the Western order that kept Germany and Japan bound to a larger American-
led alliance system. See Jerry Hough, *Russia and the West: Gorbachev and the Politics of Reform*
(New York: Simon and Schuster, 1990), pp. 219–20; and Michael J. Sodaro, *Moscow, Germany,
and the West from Khrushchev to Gorbachev* (Ithaca: Cornell University Press, 1990), pp. 341–
42. For a discussion of recent historical works that emphasize the Soviet worry over the revival
of German militarism more than American power during the Cold War, see Melvyn P. Leffler,

tally defensive alliance that served to stabilize and limit German military power. To get Gorbachev's consent, the binding character of the alliance and Western institutions had to have some credibility. There had to be some confidence that NATO would restrain German military power and keep the American military connected to Europe. NATO had to be seen as fundamentally a *pactum de controhendo*—as a pact of restraint. To get to this point, the operation of the Western order itself mattered. The "push" and "pull" of the Western leaders as they themselves worried about a unified Germany and about how to reassure the Soviets served to restrain the process. The Soviets were not faced with an aggressive and unified front that sought to roll back the weakening Soviet order.[58]

Institution Building after the Cold War

The end of the Cold War has had the effect of sharply increasing American power. The collapse of bipolarity left the United States the world's dominant power, in terms of both economic and military capability. A decade of strong economic growth in the United States—and economic stagnation in Russia, Japan, and parts of Europe—has further strengthened its relative position.[59] In the 1990s, like a victor in a great war, the United States faced choices about how to use its newly acquired power.

"The Cold War: What Do 'We Now Know'?" *American Historical Review*, Vol. 104, No. 2 (April 1999), pp. 515–16.

[58] The multisided process of negotiations also allowed Soviet leaders ample opportunity to press their views. In 1990, Baker and Shevardnadze met ten times, Baker and Genscher met eleven times, and Genscher and Shevardnadze met eight times in May and June alone. The diversity of views and agendas among the Western allies also provided openings for the Soviets to maneuver and gain concessions on guarantees and assurances. These voice opportunities both influenced Western policies toward German unification—particularly the larger package of assurances that came with it—and gave Gorbachev a chance to alter his thinking about German membership in NATO. Moens, "American Diplomacy and German Unification," p. 538; and Hutchins, *American Diplomacy and the End of the Cold War*, p. 92. The importance of this intense series of meetings is stressed in Shevardnadze, *The Future Belongs to Freedom*, p. 83.

[59] The heightened power asymmetry between the United States and the other major states during the 1990s is reflected in various economic and military indicators. Between 1990 and 1998, United States' economic growth (27 percent) was almost twice that of the European Union (15 percent) and three times that of Japan (11 percent). Calculated from OECD statistics (November 1999 web edition: www.oecd.org/std/gdp.htm). GDP measures are figured at 1990 prices and exchange rates. The United States also reduced defense spending at a slower rate after the Cold War than the other major powers, resulting in greater relative military capabilities by the end of the 1990s. See International Institute for Strategic Studies, *The Military Balance 1999/2000* (London: Oxford University Press, 1999). For additional measures that indicated an intensification of American power, see William C. Wohlforth, "The Stability of a Unipolar World," *International Security*, Vol. 24, No. 1 (Summer 1999), pp. 5–41, and Appendix Two below.

In this advantaged position during the 1990s, the United States pursued an institution-building agenda.[60] Across security and economic areas, the United States sought to build and expand regional and global institutions. NATO expansion and the creation of the North American Free Trade Agreement (NAFTA), Asia Pacific Economic Cooperation (APEC), and the World Trade Association (WTO) were elements of this agenda. This pattern of policy was consistent with the institutional model of order building. The United States employed institutions as a mechanism to lock in other states to desired policy orientations, and it was willing to exchange some limits on its own autonomy to do so. Other states also seized upon these institutions as ways to gain access to America—either its markets or its policy making.

In the immediate aftermath of the Cold War, the Bush administration pushed forward a variety of regional institutional initiatives. In relations toward Europe, State Department officials articulated a set of institutions steps: the evolution of NATO to include associate relations with countries to the east, the creation of more formal institutional relations with the European Community, and an expanded role for the Conference on Security Cooperation in Europe (CSCE).[61] In the Western Hemisphere, the Bush administration pushed for NAFTA and closer economic ties with South America. In East Asia, APEC was a way to create more institutional links to the region, demonstrating American commitment to the region and insuring that Asian regionalism moved in a trans-Pacific direction.[62] The idea was to pursue innovative regional strategies that resulted in new institutional frameworks for post-Cold War relations.

These institutional initiatives, Baker later observed, were the key elements of the Bush administration's post-Cold War order-building strategy, and he likened its efforts to American strategy after 1945. "Men like Truman and Acheson were above all, though we sometimes forget it, *institution builders*. They created NATO and the other security organizations that eventually won the Cold War. They fostered the economic institutions . . . that brought unparalleled prosperity. . . . At a time of similar opportunity and risk, I believed we should take a leaf from their book."[63] The idea was

---

[60] American foreign policy has been sufficiently inconsistent and ambiguous during the 1990s to make definitive descriptions of an underlying post-Cold War pattern—or strategy—difficult at best. The United States supported various global and regional institutional proposals, but it also withheld support for others, such as the Kyoto protocol on global warming and the International Criminal Court, and imposed unilateral sanctions on various countries. American support for regional economic institutions, such as NAFTA and APEC, can also be seen as evidence of a waning commitment to multilateralism.

[61] See Baker, *The Politics of Diplomacy*, pp. 172–73.

[62] Interview, Robert B. Zoellick, 28 May 1999.

[63] Baker, *The Politics of Diplomacy*, pp. 605–6. Emphasis in original.

to "plant institutional seeds"—to create regional institutional frameworks that would extend and enhance America's influence in these areas and encourage democracy and open markets.[64]

An institution-building agenda was also articulated by the Clinton administration in its strategy of "enlargement." The idea was to use multilateral institutions as mechanisms to stabilize and integrate the new and emerging market democracies into the Western democratic world. In an early statement of the enlargement doctrine, National Security Advisor Anthony Lake argued that the strategy was to "strengthen the community of market democracies" and "foster and consolidate new democracies and market economies where possible." The United States would help "democracy and market economies take root," which would in turn expand and strengthen the wider Western democratic order.[65] The target of this strategy was primarily those parts of the world that were beginning the process of transition to market democracy: countries of Central and Eastern Europe and the Asia-Pacific region. Promising domestic reforms in these countries would be encouraged—and locked in if possible—through new trade pacts and security partnerships.[66]

NATO expansion embodied this institutional logic.[67] At the July 1997 NATO summit, Poland, Hungary, and the Czech Republic were formally invited to join the alliance. These invitations followed a decision made at

[64] American officials working on these regional initiatives saw a strong relationship between economics and security. American presence and commitments to these regions after the Cold War would increasingly hinge on economic interests. To the extent that regional frameworks facilitated greater economic interdependence, American stakes in the regions increase and America's security role becomes more important. Interview, Robert B. Zoellick, 28 May 1999.

[65] Anthony Lake, "From Containment to Enlargement," *Vital Speeches of the Day*, Vol. 60, No. 1 (15 October 1993), pp. 13–19. See also Douglas Brinkley, "Democratic Enlargement: The Clinton Doctrine," *Foreign Policy*, No. 106 (Spring 1997), p. 116.

[66] In 1994, the Clinton White House provided a formal statement of its strategy of engagement and enlargement, calling for a multilateral approach to major foreign policy challenges: "Whether the problem is nuclear proliferation, regional instability, the reversal of reform in the former Soviet empire, or unfair trade practices, the threats and challenges we face demand cooperative, multinational solutions. Therefore, the only responsible U.S. strategy is one that seeks to ensure U.S. influence over and participation in collective decision-making in a wide and growing range of circumstances." White House, *A National Security Strategy of Engagement and Enlargement* (Washington, D.C.: White House, July 1994), p. 6.

[67] NATO expansion was intensely debated by the American foreign policy establishment. Some opponents argued that, regardless of its usefulness in locking in democratic and market reforms in Eastern Europe, it would provoke serious and long-term problems with Russia. Likewise, some proponents of NATO expansion were less interested in the institutional lock-in opportunities of an eastward spread of the alliance, and more interested in it as a precautionary balancing move against Russia. The discussion here does not seek to assess the merits of these various positions but only to describe the thinking of Clinton administration officials who championed it.

the January 1994 NATO summit in Brussels to enlarge the alliance to include new members from Eastern and Central Europe. Led by the United States, the alliance embarked on the most far-reaching and controversial reworking of institutional architecture in the post-Cold War era.[68]

The Clinton administration offered several basic rationales for NATO expansion, but it consistently emphasized its importance in consolidating democratic and market gains in Eastern and Central Europe and building an expanded Western democratic community. Secretary of State Madeline Albright advanced three arguments in support of NATO enlargement. One was that a larger alliance would expand "the area in Europe where wars do not happen." By extending security guarantees to the new states, it was less likely that war would in fact occur in the region. Albright and other administration officials downplayed Russia as a potential threat, although they acknowledged that Russia's future remained uncertain. The threats that administration officials identified were more diffuse and less specific, such as the rise of ethnic conflict and rogue states.[69]

Albright and other officials made it clear that a Russian threat did not actually exist and that such a threat was not necessary to justify enlargement. "NATO is not taking place in response to a new Russian threat," she argued, and those "who ask 'where is the threat?' mistake NATO's real value."[70] This view was not entirely shared by the new members of NATO, who were eager to join for a variety of reasons, including the fear of a renewal of Russian imperialism.[71] The second reason for NATO enlargement was that it would make NATO itself stronger and more cohesive. Albright argued that "our prospective allies are passionately committed to NATO." These new democracies saw NATO as a way to establish an unbreakable tie to Europe and the West. Their determined participation in the security organization would reinvigorate and add "strategic depth" to the alliance.[72]

The third and most important reason for NATO enlargement is that it would provide an institutional framework to stabilize and encourage democracy and market reform in these reforming countries. NATO would

[68] For a study of the American decision to expand NATO, see James M. Goldgeier, *Not Whether but When: The U.S. Decision to Enlarge NATO* (Washington, D.C.: Brookings Institution, 1999).

[69] Secretary of State Madeline K. Albright, Statement on NATO Enlargement before the Senate Foreign Relations Committee, 24 February 1998, as released by the Office of the Spokesman, U.S. Department of State, pp. 2–3.

[70] Madeline K. Albright, "Why Bigger Is Better," *Economist*, Vol. 342 (15 February 1997), pp. 21–23.

[71] Strobe Talbott, "Why NATO Should Grow," *New York Review of Books*, Vol. 42, No. 13 (August 10, 1995), pp. 27–30.

[72] Albright, Statement on NATO Enlargement, 24 February 1998, p. 3.

help lock in the domestic transitions under way in Eastern and Central Europe. The prospect of membership would itself be an "incentive" for these countries to pursue domestic reforms in advance of actually joining the alliance. This was an argument emphasized by the early proponents of NATO expansion within the Clinton administration.[73] In their view, "the prospect of NATO membership was a huge incentive for reformers in the East, since it would give them credibility with their populations yearning to be part of the West and might also assist them with membership in the European economic community which they craved."[74]

This argument featured prominently in the Clinton administration's defense of NATO expansion. "To align themselves with NATO," Albright argued, "aspiring allies have strengthened their democratic institutions, improved respect for minority rights, made sure soldiers take orders from civilians, and resolved virtually every old border and ethnic dispute in the region."[75] Undersecretary of State Strobe Talbott echoed this view in a prominent essay that made the case for NATO expansion: opening NATO to new members would create incentives for candidate countries to strengthen democratic institutions, liberalize their economies, ensure civilian control of the military, and enhance respect of human rights.[76]

Administration officials pointed to several mechanisms that would lead NATO expansion to lock in democratic and market reforms. One mechanism was political conditionality. To gain NATO membership, candidate countries must engage in requisite institutional reform.[77] Because the benefits of membership are assumed to be great, the political standing of political groups and parties committed to institutional reforms is strengthened and the domestic consensus in favor of domestic reform is expanded. "In Hungary and Poland," Talbott argued, "the prospect of NATO membership has helped to solidify the national consensus for democratic and market reforms."[78] The same argument was made by Albright in support of keeping the door open to more NATO members: it creates incentives to continue progress toward democratic and market reform. "They know they have ways to go before they can be considered. Yet just the possibility of

---

[73] According to Anthony Lake, this objective was "absolutely critical" to the thinking of the proponents of NATO enlargement within the Clinton administration. Interview, 20 September 1999.

[74] Goldgeier, *Not Whether but When*, p. 23.

[75] Albright, Statement on NATO Enlargement, 24 February 1998, p. 3.

[76] Talbott, "Why NATO Should Grow," p. 27.

[77] Certain steps were specified as a necessary prelude to admission to the alliance: democratic institutions, progress a toward market economy, armed forces in civilian hands, settled territorial borders, and movement toward interoperability with NATO forces. See Fact Sheet prepared by the Bureau of European and Canadian Affairs, 15 August 1997.

[78] Talbott, "Why NATO Should Grow," pp. 27–28.

joining has inspired them to accelerate reform, to reach out to their neighbors, and to reject the destructive nationalism of their region's past."[79] The political groups in favor of reform are reinforced, increasing their chances of success in domestic struggles with opponents of reform.

In qualifying for NATO membership, for example, Poland took steps to ensure civilian control of its military. Before the ratification of a new constitution in 1997, the Polish General Staff operated with considerable autonomy from the Defense Ministry and civilian executive authority. To meet the requirements of NATO membership, Polish leaders took steps to establish civilian control of the military. The National Defense Law passed in 1996 subordinated the Chief of the General Staff to the minister of defense and shifted control of the budget, planning, and military intelligence from the General Staff to the Defense Ministry. These steps to strengthen civilian control were at least in part promoted by the requirements of NATO membership. In a speech before the Belgian Parliament in 1997, Poland's Minister of Defense Stanislaw Dobranski indicated that "Ensuring civilian control of the armed forces has been the Polish government's priority since it declared Poland's desire to join NATO."[80] The prospect of alliance membership stimulated Polish leaders—and their counterparts in Hungary and the Czech Republic—to pursue institutional reforms that would ensure civilian control and parliamentary oversight of the military along Western lines.[81]

Once admitted to NATO, the process of alliance integration was assumed to reinforce institutional reforms. Membership entailed a wide array of organizational adaptations, such as standardization of military procedures, steps toward interoperability with NATO forces, and joint planning and training. By enmeshing themselves within the wider alliance institutions, the ability of the new NATO members to revert to old ways was reduced, and ongoing participation in alliance operations tended to reinforce the governmental changes that were made on the way toward membership. "For more than three years," according to one report, "military leaders from Poland, Hungary, and the Czech Republic have been drawn

[79] Albright, Statement on NATO Enlargement, 24 February 1998, p. 6.

[80] Stanislaw Dobranski, "Toward a Pan-European Security System," address to the committees of National Defense and Foreign Affairs of the Belgian parliament, 29 April 1997.

[81] Eastern and Central European leaders rarely argue that NATO membership was necessary to defend against a resurgent Russia but rather that it was part of a larger "European package," also involving eventual membership in the European Union, which was essential to the success of democratic and market reform. The security threat to these countries was not Russia but exclusion from Europe. See Christopher Jones, "NATO Enlargement: Brussels as the Heir of Moscow," *Problems of Post-Communism*, No. 6 Vol. 45, No. 4 (July/August 1998), p. 52; and Jan Arveds Trapans, "National Security Concepts in Central and Eastern Europe," *NATO Review* No. 6 (November/December 1997), pp. 23–26.

into the web of NATO seminars, planning sessions and military exercises that drive the alliance."[82] Integration into the alliance entailed a sweeping set of adjustments and requirements. As one NATO official remarked, "We're enmeshing them in the NATO culture, both politically and militarily so they begin to think like us and—over time—act like us."[83] NATO membership rewarded steps toward democratic and market reform, pushed it forward, and locked it in.

These arguments for NATO expansion echoed arguments advanced during the earlier post-1945 debate on NATO creation. The alliance was seen to serve political as well as security purposes.[84] It established an organizational structure that would help stabilize and embed postwar democratic institutions. "NATO gave hope to democratic forces in West Germany that their country would be welcome and secure in our community if they kept making the right choices," Albright argued, and it would do the same for the Eastern democracies today.[85] National Security Advisor Anthony Lake similarly argued in 1996 that "NATO can do for Europe's east what it did for Europe's west: prevent the return to local rivalries; strengthen democracy against future threats; and provide the conditions for fragile market economies to flourish."[86] NATO bound states together, thereby creating greater security among alliance partners and reinforcing democratic and market institutions.

A similar—if less encompassing—logic stood behind the American embrace of NAFTA and APEC. These regional economic initiatives had their origins in a worldwide movement in the late 1980s toward economic and trade liberalization. American government officials saw a variety of virtues in these agreements—not least the expectation of expanded trade and economic growth—but they were also embraced as institutional devices that would reinforce and lock in the commitments of other governments to market and political reform.

The NAFTA agreement signed by Mexico, Canada, and the United States in late 1992 culminated a decade of economic liberalization in Mexico. Departing from its long-standing protectionist and inward-looking orientation, the Mexican government worked steadily during the 1980s to

---

[82] Pat Towell, "Aspiring NATO Newcomers Face Long Road to Integration," *Congressional Quarterly*, Vol. 56, No. 6 (7 February 1998), p. 275.

[83] Quoted ibid.

[84] See Ronald D. Asmus, Richard K. Kugler, and F. Stephen Larrabee, "NATO Expansion: The Next Steps," *Survival*, Vol. 37, No. 1 (Spring 1995).

[85] Albright, Statement before the Senate Foreign Relations Committee, U.S. Senate, Hearings on NATO Enlargement, 7 October 1997 (http:/frwebgate.access.gpo.gov/cgi-bin/getdoc.cgi?dbname=105_senate_hearings&docid=f.46832.wais, p. 2.

[86] Anthony Lake, "Laying the Foundation for a New American Century," remarks to the Fletcher School of Law and Diplomacy, 25 April 1996.

deregulate the economy and reduce trade barriers. This sharp turnabout in policy was facilitated by a variety of economic and political developments: the debt crisis of the early 1980s provided an initial inducement for policy change, facilitated by the rise of new business constituencies in favor of liberalization and political reform that insulated reformist policy makers from protectionist pressures. The ruling party itself also underwent transformation, aligning itself increasingly with internationalist interests and developing social programs to maintain the support of the urban poor and peasants.[87] By 1990, with commercial liberalization largely complete, the government of President Carlos Salinas de Gortari surprised many officials in Washington by initiating NAFTA negotiations with the United States and Canada.

NAFTA offered economic gains to both countries, but it was a political tool that both governments could use to lock in—or institutionalize—the outward-looking policy orientation that Mexico had struggled to achieve. To the Salinas government, NAFTA was useful in creating more predictable and credible domestic rules to attract foreign investment. By 1990, Salinas had determined that domestic economic reforms alone were not successful in attracting new foreign capital. "Policies that would increase the expected rate of return on investment and boost confidence were the essence of this strategy," one analyst noted. "An FTA [free trade agreement] with the United States would certainly do that, for it would ensure both future access to the U.S. market and the durability of Mexico's open economic strategy."[88] Trade liberalization itself had not completely erased the suspicions that Mexico might revert to more restrictive policies. A free trade agreement with the United States was attractive to Salinas because—beyond the specific economic gains—it would tie his successors to a policy of economic liberalization. It would make backsliding more difficult, and this would improve the attractiveness of Mexico to foreign investors and traders.

NAFTA, as Peter Smith argues, offered Salinas "an opportunity to institutionalize and perpetuate his economic reforms. . . . In order to preserve his innovations, Salinas wanted to insulate them from the historic vagaries

[87] See Manuel Pastor and Carol Wise, "The Origins and Sustainability of Mexico's Free Trade Policy," *International Organization*, Vol. 48, No. 3 (Summer 1994), pp. 459–89; Michael Lusztig, *Rising Free Trade: The Politics of Trade in Britain, Canada, Mexico, and the United States* (Pittsburgh: University of Pittsburgh Press, 1996), chapter five; M. Delal Baer, "Mexico's Second Revolution: Pathways to Liberalization," in Riordan Roett, ed., *Political and Economic Liberalization in Mexico: At a Critical Juncture?* (Boulder, Colo.: Lynne Rienner, 1993), pp. 51–68.

[88] Nora Lustig, "NAFTA: A Mexican Perspective," *SAIS Review*, Vol. 12, No. 1 (Winter-Spring 1992), p. 59. See also Jorge G. Castaneda, "Can NAFTA Change Mexico?" *Foreign Affairs*, Vol. 72, No. 4 (September/October 1993), pp. 73–74.

of presidential succession, which permitted each new chief executive to reverse or ignore predecessor policies. Under NAFTA, however, the Salinas program of 'structural readjustment' now became part of an international treaty—one that was subscribed to by the world's only remaining superpower. These circumstances would sharply narrow the plausible range of choice for opponents of this model and for Salinas' successors. With NAFTA, the Salinista reforms were cast in bronze."[89] Mexican leaders were limited to one six-year term. To ensure the continuation of his policies into the future and to establish sufficient guarantees on openness to attract trade and investment, NAFTA provided a useful institutional mechanism. It was attractive to Salinas precisely because it tied his—and his successor's—hands.[90]

Likewise, the NAFTA agreement would provide some insurance against American protectionism. The United States was Mexico's most important export market. NAFTA would not just expand access to that market but—just as importantly—it would make access more predictable. In 1988, the U.S. Congress had passed legislation that would allow trade officials to act more aggressively against unfair trade practices. NAFTA's treaty-mandated market integration provided Mexico insurance against American unilateral sanctions.[91] Mexico sought to make economic relations with its largest trade partner more predictable by tying itself more closely to it.

A similar logic was part of American official thinking. NAFTA was a mechanism to ensure that Mexico's movement toward market capitalism would continue. In the same way that NATO expansion was seen as a way to bolster the political standing of pro-Western coalitions in Central and Eastern Europe, NAFTA was championed as a way to reward and strengthen Mexico's free trade coalition and institutionalize the changed policy orientation.[92] As one State Department official noted later, NAFTA was "a way of supporting the modernization of Mexico," and taking advantage of this "historic shift" to connect it more fully with North America.[93] This attraction of NAFTA was identified by the American ambassador to Mexico, John D. Negroponte, in a confidential memorandum to Washing-

[89] Peter H. Smith, *Talons of the Eagle: Dynamics of U.S.-Latin American Relations* (New York: Oxford University Press, 1996), p. 248.

[90] For a discussion of NAFTA as a "commitment device" by the Mexican government, see Aaron Tornell and Gerardo Esquivel, "The Political Economy of Mexico's Entry into NAFTA," in Takatoshi Ito and Anne O. Krueger, eds., *Regionalism versus Multilateral Trade Arrangements* (Chicago: University of Chicago Press, 1997), p. 27, 54.

[91] Guy Poitras and Raymond Robinson, "The Politics of NAFTA in Mexico," *Journal of Interamerican Studies and World Affairs* Vol. 36, No. 1 (Spring 1994), p. 7.

[92] See Morton Kondracke, "Mexico and the Politics of Free Trade," *National Interest*, No. 25 (Fall 1991), pp. 36–43.

[93] Interview, Robert B. Zoellick, 28 May 1999.

ton in April 1991: "Mexico is in the process of changing the substance and image of its foreign policy. It has switched from an ideological, nationalistic and protectionist approach to a pragmatic, outreaching and competitive view of world affairs. . . . The proposal for an FTA is in a way the capstone of these new policy approaches. From a foreign policy perspective, an FTA would institutionalize acceptance of a North American orientation to Mexico's foreign relations."[94] Regardless of its economic gains, the treaty was supported in the American government in part because it would reinforce and lock in a favorable policy orientation.

During the early 1990s, a regional economic scheme also began to take shape in the Asia Pacific. Proposals for a loose regional multilateral economic association were put forward by both Australia and Japan. A decade of robust economic growth, the waning of the Cold War, the increasing congruence of outward-oriented economic policies in the region, and the intensification of regional economic cooperation in Europe and North America contributed to growing interest among Asia Pacific countries in a cooperative regional economic body. Australia and Japan also wanted to diversify their economic relations and integrate their economies more fully within their own economically dynamic region.[95] After a flurry of consultations by regional foreign ministers, the first ministerial meeting was held in November 1989 in Canberra.[96]

A diversity of political and economic agendas stood behind agreement by regional leaders to launch an intergovernmental gathering. Disagreements existed regarding the precise boundaries of the Asia Pacific region and whether to include North American countries. But the eventual agreement to move toward a trans-Pacific grouping was motivated in part to tie the United States into a regional institution that would make its economic policies more predictable and available for regional multilateral scrutiny. Japanese officials insisted that the United States be included. In an exchange with an Indonesian minister, the Japanese official leading the push for a regional cooperative initiative argued: "It would perhaps be more effective to combat and contain US unilateral actions on trade issues if we could include the United States in the forum." The ASEAN countries, who

[94] Quoted in Smith, *Talons of the Eagle*, p. 247.

[95] On the origins of APEC, see Yoichi Funabashi, *Asia Pacific Fusion: Japan's Role in APEC* (Washington, D.C.: Institute for International Economics, 1995), chapter three; and Peter Drysdale and Andrew Elek, "APEC: Community-Building in East Asia and the Pacific," in Donald C. Hellmann and Kenneth B. Pyle, eds., *From APEC to Xanadu: Creating a Viable Community in the Post-Cold War Pacific* (Armonk, N.Y.: M.E. Sharpe, 1997), pp. 37–69.

[96] The initial participants were the six ASEAN countries along with Japan, Korea, Australia, New Zealand, Canada, and the United States. Other countries, including Taiwan, Hong Kong, and China, joined later.

had been most reluctant to expand the regional organization to include non-Asian countries, ultimately accepted this rationale.[97] As a country subject to intense bilateral pressure for trade liberalization, Japan saw APEC as a useful mechanism to broaden debate on trade and moderate American unilateral tendencies.

Much as Mexico saw NAFTA as a mechanism to gain stable access to the American market and attract foreign investment, the smaller countries of Southeast Asia saw APEC in a similar way. Newly opened Eastern Europe threatened the continued flow of American and Japanese capital into the region. APEC would encourage an ongoing Japanese and United States commitment to Southeast Asia and stabilize the flow of capital and trade. Worries about North American and European regionalism reinforced the attraction of a regional institution that steadied and regularized American economic involvement in the Asia Pacific area.[98]

During this period, United States officials were also debating the merits of more institutionalized Asia Pacific economic cooperation. At the same time that NAFTA was under negotiation, Bush administration officials were discussing the idea of a regional trade agreement with Asia Pacific partners.[99] When the Australian and Japanese proposals for a regional ministerial meeting were announced, the United States quickly agreed to participate. American thinking paralleled the logic of the NAFTA agreement. An APEC grouping dedicated to open economic relations would reinforce and lock in the recent commitments by governments to outward-oriented economic development. Such a grouping would also ensure that the United States would not be excluded from the growing interest within the Asia Pacific area in economic regionalism.[100] Proposals from Malaysia and elsewhere to build an exclusive Asian regional grouping were clearly contrary to American interests and were roundly criticized by the Bush administration. A loosely organized and open regional forum—such as APEC—would ensure that the region evolved in a trans-Pacific direction,

[97] Quoted in Funabashi, *Asian Pacific Fusion*, p. 58.

[98] See ibid., pp. 67–68.

[99] As early as the summer of 1988, the Bush foreign policy team floated the idea of creating an East Asian finance ministers group that would meet on an ongoing basis to foster policy cooperation on regional economic issues. See Walter S. Mossberg and Alan Murray, "Departure of Treasury Secretary Baker Would Bring Halt to Initiative in Asia," *Wall Street Journal*, 3 August 1988, Section One, p. 22.

[100] As economic regionalism gained momentum during this period in Europe, Asia, and the Americas, the Bush administration wanted to be sure it was in as many of them as possible. Economic and political access went hand in hand. Moreover, by being the only major country in multiple regional groupings, the United States would have unique leverage to ensure that regional economic developments were compatible with wider multilateral economic openness. Interview, Robert B. Zoellick, 28 May 1999.

reinforcing market openness and creating a voice for American policy in the region.[101]

APEC got another push from the Clinton administration. In the first year of his term, Clinton convened the leaders of the fifteen APEC countries in Seattle to gain agreement on the goal of creating a regional free-trade zone. The idea was to strengthen the APEC process by turning the annual ministerial gathering into a meeting of heads of state and put these summits in the service of a trade-liberalizing agenda. APEC was useful to all its parties. Japan and the smaller Asia Pacific countries could use the APEC process to guard against American unilateralism and discriminatory economic practices. APEC also provided a way for the ASEAN countries to strengthen their ties to Japan. These countries could exchange their pledge to move toward freer trade for an American commitment to more multilateral dispute settlement mechanisms and a predictable American presence in the region.[102]

The creation of the WTO in 1995 is perhaps the clearest and certainly most controversial example in the post-Cold War era of the United States binding itself to an international institution. Agreed to as part of the Uruguay Round trade negotiations that culminated in 1993, the WTO formalized and strengthened General Agreement on Tariffs and Trade (GATT) rule-making and dispute-settlement mechanisms.[103] The new institution marked a major step in establishing a judicial basis for international trade law. A formal organization was established with a legal personality, an independent secretariat, and an expanded institutional framework for international trade cooperation. By creating procedures for rendering binding decisions, the WTO constitutes a form of compulsory jurisdiction in international trade law. The WTO was championed by countries that

---

[101] Baker, *The Politics of Diplomacy*, pp. 44–45. See also Andrew Mack and John Ravenhill, eds., *Pacific Cooperation: Building Economic and Security Regimes in the Asia-Pacific Region* (Boulder, Colo.: Westview, 1995).

[102] As National Security Advisor Anthony Lake argues, APEC was seen in part as a "device to get the states in East Asia committed to the type of economic relationships that are in everybody's long-term interest." Interview, Anthony Lake, 20 September 1999.

[103] For descriptions of the WTO agreement, see Raymond Vernon, "The World Trade Organization: A New Stage in International Trade and Development," *Harvard International Law Journal*, Vol. 36, No. 2 (Spring 1995), pp. 329–40; Ernest H. Pregg, *Traders in a Brave New World: The Uruguay Round and the Future of the International Trading System* (Chicago: University of Chicago Press, 1995); John H. Jackson, "Managing the Trading System: The World Trade Organization and the Post-Uruguay Round GATT Agenda," in Peter B. Kenen, ed., *Managing the World Economy* (Washington, D.C.: Institute for International Economics, 1994), pp. 131–51; Jackson, "The World Trade Organization, Dispute Settlement, and Codes of Conduct," in Susan M. Collins and Barry P. Bosworth, eds., *The New GATT: Implications for the United States* (Washington, D.C.: Brookings Institution, 1994), pp. 63–75; and Gilbert R. Winham, "The World Trade Organization: Institution-Building in the Multilateral Trade System," *World Economy*, Vol. 21, No. 3 (May 1998), pp. 349–68.

sought to strengthen the legal basis of trade policy obligations as a way to discipline the resort to unilateral measures, particularly by the United States.

The most far-reaching change introduced by the WTO was the mechanism for the resolution of trade disputes. The earlier GATT dispute settlement approach operated according to consensus practices that allowed losing parties in trade disputes to block reports. Under the WTO framework, dispute settlement is upgraded by providing for cross-retaliation and the automatic adoption of panel reports.[104] The dispute-settlement constraints on national policy autonomy are quite specific. States are only bound to settlements that involve disputes over agreements they have already made on more general trade policy rules. The WTO cannot create obligations that states do not themselves agree to in principle. But member states are obliged to obey rules in practice that they negotiate in principle. States may also lose some sovereign right to determine the standing of the dispute: they agree that rules will be applied by a legal/technical body that they do not control. As a result, as one analyst concludes, "under the WTO it will be less easy for the United States and other countries to avoid the implementation of trade rules they agreed to in the past, with some resulting loss of flexibility in national commercial policy-making."[105]

The United States supported the launch of the WTO because it advanced its long-standing goal of strengthening the dispute settlement system, which administration officials argued would help protect American business and reinforce multilateral trade rules.[106] The Europeans saw the WTO dispute settlement proposal as a way to guard against the unilateral excesses of the United States, and to gain agreement they dropped their long-standing objection to the automatic adoption of GATT panels. Other middle and smaller trading countries also supported it because it was seen as a step forward in the development of a rule-based system that would protect them against arbitrary trade discrimination by stronger states.[107] In the end, the United States made the determination that the gains from the Uruguay Round trade negotiations and the strengthening of the system of trade rules would override the restrictions on its policy discretion.

NATO expansion, NAFTA, APEC, and the WTO can be seen as part of a general pattern of policy. The United States sought ways to reinforce and lock in political and market reforms in countries and regions that were

[104] See Preeg, *Traders in a Brave New World*, pp. 207–10.

[105] Winham, "The World Trade Organization," p. 363.

[106] See testimony of U.S. Trade Representative Michael Kantor, Hearings, "Overview of the Results of the Uruguay Round," before the Committee on Commerce, Science, and Transportation, United States Senate, 16 June 1994 (Washington, DC: U.S. Government Printing Office, 1995), pp. 9–19.

[107] Winham, "The World Trade Organization," pp. 352–53.

undergoing political and economic transformations. The United States could ensure its involvement in these regions and exchange its institutional commitments for assurances from these emerging countries that reforms would continue. Reflecting back, Secretary of State Baker concluded that "much of our time at State was spent creating new institutions (APEC), adapting old ones (NATO), or creating interim quasi-institutional arrangements (for example, the 'Two-plus-Four' process for German unification."[108] The Clinton administration, wielding notions of enlargement and engagement, did the same thing. "We live in an era without power blocs in which old assumptions must be re-examined, institutions modernized and relationships transformed," Albright noted in December 1996.[109] NATO enlargement and regional trade alliances were at the core of an American strategy to expand the institutional foundations of post-Cold War order.[110]

This pattern of institution building can be seen as a continuation of the logic that underlay the Western postwar settlement. Institutional agreements were pursued in order to reinforce domestic governmental and economic changes which, in turn, tended to fix into place desired policy orientations. As a leading State Department official describes the institutional strategy, "Our intention was to create institutions, habits, and inclinations that would bias policy in these countries in our direction."[111] The United States was able to ensure political and economic access to these countries and regions and gain some confidence that these countries would remain committed to political and market openness. In exchange, these countries gained some measure of assurance that American policy would be steady and predictable. The United States would remain engaged and do so through institutions that would leave it open to market and political access by these countries.

THE STABILITY OF POST-COLD WAR ORDER

The persistence of stable and cooperative relations among the advanced industrial countries is one of the most striking features of world politics

---

[108] Baker, *The Politics of Diplomacy*, p. 45.

[109] Quoted in Brinkley, "Democratic Enlargement," p. 121.

[110] Although both the Bush and Clinton administrations pursued enlargement-oriented institution-building strategies, their styles differed. Bush officials focused primarily on regional economic institution building and did not articulate a general post-Cold War strategy. The Clinton administration picked up many of these regional institution-building policies (NATO expansion and APEC) and articulated a more sweeping and less regionally differentiated grand strategy. See Michael Cox, *U.S. Foreign Policy after the Cold War: Superpower without a Mission?* (London: Royal Institute of International Affairs, 1995).

[111] Interview, Robert B. Zoellick, 28 May 1999.

after the Cold War. Despite the collapse of bipolarity and dramatic shifts in the global distribution of power, America's relations with Europe and Japan have remained what they have been for decades: cooperative, stable, interdependent, and highly institutionalized. This is surprising. Many observers expected dramatic shifts in world politics after the Cold War—such as the disappearance of American hegemony, the return of great-power balancing, the rise of competing regional blocs, and the decay of multilateralism. Yet even without the Soviet threat and Cold War bipolarity, the United States along with Japan and Western Europe have reaffirmed their alliance partnerships, contained political conflicts, expanded trade and investment between them, and avoided a return to strategic rivalry and great-power balance.

The persistence of the postwar Western order is particularly a puzzle to neorealist theories of order. Neorealist theories of balance expect alliance cohesion and cooperation in the West to decline with the disappearance of the Soviet threat. Without a unifying threat, balance-of-power theory predicts that strategic rivalry among the Western states will reemerge, and specifically that the major postwar alliances—NATO and the U.S.-Japan pact—will slowly unravel.[112] Neorealist theories of hegemony expect order also to unravel with the decline of American hegemony.[113] Others have argued more recently that it is not the decline of American power that presages disorder but the intensification of American power. In this view, the revival of American power has created a unipolar distribution of power that is not stable. American predominance will inevitably trigger counter-balancing responses.[114]

Both the balance-of-power and hegemonic arguments expect similar outcomes. Without a common external threat the security alliances should loosen, cooperation among former Cold War partners should decline, and

---

[112] See, for example, John Mearsheimer, "Back to the Future: Instability of Europe after the Cold War," *International Security*, Vol. 15 (Summer 1990), pp. 5–57; Kenneth Waltz, "The Emerging Structure of International Politics," *International Security*, Vol. 18 (Fall 1993), pp. 44–79; Pierre Hassner, "Europe beyond Partition and Unity: Disintegration or Reconstruction?" *International Affairs*, Vol. 66 (July 1990), pp. 461–75; Hugh DeSantis, "The Graying of NATO," *Washington Quarterly*, Vol. 14 (Autumn 1991), pp. 51–65; Ronald Steel, "NATO's Last Mission," *Foreign Policy*, No. 74 (Fall 1989), pp. 83–95; Christopher Layne, "Superpower Disengagement," *Foreign Policy*, No. 78 (Spring 1990), pp. 3–25; and Stephen Walt, "The Ties That Fray: Why Europe and America Are Drifting Apart," *National Interest*, No. 54 (Winter 1998/99), pp. 3–11.

[113] Robert Gilpin, "American Policy in the Post-Reagan Era," *Daedelus*, Vol. 116, No. 3 (Summer 1987), pp. 33–67. Also Paul Kennedy, *The Rise and Fall of the Great Powers: Economic Change and Military Conflict from 1500–2000* (New York: Random House, 1987).

[114] For an overview of this view, see Michael Mastanduno, "Preserving the Unipolar Moment: Realist Theories and U.S. Grand Strategy after the Cold War," *International Security*, Vol. 21, No. 4 (Spring 1997), pp. 49–88.

strategic rivalry among the traditional great powers should increase. The recent intensification of American predominance should create additional incentives for the allies to pull away from the United States. Weaker states should be wary of a unipolar world power which, without counterbalancing restraints, is unpredictable and capable of domination. A corollary expectation is that Japan and Germany will abandon their "civilian" greatpower roles and reacquire the full trappings of great-power capabilities and ambitions.[115]

The persistence of stable order among the Cold War allies—and indeed the expansion of cooperative and institutionalized relations among these countries—does not necessarily validate any particular theory, but it does provide some support for the institutional theory of order.[116] The shifts in the underlying distribution of power—and in particular the heightened asymmetry of power during the 1990s—are rendered less consequential and threatening because binding institutions restrain and regularize that power. Weaker and secondary states have fewer incentives to pull away from or balance against the dominant power, even when that power has reached unprecedented proportions.

It has been only a decade since the Cold War ended, so recent events can only be seen as preliminary evidence of the evolving order among the industrial countries. But it is striking how stable and cooperative those relations have remained despite the end of the Cold War and shifting power disparities. It is difficult to argue that the scope and intensity of conflict between the Western countries or between the United States and Japan has increased significantly in the last decade. On the contrary, trade and investment across these countries have continued to rise, security alliances have been reaffirmed and expanded, and intergovernmental ties have continue to deepen ongoing political relations. Fears of antagonistic regional blocs or even seriously frayed relations have not been realized.

Contrary to neorealist expectations, NATO has not shown signs of decay but has actually undergone political renewal and expansion. NATO continued to play a role after the Cold War as a stabilizing institution that binds together and reassures its partners.[117] When the alliance marked its fiftieth anniversary in April 1999, it was widely seen by its members as the dominant provider of order in the West. Even France, which remained disconnected from NATO during the Cold War, announced in 1995 that it in-

---

[115] See Christopher Layne, "The Unipolar Illusion," *International Security*, Vol. 17, No. 4 (Spring 1993), pp. 5–51.

[116] For realist efforts to explain this persistence, see William Wohlforth, "The Stability of a Unipolar World."

[117] John Duffield, "NATO's Functions after the Cold War," *Political Science Quarterly*, Vol. 119, No. 5 (1994/95), pp. 763–87.

tended to rejoin NATO's integrated military structures.[118] Disagreements did emerge between the United States and France over the conditions under which France would rejoin the military structure, including a dispute over whether an American or a European would head NATO's Southern Command, and France joined only NATO's Military Committee and several other bodies and not the integrated command. It is revealing that in the disagreement between the United States and France over the Southern Command, France's closest military ally, Germany, sided with the United States.[119]

The NATO bombing campaign in Kosovo during the spring of 1999 was another episode that tested alliance cohesion. Surprising many observers, the NATO partners remained quite unified on the basic aims of the military operation, although there were disagreements over the option of using ground forces and specific diplomatic proposals. As the first military operation undertaken by NATO and the most significant use of force in Europe since the end of World War II, its impact on the alliance will be felt for years to come. It could trigger, for example, a move by European governments to develop more independent military capabilities, thereby setting the stage for a loosening of alliance ties.[120] Nonetheless, during the 1990s, the Atlantic alliance has essentially remained as unified and integrated as it had been during the Cold War.

An equally striking development has been NATO enlargement. The United States and its NATO partners supported enlargement in large part to reinforce and lock in the democratic and market reforms of its new members. NATO is doing what it has always done; it has only expanded this institutional logic to additional countries to the east.[121] Both the old and new alliance members have affirmed a central purpose of the alliance: to provide an institutional structure that will facilitate integration and stability among its members as well as in the surrounding area.

The U.S.-Japan alliance has also undergone renewal in recent years. Rather than loosening alliance ties, the two countries have reaffirmed their security partnership and developed more sophisticated forms of military

[118] Roger Cohen, "France to Rejoin Military Command of NATO Alliance," *New York Times*, 6 December 1995, p. A1. A variety of considerations informed French rethinking of its NATO involvement: a view that a European defense identity could more effectively be promoted from within the alliance rather than from outside, the French experience in the Gulf War and in Bosnia, and opportunities to reduce defense spending.

[119] See Geir Lundestad, " 'Empire by Invitation' in the American Century," *Diplomatic History*, Vol 23, No. 2 (Spring 1999), p. 204.

[120] See Roger Cohen, "Uncomfortable with Dependence on U.S., Europe Aims for New Parity," *New York Times*, 15 June 1999, pp. A1, A14..

[121] This rationale for NATO enlargement reinforces the claim made in the last chapter that the alliance was originally supported by its members in part as an institutional structure to bind the allies together and reduce strategic rivalry among them. For a similar argument

cooperation, contingency planning, and burden sharing. Ten years after the Cold War, the bilateral U.S.-Japan alliance appears to be as stable as it ever has been.[122] The revision of the U.S.-Japan security treaty in May 1996 is an indication that both countries see virtues in maintaining a tight security relationship, regardless of the end of the Cold War or the rise and fall of specific security threats in the region.[123] Even though the threats to the region have become less tangible or immediate, the alliance has taken on a semipermanent character. Part of the reason is that the alliance is still seen by many Japanese and American officials as a way to render the bilateral relationship more stable by binding each to the other.[124]

The constitutional features of the Western order have been particularly important for Germany and Japan. Both countries were reintegrated into the advanced industrial world as "semisovereign" powers: that is, they accepted unprecedented constitutional limits on their military capacity and independence.[125] As such, they became unusually dependent on the array

---

relating specifically to Germany, see Josef Joffe, "Where Germany Has Never Been Before," *National Interest*, No. 56 (Summer 1999), pp. 45–53.

[122] With the rise of Chinese power in the Asia-Pacific, the persistence of the U.S.-Japan alliance presents less of a puzzle to neorealist theories of order. The end of the Cold War may have actually contributed to Japanese and American worries about security because, with the collapse of the Soviet Union, the American security partnership with China is no longer needed.

[123] President Bill Clinton and Prime Minister Ryutaro Hashimoto signed a Joint Declaration on Security on 17 April 1996, which was a revision of the 1978 Guidelines for U.S.-Japan Defense Cooperation. The agreement declared that the U.S.-Japan security treaty of 1960 "remains the cornerstone" of their policies, that their combined forces in Japan would engage in policy coordination for dealing with regional crises, and on a reciprocal basis provide equipment and supplies. The Japanese even made a commitment to move toward closer security relations with the United States: in May 1999 the Japanese parliament approved legislation that further expanded the country's military partnership with the United States. See Mary Jordan, "Japan Approves Expanded Military Alliance with U.S.," *Washington Post*, 25 May 1999, p. A10.

[124] Peter J. Katzenstein and Yutaka Tsujinaka argue that "the security relationship between the United States and Japan is best described by 'binding,' with the United States doing most of the 'advising' and Japan most of the 'accepting.' By and large since the mid-1970s defense cooperation has increased smoothly and apparently to the satisfaction of both militaries. Since that cooperation involved primarily governments and sub-units of governments implementing policy, 'binding' results primarily from transgovernmental relations." Katzenstein and Tsujinaka, "'Bullying,' 'Buying,' and 'Binding': U.S.-Japanese Transnational Relations and Domestic Structures," in Thomas Risse-Kappen, ed., *Bringing Transnational Relations Back In: Non-State Actors, Domestic Structures, and International Institutions* (Cambridge: Cambridge University Press, 1995), p. 80.

[125] On the notion of semisovereignty, see Peter J. Katzenstein, *Policy and Politics in West Germany: The Growth of a Semi-Sovereign State* (Philadelphia: Temple University Press, 1987). On the importance of European institutions for German political identity and stability, see Peter J. Katzenstein, ed., *Tamed Power: Germany in Europe* (Ithaca: Cornell University Press, 1997). For a discussion of Japanese semisovereignty and the postwar peace constitution, see

of Western regional and multilateral economic and security institutions. The Western political order in which they were embedded was integral to their stability and functioning. The Christian Democrat leader Walther Leisler Kiep argued in 1972 that "the German-American alliance . . . is not merely one aspect of modern German history, but a decisive element as a result of its preeminent place in our politics. In effect, it provides a second constitution for our country."[126] This logic of Germany's involvement in NATO and the EU was reaffirmed in 1997 by the German political leader Karsten Voigt: "We wanted to bind Germany into a structure that practically obliges Germany to take the interests of its neighbors into consideration. We wanted to give our neighbors assurances that we won't do what we don't intend to do."[127] Western economic and security institutions provide Germany and Japan with a political bulwark of stability that far transcends their more immediate and practical purposes.

The special status of Germany and Japan within the Western security system appears to be quite stable. The fact that German and Japanese defense spending has fallen more rapidly than American spending is a telling indication that these states are not pursuing great-power ambitions and capabilities. As one study indicates, "Germany, of all the states in Europe, continued to promote its economic and military security almost exclusively through multilateral action. . . . [B]edrock institutional commitments were never called into question, and many reform proposals, notably in connection with the EC, aim to strengthen international institutions at the expense of the national sovereignties of member states, including, of course, Germany itself."[128] Although Germany and Japan have been seeking a greater political role in international institutions, most notably the UN Security Council, the two countries have resisted a more dramatic redefinition of their security roles within the wider Western order.

Trade conflicts periodically break out between the United States and its European and Japanese partners, but they do not appear to be any more severe than economic conflicts during the Cold War. The successful completion of the Uruguay multilateral trade round and the evolution of

---

Masaru Tamamoto, "Reflections on Japan's Postwar State," *Daedalus*, Vol. 124, No. 2 (Spring 1995), pp. 1–22.

[126] Quoted in Thomas A. Schwartz, "The United States and Germany after 1945: Alliances, Transnational Relations, and the Legacy of the Cold War," *Diplomatic History*, Vol. 19 (Fall 1995), p. 555.

[127] Quoted in Jan Perlez, "Larger NATO Seen as Lid on Germany," *International Herald Tribune*, 8 December 1997.

[128] Jeffrey J. Anderson and John B. Goodman, "Mars or Minerva? A United Germany in a Post-Cold War Europe," in Robert O. Keohane, Joseph S. Nye, and Stanley Hoffmann, eds., *After the Cold War: International Institutions and State Strategies in Europe, 1989–1991* (Cambridge: Harvard University Press, 1993), p. 34.

GATT into the WTO mark a major widening and deepening of the international trade regime. Expectations of the rapid emergence of exclusionary and antagonistic trade blocs have not been fulfilled. The long-standing economic disputes between the United States and Japan have also failed to take a more serious turn. The United States has continued to insist that Japan open its markets and economic practices, and Japan has not responded with increased intransigence but rather has taken steps toward openness and deregulation. Despite expectations that the post-Cold War domestic realignment in Japan would lead to a strengthened commitment to mercantilist policies and a weakening of U.S.-Japan security arrangements, in 1999 the Japanese prime minister reaffirmed both a commitment to deregulation and greater openness and the primacy of its security treaty with the United States.[129]

The dominance of the United States has sparked complaints and resistance in various quarters of Europe and Asia, but it has not triggered the type of counterhegemonic balancing or competitive conflict that might have been expected. Some argue that complaints about America's abuse of its commanding power position have grown in recent years.[130] Unwillingness to pay United Nations dues, the Helms-Burton Act (which inhibits trade with Cuba), and resistance to commitments to cut greenhouse gases—these and other perceived failures are the grist of European and Asian complaints about American predominance. But such complaints about the arrogance of American power have been a constant minor theme across the postwar period. Episodes include the "invasion" of U.S. companies into Europe in the 1950s, the dispute over the Suez in 1953, the "Nixon shocks" in 1971 over the surprise closure of the gold window, failure of America to decontrol oil prices during the 1970s energy crisis, and the Euro-missiles controversy of the early 1980s. Seen in postwar perspective, it is difficult to argue that the level of conflict has risen. Today, as in the past, the differences tend to be negotiated and resolved within intergovernmental channels—even while the Europeans, Americans, and Japanese agree to expand their cooperation in new areas, such as international law enforcement, the environment, and nonproliferation.

---

[129] See remarks by President Clinton and Prime Minister Obuchi at their May 1999 joint press conference. The White House, Office of the Press Secretary, "Press Conference of the President and Prime Minister Obuchi," 3 May 1999.

[130] A reporter for the *Washington Post* summarized this view: "The chorus of dismay with America's overwhelming power has grown louder lately as the United States finds itself increasingly accused of bullying the rest of the world. Indeed, the United States is discovering that its behavior has come under sharpest scrutiny from friendly nations that no longer feel prevented by Cold War loyalties from expressing their disagreements with Washington." William Drozdiak, "Even Allies Resent U.S. Dominance," *Washington Post*, 4 November 1997, pp. A1, A13.

Despite complaints about the American abuse of its hegemonic position, there are no serious political movements in Europe or Japan that call for a radical break with the existing Western order organized around American power and institutions. Indeed, there is evidence of an ongoing demand for American leadership. It is striking that the most pointed European criticism of the United States has not been about coercion or heavy handedness but rather about perceptions of American unwillingness to lead.[131] It is the stability of the order, in spite of policy struggles and complaints, that is more remarkable than any changes in the character of the struggles or complaints.

The bargains struck and institutions created in the early moments of post-1945 order building have not simply persisted for fifty years, but they have actually become more deeply rooted in the wider structures of politics and society of the countries that participate in the order. That is, more people and more of their activities are connected to the institutions and operations of the American postwar order. A wider array of individuals and groups, in more countries and more realms of activity, have a stake—or a vested interest—in the continuation of the system. The costs of disruption or change in this system have grown steadily over the decades. Together, this means that "competing orders" or "alternative institutions" are at a disadvantage. The system is increasingly hard to replace.

When institutions manifest increasing returns, it becomes very difficult for potential replacement institutions to compete and succeed.[132] American post-1945 order has exhibited this phenomenon of increasing returns to its institutions. In the early period after 1945, when the imperial, bilateral, and regional alternatives to America's postwar agenda were most imminent, the United States was able to use its unusual and momentary advantages to tilt the system in the direction it desired. The pathway to the present liberal hegemonic order began at a very narrow passage when really only Britain and the United States—actually a few top officials in each—could shape decisively the basic orientation of the world political economy. But once the institutions, such as Bretton Woods and GATT, were established, it became increasingly hard for competing visions of postwar order to have any viability. America's great burst of institution building after World War II fits a general pattern of international continuity and change:

---

[131] Michael Mastanduno summarizes this pattern: "Rather than edging away from the United States, much less balancing it, Germany and Japan have been determined to maintain the pattern of engagement that characterized the Cold War. . . . Neither China nor Russia, despite having some differences with the United States, has sought to organize a balancing coalition against it. Indeed, a main security concern for many countries in Europe and Asia is not how to distance from an all-too-powerful United States, but how to prevent the United States from drifting away." Mastanduno, "Preserving the Unipolar Moment," p. 58.

[132] The phenomenon of "increasing returns" to institutions is discussed in Chapter Three.

crisis or war opens up a moment of flux and opportunity, choices get made, and interstate relations get fixed or settled for a while.

The notion of increasing returns to institutions means that once a moment of institutional selection comes and goes, the cost of large-scale institutional change rises dramatically, even if potential institutions, when compared with existing ones, are more efficient and desirable.[133] In terms of American hegemony, this means that, short of a major war or a global economic collapse, it is very difficult to envisage the type of historical earthquake needed to replace the existing order. This is true even if a new would-be hegemon or coalition of states had an interest in and agenda for an alternative set of global institutions—which they do not.[134]

The open and penetrated character of the United States and the other advanced democracies encourages the proliferation of connecting groups and institutions. A dense set of transnational and transgovernmental channels are woven into the trilateral regions of the advanced industrial world. A sort of layer cake of intergovernmental institutions extends outward from the United States across the Atlantic and Pacific.[135] Global multilateral economic institutions, such as the International Monetary Fund (IMF) and WTO, are connected to more circumscribed governance institutions, such as the G–7 and G–10, which bring finance ministers and other officials of the leading industrial states together for periodic consultations. Private groups, such as the Trilateral Commission and hundreds of business trade associations, are also connected in one way or another to individual governments and their joint management institutions. The steady rise of trade and investment across the advanced industrial world has made these countries more interdependent, which in turn has expanded the constituency within these countries for a perpetuation of an open, multilateral system.

Not only have more and more governments and groups become connected to the core institutions of the Western order, still more are seeking to join. Almost every country in the world has now indicated a desire to join the WTO, including China, and the line for membership in NATO stretches all the way to Moscow. In the recent Asian currency crisis, even

[133] This notion of breakpoint or critical juncture is not developed in the increasing returns literature, but it is implicit in the argument, and it is very important for understanding the path dependency of the 1945 Western settlement.

[134] Major or great-power war is a uniquely powerful agent of change in world politics because it tends to destroy and discredit old institutions and force the emergence of a new leading or hegemonic state. Robert Gilpin discusses the possibility that with the rise of nuclear weapons, this sort of pattern of global change may end, thereby leaving in place the existing hegemonic order. See Gilpin, *War and Change in World Politics*, Epilogue, pp. 231–44.

[135] See Cheryl Shanks, Harold K. Jacobson, and Jeffrey H. Kaplan, "Inertia and Change in the Constellation of International Governmental Organizations, 1981–1992," *International Organization*, Vol. 50, No. 4 (Autumn 1996), pp. 593–628.

countries with little affinity for the IMF and its operating methods have had little choice but to negotiate with it over the terms of loans and economic stabilization. Russia has joined the annual G–7 summit, turning it into the Summit of the Eight, and the eventual inclusion of China is quite likely. In the meantime, the G–7 process in the 1990s has generated an expanding array of ministerial and intergovernmental bodies in a wide variety of functional areas, including organized crime, energy, terrorism, the environment, aid to the Ukraine, and global finance.[136] Together, relations among the advanced industrial countries since the end of the Cold War are characterized by an increasingly dense latticework of intergovernmental institutions and routinized organizational relationships that are serving to draw more governments and more functional parts of these governments into the extended postwar Western political order.

CONCLUSION

The end of the Cold War is a type of "historical break" different from the other major historical cases, but it does help sharpen the book's theory and illuminate aspects of Western political order. The end of the Cold War— the decision of the Soviet leaders in the late 1980s to allow peaceful change in Eastern Europe and in the Soviet Union itself—shows evidence of the ability of the United States and the other Western democracies to establish institutionalized restraint in great-power and superpower relations. It was precisely because the United States was institutionally restrained within and outside the Western alliance in pursuing a hard-line and aggressive foreign policy toward the Soviet Union that made Gorbachev's reforms and accommodations less risky. Germany also took advantage of European and Atlantic institutions to reassure its neighbors that a unified and more powerful Germany would not threaten its neighbors.

American foreign policy after the Cold War is largely consistent with the institutional model of order building. As a rising post-Cold War power the United States had incentives to use institutions to lock in favorable policy orientations in other states. NATO expansion, NAFTA, and APEC all contain elements of this thinking. American officials calculated that bringing newly reforming countries into these organizations would help reinforce domestic institutions and political coalitions in these countries that were committed to political and market liberalization. In return, the United States accepted some additional obligations to these countries in the form of security commitments (NATO expansion) or institutionalized access to American markets (NAFTA, APEC, and the WTO).

---

[136] See Peter I. Hajnal, *The G7/G8 System: Evolution, Role and Documentation* (Brookfield, Vt.: Ashgate, 1999).

The end of the Cold War also eliminated what many observers argue was the key source of cohesion and stability among the industrial democracies, and this allows us to assess the importance of external threat for order within the West. The persistence of cooperation between the industrial democracies despite the end of the Cold War strengthens the claims of this book, that there was an internal institutional logic to postwar order in the West, which was reinforced but not caused by the Cold War. Despite an intensification of American power during the 1990s, the relations among the advanced industrial countries have remained stable—trade, investment, and intergovernmental cooperation have all expanded. The scope or intensity of political or economic conflict has not risen. The absence of significant steps by European and Asian democracies to pull away from or balance against the United States is consistent with the expectation of the model of institutional order: power disparities are rendered less consequential, reducing the incentives for states to move toward traditional hegemonic and balance-of-power orders.

Chapter Eight

CONCLUSION

"ONE KNOWS where a war begins but one never knows where it ends." So remarked Prince von Bulow, looking back at the bloodiest war in history, the collapse of Europe's great empires, and the chaotic spectacle of Versailles—all of which seemed to follow from shots fired by a lone gunman in Sarajevo.[1] States rarely finish wars for the same reasons that they start them. The destruction of war extends far beyond the battlefield. States, societies, and political institutions are inevitably changed by war and sometimes destroyed. War is also one of history's great catalysts in rearranging the international distribution of power. States rise and decline over long stretches of time, but war can speed the process, pushing some great powers dramatically upward and others dramatically downward. Wars do not just produce winners and losers on the battlefield; they also break apart international order and alter the power capacities of states.

This book has posed three questions about order building after major wars: What is the logic of choice that newly powerful states face at this juncture? What explains the increasing use of institutional strategies, by leading states in order building in the 1815, 1919, and 1945 settlements? And what accounts for the remarkable durability of the 1945 order among the industrial democracies despite the end of the Cold War?

This chapter reassesses the institutional theory in light of the historical cases. The cases do show newly powerful states at postwar junctures responding to incentives captured in the model. An institutional bargain between the leading and secondary states was part of each of the major settlements, although the institution's specific character, the extent to which it was actually realized, and the impact it had on the eventual postwar order differed from case to case. The variation in the extent to which the leading state used institutions to lock in other states and signal its own restraint and commitment is also at least partially explained by the variables identified in the model. The 1945 postwar juncture provided the greatest incentives and opportunities for an institutional settlement, and the order created among the Western industrial countries most fully exhibits the institutional logic. Because the Cold War also fostered cohesion among the industrial democ-

[1] On 28 June 1914, Gavrilo Princip, a Serbian freedom fighter, shot and killed Archduke Franz Ferdinand, whose automobile had stopped on a street in Sarajevo.

racies, the pattern of relations among these countries after the Cold War is critical in determining the institutional sources of Western order.

Building on the institutional model, this chapter goes on to offer an argument about the general sources of stable political order, domestic and international. Stable orders are those in which the returns to power are relatively low and the returns to institutions are relatively high. These are precisely the circumstances that characterize the most fully developed constitutional polities. There is at least some reason to conclude that contemporary international relations increasingly exhibit low returns to power and high returns to institutions.

The chapter ends by examining the implications that emerge from the theoretical and historical analysis for American foreign policy. The United States begins a new century as an unrivaled global power. If the argument in this book is correct, American foreign policy makers need to be reminded what characteristics of the postwar order have made American power reasonably acceptable to other states and peoples during and after the Cold War. American power is not only unprecedented in its preponderance but it is also unprecedented in the way it is manifest within and through institutions. This helps explains why it has been so durable. If American policy makers want to perpetuate America's preeminent position, they will need to continue to find ways to operate within international institutions, and by so doing restrain that power and make it acceptable to other states.

The Institutional Bargain

The institutional model of order building is based on a potential bargain between unequal states after the war. The leading state—driven by a basic incentive to conserve its power—wants a legitimate order that will reduce its requirements to coerce. The greater the asymmetries of power after the war, the more this circumstance should be at the front of the leading state's postwar thinking. Likewise, the sharper the power asymmetries, the more weaker and secondary states will be worried about domination and abandonment. This is where the possibility for an institutional bargain enters, particularly if other circumstances exist that allow states to be confident that institutions will in fact restrain power and lock in policy commitments.

In the institutional bargain, the leading state wants to reduce compliance costs and weaker states want to reduce their costs of security protection—or the costs they would incur trying to protect their interests against the actions of a dominating lead state. This is what makes the institutional deal attractive: the leading state agrees to restrain its own potential for domination and abandonment in exchange for greater compliance by subordinate states. Both sides are better off with a constitutional order than in an order based on the constant threat of the indiscriminate and arbitrary exercise of power.

Additional calculations reinforce this potential bargain. The leading state has an interest in locking in gains over the long term. It has received a windfall of power and it wants to use it efficiently over the long haul. Weaker states receive early returns on their power even if they give up full capacity to take advantage of their rising power in the future. This institutional bargain will be most wanted and available when power is highly concentrated in the hands of a single state, and where democratic states can employ institutions to establish credible restraints and commitments.

It is useful to think of the ability of the leading state to restrain and commit its power credibly as, paradoxically, a type of power.[2] It wants to lock other states into specific types of postwar institutional commitments; it could use its power to coerce them, but in doing so it loses any chance of building a legitimate order. If the leading state can bind itself and institutionalize the exercise of its power, offering to do so becomes a bargaining chip it can play as a way to obtain the institutional cooperation of other states. But it is only a bargaining chip when the power disparities make limits and restraints desirable to other states, and when the leading state can in fact establish such limits and constraints. In 1815, 1919, and 1945, the leading states differed in their ability to use this bargaining chip, thereby shaping the institutional bargains and postwar orders that followed.

INSTITUTIONS, COMMITMENT, AND RESTRAINT

The postwar cases show the leading state in each instance seeking an institutional bargain. The scope and depth of the proposed postwar bargain, however, expanded considerably with each succeeding settlement. This, in turn, reflected changes in the character of postwar power asymmetries (which shaped the goals and capabilities of the leading state and the extent to which weaker states worried about domination and abandonment) and the democratic character of the states (which shaped their ability actually to use institutions to establish commitment and restraint).

A common desire by the leading states across the settlements was to establish a postwar order that would allow that leading state to engage in very little direct management or active balancing of relations within the order. Castlereagh was eager to stabilize Europe in a way that would allow the British to avoid playing a direct balancing role on the continent, and thereby maintain its strategic emphasis on the empire and maritime su-

---

[2] See the discussion by Thomas Schelling on "the power to bind oneself." Schelling, *The Strategy of Conflict* (Cambridge: Harvard University Press, 1960), pp. 22–28.

premacy. Wilson wanted to transform European politics, creating a liberal democratic order that would be structurally and inherently pacific. This is the paradox of Wilson's agenda: he wanted to avoid involvement in European politics, so he pursued a vision that entailed the utter transformation of European politics. Roosevelt in 1945 was less ambitious in his proposals for a universal postwar peacekeeping institution, but he held many of the same reservations about actively intervening in European politics. His secretary of state, Cordell Hull, wanted a postwar system of free trade partly because he believed it would set in motion global economic dynamics that would make peace and order self-reinforcing.

What these patterns suggest is that Britain and the United States were not biased toward direct hegemonic domination of the postwar system. Restraint was partly built into the way these states wanted to establish an "automatic" order. But commitment and restraint were both necessary. In America's dealings with Europe in 1919 and 1945, the challenge was to reassure Britain and France that American power would be predictable and tied to Europe in an ongoing and institutionalized commitment.

Despite these similarities, the strategies and postwar outcomes evolved across these major settlements. In 1815, Britain was primarily a maritime power and it did not have specific territorial objectives after the war. This relative detachment from continental Europe, combined with its economic and naval supremacy, gave it options unavailable to the other postwar states. Prussia and Austria were forced into strategies of maneuver, seeking alliances and balancing arrangements that protected their more precarious positions. Russia was a dominant power, especially because the tsar's army had played a decisive role in defeating Napoleon, but Russia also was vulnerable to being pushed out of Europe into the periphery. These circumstances made at least some level of institutionalized commitment among the great powers attractive.

The initiative to bind the great powers together in a postwar security institution came from Britain. Its goal was to lock the other European powers into predictable security relations and provide mechanisms for the management of territorial disputes. This was all the more appealing to Britain because such a settlement would minimize its direct role in actively balancing the other European powers. It conserved British power. This British thinking was reflected in Castlereagh's efforts during the war to maintain the alliance and set the stage for a postwar institutional agreement to manage security relations. The wartime alliance itself was the seedbed for the postwar concert. Britain's manipulation of war aims and management of the coalition was a remarkable example of using the alliance as a mechanism of power management and restraint. The Vienna settlement was really an extension of this wartime alliance practice.

In 1815, the binding character of the proposed postwar institutions was limited, particularly when contrasted with 1919 and 1945. Yet the logic was clear: to connect the great powers together in an institution that facilitated security consultations, thereby allowing rival and potentially threatening states to keep close ties to one another. The failure of the proposal for a more far-reaching set of security guarantees revealed the limits of the restraints on the power of the major states. The unwillingness of the British government to make more formal guarantees was both a reflection of its own reluctance to become more fully committed to security conflicts on the continent and the lack of credibility of the other nondemocratic states. Castlereagh and other British officials were explicit in their skepticism of the soundness and credibility of Tsar Alexander's government. This placed limits on how far institutions and formal guarantees could be established to maintain postwar order.

In 1919, the United States and its European partners had more demanding goals for the establishment of postwar power restraint and commitment. Much like Britain in 1815, the United States wanted to dominate the settlement precisely because it wanted to institute an order that would not require direct involvement or the active management of the balance of power. The United States wanted to lock in a settlement that ensured a durable order organized around democratic government and a global collective security organization. In this sense, Wilson's postwar institutional strategies were much more ambitious than Castlereagh's. The expectations and obligations on the great powers were greater, and the institutional mechanisms for joint management of territorial disputes, economic dislocations, and peacekeeping were much more elaborate.

The United States also saw the League of Nations as a mechanism that would allow German postwar reconstruction and power to be monitored and restrained. This was reflected in the American position on the admission of Germany to the League of Nations. In discussions at the Paris peace conference, Wilson argued that Germany should be admitted after a period of probation: "It was a question of whether they were to be pariahs, or to be admitted into the League of Nations." Wilson went on to agree with Lloyd George that one of the arguments in favor of admission was that "Germany could be better controlled as a member of the League than outside it."[3] This was an echo of the binding logic that emerged in Vienna. The strategy was to bring Germany into the institutional fold, allowing the allies to monitor and restrain any German military resurgence. French resistance to German membership and the Rhineland compromises at Ver-

---

[3] Quoted in Lloyd E. Ambrosius, *Woodrow Wilson and the American Diplomatic Tradition: The Treaty Fight in Perspective* (New York: Cambridge University Press, 1987), p. 133.

sailles ensured that this particular use of the League of Nations as a restraining institution would be minor at best.

With the rise of Germany and the geographically remote position of the United States, the character and extent of American postwar commitments to Britain and France were even more critical than Britain's commitments to Europe after 1815. British cultivation of American participation in postwar Europe began even before the United States entered the war. The 1915 messages between Grey and House, and the Lloyd George government's interest in a postwar peacekeeping organization, were indications of this consistent British interest in establishing a American security link to Europe. The French were even more concrete and specific in proposing a formal security alliance with joint administration and soldiers under a common command. Wilson's reluctant agreement to a Anglo-French-American security accord (never ultimately ratified) during the Paris peace negotiations was a last-ditch concession made to appease the French and gain their agreement on the League of Nations.

The American inability to overcome European fears of abandonment was also due to a factor not captured in the model: Wilson's own personal view about commitments and restraints in international relations. Wilson put limited stock in specific institutional guarantees for two reasons. First, the most significant source of power restraint, in his view, was worldwide democracy. Governments that truly embodied the will of the people would not be able to engage in military aggression. An anticipated democratic revolution, overturning the political structures of Old World militarism, would do more than anything else to restrain state power after the war. Second, the League of Nations would reinforce this democratic peace by providing mechanisms to adjudicate conflict and nurture norms of peaceful settlement of disputes. Wilson understood that the viability of these mechanisms and the strength of norms of conflict resolution would emerge slowly. His belief—probably actually his hope—was that the League of Nations would not be put to the test immediately after the war. As he confided to one colleague, if the world could have twenty years of peace after Versailles, the covenant would have a chance really to take root. In both these ways, Wilson's thinking about democracy, law, and norms of restraint diminished the practical importance of specific institutional commitments to Europe.

After 1945, the problem of establishing commitments and restraints was more acute than in previous settlements, but the opportunities to do so were also more readily available. In contrast to 1919, the United States emerged in a more fully hegemonic position, Britain and France were economically weaker, and the military defeat of Germany was more complete. As in 1919, European allies were worried about both restraining American postwar power and ensuring a reliable commitment. Chapter Six argued that the United States was "doomed" to reassure Britain and France. The American aversion to active involvement on the continent was itself a signal that the United States was not eager to exploit its position or actively dominate Europe. It meant that the Europeans would need to cultivate American power rather than resist it. The efforts by the British—particularly the diplomacy of Foreign Minister Ernest Bevin—to blunt the emergence of a distinct European "third force" in favor of a transatlantic security institution was the most vivid example of this postwar dynamic.

The remarkable variety of schools of thought within the American government on postwar economic and security order also provided opportunities for the Europeans to engage the American government and encourage the development of congenial policy. The simple fact of so many official plans and agendas was a characteristic of a large and relatively open American government that served to soften the hard face of American hegemonic power. But it also provided opportunities for European officials to maneuver among the various positions and actively help shape the policies and commitments that finally emerged. The evolution of postwar economic and security policy, traced in Chapter Six, demonstrated this characteristic and its implication for postwar agreement.

More generally, the United States had more ways to establish a commitment to Europe in 1945 than it had in 1919. The postwar order-building agenda was a more protracted and multidimensional process than it was in 1919. Postwar economic planning unfolded in one realm, European reconstruction in another, security discussions in yet another, and the negotiations over the United Nations proceeded on yet another track. They were all related, but the sheer architectural scope of the postwar transition provided many more opportunities for the United States to reassure its partners with commitments to participation and mechanisms to ensure restraint. The United States was able to obtain agreement on postwar economic organization and lock in European participation in an open and managed system. The Europeans, in return, were able to obtain compromises on the initial American free-trade plans and commitments by the United States to play an active role in stabilizing the system.

The establishment of commitments and restraints was a rolling process, not tied as the 1919 settlement was to the passage or defeat of a single treaty. Bretton Woods provided one opportunity to institutionalize postwar commitments but so, too, did assistance for the reconstruction of Europe and the ongoing security discussions. Both the Americans and Europeans initially underestimated the extent of the economic collapse of Europe after the war—a weakness that was revealed most dramatically with the ill-fated British move, with American pressure, to make its currency convertible in 1946. The economic distress in Europe in 1947, coupled with the deterioration of relations with Stalin, provided the impetus for massive American aid to Europe, announced in Secretary of State George Marshall's celebrated speech in June 1947. Ernest Bevin's reaction to the announcement was reported by Lord Franks: "The first thought that came into his mind was not that this gave a prospect of American economic help for Europe. He saw that, and grasped the chance with both hands; but first came the realization that his chief fear had been banished for good. The Americans were not going to do as they had done after the First World War and retreat into their hemisphere. They had enlarged their horizon and their understanding of the intention of the United States to take in the Atlantic and the several hundred million of Europeans who live beyond it. The keystone of Bevin's foreign policy had swung into place."[4]

The Marshall Plan served both American and European purposes. The $13 billion dollars in Marshall Plan assistance to Europe were massive and unprecedented. The United States was forgoing some current economic gains in favor of investment in future gains. It would speed up the process of European recovery and dampen support within Europe for the communist opposition. It also provided a tool to get the Europeans to cooperate among themselves to administer the program, and this was seen by American officials as an important step in building Europe-wide institution for economic cooperation.[5]

NATO provided an even more significant opportunity for Europe and the United States to tie each other down and together. European efforts to bind American power to Europe were persistent in the years after the war. But the United States was also seeking to use postwar economic and security institutions to bind the Europeans together. This was the thinking of George Kennan in a 1948 strategic overview of American postwar foreign policy, particularly in reference to Germany's future role in Europe. "In the long run there can be only three possibilities for the future of western and central Europe," Kennan argued. "One is German domination. Another is Russian domination. The third is a federated Europe, into which the parts of Germany are absorbed but in which the influence of the other countries is sufficient to hold Germany in her place." The solution to the German problem had to be some type of European union. Kennan argued that it is "evident that the relationship of Germany to the other countries of western Europe must be so arranged as to provide mechanical and automatic safeguards against any unscrupulous exploitation of Germa-

---

[4] Sir Oliver Franks, in *Listener*, 14 June 1956. Quoted in John W. Wheeler-Bennett and Anthony Nicholls, *The Semblance of Peace: The Political Settlement after the Second World War* (London: Macmillan, 1972), p. 573.

[5] The Organization for European Economic Cooperation was established in Paris on 16 April 1948 for the implementation of the Marshall Plan.

ny's preeminence of population and in military-industrial potential."[6] Binding Germany to Europe was necessary regardless of the fate of relations with the Soviet Union.

The United States was determined—particularly as relations with the Soviet Union deteriorated—to rehabilitate and integrate the allied zones of Germany into the West, and American officials searched for an institutional solution to this problem. Europeans resisted initially, and ultimately tied the binding of Germany to Western Europe to the binding of the United States to Western Europe. Both these great challenges—establishing an American commitment to Europe and protecting Europe from German resurgence—existed prior to the Cold War. The rise in tensions with the Soviet Union was critical in gathering sufficient political support in both the United States and Europe to achieve a final institutional bargain. It is also doubtful that Congress would have appropriated the great bulk of Marshall Plan aid without the added worry of communist penetration of Western Europe. But the dilemmas of commitment and restraint existed even without the Soviet threat.

The basic logic of the settlement was represented in an institutional bargain: the United States gained agreement with the Europeans that locked them into an American-led postwar order, which was made certain and durable by an array of security and economic institutions. In return, the Europeans were able to gain American institutionalized participation in the economic reconstruction and security protection of Europe. American power was both tied down and bound to Europe. The United States achieved a highly institutionalized postwar order that provided continuous and predictable relations with the industrial democratic world well into the future. The war-weakened Europeans locked themselves into the postwar order and in return received immediate economic benefits and institutional assurances that they would not be dominated or abandoned.

Finally, in the 1945 settlement—and again after 1989—the proposals to engage or expand binding institutions were explicitly tied to the democratic character of the states involved. The launching of NATO was understood by European and American officials as more than a security alliance; it was a way of binding the democracies together to concentrate their power but also to overcome internal security dilemmas and reinforce wider realms of postwar cooperation. Later, West German leaders understood that democracy was a necessary condition for NATO membership and full integration into Europe. Throughout the postwar period, Europeans were more will-

---

[6] George Kennan, "Review of Current Trends—U.S. Foreign Policy," Report by the Policy Planning Staff, 24 February 1948. *Foreign Relations of the United States* (Washington, D.C.: U.S. Government Printing Office, 1948), Vol. 1, Part 2, pp. 515, 517.

ing to accept American leadership within NATO and other Western institutions because its domestic democratic institutions created openness and access. Postwar institutions created conduits into the American policymaking system. After 1989, American and European leaders celebrated the binding character of the institutions that linked the Atlantic states, and drew direct connections between democracy and the stability and permanence of Western alliance ties. Despite the end of the Cold War, the asymmetries of power among these countries provided incentives to increase rather than lessen their mutual commitments. The democratic character of these states increased their capacity to do so.

THE SOURCES OF POLITICAL STABILITY

The foregoing argument raises the final question: what makes some political orders stable and others not? This is an old question in politics, and it has no simple answer. Different types of political order—order built on balance of power, hegemony, and constitutionalism—have all exhibited stability and instability in various historical settings.

In the terms of the argument presented earlier, stable political orders tend to be those that have low returns to power and high returns to institutions. When political orders are organized in ways that constrain the ability of one actor or group to dominate or to wield power arbitrarily or indiscriminately, others actors and groups are more likely to abide by the rules and outcomes that the political order generates at the moment. Likewise, when political institutions are deeply entrenched and difficult to overturn or replace, this also reduces the returns on power and increases the continuity of the existing order. These two characteristics of constitutional orders tend to go together: the returns to power are reduced where strong institutions exist, which limit when and how particular aggregations of wealth and power can be used. So in circumstances where institutions are durable—when the returns to institutions are high—the institutions are most likely to have a shaping and constraining impact on power.

Orders that have low returns to power are those in which systematic institutional limits are set on what actors can do with momentary advantages of power and wealth. Unequal gains in power or wealth—or winning more than others in a specific distributive struggle—cannot be translated into a permanent advantage. Because winning is always limited and temporary, gains by one group cannot be used to engage in the permanent domination of other groups. Where the returns to power are low, the stakes in political battles are low. The implications of winning and losing are less significant: to win is not to gain a permanent position of superiority and to lose is not to risk everything. Political orders with low returns to power are more stable than high return systems because the risks of domination and coercion are reduced. Because of this, losers are more likely to agree to their losses and prepare for the next round.[7]

Reducing the returns to power is precisely what constitutions do in domestic political orders. Even where the underlying social and economic conditions are very unequal, a political order with low returns to power means that there are clearly circumscribed limits on how those social and economic advantages can be used within the political order. Indeed, constitutions emerged historically as economic change and the evolution of society produced more class divisions and greater economic and social inequality; under these conditions, the role of constitutional arrangements and political institutions rose in importance.[8] More generally, the rise of modern societies has been marked by the institutionalization of inequality—that is, the creation of categories of inclusion and exclusion, rights and rewards, that perpetuate but also differentiate and circumscribe inequality in a particular area.[9] It is not that constitutional orders banish social or economic inequality; rather, they channel and differentiate the ways in which resources and opportunities can be pursued to achieve political gains.

Of course, the underlying operation of the economy and society can also work to constrain and limit the monopoly of political power. In international relations, if the underlying evolution of the world economy works to rotate and distribute wealth, technology, and economic growth to widely different countries, and does so continuously, momentary gains and advantages enjoyed by one country will be more acceptable to others. This will be true because the losing states realize that their turn will come.[10]

Going beyond the argument presented earlier, one can think of two different distributional situations presented to states by the world economy. In one, economic gains are derived largely by a single wealthy country and the unequal and disproportionate gains that this one country receives can be used by it to solidify its future ability to gain disproportionately.

---

[7] See Adam Przeworski, "Democracy as a Contingent Outcome of Conflict," in Jon Elster and Rune Slagstad, eds., *Constitutionalism and Democracy* (New York: Cambridge University Press, 1988).

[8] The importance of political institutions—of which constitutional structures are the most fundamental—to the mediation and muting of dynamic social forces in evolving societies is stressed by Samuel Huntington, *Political Order in Changing Societies* (New Haven: Yale University Press, 1968).

[9] For discussions of this process, see Charles Tilly, *Durable Inequality* (Berkeley and Los Angeles: University of California Press, 1998); and Jack Knight, *Institutions and Social Conflict* (New York: Cambridge University Press, 1992).

[10] In a lighthearted snapshot of this logic, at a recent meeting of the Trilateral Commission an American participant indicated to a French participant that he was very upset that the Europeans had beaten the Americans to a big airplane deal with China. The French gentlemen responded: "Don't worry, next time it will be your turn."

Other countries are effectively doomed to unfavorable current and future economic returns. In the other situation, the gains rotate rapidly from one country to the next, a result of constant changes in the world economy that are largely outside of the control of governments. Moreover, in this second situation, there is both high rotation and high segmentation of economic winning and losing. States can be winning in some areas and losing in others. This second situation obviously operates in a way that lowers the returns to power more than the first does. That is, in the second situation there is less pressure on states to create institutions that lower the returns to power, whereas in the first case, if the political order is to be stable and mutually acceptable, institutions will be necessary in order to limit and constrain how the leading state can use its disproportionate and perpetual gains.

In the first situation, a losing country has a very strong incentive to make a fundamental break with the order, where it has no chance of ever competing and succeeding. It will always be in a position of inferiority—the risks of domination by the leading state are high and ever present. In the second situation, even without institutions that limit the returns to power, it is harder for states to conclude that the basic structure of the order works to their permanent disadvantage. Where winning and losing rotates and is highly differentiated into narrow markets and segments, the larger political order is likely to be more stable. Arguably, this second situation seems to better represent the world economy within which the advanced industrial countries operate today than does the first situation. The underlying world economic conditions reinforce stability of the postwar political order.

Political orders with high returns to institutions are those with sticky institutions difficult to overturn or replace. "High returns to institutions" refers to built-in, structural restraints and costs associated with wholesale changes in those institutions. Likewise, in political orders where the political institutions are durable, the political order itself is likely to be more stable. The institutions stay in place and operate to reduce the returns to power. Where institutions are not sticky, they are more subject to manipulation by powerful groups within the order; the order operates more directly on the struggle between groups and actors based on the underlying distribution of power and wealth. Where institutions are more easily overturned or replaced, weaker actors who are disadvantaged have less confidence that the political order will not work to their continuous disadvantage; the risks of domination based on the underlying distribution of power rises.

The returns to institutions will depend on the character of the institutions themselves and on the political environment in which they operate. Intergovernment institutions created between liberal democracies are more likely to become connected to adjacent institutions and create expanding mutual dependencies that make institutional change more difficult. A positive feedback loop is established: because people and organizations believe that the initial institution will persist into the future, they arrange their lives and activities to accommodate the institution. These webs of interdependence, even if not formally part of the initial institution, gives it a more extended and embedded existence, and disruption costs of institutional replacement increases.

Beyond this, the more complex, adaptable, and autonomous the institution, the more durable it will be and the more it can play a role in lowering the returns to power. The more complex an institution, the more multidimensional are its layers and units, the greater its tasks and functional relationships, and the more decentralized and diversified are the individuals and groups who operate within it. The more adaptable an institution, the more that it can cope with changing conditions in its environment. It embodies principles and mechanisms that allow it to respond to a wide range of problems and circumstances. The autonomy of an institution is a measure of the degree to which the institution is insulated from the dictates of classes and interest groups that have a stake in its operation.[11] The greater the ability of the institution to function independently of the groups that created it or who have the most to gain or lose by its operation, the more durable it will be.

Why some international institutions are more durable and autonomous than others is an ongoing question for research.[12] But it is clear that at sharp historical junctures, when old institutions break apart because of economic crisis, political conflict, or war, a rare and momentary opportunity is created to construct new institutions. Later, after the institutions are in place, the costs and constraints on replacing those institutions grow considerably. When those institutions are established between mature liberal democracies—which are themselves complex, adaptable, and autonomous institutions—this reinforces the stickiness of these intergovernmental institutions, and the implications for political stability follow in turn.

This theory of political stability is useful in explaining the remarkable durability of the Western postwar order. The durability of this order is built on two core logics. First, the array of institutions and practices of the order serve to reduce the returns to power—or more precisely, to regularize that power and extend the returns on power further into the future—which lowers the risks of participation by strong and weak states alike. American power is made less threatening, more restrained, and more acces-

[11] See Huntington, *Political Order in Changing Societies*, pp. 12–24.

[12] See Stephen D. Krasner, *Sovereignty: Organized Hypocrisy* (Princeton: Princeton University Press, 1999), chapter two.

sible. This, in turn, makes a resort to balancing less necessary. Second, the institutions also exhibit an increasing returns character, which makes it more and more difficult for would-be orders and would-be hegemonic leaders to compete against and replace the existing order and leader. Although the Cold War reinforced this order, it was not triggered by it or ultimately dependent on the Cold War for its functioning and stability.

This argument about the sources of political stability leads to an optimistic view of the future stability of the Western order. It is not the preponderance of American power that keeps the system intact but its unique ability to engage in strategic restraint, thereby reassuring partners and facilitating cooperation. Because of its distinctively open domestic political system and because of the array of institutions that establish restraint and commitment, the United States has been able to remain at the center of a large and expanding world political order. Its capacity to win in specific struggles with others within the system may rise and fall, but the larger order remains in place with little prospect of decline.

AMERICAN POWER AND THE PROBLEM OF ORDER

American power in the 1990s is without historical precedent. No state in the modern era has ever enjoyed such a dominant global position. The decline in rival ideologies and the economic failings of other major states have added to the reach and pervasiveness of American power. "The United States of America today predominates on the economic level, the monetary level, on the technological level, and in the cultural area in the broad sense of the word," the French foreign minister, Hubert Vedrine, observed in a speech in Paris in early 1999. "It is not comparable, in terms of power and influence, to anything known in modern history."[13] It is the multidimensional character of American power that makes it unprecedented.

But if the past is a guide, American primacy should produce resistance and counterbalancing. One of the great puzzles today is why these reactions have not yet made a serious appearance. The argument advanced here is that asymmetrical power relations are not only compatible with stable political order but—when constituted by democratic states—power disparities can even be a catalyst for institutionalized cooperation. In today's one-superpower world, this hypothesis will be severely put to the test.

This institutional theory of order is relevant to explaining why international order has remained so stable after the Cold War despite these heightened power asymmetries. But it also contains a note of caution to policy makers who wield that power. How policy makers think about power and

---

[13] Quoted in Craig R. Whitney, "NATO at 50: With Nations at Odds, Is It a Misalliance?" *New York Times*, 15 February 1999, p. A7.

institutions will have an impact on the workings and future of American power and the post-Cold War order.

American power is made more acceptable to other states because it is institutionalized. NATO and the other security treaties establish some limits on the autonomy of American military power, although these limits are only partial. Other regional and global multilateral institutions also function to circumscribe and regularize America's power in various economic and policy realms. Restraints are manifest through some institutionalized limits on policy autonomy and mechanisms that allow other states to have a voice in policy making. As one former American State Department official describes the operation of this postwar order: "The more powerful participants in this system—especially the United States—did not forswear all their advantages, but neither did they exercise their strength without substantial restraint. Because the United States believed the Trilateral system was in its interest, it sacrificed some degree of national autonomy to promote it."[14]

The implication of this argument is that the more that power peeks out from behind these institutions, the more that power will provoke reaction and resistance. American leaders are indeed ambivalent about entangling the country in restraints and commitments. This is seen most clearly in the trade area, where congressional legislation such as Super 301 authorizes the executive to take unilateral action against countries that the United States government judges to be engaged in unfair trade. In contentious trade disputes with Japan and other countries, the United States has used this legislation to threaten unilateral tariffs unless the offending country opens its markets.[15] It was the power of the American market—the ability to inflict more economic harm on Japan than the latter could inflict in return—that moved the dispute to a settlement.[16] In 1996, the Clinton administration signed the so-called Helms-Burton Act, which authorized the American government to punish foreign companies that operate or trade with factories in Cuba that were confiscated by the Cuban govern-

[14] Robert B. Zoellick, "The United States," in Zoellick, Peter D. Sutherland, and Hisashi Owada, *21st Century Strategies of the Trilateral Countries: In Concert or Conflict?* (New York: Trilateral Commission, 1999), p. 5. The Trilateral system refers to the postwar relations among Europe, Japan, and the United States.

[15] Super 301 was invoked by the United States in its automobile dispute with Japan in 1995, although an agreement was reached before the American tariffs were imposed. See David E. Sanger, "A Deal on Auto Trade: The Agreement," *New York Times*, 29 June 1995, p. 1.

[16] On the wider pattern of American unilateral trade policy, see Benjamin J. Cohen, " 'Return to Normalcy'? Global Economic Policy at the End of the Century," in Robert J. Lieber, ed., *Eagle Adrift: American Foreign Policy at the End of the Century* (New York: Longman, 1997), pp. 73–99; and Robert Gilpin, *The Challenge of Global Capitalism: The World Economy in the 21st Century* (Princeton: Princeton University Press, 2000), chapter 3.

ment.[17] Officials in Europe, Canada, and Mexico have denounced the act as a violation of international trade law. One American official captured the view of governments around the world that have been subject to treats of unilateral trade discrimination: "You hear a lot of smaller countries calling this economic imperialism, and sometimes you have to wonder whether our very aggressive approach creates more ill will than it is worth."[18] The American government's embrace of multilateral trade rules is decidedly ambivalent. It has championed the established of the WTO and its rule-based approach to trade, but it has also acted in violation of at least the spirit of the WTO with its unilateralist trade policy.

The United States has also left itself institutionally unencumbered in other areas. It has failed to ratify various multilateral agreements and conventions dealing with land mines, environmental protection, and the proposed International Criminal Court.[19] In its relations with the United Nations, the United States has failed to pay its dues fully, and it acted in what many observers thought was a heavy-handed manner to prevent Secretary General Boutros Boutros-Ghali from returning for a second term. The frequent American military interventions in recent years—Somalia, Haiti, Iraq, and Kosovo—also underscore America's singular capacity to project military power with modest international institutional constraints. This pattern of American policy leads some to worry openly about what appears to be an increasingly unrestrained world power. A French former ambassador remarked in the spring of 1999 that the great menace in world politics was American "hyperpower." During the Cold War, the United States and the Soviet Union restrained each other, whereas now "the U.S. can do anything it wants."[20] Even an American ally, German Chancellor Gerhard Schroder, has raised concerns: "That there is a danger of unilateralism, not by just anybody but by the United States, is undeniable."[21]

The NATO bombing campaign in Serbia in 1999 may also have implications for the way American power is perceived around the world. One virtue of the Western alliance during the last years of the Cold War is that it was ultimately seen by Soviet leaders as a defensive security partnership. It served to restrain American and Western military power. This was the judgment that Gorbachev and his colleagues made in the final stage of negotiations over the unification of Germany. The alliance tied rising Ger-

[17] Michael Wines, "Senate Approves Compromise Bill Tightening Curbs on Cuba," *New York Times*, 6 March 1996, p. 7.

[18] David E. Sanger, "Play the Trade Card," *New York Times*, 17 February 1997, p. 1

[19] See Laura Silber, "Divisions Are Deep over New War Crimes Court," *Financial Times*, 6 April 1998, p. 6.

[20] Flora Lewis, "Uncomfortable with U.S. Power, Real or Illusory," *International Herald Tribune*, 14 May 1999, p. 5.

[21] Whitney, "NATO at 50."

man power down within a dense set of Atlantic institutional links, and insured that American power would remain connected to Europe. If NATO was partly attractive to alliance members because it lessened European fears of American domination or abandonment, it also reassured outside states to some extent by restraining abrupt and offensive shifts in Western military policy. But the NATO bombing in Serbia takes the alliance along a new path of military intervention outside alliance territory. China and Russia—along with other countries—publically condemned the NATO actions pursued without UN Security Council sanction.[22] If NATO was an alliance that bound power together and down—thereby reassuring both its members and its neighbors—it looks very different today. The impact of the NATO action on Western and non-Western views of American power will take years to fully appreciate.

The lesson of American order building in this century is that international institutions have played a pervasive and ultimately constructive role in the exercise of American power. Traditional realist theory misses the way institutions relate to power. The conventional view is that they tend to be antithetical: more of one entails less of the other and, because power is the ultimate determinant of outcomes in international relations, institutions do not matter. But power and institutions are related to each other in a more complex way. Institutions can both project and restrain state power. If the United States had not endeavored to build the array of regional and global institutions that it did in the 1940s, it is difficult to imagine that American power would have had the scope, depth, or longevity that it in fact has had. International institutions can make the exercise of power more restrained and routinized, but they can also make that power more durable, systematic, and legitimate.

When American power holders bridle at the restraints and commitments that international institutions often entail, they might be reminded that these features of institutions are precisely what has made American power as durable and acceptable as it is today. If the American postwar order persists in the new century, it will be due in no small measure to the way power and institutions operate together to create stable and legitimate relations among the industrial democracies.

---

[22] Anthony Faiola, "Bombing of Yugoslavia Awakens Anti-U.S. Feeling around the World," *Washington Post*, 18 May 1999, p. A1; and Carla Anne Robbins, "Fears of U.S. Dominance Overshadow Kosovo Victory," *Asian Wall Street Journal*, 7 July 1999, p. A1; Robert F. Ellsworth and Michael M. May, "An Overreaching U.S. Spurs Fears Worldwide," *Korea Herald*, 20 July 1999, p. A2. See also François Heisbourg, "US Hegemony? Perceptions of the US Abroad," paper presented at International Institute for Strategic Studies Conference, San Diego, Cal., 8–11 September 1999.

APPENDIX ONE

Postwar Settlements

War	Great Power Battle Deaths	Principal Settlement
Thirty Years' (1618–48)	2,071,000	Treaty of Westphalia
Franco-Spanish (1648–59)	180,000	Treaty of Pyrenees
Ottoman (1657–64)	109,000	Truce of Vasvar
Franco-Dutch (1672–78)	342,000	Treaty of Nimwegen
Ottoman (1682–99)	384,000	Treaty of Karlowitz
League of Augsburg (1688–97)	680,000	Treaty of Ryswick
Spanish Succession (1701–13)	1,251,000	Treaty of Utrecht
Austrian Succession (1739–48)	359,000	Treaty of Aix-la Chapelle
Seven Years' (1755–63)	992,000	Treaty of Paris, Hubertusburg
Ottoman (1787–92)	192,000	Treaty of Jassy
French Revolutionary (1792–1802)	663,000	Treaty of Amiens
Napoleonic (1803–15)	1,869,000	Congress of Vienna
Crimean (1853–56)	217,000	Congress of Paris
Franco-Prussian (1870–71)	180,000	Treaty of Frankfurt
Russo-Turkish (1877–78)	120,000	Treaty of San Stefano, Congress of Berlin
World War I (1914–18)	7,734,300	Treaties of Brest-Litovsk, Versailles, St. Germain, Neuilly, Trianon
Sino-Japanese (1937–41)	250,000	merged into WWII
World War II (1939–45)	12,948,300	no general settlement
Korean (1950–53)	954,960	armistice: no settlement

Source: Derived from data presented in Jack S. Levy, *War and the Modern Great Power System, 1495–1975* (Lexington: University Press of Kentucky, 1983).

APPENDIX TWO

Power Rankings of the Great Powers

Country	Military Expeditures[a]	Percent of Lead State[b]	C.O.W. Index[c]	GDP[d]	Percent of Lead State[e]
1816					
United States	3,823	23	7.5		
United Kingdom	16,942	100	28.6		
France	10,554	62	15.3		
Germany	13,516	80	8.6		
Hungary	n/a	n/a	12.6		
Russia	10,582	62	24.7		
1820					
United States	1,556	13	6.9	12,432	36
United Kingdom	11,748	100	26.5	34,829	100
France	9,414	80	18.2	38,071	106
Germany	3,714	32	8.6	16,393	47
Hungary	6,175	53	15.2	n/a	n/a
Russia	9,317	79	24.6	37,873	109
1825					
United States	1,336	13	6.8		
United Kingdom	10,568	100	27.1		
France	10,609	100	18.9		
Germany	3,085	29	8.0		
Hungary	5,087	48	14.5		
Russia	7,476	71	24.8		
1830					
United States	1,687	20	7.4		
United Kingdom	8,491	100	26		
France	12,618	149	20.1		
Germany	3,096	36	8.1		
Hungary	4,567	54	13.8		
Russia	7,780	92	24.7		

continued on page 278

Country	Military Expeditures[a]	Percent of Lead State[b]	C.O.W. Index[c]	GDP[d]	Percent of Lead State[e]
1910					
United States	55,880	91	27.2	461,011	233
United Kingdom	61,417	100	14.7	197,736	100
France	49,539	81	9.9	121,084	61
Germany	60,416	98	17.6	128,676	65
Hungary	23,208	38	6.5	n/a	n/a
Russia	62,099	101	18.6	n/a	n/a
Japan	18,516	30	5.4	62,108	31
1915					
United States	257,648	6	22.4	491,573	210
United Kingdom	4,651,398	100	15.2	233,981	100
France	3,525,000	76	8.9	130,244	56
Germany	5,014,000	108	15.6	117,360	50
Hungary	2,013,000	43	11.6	n/a	n/a
Russia	4,524,000	97	14.4	n/a	n/a
Japan	107,515	2	3.2	73,069	31
1920					
United States	1,657,118	100	37.1	594,135	100
United Kingdom	1,475,661	89	17.5	203,312	34
France	361,910	22	9.7	124,662	21
Germany	79,025	5	10.2	114,024	19
Hungary	n/a	n/a	n/a	13,585	2
Russia	1,183,426	71	18.6	n/a	n/a
Japan	449,471	27	6.9	91,060	15
1925					
United States	589,706	100	35.1	731,402	100
United Kingdom	580,411	98	14.9	221,327	30
France	324,761	55	10.8	167,599	23
Germany	147,858	25	11.8	149,420	20
Hungary	n/a	n/a	n/a	18,914	3
Russia	1,447,885	246	19.3	n/a	n/a
Japan	181,598	31	8	107,948	15
1935					
United States	806,400	100	27.1	699,805	100
United Kingdom	646,350	80	11	259,502	37
France	867,102	108	8.7	169,746	24
Germany	1,607,587	199	15.3	174,662	25
Russia	5,517,537	684	29.1	334,818	48
Japan	295,113	37	8.8	141,243	20

Country	Military Expeditures[a]	Percent of Lead State[b]	C.O.W. Index[c]	GDP[d]	Percent of Lead State[e]
1940					
United States	1,657,000	100	26.6	930,828	100
United Kingdom	9,948,329	600	12.2	233,981	34
France	5,707,762	344	11	164,164	18
Germany	21,200,000	1,279	22.6	242,844	26
Russia	6,145,214	371	20.4	420,091	45
Japan	1,863,181	112	7.3	201,766	22
1945					
United States	90,000,000	100	42.9	1,646,690	100
United Kingdom	17,002,048	19	17.5	331,347	20
France	1,230,509	1	4.7	101,189	6
Germany	n/a	n/a	n/a	194,682	12
Russia	8,589,076	10	25.5	333,656	20
Japan	4,002,481	4	11.3	98,711	6
1950					
United States	14,559,000	100	38.7	1,457,624	100
United Kingdom	2,376,154	16	14.1	344,859	22
France	1,489,278	10	7.7	218,409	15
Germany	n/a	n/a	n/a	213,976	15
Russia	15,510,433	107	37.6	510,243	35
Japan	n/a	n/a	n/a	156,546	11
1955					
United States	40,518,000	100	41.2	1,816,591	100
United Kingdom	4,363,684	11	12.2	397,402	22
France	2,948,000	7	7.2	271,508	15
Germany	n/a	n/a	n/a	336,848	19
Russia	29,542,096	73	39.4	648,027	36
Japan	n/a	n/a	n/a	242,022	13
1975					
United States	90,948,000	100	20.2	3,468,461	100
United Kingdom	11,475,228	13	6.2	657,762	19
France	13,034,714	14	5	690,434	20
Russia	128,000,000	141	28	1,561,399	45
China	28,500,000	31	28.2	1,145,317	33
Japan	4,535,240	5	12.3	1,223,760	33

continued on page 280

Country	Military Expeditures[a]	Percent of Lead State[b]	C.O.W. Index[c]	GDP[d]	Percent of Lead State[e]
1980					
United States	143,981,000	100	19.8	4,161,014	100
United Kingdom	26,757,385	19	5.3	719,528	17
France	26,424,988	18	5.1	807,081	19
Russia	201,000,000	140	29	1,709,174	41
China	28,500,000	20	28.8	1,434,204	34
Japan	9,297,521	6	12	1,531,612	37
1985					
United States	252,700,000	100	18.9	4,797,624	100
United Kingdom	24,200,000	10	4.5	795,233	17
France	20,800,000	8	4.2	870,199	19
Russia	275,000,000	109	31.4	1,940,363	41
China	24,870,000	10	29.9	2,189,825	34
Japan	12,480,315	5	13.9	1,839,879	37
1996 (f)					
United States	265,700,000	100	28	7,636,000g	100
United Kingdom	34,500,000	13	4	1,158,921	15
France	46,400,000	17	5	1,538,794	20
Russia	71,000,000	27	12	429,620	6
China	8,600,000	3	33	834,000	11
Germany	39,000,000	15	6	2,352,472	31
Japan	44,000,000	17	10	4,595,200	60

Notes:

[a] Military expenditure in 1984 U.S. dollars; unless otherwise noted, all dollar figures are in thousands of dollar units.

[b] Percentage of spending in relationship to the lead state, whose percentage is set at 100.

[c] C.O.W. stands for Correlates of War, an index of a state's warmaking potential based on six major warmaking capabilities: Military Personnel, Military Expenditure, Energy Production, Iron and Steel Production, Urban Population, and Total Population. For more information on the C.O.W. index, see J. D. Singer and Paul Diehl, eds. *Measuring the Correlates of War* (Ann Arbor: University of Michigan Press, 1990).

[d] GDP figures are in million 1990 Geary-Khamis dollars. These figures can be found in Angus Maddison, *Monitoring the World Economy: 1820–1992* (Paris: Developmental Centre of the Organiation for Economic Co-operation and Development, 1995)

[e] Percentage of GDP in relationship to the lead state, whose percentage is set at 100.

f 1996 figures can be found in *The Military Balance* (London: Institute for Strategic Studies, 1998). These figures are in 1996 dollars.

[g] Figures taken from International Statistics Yearbook 1998 (Washington, D.C.: World Bank Group, 1999), and are in current market prices.

High Technology Indicators for Major Powers

Country	High Technology Manufacturing (Percent 1995)[a]	Total R&D Expenditures (Percent 1995)[a]	Defense R&D Expenditures (Percent 1995–96)[a]	PCs per 1,000 people (1996)[b]
United States	41	53	80	362
United Kingdon	6	6	7	149
Japan	30	22	2	75
France	5	58	8	150
Russia	n/a	n/a	n/a	23.7
China	8	n/a	n/a	3
Germany	10	11	3	232

Notes:

[a] Obtained online in the National Science Foundation's *Science and Technology Indicators 1998* (www.nfs.gov/sbe/seind98/start.htm).

[b] In the World Bank's *World Development Indicator, 1998* (Washington, D.C.: International Bank for Reconstruction and Redevelopment, 1998).